SIMPSON

IMPRINT IN HUMANITIES

The humanities endowment
by Sharon Hanley Simpson and
Barclay Simpson honors
MURIEL CARTER HANLEY
whose intellect and sensitivity
have enriched the many lives
that she has touched.

*The publisher gratefully acknowledges the generous support
of the Simpson Humanities Endowment Fund
of the University of California Press Foundation.*

Contesting Indochina

FROM INDOCHINA TO VIETNAM: REVOLUTION
AND WAR IN A GLOBAL PERSPECTIVE

Edited by Fredrik Logevall and Christopher E. Goscha

1. *Assuming the Burden: Europe and the American Commitment to War in Vietnam,* by Mark Atwood Lawrence
2. *Indochina: An Ambiguous Colonization, 1858–1954,* by Pierre Brocheux and Daniel Hémery
3. *Vietnam 1946: How the War Began,* by Stein Tønnesson
4. *Imperial Heights: Dalat and the Making and Undoing of French Indochina,* by Eric T. Jennings
5. *Catholic Vietnam: A Church from Empire to Nation,* by Charles Keith
6. *Vietnam: State, War, and Revolution, 1945–1946,* by David G. Marr
7. *Hanoi's Road to the Vietnam War, 1954–1965,* by Pierre Asselin
8. *Contesting Indochina: French Remembrance between Decolonization and Cold War,* by M. Kathryn Edwards

Contesting Indochina

FRENCH REMEMBRANCE BETWEEN
DECOLONIZATION AND COLD WAR

M. Kathryn Edwards

UNIVERSITY OF CALIFORNIA PRESS

University of California Press, one of the most distinguished university presses in the United States, enriches lives around the world by advancing scholarship in the humanities, social sciences, and natural sciences. Its activities are supported by the UC Press Foundation and by philanthropic contributions from individuals and institutions. For more information, visit www.ucpress.edu.

University of California Press
Oakland, California

© 2016 by The Regents of the University of California

Library of Congress Cataloging-in-Publication Data

Names: Edwards, M. Kathryn, 1979– author.
  Title: Contesting Indochina : French remembrance between decolonization and Cold War / M. Kathryn Edwards.
  Other titles: From Indochina to Vietnam ; v. 8.
  Description: Oakland, California : University of California Press, [2016] | "2016 | Series: From Indochina to Vietnam ; 8 | Includes bibliographical references and index.
  Identifiers: LCCN 2016009422 (print) | LCCN 2016010585 (ebook)
  ISBN 9780520288607 (book/cloth : alk. paper)
  ISBN 9780520288614 (book/paper : alk. paper)
  ISBN 9780520963467 (EBook Format/ePub + PDF)
  Subjects: LCSH: Indochinese War, 1946–1954. | Decolonization— Indochina. | France—Colonies—Indochina.
  Classification: LCC DS553.7 .E37 2016 (print) | LCC DS553.7 (ebook) | DDC 959.05/3—dc23
  LC record available at http://lccn.loc.gov/2016009422

25 24 23 22 21 20 19 18 17 16
10 9 8 7 6 5 4 3 2 1

For Chris

In France, one cannot address the history of colonialism, of anticolonialism, of communism, or of anticommunism, without provoking—or unleashing—some passion.

ALAIN RUSCIO, *Les communistes français et la guerre d'Indochine, 1944–1954*

CONTENTS

List of Illustrations ix
Institutional Acronyms xi
Acknowledgments xv
Map of France xviii

Introduction 1

1 · French Indochina from Conquest to Commemoration 12

2 · Remembrance and Rehabilitation: The ANAI
and the Anticommunist Narrative 34

3 · From Activism to Remembrance: The Anticolonial Narrative 54

4 · *Morts pour la France?* Official Commemoration
of the Indochina War 88

5 · "The Forgotten of Vietnam-sur-Lot": Repatriate Camps
as Sites of Colonial Memory 116

6 · *"La sale affaire"*: Collaboration, Resistance,
and the Georges Boudarel Affair 145

7 · Missing in Action: The Indochina War and French Film 167

Conclusion 208

Notes 215
Bibliography 277
Index 297

ILLUSTRATIONS

1. Bust of Ho Chi Minh, Parc Montreau, Montreuil *85*
2. Rolf Rodel's monument at Dien Bien Phu *91*
3. Bas-relief on the Monument to the Dead of Indochina (1983), Fréjus *96*
4. Memorial to the Indochina Wars, Fréjus *100*
5. Memorial wall (1996), Fréjus *103*
6. Permanent exhibit of the Memorial *111*
7. Entrance to the Reception Center for the French of Indochina (CAFI) *123*
8. Barracks and water tower at the CAFI *123*
9. Brigadier General de Castries's bunker, Dien Bien Phu *212*
10. Military cemetery in Dien Bien Phu *213*

INSTITUTIONAL ACRONYMS

AAFV	Franco-Vietnamese Friendship Association (Association d'amitié franco-vietnamienne)
ACUF	Association of the Combatants of the French Union (Association des combattants de l'Union Française)
ACVGI	Association of Veterans and Victims of the Indochina War (Association des anciens combattants et victimes de la guerre d'Indochine)
AEMNAI	Association for the Construction of a National Monument to the *Anciens* of Indochina, Combatants and Victims of War (Association pour l'érection d'un monument national des anciens d'Indochine, combattants et victimes de guerre)
AEMSI	Association for the Construction of a Memorial to the Soldiers of Indochina and the Victims of War (Association pour l'érection d'un mémorial aux soldats d'Indochine et victimes de guerre)
AFV	France-Viet Nam Association (Association France-Viet Nam)
ANAI	National Association of Veterans and Friends of Indochina (Association

	nationale des anciens et amis de l'Indochine)
ANAPI	National Association of Former Prisoners and Internees in Indochina (Association nationale des anciens prisonniers et internés d'Indochine)
ARAC	Republican Veterans' Association (Association républicaine des anciens combattants). *Also:* Association of Residents and Friends of the CAFI (Association des résidents et amis du CAFI)
ARINA	Association of Repatriates of Noyant d'Allier (Association des rapatriés de Noyant d'Allier)
CAFI	Reception Center for the French of Indochina (Centre d'accueil des Français d'Indochine)
CEFEO	French Far East Expeditionary Corps (Corps expéditionnaire français en Extrême-Orient)
CEP-CAFI	Eurasian Association of Paris-CAFI (Coordination des Eurasiens de Paris-CAFI)
CGT	General Confederation of Labor (Confédération générale de travail)
CID-Vietnam	Center for Information and Documentation on Vietnam (Centre d'information et de documentation sur le Vietnam)
CIMADE	Inter-Organizational Committee in Support of Evacuees (Comité inter-mouvements auprès des évacués)
CNC	National Combattants' Circle (Cercle national des combattants)
CNE	National Franco-Vietnamese, Franco-Cambodian and Franco-Lao Aid Committee (Comité national d'entraide

	franco-vietnamien, franco-cambodgien et franco-laotien)
CNRS	National Center of Scientific Research (Centre national de la recherche scientifique)
DRV	Democratic Republic of Vietnam
ECPAD	Institute of Communication and Audiovisual Production of the Ministry of Defense (Établissement de communication et de production audiovisuelle de la Défense)
EFEO	French School of the Far East (École française d'Extrême-Orient)
FLN	Algerian National Liberation Front (Front de libération nationale)
FNACA	National Federation of Veterans of Algeria, Morocco and Tunisia (Fédération nationale des anciens combattants d'Algérie, Maroc et Tunisie)
FTEO	Far East Ground Force (Force terrestre d'Extrême-Orient)
FTNV	North Vietnam Ground Force (Force terrestre du Nord Vietnam)
IAO	Institute for East Asian Studies (Institut d'Asie orientale)
IFOP	French National Institute of Public Opinion (Institut français d'opinion publique)
IHTP	Contemporary History Institute (Institut d'histoire du temps présent)
INALCO	National Institute for Asian Languages and Civilizations (Institut national des langues et civilisations orientales)
MHV	Museum of Living History (Musée de l'histoire vivante)
PCF	French Communist Party (Parti communiste français)

PRG	Provisional Revolutionary Government (of South Vietnam)
SIRPA	Army Information and Public Relations Service (Service d'information et de relations publiques de l'armée)
SRV	Socialist Republic of Vietnam
UFAC	French Union of Veterans' and War Victims' Associations (Union française des associations de combattants et de victimes de guerre)
UNC	National Union of Combatants (Union nationale des combattants)
VCP	Vietnamese Communist Party

ACKNOWLEDGMENTS

This book has been a long time in the making and could not have come to fruition without the extensive support of many friends, family members, colleagues, and organizations. Norman Ingram's patience as I muddled my way from a general interest in French historical memory to a focus on the Indochina War as a master's student was essential to the genesis of this project. Eric Jennings has provided unqualified support for this project since agreeing to supervise my doctoral dissertation; he has read countless iterations of the chapters in this book, long after I completed the dissertation, and has consistently provided incredibly thoughtful feedback. I could not have asked for a better advisor and colleague. Nhung Tuyet Tran has been a mentor for my research and professional development since I began my doctoral studies, and secured both the funding and research contacts that made it possible for me to undertake a research trip to Vietnam. Christopher Goscha has provided invaluable advice, guidance, and feedback on this project as it evolved from a dissertation to a monograph. Along with Fredrik Logevall, he strongly encouraged me to submit the manuscript for consideration in the present series; I am grateful to both of them for their sustained support of this project. Pierre Brocheux provided much-needed advice and a sense of direction when this project was just getting off the ground and also shared materials from his personal collection. Alain Ruscio provided valuable insights and contacts when I was undertaking new research on the anticolonial narrative. Agathe Larscher-Goscha generously shared unpublished conference papers that were immensely helpful for the section on the faculty of the University of Paris VII. Judith DeGroat, David Del Testa, Nathalie Dessens, Susan Dixon, Christina Firpo, Ruth Ginio, Caroline Herbelin, Charles Keith, Jean-François Klein, and Ken Orosz have all provided critical leads, feedback, and encouragement.

I have presented my work in many venues and am grateful for all of the feedback I received. I was fortunate to have presented my first conference paper from this project at an annual meeting of the French Colonial Historical Society, which is an exceptionally welcoming and vibrant intellectual community. I have presented material from virtually every chapter of this book to audiences at FCHS meetings, and my thanks go to copanelists, commentators, and audience members for their remarks. In Toronto the French History Seminar was a warm and inviting forum for discussing and presenting research, and I thank the organizers and participants for their comments on my analysis of the Georges Boudarel affair. I would also like to thank the members of the Modern European Reading Group at the University of Toronto for their constructive criticism of dissertation chapters.

I am grateful to the institutions and agencies that provided generous funding for my research, to the archivists who provided extensive guidance, and to the associations who opened their collections (and sometimes even their homes) to me. My doctoral research was made possible by the financial support of the University of Toronto, the Social Sciences and Humanities Research Council of Canada, and the Leonard and Kathleen O'Brien Humanitarian Trust. I was able to undertake subsequent research thanks to a fellowship with the Memory and Memorialization Program cosponsored by the Centre national de recherche scientifique and New York University. François Guillemot at the Institut d'Asie Orientale kindly granted me access to the Fonds Georges Boudarel, then still in the process of being catalogued. Sandrine Lacombe and Pascal de Toffoli at the Archives départementales du Lot-et-Garonne, Lucette Vachier at the Centre d'Archives d'Outre-mer, Sébastien Colombo at the Archives départementales Seine-Saint-Denis, and Éric Lafon at the Musée de l'Histoire vivante also provided access to crucial materials and guidance. I am also immensely grateful to Daniel Frêche, Nina Sinouretty, and the other members of the Coordination des Eurasiens de Paris; General Guy Simon and the members of the Association nationale des anciens and amis de l'Indochine; and Marie-Hélène Lavallard and the Association d'amitié franco-vietnamienne. I would also like to thank my former colleagues at Amherst College, Bucknell University, and the University of Louisiana at Lafayette for their support. Bucknell students Marcus Hernandez and Maddie Harrison provided significant assistance on various aspects of the manuscript.

At the University of California Press, I would like to thank Niels Hooper and his editorial team for their excellent work. Special thanks go to Bradley

Depew and Kate Hoffman for shepherding me through the production process with such care and attention, and to Jeff Wyneken for his excellent copyediting. I am also deeply grateful to my two anonymous readers, whose insights, feedback, and suggestions have significantly improved this book.

Finally, this project would not have been possible without the unflagging support of friends and family. Bayne MacMillan, whose classroom impersonation of a flying buttress I will never forget, encouraged my passion for the study of history, beginning in the tenth grade. Through countless coffee breaks and shared meals, Claire Eldridge and Sara Barker were wonderful companions on the journey through the ins and outs of French archives during my research year in Paris. Erin Hochman provided regular and insightful comments on many of the chapters of this book along with a healthy dose of encouragement. My fellow French historians in Toronto, Valerie Deacon and Laura Godsoe, with whom I shared many a delicious meal and late night during my graduate studies, have been an essential source of moral and intellectual support. Ukupa McNally, Kate Parizeau, Missy Roser, and Jamie Sedgwick have all been cheerleaders along the way. My parents, Peter Edwards and Kathy Hamer, instilled in me a love of history and of French language and culture. They, along with my sister Meghan, have been unfailing in their encouragement. And finally, this book is for Chris, who accompanied me on seemingly endless research trips, provided invaluable editorial feedback, and was always willing to act as a sounding board, even at the most inconvenient times.

An early version of chapter 1 appeared as "Traître au colonialisme? The Georges Boudarel Affair and the Memory of the Indochina War" in *French Colonial History* 11 (2010), published by Michigan State University Press. Sections of chapter 2 appeared as "The National Association of Veterans and Friends of Indochina, the Commemoration of the Indochina War and the 'Positive' Role of Colonialism" in *Hagar: Studies in Culture, Polity and Identities* 9, no. 2 (2010), 30–48, published by Ben Gurion University of the Negev.

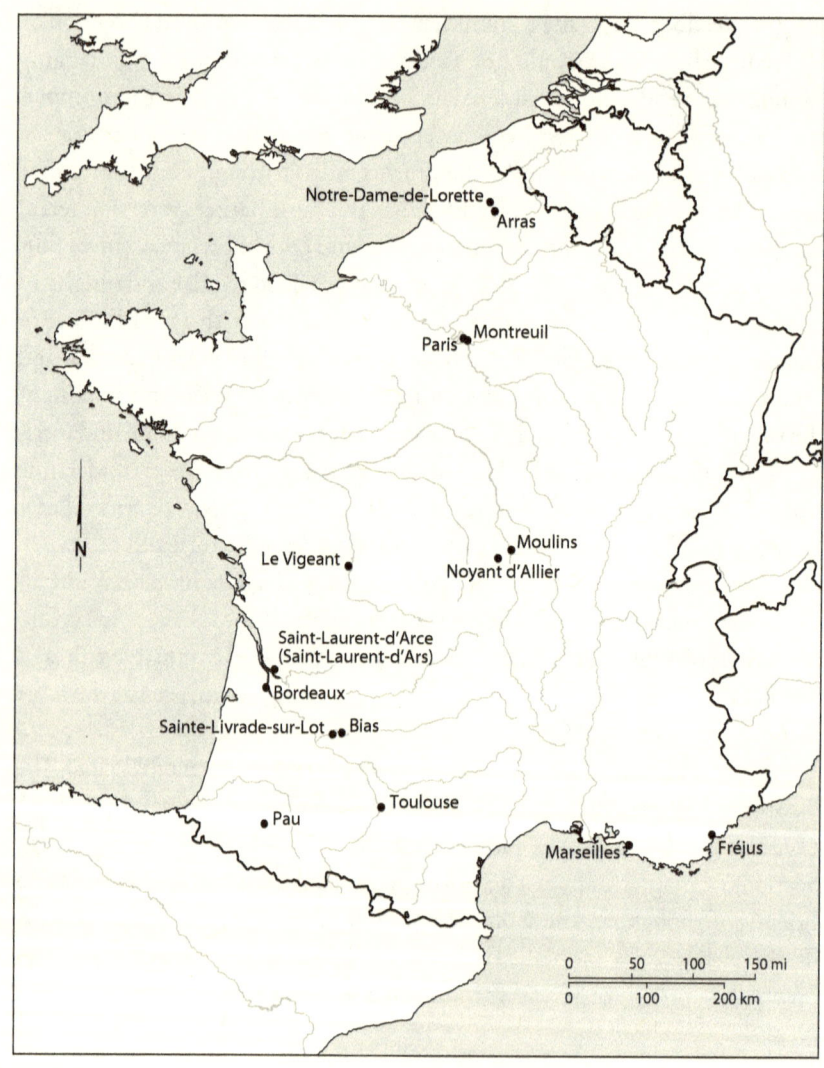

France

Introduction

> Indeed, with memory as with strategy, the French are often one war behind. The point of reference [for the Algerian War] is not the forgotten war in Indochina, or even the Great War of 1914–1918. [...] The memory of the Algerian War has more in common with that of the Second World War: bitter memories of defeat and less than glorious events that people would prefer to bury, undercurrents of civil war, and disgraceful acts perpetrated by fellow countrymen.[1]
>
> ROBERT FRANK

THE FRENCH INDOCHINA WAR presents an immediate dilemma for the scholar of historical memory: it is a "forgotten" war and yet has left indelible traces in the French imaginary. It has not captured public attention as have the German Occupation and the Algerian War; and while the Algerian War is the "war without a name" (*la guerre sans nom*), the Indochina War has rightly been described as the "overshadowed war" (*la guerre occultée*).[2] Explanations for this state of affairs are readily available: it was a faraway conflict; it was met with the general indifference of the metropolitan public; it was fought not by conscripts but by a professional army in which colonial troops, local auxiliaries, and the Foreign Legion outnumbered metropolitan French soldiers. It was fought in a colony with a relatively small settler population (in distinction to Algeria).[3] It was largely overshadowed by the Second World War, which preceded it, and the Algerian War, which followed it, and that despite its contentious nature among government officials, political groups, and intellectuals. Its identity was lost among these and other wars. It was eclipsed by the American war in Vietnam with respect to media coverage, global interest, and large-scale protest; and the American Vietnam War is often understood in France as being the equivalent of the Franco-Algerian war without any apparent awareness that France actually *had* its own Vietnam War.[4] Lastly the Indochina War is rarely presented as a worthwhile subject of investigation despite acknowledgment of its forgotten nature, as the epigraph to this introduction shows.[5]

Certainly the war was not utterly forgotten. Serge Tignères and Alain Ruscio have demonstrated that the battle of Dien Bien Phu has remained a potent symbol over the decades since the French defeat.[6] Like Sedan and Verdun it was disastrous: Ruscio even calls it "the greatest blunder in centuries and centuries of strategy."[7] Whatever prominence Dien Bien Phu has acquired stands in sharp contrast to the general obscurity of the Indochina War as a whole. And indeed the battle's mythical status may help to explain that obscurity.[8] The conflict has seen no resurgence in public awareness as there was for France's other "black holes" of memory. There was no "breaking of the mirror" for Indochina as there was for the Vichy period.[9]

And yet comparable memorial processes and commemorative practices abound. Veterans and various members of the political right and extreme right have held commemorative events since the 1950s and have actively lobbied the government for greater public and official recognition of those who fought in the war.[10] Groups with a fundamentally different understanding of the war, most often from the political left and extreme left, have staged commemorations of their own and have sought to challenge what they deem to be the colonial nostalgia of the right. Debate over the Indochina War and the colonial legacy in Southeast Asia has typically eluded public awareness even as such debate has on occasion erupted onto the public stage.

Although its significance as a historical event and as the subject of historical remembrance has often been overlooked, recent scholarship has refocused attention on the Indochina War as a turning point in the histories of France, decolonization, and the emergence of the Cold War. The Indochina War sat squarely "at the intersection of the grand political forces that drove world affairs during the century";[11] more specifically, "the Cold War and decolonization collided most intensely at first in Asia."[12] These dual political forces make the Indochina War an excellent case study for historical remembrance: it provides the opportunity to engage with and provide new perspectives on the politics of remembrance of both French decolonization and the Cold War, and more importantly of the overlap between these contexts. The Algerian War has dominated scholarship on the remembrance of French decolonization, and little scholarship exists on the remembrance of the Cold War in Western Europe.[13] This book helps to redress the imbalance.

The remembrance of the Indochina War is an integral part of the study of the Cold War and of French decolonization. The intersection of these two contexts complicates our understanding of both the events themselves and the ways in which they have been remembered. One context typically overshadows the other. A focus on decolonization often causes the ideological framework of the Cold War to recede into the background, while emphasis on Cold War discourse frequently obfuscates the colonial dimension of the conflict. The characterization of the war as a struggle to protect the "Indochinese" from communism distracts from the murkiness of the aims and tactics of colonial war; such mischaracterization was not possible to the same extent in the Algerian context.[14] The members of the Algerian National Liberation Front (FLN; Front de libération nationale) were cast as terrorists and rebels much like the Viet Minh, but whereas the FLN was often linked with global communism by its detractors, the Viet Minh unmistakably represented it. The overt connection to communism subsumed the Indochina War into a broader global conflict that was (and often still is) understood as a clear-cut confrontation between the forces of good and evil. This study highlights the influence of Cold War rhetoric and offers a new perspective to the growing historiography of the remembrance of empire.

Beyond the Cold War framework, the unique memorial processes of the Indochina War deserve further study. This traumatic event has not experienced a real resurgence in the public sphere on the model of the Vichy period or the Algerian War.[15] This neglect should not be taken for insignificance, since scholars now recognize the complex spectrum between "remembering" and "forgetting" as well as the social, cultural, and political manifestations of silence.[16] This study demonstrates that even in the absence of sustained public engagement "memory work" (*travail de mémoire*) is an ongoing process. Scholars have come to understand the model of repression followed by overexposure as the normative model for the collective remembrance of contentious events. The Indochina War offers a counter-model to this tendency, thereby enriching our understanding of the workings of collective remembrance.

Public and political engagement with the history and legacies of the Indochina War has ebbed and flowed in the sixty years following the end of the conflict. The stakes are high for those actors and interest groups who are most invested in the remembrance of the Indochina War. They have long lobbied for more commemorative events and for greater acceptance of their narrative of events. But without a strong public investment in the subject the dominant narratives have changed little. Rather, old ideological divisions have continued to play themselves out in commemorative arenas. Certain aspects of this ideological division are reminiscent of the American remembrance of the Vietnam War, which remains divided between those who are convinced that the struggle against communism had been a "noble cause," and those who maintain that the war had been an illegitimate conflict.[17]

This book examines the ongoing social and cultural impacts of the Indochina War on French society.[18] It casts its net widely: state-sponsored commemorative sites and practices, media coverage related to the war, film, cultural organizations, and museums. Moreover, the book delves into the lived experience of the consequences of war through the analysis of several veteran and settler associations, as well as the so-called repatriate camps that as of 1955 housed French citizens of "Indochinese" origin.[19] The book is divided into chapters that reflect established categories in the field of historical remembrance, such as "official memory," "popular memory," and "cultural memory," yet it also demonstrates the considerable overlap of these categories. Each chapter shows how various agents including the state, veterans, filmmakers, scholars, and politicians shape specific narratives, or "myths," about the war. As Samuel Hynes argues, such myths help to "make sense of [a war's] incoherences and contradictions."[20] As such these myths are not mere accounts of the war but also reflect contemporary political and cultural concerns. Furthermore, the contents of these myths cannot be isolated from their construction: "story and way of telling converge, tone determining the selection of events and events determining tone, until a complete, coherent story emerges."[21]

The remembrance of the Indochina War in France has actually been characterized not by a single myth or story but rather by two distinct and competing narratives, which reflect the dual contexts of decolonization and Cold War. One account maintains that the Indochina War was first and foremost a struggle against communism; the other, that the war was motivated by a desire to reconquer the colony and to thwart legitimate national independence movements. The proponents of each seek to impose their interpretation as the standard for collective remembrance. Furthermore, while these narratives appear to separate the colonial from the ideological aspects of the conflict, the two in fact are inextricably linked. As a result the subject of controversy or debate is never solely the Indochina War but inevitably comes to include the colonial system and the imperial project.

The first of these narratives, which I call the "anticommunist narrative," finds the greatest support from veterans[22] and members of the political right and extreme right as well as some members of the Vietnamese diaspora; it has also had significant influence on state-sponsored commemoration. It focuses overwhelmingly on the Cold War context of the conflict often to the exclusion of its colonial dimension.[23] The French expeditionary corps is depicted as having fought alongside full-fledged Indochinese partners to defend them from the horrors of a totalitarian system.[24] The Viet Minh are understood as fighting not for independence from oppressive French rule but to establish communist dominance. Many proponents of this perspective seek to rehabilitate France's colonial reputation, not only by portraying the French forces as fighting to defend their longtime colonial partners but also by contrasting life under colonial control with life under communist control. The plight of refugees fleeing the peninsula in the mid- to late 1970s following the establishment of communist regimes is frequently used as evidence for the claim that the French had been good caretakers. Former air ambulance nurse Geneviève de Galard articulated this perspective quite succinctly in a 1992 interview:

> It's horrible to think that it took the boat people and the fall of the Berlin wall to open the eyes of those last few who still believed that in 1954 the Indochina War was a colonial war. For my part, I never felt that I was participating in a colonialist battle, but rather that I was helping the Vietnamese combat communism—a war of liberation.[25]

In addition to this emphasis on anticommunism and a Franco-Indochinese partnership, a third major feature of this narrative is the heroism of those who fought for the French cause. In the postwar period the heroism of French troops was transformed into a narrative of victimhood and even martyrdom.[26] The claim of heroism is reinforced by the belief that the French expeditionary corps was in fact fighting to protect the Indochinese people, as well as by the conviction that the military had been all but abandoned by the government and the French public. This claim of a general abandonment is, to be sure, not entirely unwarranted. The succession of French governments in power from 1946 to 1954 did not elaborate consistent and clear objectives for the war effort, and there were frequent miscommunications, even outright clashes, between authorities in Paris and civilian and military authorities in Saigon and Hanoi. The general public was both ill informed and often indifferent to the war and those who were fighting it. Additionally, and not unlike the experiences reported by their American counterparts, many veterans felt victimized by protesters as they were returning from or departing for Indochina.[27] They claim to have been verbally or physically attacked and maintain that even the wounded were subjected to this treatment.[28]

The proponents of the anticommunist narrative—veterans, in particular—have also tended to emphasize the fact that the war and those who fought it are often overlooked or forgotten. For them this extends a pattern of victimization begun during the war itself: first, soldiers were the victims of the French state and the metropolitan public, who at best failed to support them and at worst jeopardized their lives with their indifference (or in the extreme, by committing sabotage). Second, they were the victims of the Viet Minh, especially as prisoners of war who faced the dire conditions of the POW camps—camps which have often been compared to those of other totalitarian regimes. Third, they have been the victims of a nationwide "forgetting" (*oubli*) since the conclusion of the war, a theme evident in Erwan Bergot's *Secret Services in Indochina: The Forgotten Heroes* (1979), Louis Stien's *The Forgotten Soldiers* (1993), and Alain Vincent's *Indochina: The Forgotten War* (2007).[29] These claims of victimhood can be further reinforced by the nature of asymmetrical warfare, which defined the first years of the conflict: with limited military equipment the Viet Minh relied primarily on guerrilla tactics to target French soldiers and civilians. The French, though much better equipped, nonetheless resorted to counterinsurgency measures. As Stef Scagliola has argued with respect to the Dutch-Indonesian War (1945–49), "the problematic categorisation of victims and perpetrators"[30] and the blurred lines of guerrilla warfare can facilitate the casting of veterans as victims rather than occupiers. Moreover, the use of guerrilla tactics on the part of the "enemy" allows soldiers to justify their own use of violence (and avoid taking responsibility for any excesses).[31]

Standing in stark opposition to this anticommunist narrative is the anticolonial narrative, which characterizes the conflict as a "dirty war" (*sale guerre*) of colonial reconquest on the French side, and as a war for Indochinese (primarily Vietnamese) independence on the other side. This interpretation, which has been maintained primarily by members of the political left and extreme left,[32] also tends to highlight the abuses of the colonial system and celebrates both anticolonial and antiwar activism. Antiwar protesters like Henri Martin and Raymonde Dien play an important symbolic role in the anticolonial narrative. Ho Chi Minh is often admired—occasionally even lionized—and the Democratic Republic of Vietnam (DRV) is cast as the legitimate representation of the will of the Vietnamese people. There is a tendency among some proponents of this narrative to overlook the dark side of the DRV, including the devastating impact of land reform and the repression of dissidents. In contrast to the anticommunist narrative, which is maintained by groups and individuals who are quite united in their views and their commitments to lobbying efforts, the anticolonial narrative is promoted by far more disparate parties. Some of the groups and individuals who fall under the broad umbrella of the anticolonial narrative have close connections with the French Communist Party (PCF; Parti communiste français), which was a dominant force behind the antiwar movement. Though the PCF has not maintained an active commemorative agenda on par with its commitment to the antiwar cause, it has nonetheless supported the activities of these affiliated actors.

These two narratives of the Indochina War are clearly and fundamentally at odds. For many, Cold War politics continue to play themselves out despite the end of the Cold War and the collapse of the Soviet bloc. Moreover, since this collapse there has been a persistent indictment of communism from some quarters and an attempt to quantify its victims. In the absence of any legal reckoning—an equivalent to the Nuremberg trials for Nazism, for example—this project has manifested itself in other forms. The unremitting attacks in the early 1990s on Georges Boudarel, a university professor accused of having crossed over to the Viet Minh (see chapter 6), and the staunch anticommunism of the National Association of Veterans and Friends of Indochina (ANAI; see chapter 2) both illustrate this trend. In 1997 French historian Stéphane Courtois edited a volume entitled *The Black Book of Communism: Crimes, Terror, Repression*.[33] This highly controversial book garnered considerable criticism, much of which targeted Courtois's claim that globally, communism had caused the deaths of one hundred million people.[34] While his introduction deliberately courted controversy, the other scholars who contributed chapters sought to present academically rigorous analyses of communist systems around the world.[35] Though equally critical of communist regimes, this scholarship should be distinguished from those who were in many ways continuing to wage Cold War battles; rather than being motivated purely by ideology, these scholars have sought to provide informed critiques of the regimes in question.

Similarly, debates over the legitimacy and impacts of the colonial project have carried over to the postcolonial period and have arguably grown more heated. The fundamental disagreement over the nature of the Indochina War as either a battle against communism or a war of colonial reconquest has contributed to the extensive debates over the relative merits of the colonial project and its putative resurrection in 1945. The legacy of colonialism in France has gained increasing prominence in public discourse in recent years. Arguments have run the gamut from the belief that France has insufficiently addressed the detrimental side of its colonial policy, to calls to put an end to a culture of colonial repentance. In 2003, Éditions Robert Laffont published *The Black Book of Colonialism,* edited by Marc Ferro, which was clearly intended as a counterpart to Courtois's volume. Though far less controversial, the book's motivations were nonetheless implicated in a broader debate over how to adequately come to terms with the colonial past. Historian of French colonial Algeria Daniel Lefeuvre, for example, became the standard-bearer for a movement that sought to bring "an end to colonial repentance," which was portrayed as an unproductive and even damaging process.[36] These opposing beliefs were brought into direct conflict with the passing of the now infamous law of February 2005, which included an article legislating the teaching of the "positive aspects" of colonialism in schools and universities.[37] While this article was later presidentially repealed, it nonetheless prompted considerable controversy among the academic community and the broader public; what is less well known is that veterans of the Indochina War were a driving force in this political offensive.

Not only do the anticommunist and anticolonial narratives reflect old ideological divides, but they have also remained virtually static since their creation in the postwar years. Groups and individuals have been more or less vocal about their interpretations of the war depending on context and circumstances, but even these ebbs and flows have not contributed to any significant questioning or reevaluation of the narratives. The static nature of these narratives is also evident in individual testimony. The case of Geneviève de Galard illustrates this phenomenon, as the narrative *about* her appears as unchanging as the testimony that she herself relates to the public. Hailed during the siege at Dien Bien Phu as a hero for her medical assistance to and moral support of the wounded, she was also presented as the only woman on site despite the fact that there was at least one group of prostitutes (the women of the *bordel militaire de campagne,* or BMC) who became makeshift nurses,[38] not to mention the Vietnamese women who worked as porters for the Viet Minh troops. Even as this fact became more widely known, de Galard continued to be referred to as the only woman at Dien Bien Phu. This phenomenon reflects the desire to cast the heroes of the story as those who were morally beyond reproach; the question of honoring prostitutes has been contentious. Moreover, the focus on de Galard reveals the construction of a predominantly masculine collective remembrance of the war; she is described, and often describes herself, in nothing but the most feminine terms.[39] She was a nurse, a friend, and a mother who helped ease the suffering of the wounded, never a "masculine" woman fighting alongside the men. Much like the public image thus constructed, de Galard's narrative of her experiences is remarkably unchanging; her stories are drawn from a select number of incidents such as the story of the young soldier who had lost both arms and a leg but who was convinced that when the war was over he would take her dancing.[40]

This study is structured thematically to allow for thorough investigation of specific themes and vectors of remembrance. Chapter 1 surveys the colonial era, the Indochina War, and the key periods of collective remembrance of the conflict. Given the thematic structure, the latter section is intended to provide a framework in which to situate the remaining chapters. Chapters 2 and 3 establish the contours of the anticommunist and anticolonial narratives through detailed analyses of their primary proponents. Chapter 2 examines the National Association of Veterans and Friends of Indochina (ANAI; Association nationale des anciens et amis de l'Indochine). This was one of the most prominent associations with a connection to French Indochina and the war and was also a driving force behind the anticommunist narrative. Until it disbanded in 2012, the ANAI boasted a uniquely diverse membership of former settlers, veterans, and as of the late 1980s anyone with an interest in the region. The ANAI's commitment to promoting public awareness of the Indochina War and a positive interpretation of the colonial project through commemorative activities and pedagogical initiatives makes it a particularly illuminating case study for the creation and transmission of collective remembrance. Its narrative of the war aligns with that maintained by many other veterans and members of the political right and the extreme right. In broader terms this case study illustrates the processes by which special interest groups impact official and public discourses.

Chapter 3 provides an analysis of the anticolonial narrative as it has been shaped by diverse groups of individuals and organizations. Each of the actors examined contributes to the interpretation of the war that emphasizes its colonial dimension, justifies it as a legitimate war of independence, and celebrates the antiwar movement in France. Central to the analysis are the following actors: a core group of scholars who have been central to the development of the anticolonial narrative as well as to the development of the field of Southeast Asian studies in France more generally; the left-wing Republican Veterans' Association (ARAC; Association républicaine des anciens combattants) and its affiliate, the Association of Veterans and Victims of the Indochina War (ACVGI; Association des anciens combattants et victimes de la guerre d'Indochine); the Franco-Vietnamese Friendship Association (AAFV; Association d'amitié franco-vietnamienne), a civilian organization dedicated to developing strong cultural, economic, and diplomatic ties with Vietnam; and the city of Montreuil, a Paris suburb that has maintained a long and unique relationship with Vietnam and features commemorative sites honoring Ho Chi Minh. Although they all pursue individual initiatives, these groups often collaborate. Each year, for example, they participate in a commemoration of the signature of the Geneva Accords, a practice that is vehemently opposed by right-wing veterans and politicians.

Chapters 4 and 5 examine sites of memory, both official and unofficial. Chapter 4 focuses primarily on state-sponsored commemorative sites and activities as well as surveying veterans' commemorative practices. The state's involvement in official commemoration of the war began in 1980 with the burial of an unknown soldier and gained momentum with the construction of the Memorial to the Indochina Wars in Fréjus in 1988. Special attention is paid to the impact of lobbying efforts undertaken by the ANAI and other organizations as well as the degree to which state commemoration has been influenced by the anticommunist narrative. Chapter 5 moves beyond official commemoration to address "unofficial" sites of memory, namely the so-called repatriate camps (*camps de rapatriés*). These camps, or "reception centers" (*centres d'accueil*), were converted military barracks or former workers' complexes which housed French citizens of Indochinese origin. The small communities of Noyant d'Allier (Allier) and Sainte-Livrade-sur-Lot (Lot-et-Garonne) hosted the two largest centers. Informed by the extensive files on the camps and their residents maintained at the departmental archives of the Allier and the Lot-et-Garonne, as well as material from current and former residents' associations and the municipal library of Sainte-Livrade, this chapter explores the tangible legacies of the Indochina War and the decolonization of the peninsula through the lived experiences of these repatriates. In addition to examining the camps as sites of memory of French decolonization, the chapter makes contributions to the broader history of immigration to France.

Chapters 6 and 7 explore public and cultural manifestations of war remembrance. Chapter 6 presents an in-depth examination of the Georges

Boudarel affair of 1991. Boudarel was a professor of Vietnamese studies at the University of Paris VII (Jussieu) and a former member of the French Communist Party accused of having been a political commissar at a Viet Minh camp that housed French prisoners of war, a staggering number of whom died in captivity. Although Boudarel admitted to having spent time at the camp, he claimed that his role as a low-level political instructor did not permit him to effect any real change in the prisoners' living conditions. The denunciation and Boudarel's admission provoked a media scandal that lasted several months. This "flashpoint" of collective remembrance resulted in significant debates over the nature of the Indochina War and the relative merits of the colonial project. Chapter 7 turns to representations of the Indochina War in key films and to a lesser extent works of literature. Some of these films enjoyed commercial success and critical acclaim, while others were a source of controversy. Henri de Turenne's documentary series *Vietnam* met with particularly violent criticism when it aired on French television in January and February of 1984, and the three major films released in 1992 prompted similar, though far more muted reactions.[41] Whereas the majority of the films offer a sympathetic portrayal of the soldiers and a muted critique of colonialism, one film stands out for its focus on antiwar protest. Paul Carpita's *Le rendez-vous des quais* (*Protest on the Docks*) is significant not only for its subject matter but also for its trajectory, having been censored, forgotten, and rediscovered. Together this collection of films and their reception reveals a great deal about the two dominant narratives of the war and the ongoing debates over the colonial project.

ONE

French Indochina from Conquest to Commemoration

IN 1924 THE GOVERNOR GENERAL OF INDOCHINA, Martial Merlin, proclaimed that French Indochina "is increasingly active, its influence grows, and its role as a Second Metropole, an outpost of France in Asia [...] grows stronger."[1] This "Pearl of Empire," as French Indochina was known, occupied an important place in the colonial imaginary. With its lush tropical landscapes, its temples, and its opium, it served as the exotic setting for novels by Pierre Loti, André Malraux, and Marguerite Duras. Like the rest of the French empire it was also the focus of modernization projects, often under the guise of the humanitarian ideals of the civilizing mission. As another governor general, Paul Doumer, wrote in 1905, "The new Indo-China can attain a level of prosperity and glory that the ancestors of our colonial subjects would never even have dared to dream of."[2] In fact this "new Indochina" had only formally come into being eighteen years earlier in 1887. The consolidation of French control over the territories had been a slow process: French forces had first arrived in southern Vietnam in 1858 and Laos was not incorporated until 1893. The federation of French Indochina lasted until 1945, when the region erupted into a full-scale war of independence that would evolve into a hot spot of the Cold War. The war came to an end in 1954 with the stunning defeat of French Union forces at Dien Bien Phu. The Geneva Accords confirmed the independence of Cambodia, Laos, and Vietnam (divided at the 17th parallel), all of which would face further domestic upheaval, civil war, and foreign intervention in subsequent decades. France too would continue to face turmoil as decolonization gained momentum; barely three months after the Geneva Accords, the French would be embroiled in a second colonial war, this time in Algeria.

This chapter provides an overview of French Indochina from the first French forays into the region to the conclusion of the Indochina War,[3] for those readers who are less familiar with these events. This is followed by a chronological overview of the evolution of the remembrance of the war, which will provide a framework in which to situate the thematically oriented chapters of this study.

COLONIAL CONQUEST TO THE SECOND WORLD WAR

In September 1858 French troops landed in Da Nang (known as Tourane to the French), ostensibly to protect Catholic missionaries and Vietnamese converts from persecution. In reality this intervention was guided as much by Napoleon III's desire to reassert French power on the global stage as it was by any desire to protect Catholics abroad. This was not the first French or European involvement in Southeast Asia: French and Portuguese missionaries had established themselves in the region since the early seventeenth century.[4] Despite this long history of Catholic involvement in Southeast Asia, Catholicism in Vietnam has often erroneously been identified as a product of the French colonial period.[5] Above and beyond the missionary connection, the French strengthened their relationship with the Vietnamese through the 1787 Treaty of Versailles, according to which Louis XVI promised support to the beleaguered Nguyen Phuc Anh,[6] who would later rule a unified Dai Viet as Gia Long (1802–20) in exchange for trade rights and a concession over Da Nang.[7] Diplomatic relations evolved little over the next half century, although the missionary presence remained strong.

The French "protection" that arrived in central Vietnam in the fall of 1858 was quickly transformed into a force of outright conquest, beginning with the southernmost tip of the country. By 1862, following intense combat, Emperor Tu Duc was forced to cede three provinces to the French, which became the colony of Cochinchina. This was followed by the establishment of a protectorate over Cambodia (1863); successive campaigns, which met with varying degrees of resistance,[8] resulted in the expansion of French control throughout much of the peninsula. A brief war with China in 1884–85 resulted in the Chinese recognition of French protectorates over Annam and Tonkin. Finally in 1887 the Indochinese Union was formally established. Territorial expansion was essentially completed with the consolidation of control of Laos in 1893 following the Franco-Siamese war, although French and Siamese authorities continued to quarrel over borderlands. Despite the common reference to Indochina as a single entity, union, or federation, it was anything but that; rather, it was characterized by a patchwork of governing statutes ranging from formal colonies and protectorates to mixed regimes. A French governor general oversaw the administration of the union, and a resident superior was in charge of each region, with a lieutenant governor presiding over Cochinchina. The administration was rounded out by French civil servants and a significant number of indigenous subordinates.[9]

In their foundational study of colonial Indochina, Pierre Brocheux and Daniel Hémery characterize the French colonization as decidedly "ambiguous"; that is, it was pursued with a mix of nominally good intentions and exploitative agendas.[10] French colonial society in Indochina, much like that in other European colonies, was characterized by entrenched inequalities and abuses. The so-called civilizing mission deemed necessary for improving the "backward" and "stagnant" Asian societies dictated the introduction of Western theories and infrastructure in the spheres of politics, economy, medicine, industry, and education, among others. Proponents of imperialism lauded the building of schools, hospitals, and roads. The conviction that France brought progress to Indochina and to the rest of its colonies has been sustained long past the era of decolonization, and defenders of the colonial project have tended to emphasize these same areas.[11]

It is true that French modernization projects contributed to an increase in production output,[12] led to decreased infant mortality rates in some urban areas,[13] and expanded the number of public schools.[14] Most scholars acknowledge, however, that these developments were rooted in a system that was at best fundamentally unequal and at worst brutally exploitative. From quotidian harassment and mistreatment, to the harsh working conditions on plantations and in mines, to heavy prison sentences in the infamous Poulo Condore prison—sometimes for minor infractions—many French colonial subjects were relegated to second-class status.[15] As Tran Tu Binh wrote of his experience on the Phu Rieng rubber plantation (owned by Michelin), "not only were rubber workers exploited and repressed in the extreme on the rubber plantations, but they were even exploited and repressed while they were on the road to those hells on earth."[16] Such disparate perceptions of the impact of French colonization have weighed heavily on postcolonial debates over the legacy of the colonial era.

The Second World War brought a new dimension to colonial rule in Indochina with the fall of France in 1940 and the establishment of the Vichy regime. A power-sharing agreement was reached with imperial Japan, which by 1942 wielded control over much of Southeast Asia. In fact French Indochina soon became the only Western colonial regime left in East and Southeast Asia—in the Dutch Indies, Hong Kong, Burma, Malaysia, Singapore, the Philippines, and elsewhere, the Japanese removed the ruling powers. This unique situation lasted only a few years: on 9 March 1945 the Japanese regime staged a coup against the French colonial government led by Admiral Jean Decoux. The French population, both military and civilian, faced internment camps or restricted living quarters, brutal attacks, and even execution; this period is recalled as one of senseless violence and even martyrdom by many former settlers. Nor were victims of the Japanese limited to the French: hundreds of thousands of northern Vietnamese died as the result of a famine provoked by a poor rice harvest and Japanese requisitions of the dietary staple. In April Japanese officials granted nominal independence to Cambodia, Laos, and Annam-Tonkin, leaving Cochinchina's fate to be decided at a future date. Barely five months later the American bombing of Hiroshima and Nagasaki forced Japan's capitulation. This created a unique situation in Indochina, particularly in Vietnam: the French and the Japanese had been knocked out of power, but the presumed successor in Vietnam—Emperor Bao Dai—was seen as having compromised himself by working with both foreign powers.

Taking advantage of this power vacuum, the Viet Minh (an abbreviation of Viet Nam Doc Lac Dong Minh, or League for the Independence of Viet Nam) under the leadership of Ho Chi Minh established a new government on 16 August 1945. Unlike Bao Dai, the Viet Minh was backed by considerable popular support, gained in part by the group's actions to mitigate the impact of the famine of 1945. Bao Dai abdicated on 25 August, transferring his authority to the new government. Ho Chi Minh proclaimed Vietnamese independence on 2 September 1945,[17] the same day that the Japanese formally surrendered. Chinese nationalist and British forces were dispatched to the northern and southern regions, respectively, to oversee the transition from Japanese control. Viewing the French as the legitimate authority over Indochina, the British forces in the south under the command of General Douglas Gracey released the French prisoners of the Japanese and re-armed some one thousand French, many of whom attacked and terrorized Vietnamese at random. Acting partly out of retaliation, "Vietnamese bands of various political stripes" initiated an attack on the Cité Hérault in Saigon, massacring French civilians.[18] The French Far East Expeditionary Corps (CEFEO; Corps expéditionnaire français en Extrême-Orient), led by General Philippe Leclerc, arrived in October 1945 to the relief of the French population. The CEFEO had been sent to defeat the Japanese, but given the evolving situation in September was instead entrusted with eliminating the Viet Minh threat. With British support the CEFEO was able to reestablish control over Cochinchina with relative ease, though not, as the above incidents indicate, without bloodshed.

In the meantime the French provisional government under the leadership of Charles de Gaulle had outlined the postwar plan for Indochina in the declaration of 24 March 1945.[19] This statement called for the creation of an Indochinese Federation, which would be part of the new French Union, all of which fell in line with the policies presented at the conference convened in Brazzaville in 1944 to discuss imperial reform. The Lao and Cambodian monarchies initially agreed to work with the French, though both countries would press for greater independence subsequently.[20] Ho Chi Minh and other representatives of the Democratic Republic of Vietnam (DRV), however, proved less enthusiastic.

Negotiations between Ho Chi Minh and French delegate Jean Sainteny began in September 1945, resulting in an agreement on 6 March 1946. This agreement established the French government's recognition of the DRV as a free state (*état libre*) within the context of the Indochinese Federation and the French Union,[21] and the DRV's acceptance of the replacement of Chinese troops with French soldiers as required by international agreements. Finally the agreement required that both parties agree to pursue future negotiations. The agreement was plagued with ambiguities: what was meant by "free state"? What were the territorial boundaries of the DRV? Furthermore the DRV was committed to the reunification of all three *ky* (the regions of Tonkin, Annam, and Cochinchina), which was out of the question for the French. These ambiguities were to be resolved through negotiations at Dalat (beginning in April 1946) and Fontainebleau (beginning in July the same year), but no firm conclusions were reached despite the signing of a partial agreement in the form of a modus vivendi in September. For many contemporaries (and several historians), the failure of these negotiations represented a missed opportunity for peace.[22]

THE FRENCH INDOCHINA WAR, 1945 TO 1954

Tensions between the French and the DRV were thus escalating rapidly in 1946 and were complicated by the differences in opinion of French leaders; while Leclerc and Sainteny favored negotiation, High Commissioner

Admiral Georges Thierry d'Argenlieu maintained that force was necessary.[23] The French conviction that the Viet Minh was preparing an attack and the Viet Minh conviction that the French intended to reestablish colonial authority left little room for maneuver. Pinpointing the actual beginning of the war is, as Alain Ruscio states, "not so easy."[24] The first incident to cause a significant escalation of tensions was the French bombing of Haiphong on 23 November 1946, which caused extensive damage to the port city and killed between 1,500 and 3,000 Vietnamese.[25] Barely a month later on 19 December the Viet Minh launched attacks on French civilians and soldiers in Hanoi. Each of these events has been identified as constituting the "true" beginning of the war, though most historians recognize that a sequence of events rather than a single incident led to its outbreak. Other scholars, like Michel Bodin, argue that while these events were critical, the war really began with the first skirmishes between the Viet Minh and French parachutists in August 1945,[26] or with the arrival of Leclerc's forces on 5 October. Fredrik Logevall suggests that the September 1945 Cité Hérault massacre is "as plausible a start date as any."[27] Naturally the debate over the war's origins is anything but neutral: the choice fuels the debates over the very nature of the war either as a process of colonial reconquest (and thus a war instigated by the imperialist French) or as a rebellion instigated by the Viet Minh, who were intent on imposing a communist society. More than thirty years after the end of the conflict the question still hung in the air: in a 1990 discussion of the national memorial under construction in Fréjus, Socialist deputy Jean-Louis Dumont asked his peers in the National Assembly "which date to use as the starting point of the aforementioned Indochina War."[28] Ultimately the complexity of the situation is such that regardless of which date one accepts, it is still difficult to assign firm responsibility to one side or the other.[29]

The war itself can be divided into two major phases: 1945 to late 1949, and early 1950 to 1954.[30] The first phase is best characterized as a war of colonial reconquest, which pitted the French expeditionary corps against the guerilla tactics of the Viet Minh.[31] Fighting an enemy who relied on terrorist tactics and ambushes and who blended into the civilian population—a situation the French would encounter again in Algeria, as would the Dutch in Indonesia and the Americans in Vietnam—presented extraordinary logistical challenges and took a serious psychological toll on combatants, many of whom were trained for traditional combat. What we now call counterinsurgency measures were used to combat Viet Minh tactics, including "gridding" (*quadrillage*) and "cleaning" (*nettoyage*) operations intended to break support networks supplying "rebel" forces with food and weapons. As is often the case in such circumstances, it was Vietnamese civilians who paid the highest price, as they were torn between the demands of the Viet Minh and the demands of French forces. Both sides used harsh interrogation methods, torture, and the torching of villages (among other tactics) to acquire information and intimidate combatants and civilians. Moreover the difficulty of distinguishing between combatants and noncombatants led some French Union soldiers to use violence indiscriminately.[32] The need to weed out foe from friend using whatever tactics were necessary was deemed all the more important in those regions where control shifted frequently from the CEFEO to the Viet Minh; one of the most entrenched images of the Indochina War is the French control of rural areas by day and Viet Minh control by night.[33]

By 1948 the objective of reestablishing French control over the peninsula had been largely abandoned as impractical and the war was increasingly being defined in Cold War terms. The second phase (1950–54) was heavily influenced by the internationalization of the conflict and was characterized by more traditional military engagements. The victory of the Communists in neighboring China in October 1949 had a significant impact on international power politics in general and on the parameters of the Indochina War in particular. The DRV gained not only military and ideological support, but the new Chinese government also officially recognized the DRV on 19 January 1950, followed by the Soviet government on the thirty-first. Barely a week later the United States recognized the new State of Vietnam (État du Viet-Nam) under Bao Dai's leadership, which was created as the result of years of negotiations between the former sovereign and the French authorities. What had been primarily a colonial war thus entered firmly into the sphere of the Cold War.

Envisioned as early as 1947, the so-called Bao Dai solution was in reality an arrangement by which France could both maintain its influence in the region and have a stronger base from which to combat the communist DRV. Negotiations were officially initiated with Bao Dai in 1948 with the objective of granting nominal independence to the State of Vietnam under his control, which would be an Associated State within the French Union. The initial agreement was signed in Halong Bay in June 1948 and was confirmed through an exchange of letters between Bao Dai and French president Vincent Auriol in March 1949.[34] The State of Vietnam was envisioned as a nationalist stronghold that could combat the communist forces of Ho Chi Minh.[35] Reorienting military objectives away from the colonial framework was also intended to appeal to the United States and its growing anticommunism; it was hoped that an anticommunist agenda might override American anticolonialism.[36] Certainly this shift along with the advent of the Korean War and growing commitment to the "domino theory" contributed to American support of the French war; by 1954 the United States was bankrolling close to 80 percent of French war expenses.[37]

The second phase of the war was also marked by a change in the French high command intended to reinvigorate the CEFEO after a disastrous retreat from Cao Bang and introduce new strategy that would, it was hoped, pull the French effort out of stagnation. "One of France's great military leaders of the twentieth century,"[38] General Jean de Lattre de Tassigny, arrived in Saigon in December 1950. Among the cornerstones of his new approach were the creation of a national Vietnamese army (a process referred to as *jaunissement,* or "yellowing"), the initiation of a series of effective "cleaning up" operations (*nettoyage*), and the creation of a network of fortified posts to protect the Red River delta. By all accounts these changes and—more importantly, perhaps—his leadership style contributed to a significant if temporary increase in morale within the CEFEO. De Lattre was adamant that France was fighting to protect an independent Vietnam from communist intrusion, thus sowing the seeds of the anticommunist narrative during the war itself.[39] Despite several important victories, de Lattre was unable to turn the tide definitively in favor of the French forces before he resigned his position in late 1951. Stricken by cancer and deeply affected by the death of his son Bernard in combat, he died a few months later. He was succeeded by Raoul Salan, who would later be replaced by Henri Navarre, the architect of the plan to draw the Viet Minh into battle in the Muong Thanh valley, at Dien Bien Phu.

Operation *Castor* was initiated in November 1953 with the primary objective of establishing a strong base to block the Viet Minh's path to Laos and protecting the Lao royal capital of Luang Prabang. It was also hoped that such a base would draw the Viet Minh into a direct engagement, as a decisive victory would enable a rapid cease-fire and give France the upper hand in the upcoming negotiations in Geneva.[40] General Henri Navarre's master plan might initially appear ill considered; after all, it called for a fortified camp to be built in the middle of a valley (in French it is usually referred to as a *cuvette,* a "basin"). However, this is somewhat misleading: not only is the valley approximately twelve miles long and several miles wide, but the French positions were established on a series of hills at its center (each given a woman's name—Éliane, Isabelle, Huguette, and so on). Intricate networks of trenches and fortifications, which would later be the site of devastating death tolls, earned the camp the moniker of "tropical Verdun."[41] The valley was surrounded by hills so high and so steep that the French military command underestimated the amount of heavy artillery the Viet Minh would be able to set up there; this turned out to be one of several serious miscalculations.

General Giap, who was the mastermind behind many of the DRV's military successes, launched his first major attack on the French fortress on 13 March, targeting the outpost codenamed Béatrice.[42] Over the course of the next fifty-seven days the French positions fell one by one. By mid-March there was no longer any possibility of flying planes in or out, and supplies and reinforcements were instead parachuted in. With no way to evacuate the wounded and with limited supplies, the medical staff did what they could: Major Doctor Paul Grauwin operated for hours on end often without sufficient anesthetic, doing his best to stave off infection.[43] Heavy April rains "filled the trenches with knee deep mud, breeding disease and infections as un-evacuated corpses on both sides rotted away, giving rise to an indescribable stench matched only by the sights of the decomposing cadavers."[44] The sacrifice and hardship of those fighting to the bitter end was fuel for the mythologization of the battle both at the time and subsequently. Press coverage of the last stand held the rapt attention of the public; *Paris Match* published some 144 photographs of the fortified camp between 20 March and 15 May, featuring five of them on the cover.[45] The focus was often on a small set of heroic figures when it wasn't on the French forces as a whole: the hard-nosed Major Marcel Bigeard, who volunteered to parachute into the embattled garrison in March when all hope seemed lost; the stoic air ambulance nurse Geneviève de Galard, who assisted Grauwin in caring for the wounded; and the tenacious Brigadier General Christian de Castries.

On 7 May, with the French forces unable to protect the central command post or the remaining strongholds, a ceasefire was declared. "As on some gruesome Judgment Day," Bernard Fall would later write, "mud-covered soldiers, French and enemy alike, began to crawl out of their trenches and stand erect as firing ceased everywhere. The silence was deafening."[46] Of the fifteen thousand troops on the French side, approximately three thousand were killed, nearly ten thousand were taken prisoner, and some two thousand deserted.[47] Those taken prisoner joined long columns on forced marches to POW camps, which had been growing in number since the first major Viet Minh victories in 1950.[48] Notorious for their atrocious conditions, including malnutrition, rampant disease, and ideological indoctrination, these camps would come to symbolize the victimization of French Union soldiers by the Viet Minh.

Despite the stunning defeat at Dien Bien Phu, the French continued to hold key positions in Hanoi and the Red River delta. However, as the focus of discussions in Geneva shifted from Korea to Indochina, the French were clearly far from the position of power that had brought them to Dien Bien Phu in the first place. Ultimately the accords signed on 20 July and ratified on the twenty-first confirmed the full independence of Laos, Cambodia, and Vietnam and also provided for the temporary division of Vietnam along the 17th parallel. Finally the agreement mandated the full withdrawal of French troops by the spring of 1956. Between September 1945 and July 1954 a total of 488,560 soldiers had been sent to the Indochinese peninsula; of these there were 233,467 French, 72,833 legionnaires, 122,920 North Africans, and 60,340 Africans.[49] In addition there were hundreds of thousands of Indochinese troops that served as auxiliaries with the French forces or in associated armies. By the time of the Geneva conference between 90,000 and 113,000 troops from the French side had been killed in combat or were presumed dead.[50] The war's toll was felt not only in the former Indochina or among the ranks of the CEFEO, however; there were serious political and social consequences in metropolitan France as well.

FRENCH PUBLIC OPINION, REACTIONS, AND RESISTANCE

The Fourth Republic was born during the Indochina War and was arguably irrevocably damaged by it. The fledgling republic was faced with the void left by Charles de Gaulle's 1946 resignation from the government, extensive reconstruction, and new diplomatic alignments and initiatives in addition to turmoil in the colonies. The situation was compounded by instability: nineteen governments succeeded one another in France during the period from 1945 to 1954.[51] Politically France was divided: the French Communist Party (PCF), which had garnered considerable support in the immediate postwar period, was forced out of government in May 1947 as a result of profound disagreements over the Indochina War and the deepening of the Cold War. Although the Fourth Republic was not dissolved until 1958, many have concluded, as did the makers of the 1974 documentary *The Republic Died at Dien Bien Phu*,[52] that the Indochina War contributed to its downfall.[53]

Set against the background of this tumultuous political experience of the war, what were the reactions and opinions of the French public? Responses ranged from sustained indifference to committed protest. Both Jacques Dalloz and Alain Ruscio have used opinion polls from the French National Institute of Public Opinion (IFOP; Institut français d'opinion publique) to contend that there was general indifference on the part of the metropolitan public toward the conflict.[54] Ruscio's study in particular reveals two major trends. First, opinions of various aspects of the war shifted considerably over the period from 1945 to 1954. Polls inquiring about the measures that should be taken in Indochina were conducted several times between 1947 and 1954: in July 1947, 37 percent of respondents stated that "order should be restored and reinforcements sent" (as opposed to 15 percent who felt that France should negotiate with the Viet Minh and 22 percent who thought that France should end the war and recognize Vietnamese independence). By February 1954 only 7 percent of respondents maintained that order should be restored, while 42 percent felt that negotiating with the Viet Minh was the best approach.[55] These statistics unequivocally indicate a significant shift in the public's commitment to maintaining French involvement in Indochina.

However, Ruscio argues that this shift in public opinion must be contextualized within the larger trend of what he terms "a massive disinterest" in the Indochina War.[56] An IFOP poll conducted in January 1948 on the most significant events of 1947 resulted in so few references to the war that they were categorized with the 6 percent of "miscellaneous" answers. Furthermore a poll from May 1953 asking how often respondents followed the news from Indochina revealed that only 30 percent did so regularly, while the remaining 70 percent did so "from time to time" or not at all.[57] Overall between 20 percent and 30 percent of respondents from 1945 to 1954 declared themselves to be without an opinion on events in Indochina.[58] While these appear to be damning statistics and have been interpreted by a number of historians as such, public opinion was likely far more nuanced. Pierre Cenerelli reminds us that while there was certainly significant indifference to the war, there were equally high levels of "no opinion" responses to polls on a variety of other topics.[59] Moreover both he and Dalloz point to the poorly informed public whose ignorance—or at best flawed understanding—of the conflict was rarely corrected by politicians or the press. The public was often on the receiving end of contradictory and incomplete news reports, which naturally made it difficult to fully appreciate the intricacies of the conflict, contributing to overall disinterest.[60]

Although a significant portion of the public expressed relative indifference to the war, there was nonetheless an active movement of dissent and opposition. Protests never reached levels comparable to those against the Algerian War or the American Vietnam War, but their impact should not be underestimated. The development of a strong movement of opposition came rather late in the course of the war, and even then it was somewhat fragmented. The earliest opposition was undertaken primarily by the French Communist Party and the General Confederation of Labor (CGT; Confédération générale de travail) as well as a few smaller organizations with ties to the PCF.[61] There was also a range of Christian organizations (both Catholic and Protestant) that were actively engaged with the antiwar movement.[62] In 1948 the first collective (*mutualité*) against the war was organized by a group of communists, contributors to *Esprit*, the France-Viet Nam Association (AFV; Association France-Viet Nam), and a few socialists, though it was only able to bring together some six hundred people.[63] In 1949 the editorial team of the Christian newspaper *Témoignage chrétien* began publishing articles detailing the use of torture and other controversial aspects of the conflict.[64]

The use of torture by the French forces during the Indochina War is a topic that has yet to gain the kind of attention that it has in the context of the Algerian War.[65] Writer Jules Roy, who had a very public break with the army following his service in Indochina in 1952–53, wrote in his memoirs that "we systematically tortured suspects, we burned villages with napalm, we snuffed out everything that moved: peasants, women, children, buffalo."[66] After witnessing the use of the *gégène* (a form of torture involving electrocution) on a group of peasants, one after the other in a pagoda, Roy made his decision to leave the army.[67] Civilian Lyliane Veyrenc, a film operator, also describes the torture that she witnessed during the war.[68] Interestingly, unlike the collective memories of the Franco-Algerian and American-Vietnam wars, the use of torture in Indochina has garnered little attention.

Following its ouster from the government in 1947, the PCF became all the more vocal about its opposition to the war and became the single largest source of antiwar activism in France. By 1949 the Vietnam question was occupying a far more prominent place in party propaganda. A new slogan was launched: "Not one more man, not one more penny for the war in Indochina."[69] The party's characterization of the conflict was also shifting from one of "colonial plundering" (*guerre de rapine coloniale*) to "an element of an American-led imperialist strategy."[70] Actions against the "dirty war"[71] evolved from distributing tracts and publishing antiwar articles in

L'Humanité to workers refusing to load military equipment onto ships to be transported to the conflict. Many veterans have claimed that there was also rampant sabotage of everything from medical supplies to weapons.[72] By the end of 1949 incidents of refusal to load supplies had multiplied, and there were a number of strikes by dockworkers (of Marseilles in particular) in 1950. In fact the government perceived the potential threat of these obstructions to be severe enough to pass a law in March 1950 against "acts of sabotage against army equipment, those who obstruct the free movement of military equipment, and those who undertake the demoralization of the army."[73] This led to an increase in the incarceration rate of protestors: by July 1950 forty-four had been sentenced to time in prison. Amid the dozens of arrests it was those of Raymonde Dien and Henri Martin that really pushed the antiwar movement into the spotlight. On 23 February 1950 twenty-year-old Dien was arrested for having lain down on the railroad tracks in Saint-Pierre-des-Corps (Indre-et-Loire) to prevent the departure of a train carrying munitions. She was subsequently sentenced to a year in prison, though she was released after nine months on Christmas Eve. Henri Martin's experience was both more complicated and the subject of greater attention; he quickly became a cause célèbre for protesters and left-wing intellectuals.

A former member of the Resistance, Martin had volunteered for service in the navy, ostensibly to liberate Indochina from the Japanese. By the time he arrived, however, the Japanese had been defeated and French troops were engaged in anti–Viet Minh activity. Opposed to such actions, he asked to be repatriated, but his multiple requests were denied until he finally returned to France in December 1947. He was arrested in March 1950 and charged with the distribution of antiwar pamphlets and the sabotage of an aircraft carrier, the *Dixmude*. While he admitted the former, he strenuously denied the latter and yet was sentenced to five years in prison despite a lack of evidence. The "Henri Martin Affair" lasted until his early release in August 1953 following a pardon from President Vincent Auriol. In that time he became a symbol for antiwar protest: special issues of magazines were devoted to him,[74] poems and songs were written about him or dedicated to him,[75] Picasso and others sketched portraits of him, a play entitled *Drame à Toulon (Drama in Toulon)* was written about the events,[76] a support committee was created,[77] and numerous intellectuals rallied to the cause. Jean-Paul Sartre headed a collective that published *L'Affaire Henri Martin*, a series of essays in support of the activist.[78] Journalist and PCF member Hélène Parmelin wrote a series of columns in *L'Humanité* covering the affair and subsequently published a book on the subject entitled *Matricule 2078* after Martin's prisoner number.[79] As many have commented, Martin was the perfect poster child for the antiwar movement: he was young, handsome, and a former member of the Resistance. Moreover he received what was by far the heaviest punishment among all those convicted for their protest activities. Unsurprisingly there was significant backlash to the PCF's instrumentalization of Martin, which also targeted party militants in general.

Despite the lack of sustained public attention to the conflict, the stakes were high for soldiers, the French government, and antiwar protestors. Actors became entrenched in their ideological positions—for or against colonialism, for or against communism—and have largely remained so in the decades since, despite the end of the Cold War (if not of communism) and the decolonization of Europe's former empires.

CHRONOLOGICAL OVERVIEW OF THE REMEMBRANCE OF THE INDOCHINA WAR

For all that contemporary commentators and historians have qualified the Indochina War as having been largely ignored by the metropolitan French public, it is clear that it was a divisive war that mobilized pro- and anticolonialists, communists and anticommunists in equal parts. Likewise, although the Indochina War has not often risen to the surface of collective remembrance, this is not to say that there has not been a certain evolution of interest and awareness in the conflict and its commemoration; indeed, following decades of relative silence on the part of the state and the public, there was a wave of memorial activity in the 1980s and the early 1990s. While such public interest has declined steadily since the fiftieth anniversary of the end of the war in 2004, remembrance of the Indochina War lives on in the heated debates surrounding the legacies of colonialism that reached new levels in 2005 and have yet to be fully appeased. This section provides an overview of the evolution of the remembrance of the Indochina War in France between 1954 and 2014; this will allow readers to situate the material covered in subsequent chapters.[80]

1954 to 1963

In the last days of Dien Bien Phu and the immediate postwar period public attention focused on a handful of heroes of the siege, most notably Brigadier

General Christian de Castries, Major Doctor Paul Grauwin, air ambulance nurse Geneviève de Galard, who was heralded in France and the United States as the "angel of Dien Bien Phu," and Major Marcel Bigeard, who distinguished himself in leading counteroffensives after having been parachuted into the fortified camp. Of these four de Castries quickly drew back from the spotlight, granting only a handful of interviews before isolating himself altogether. After the initial media blitz Geneviève de Galard also stepped out of the spotlight. She would later return, however, and along with Marcel Bigeard and filmmaker Pierre Schoendoerffer would constitute a "holy trinity" of commentators on the Indochina War.[81] All three had similar perspectives on the war, and their voices—along with that of the ANAI and several other very vocal veterans—would dominate veteran discourse.[82]

The immediate postwar period was also characterized by a series of inquests and trials. First, a hearing was held in 1955 with the objective of establishing responsibility for the French defeat, which was followed by Henri Navarre's publication of *Agonie de l'Indochine,* in which he finds fault with the government and the public for abandoning the military in Indochina.[83] Second, there were numerous trials resulting from the *affaires des fuites,* a series of scandals involving official documents being leaked to and published by the media, in particular the newsmagazines *L'Express* and *France observateur.* This was only one of many affairs that had cast shadows over the French during the war: there was also the generals' affair of 1949–50, in which a critical report by General Revers ostensibly found its way into the hands of the Viet Minh, and the illegal trade in piastres (the currency of French Indochina).[84] The impact of the attention paid to these inquests and affairs was the perception of a war that had been mismanaged by the state and the elite, with the soldiers bearing the brunt of each fiasco. Few soldiers or officers spoke out about their experiences, due in part to the fact that many of them were serving in Algeria. Others simply felt that they would not be heard, given that they had not received a warm welcome upon their return to the metropole. A handful of veterans did, however, write extensively about their experiences; Roger Delpey and Erwan Bergot were both especially active.[85]

Public commemoration was minimal in this period: a small ceremony was organized by veterans at the eternal flame under the Arc of Triumph in Paris in 1955 to mark the one-year anniversary of the defeat at Dien Bien Phu, but this was not a state-led affair. Press coverage of the commemorative genre was rare, even in 1959 for the fifth anniversary. Beginning in 1955, French citizens of Indochinese origin, following on the heels of their European counterparts, arrived to start new lives in France. Frequently referred to as "repatriates" because of their citizenship, the majority of these new arrivals were of mixed French and Vietnamese, Lao, or Cambodian heritage. While they created quite a stir in the regions in which they were housed, there was little media coverage or awareness of their experience at the national level. The war in Algeria (1954–62), which mobilized public opinion to a greater degree than the Indochina War had, certainly drew some of the attention away from commemorating the earlier defeat and from the arrival of settlers and former colonial subjects from other parts of the empire.

1964 to 1975

Compared to the dearth of media attention paid to the first and fifth anniversaries of the end of the war, the tenth anniversary in 1964 garnered comparatively more attention. Publications like *Paris Match, Le Figaro, Le Monde,* as well as specialized magazines like *Historama* all published at least one article about the war. The televised current affairs show *Cinq colonnes à la une* aired a special episode on Dien Bien Phu on 8 May.[86] Pierre Schoendoerffer and Marcel Bigeard were the invited guests and were asked to comment on what was presented as Viet Minh film footage of the fall of the French-held position. Bigeard maintained a certain degree of suspicion of the segment depicting the defeat, arguing that some of the details were not accurate (a flag-bearer leading the troops; attacks in broad daylight; French prisoners waving white flags while marching to the camps). The footage it was later discovered was not in fact of the actual defeat but a reconstruction of events staged by the Soviet filmmaker Roman Karmen. This footage would be used in a number of documentaries over the decades, most controversially in Henri de Turenne's 1984 documentary *Vietnam.* The reaction was similar though on a smaller scale in 1964: the extreme right-wing publication *Minute* attacked the producers of the show in a series of articles.[87]

The joint appearance of Bigeard and Schoendoerffer on *Cinq colonnes* marked the beginning of their transition to a position of prominence where commentary on the war was concerned. Bigeard had gone on to serve in Algeria and so was not fully involved with commentary on Indochina until after 1962. Schoendoerffer, in contrast, was a relative unknown until 1964 and the release of his film *La 317ème section* based on his novel of the same name, which was quite well received. From the time of this joint interview until the deaths of the two men in 2010 and 2012, respectively, they were featured in documentaries, interviews, and special editions of magazines and television shows on the topic of Indochina. They each penned several prefaces to works on the war and were expected to comment on other historical works. Geneviève de Galard, who would become the third member of this trinity, did not return fully to the spotlight until the early 1990s, by which time she was as frequently solicited for commentary as Bigeard and Schoendoerffer. In the intervening years, however, she did make a point of publicly voicing her opinion when she felt that veterans were being badly treated. In 1984, for example, she published an open letter to documentarian Henri de Turenne in *Le Figaro,* in which she protested his recent work.[88] Bigeard's and Schoendoerffer's opinions were solicited as well. The three gained special prominence in the early 1990s and were solicited to comment on films, the Georges Boudarel affair, François Mitterrand's trip to Vietnam, and a range of other events and incidents.

Of further significance to the increased—albeit still limited—attention to the Indochina War in the 1960s was the intensification of the American war in Vietnam. Articles appeared in *Le Monde* and *Combat,* for example, tying together the tenth anniversary of the end of the first war with the contemporary American experience.[89] Scholars and journalists writing on the two conflicts, such as Bernard Fall, further contributed to this phenomenon.[90] The long-term impact of the Vietnam War on the French remembrance of the Indochina War was, however, much like that of the Algerian War: a near-total eclipse of the battles waged from 1945 to 1954.

1975 to 1994

The establishment of communist regimes in Laos, Cambodia, and the newly unified Vietnam in 1975 marked a distinct turning point for many veterans who had previously been unwilling to speak publicly about their experiences.[91] For those who had understood their objective as being the containment of communism, the establishment of totalitarian states and the flight of refugees were proof that they had been justified in pursuing that objective. Speaking to the National Assembly, Marcel Bigeard stated that

> when you see what's happened in the last ten years, when you see 500,000 Vietnamese who fled and died in the China Sea, when you see what's happening in the world, I believe—and I say this good and loud—that this war was just and that we were defending freedom.[92]

As a result of this turn there was a marked increase in veterans' willingness to speak out about their experiences, publish their memoirs, and lobby for greater state recognition and commemorative efforts. Indicative of this shift among veterans and others was the publication in July 1975 of a volume of collected works entitled *Requiem for Pnom Penh and Saigon*.[93] Within weeks of the fall of Saigon in April 1975 the publishing company *Société de production littéraire* was soliciting contributions from military officers, politicians, writers, and journalists. Among the more prominent contributors were military figures, such as Henri Navarre and Marcel Bigeard, and figures of the far right, including Jean-Marie Le Pen and Roger Holeindre. The tone was overwhelmingly anticommunist and as the title implies encouraged a collective browbeating over the loss (or abandonment) of the former colony to totalitarianism. A decade later General Bernard Lemattre would write of the events of 1975 that "it took the tragedy of the boat people for many of our compatriots to realize the purpose of our struggle in Indochina, and for the first signs of a moral rehabilitation of the combatants to emerge."[94]

The impact of the change in regimes in the former Indochina, in conjunction with domestic factors,[95] was evident in the increased coverage of the twenty-fifth and thirtieth anniversaries of the end of the war in 1979 and 1984. The years 1974 to 1979 witnessed a steady rise of media coverage culminating in an exponential increase in 1984. In 1980 veterans' groups, including the National Association of Veterans and Friends of Indochina (ANAI), had finally succeeded in their quest to have an unknown soldier of the war honored and buried alongside those of France's other major twentieth-century conflicts. This was the first state-sponsored commemorative site honoring the Indochina War. From this point forward the war experienced a relative surge in the public sphere, beginning with the extensive space devoted by the press to the war and the battle of Dien Bien Phu. Henri de Turenne's documentary series *Vietnam* aired in January and February of that year, provoking controversy and vicious criticism from many veterans and especially from the political right and extreme right. Despite the greater publicity veterans still opted to commemorate the fallen privately, away from the prying eyes of the public, as they had done each seventh of May for decades.

After 1984 interest in or at least awareness of the war snowballed.[96] In 1985 the first thesis addressing the wartime experience of soldiers, and of prisoners of war in particular, was published.[97] In 1986 an agreement was reached with the Vietnamese government providing for the repatriation of the remains of over 25,000 French and colonial soldiers, which prompted the design and construction of the Memorial to the Indochina Wars (Mémorial aux guerres d'Indochine). Ground was broken in 1988 on a site that included an earlier monument (built in 1983); the whole complex was completed in 1996. In 1989, after years of lobbying, former prisoners of war were granted legal status akin to that of those deported by the Nazis.[98] All of this activity culminated in the Georges Boudarel affair of 1991, which brought opposing interpretations of the war and the colonial period into direct confrontation. In the wake of the Boudarel affair and the attendant publicization of the experiences of prisoners of war, the fortieth anniversary of the fall of Dien Bien Phu in 1994 was far more mediatized than previous anniversaries. For the first time a highly placed representative of the government—Minister of Defense François Léotard—attended the commemorative events, which themselves were a more public affair than had long been the case. The war also maintained a heavy presence on the big screen (*L'Amant*, *Indochine*, and *Diên Biên Phu* were all released in 1992), as well as on the small screen through documentaries and special editions of current affairs programs. International affairs played their role as well: diplomatic relations between France and Vietnam changed significantly in this period. Following a period of reform in the mid- to late 1980s, Vietnam opened its borders to tourists from the West, and a number of French veterans took advantage of the opportunity to revisit the country for which they had experienced such nostalgia, commonly known as *le mal jaune*, or "the yellow sickness."[99] In 1993 François Mitterrand became the first French head of state to visit the Socialist Republic of Vietnam, and the first Western head of state to visit the country since the end of the Indochina wars.

1995 to 2005

Although the decade from 1984 to 1994 represents a high point in cultural, legal, and commemorative manifestations of the Indochina War, it was by no means a period of resurgence in the manner of the Algerian War or the Vichy period. Both of these periods were the subject of considerably more press, more public debate, and more intellectual and academic investigation. For example, Fayard published the proceedings of two major conferences held by the Contemporary History Institute (IHTP; Institut d'histoire du temps présent) in 1990 and 1992: *The Algerian War and the French People* and *The Vichy Regime and the French People*. These hefty volumes brought together contributions from top scholars, and both include sections on the politics of remembrance. The Indochina War, in contrast, has not been the subject of a comparable study, nor has it experienced a similar resurgence and integration into French politicocultural life.[100] In fact the period from 1995 to 2005 demonstrates that even as veterans made progress with respect to state recognition—the president of the Republic participated in the fiftieth anniversary events in 2004, and a national day of homage to the dead of the war was instituted in 2005—they were (and are) still fighting for the acknowledgment of the public and for their narrative of the war to gain common acceptance.

Although the state-sponsored commemorative events marking the fiftieth anniversary were, as Nicola Cooper observes, "fairly subdued,"[101] they were nonetheless significant by virtue of the level of government involvement; they were also complemented by a wide range of cultural and scholarly programming. Secretary of State for Veterans' Affairs Hamlaoui Mékachéra had originally hoped to capitalize on the fiftieth anniversary of the end of the war by collaborating with the Vietnamese government on a series of events intended to symbolize the rapprochement of the two countries and create a "shared memory."[102] However, as Alain Barluet reported in *Le Figaro,* "Hanoi was not convinced,"[103] and ultimately each state pursued its own commemorative agenda.[104] In Paris President Jacques Chirac and Defense Minister Michèle Alliot-Marie attended a ceremony at the Invalides, during which Chirac decorated several veterans. Where state collaboration for the fiftieth anniversary failed, however, academic collaboration succeeded: in 2003 and 2004 a series of three conferences on the war were held in Paris, Hanoi, and Beijing. In addition scholars of and participants in the antiwar movement held a one-day conference on the Henri Martin affair. The latter was in fact part of a broader set of commemorative events organized by the city of Montreuil, which has been an important actor in the transmission of the anticolonial narrative of the war.

In May 2005 the state responded to decades of lobbying efforts on the part of veterans by instituting the national day of homage to those who died for France in Indochina (Journée nationale d'hommage aux morts pour la France en Indochine) to be held annually on 8 June.[105] Observed for the first time a month after its creation, 8 June has supplanted 7 May in some veterans' groups, while others continue to commemorate both dates. Public ceremonies are held in a number of communities and departments across the country; in Paris they are centered on a ceremony to relight the eternal flame at the Arc de Triomphe. The question of commemorative dates has also provoked tension between veterans' groups, as two organizations with ties to the

PCF have since the late 1980s commemorated the war on 20 July in recognition of the Geneva Accords.

Despite the events of 2004 and 2005 cultural manifestations of the war between 1994 and 2006 seem to be a pale replica of the 1980s. The Boudarel affair, which dragged on through suits and countersuits until 1997, no longer prompted the violent reactions it initially had. There were two major films released in 2004 and 2006, which mirrored the films of 1992 in that one was a film by Schoendoerffer and the other was an adaptation of a novel by Marguerite Duras;[106] neither, however, was the subject of much controversy, whereas a mere mention of the Sétif massacre in Rachid Bouchareb's *Hors-la-loi* (*Outside the Law,* 2010) triggered intense controversy and soured relations between France and Algeria. The stark difference between the evolution of the place of the Algerian and Indochina wars in the French collective remembrance is evident in the publication in the early 2000s of, one the one hand, Mohammed Harbi and Benjamin Stora's *The Algerian War, 1954–2004: The End of Amnesia* and, on the other, Amédée Thévenet's *The Indochina War Told by Those Who Lived It*.[107] While the former indicates a certain collective reconciliation with a traumatic event, the latter seeks to redress "the persistent misunderstanding among the public of the significance of the Indochina War, the reasons for the struggle we undertook with great pain, but always with the goal of being worthy of the great country that sent us there,"[108] and is explicitly envisioned as part of a duty to remember (*devoir de mémoire*).

2006 to 2014

The period following the fiftieth anniversary of the end of the war has thus far been marked by a steady decline in commemorative activities. If the events of 2004 were subdued, those of 2014 were barely registered by the press or the public. Media coverage of the major anniversary years was often overshadowed by the commemoration of VE Day on 8 May, a problem that persisted even after the creation of the national day of homage, which falls two days after the anniversary of the Normandy landings of June 1944. Indeed in 2014 the major events commemorating the sixtieth anniversary of the Indochina War were moved to the week of 26 April to 4 May so as to avoid conflicting with events in honor of the seventieth anniversary of D-Day.[109] The decline in commemorative attention to the war is due in no small part to the disappearance of those who have long been considered the gatekeepers of memory. The ANAI, long the most active of the veterans' organizations, closed its national headquarters in 2012 due to the advanced age of its leadership and the issue of dwindling membership. The deaths of General Marcel Bigeard in 2010 and of filmmaker Pierre Schoendoerffer in 2012 dealt a further blow to those who have worked long and hard to promote the anticommunist narrative and to increase public awareness of the conflict more generally.

Amid this decline, however, were two high points of engagement for those most invested in the remembrance of the Indochina War. In 2013 the national Army Museum (Musée de l'armée) in Paris presented an exhibit on the French military presence in Indochina from 1856 to 1956, in which one of four sections was devoted to the period from 1940 to 1956.[110] The exhibit was part of the activities surrounding the official France-Vietnam Year (Année France-Vietnam), which marked the fortieth anniversary of the reestablishment of diplomatic relations. It was also the sequel to the museum's 2012 exhibit on Algeria from 1830 to 1962. These were the first exhibits featuring either war to be hosted by the museum and as such represent a further step in the rehabilitation of the soldiers who fought them. Moreover both exhibits were quite balanced, if not entirely impartial, in their presentation of the two conflicts; the Algerian exhibit openly engaged with the troublesome subject of torture, and the Indochina exhibit contextualized the Viet Minh and DRV within the anticolonial and nationalist movements.

More controversial was Defense Minister Gérard Longuet's 2011 proposal to transfer General Marcel Bigeard's ashes to the Pantheon. Bigeard's own wish to have his ashes dispersed over Dien Bien Phu had been firmly rejected by the Vietnamese government, prompting the decision to find an appropriate resting place for him on French soil. While many veterans and others backed Longuet's project, it met with considerable backlash from those who see Bigeard not as a hero who volunteered to parachute into Dien Bien Phu or who had helped to restore order in Algiers, but as a brute and a torturer. The debate over how (and whether) to honor Bigeard had important implications for the remembrance of the Indochina War, not least because he had become such a symbolic figure within the anticommunist narrative. If anything the challenge to his burial at the Pantheon only served to further entrench the image of him as a selfless, courageous hero among his supporters. Ultimately Bigeard was buried on the grounds of the Memorial to the Indochina Wars, a solution that was deemed acceptable even by most of those who had opposed his interment in the Pantheon.

TWO

Remembrance and Rehabilitation

THE ANAI AND THE ANTICOMMUNIST NARRATIVE

> Most veterans of Indochina keep fond memories of it in their hearts, despite the war and their suffering. Many still talk about it with great emotion, as if they could still smell the fragrances, as if they were still watching the daily performance of Indochinese life. [...] When they returned, their memories set them apart from the rest of French society. They felt as though they no longer understood their compatriots, and more importantly that they were incapable of communicating with them. [...] The entirety of these reactions is known as *le Mal jaune,* and it separates the soldiers who served in Indochina from the others.[1]
>
> MICHEL BODIN

VETERANS' ORGANIZATIONS HAVE LONG played a critical role in the commemoration of the wars in which their members fought, and in many cases in the maintenance and transmission of a particular narrative of those conflicts to the public. The First World War led to a new style and scope of war monuments and commemorations, and French veterans' organizations played a central role in these developments as well as in creating support networks and in lobbying for benefits for themselves and their families.[2] The ranks of these organizations, like the National Union of Combatants (UNC; Union nationale des combattants), were later open to veterans of the Second World War, and there was an increasingly diverse spectrum of groups representing former members of the Resistance, deportees, Jewish victims of the Holocaust, and others. The largest association of veterans of the Algerian War is the National Federation of Veterans of Algeria, Morocco and Tunisia (FNACA; Fédération nationale des anciens combattants d'Algérie, Maroc et Tunisie), which has been exceptionally active in the realm of commemoration and remembrance.[3]

Veterans of the Indochina War, however, have no formal organization that is dedicated solely to them. They are eligible for membership in the general veterans' organizations like the UNC as well as groups that are slightly more specific, such as the National Union of Veterans of Indochina, the Exterior Theaters of Operations and North Africa (Union nationale des anciens combattants d'Indochine, des TOE, et d'Afrique du Nord). There have been, however, a number of associations that exist alongside formal veterans' organizations, which provide a forum for veterans to connect, to discuss their shared experiences, and to commemorate their fallen comrades. Among them are the Association of Veterans of Dien Bien Phu (Amicale des anciens de Dien Bien Phu) for those who participated in the final battle, and the National Association of Former Prisoners and Internees in Indochina (ANAPI; Association nationale des anciens prisonniers et internés d'Indochine) for those who were prisoners of either the Japanese or of the Viet Minh.[4] Many of these associations are also members of an umbrella organization known as the National Committee of Veterans of Indochina (Comité national d'entente des anciens d'Indochine). In addition to these military organizations there are a number of civilian groups, such as the Association of Rubber Planters (Amicale des planteurs d'hévéas).

The National Association of Veterans and Friends of Indochina (ANAI), which closed its doors in 2012, was one of the largest associations with a connection to the former Indochina and featured a unique membership composed of veterans and former settlers, as well as a number of members of Vietnamese, Lao, and Cambodian origins. The group also had the distinction of being one of the main carriers of veteran remembrance.[5] The ANAI maintained a central role in state-led commemoration in pursuit of its dual memorial mandate to "honor the memory of those who died in order to defend the freedom of [the Indochinese] people" and to "demonstrate France's accomplishments there over the course of three centuries."[6] Through its internal commemorative activities and its involvement in state-sponsored commemorative projects, the group was among the most active promoters of the anticommunist narrative. The ANAI consistently presented the war as a struggle against communist forces and ideology and almost entirely ignored its colonial aspects.[7] It sought to rehabilitate veterans in the public eye and to rehabilitate the reputation of the colonial project.

Despite the emphasis of many members of the academic community on the dual nature of the conflict, the ANAI maintained its anticommunist focus. The association's narrative of the war cast French soldiers (and others fighting for France) as the partners and protectors of the nationalist Vietnamese as well as other anticommunist forces in the peninsula. In the words of longtime president General Guy Simon: "We do not accept the calls for Franco-Vietnamese reconciliation, because we were never the enemies of the Vietnamese. We fought for them, with them, alongside them, sometimes in front of them, in order to protect their independence from the international communist menace."[8] This theme of partnership extended to the group's commitment to promoting a positive view of colonialism emphasizing three centuries of Franco-Indochinese relations in addition to the ostensible progress instituted by the French. Anticommunism shaped the ANAI's perceptions of colonialism as well, insofar as the conditions imposed by communist governments in the peninsula were compared with those under the French administration of the region.

The following is a case study of the processes by which interest and advocacy groups inflect official discourse and action as well as broader public discourse and action with respect to the various iterations of the colonial past. Analysis will focus on the ANAI's two central mandates as well as on how the ANAI presented (and represented) itself and its aims, primarily through the pages of its quarterly bulletin.[9] The objective is to shed light on the ANAI's construction of particular interpretations of the Indochina War and the colonial project, as well as to examine the parallels between these interpretations and the narratives promoted by the French government, which is explored in greater detail in chapter 4.

ANAI HISTORY AND OBJECTIVES

The origins of the ANAI lie with a gathering of repatriated settlers and veterans at the Arc de Triomphe in September 1947 organized by a Monsieur Gaches, who sought to bring together victims of the Japanese coup of 9 March 1945.[10] This group became the Metropolitan Association of Veterans and Victims of the Indochina War (Association métropolitaine des anciens combattants et victimes de la guerre d'Indochine) and was presided over by Gaches. In November 1964 it merged with the Association of Support for the French of Indochina (Association amicale de prévoyance des Français d'Indochine), then under the leadership of a Docteur Vial. On 14 March 1981 the association absorbed the Souvenir Indochinois,[11] founded in 1917 to oversee the proper burial and maintenance of cemeteries for Indochinese troops who died in Europe during the First World War. This additional commemorative duty underlines the ANAI's own sense of representing the interests of all Indochinese in France, which was further exemplified by its various humanitarian and philanthropic efforts. It was closely linked to the National Franco-Vietnamese, Franco-Cambodian and Franco-Lao Aid Committee (CNE; Comité national d'entraide franco-vietnamien, franco-cambodgien et franco-laotien) created in 1975 to aid those fleeing newly established communist regimes. After 1992 the CNE was actually folded into the ANAI. It also undertook fund-raising efforts to build churches and schools, primarily in Vietnam, and oversaw a sponsorship program for children.

General Guy Simon, a graduate of Saint-Cyr and a veteran of both the Indochina and Algerian wars, was the first veteran to serve as president of the association.[12] His predecessors were lawyer Claude Thomas-Degouy, who presided from the 1964 merger until 1967, and Hélène Bastid, who occupied the post until 1986. Bastid had lived in various parts of Southeast Asia with her husband and family in the period from 1924 to 1934; her son was born in Indochina and was killed there in combat in 1947. Simon took over in 1986 and remained president until the association disbanded in 2012. Never an extremely large group, the ANAI reached a peak membership of approximately ten thousand in 1990,[13] after experiencing a small influx of members. The objective of reaching a wider audience prompted it to open membership in the late 1980s to "friends" of Indochina: "travelers, those performing civil service, investors, researchers, professors, historians [and] linguists interested in contemporary Vietnam, Cambodia, and Laos."[14] This expansion of membership was reflected in the modification of the association's name, which became the National Association of Veterans *and Friends* of Indochina. The increase in membership (specifically of veteran members) is also attributable to the renewed interest in the 1980s in the war and the colonial era described in the introduction and chapter 1.

The association's constitution specifically prohibited "all political, religious and union-related debate,"[15] yet the ANAI was repeatedly involved in a number of public debates that reveal very particular political beliefs. As President Simon stated as recently as 2004, "Communism is still the enemy."[16] In a 2001 editorial Simon argued that the defeat of the French forces led to much worse: the defeat of freedom. After communist control was consolidated in the peninsula, he maintained, "two million Cambodians and 80,000 Vietnamese were assassinated; a million and a half Vietnamese were deported to concentration camps. Three million Indochinese fled using all available means; 500,000 died as a result."[17] The organization's staunch anticommunism targeted domestic groups (such as the French Communist Party) and communist governments abroad equally. While such a position might seem untenable since the collapse of the Soviet bloc, the very fact that there continued to be communist regimes in power in Vietnam, Laos, China, and elsewhere ensured that the ANAI would continue its anticommunist struggle.

Beginning in the late 1970s, the group used a variety of methods to transmit awareness of the Indochina War and a particular vision of the colonial period. First and foremost was its quarterly bulletin, *Bulletin de l'ANAI*, which was transformed from a photocopied and stapled booklet to a glossy color magazine. This publication was intended to be a "remarkable vehicle for the transmission of memory,"[18] but it also served as means by which veterans and regional branches could stay in touch with one another and stay informed about current events in Laos, Cambodia, and Vietnam as well as campaigns undertaken by the association. Since the *Bulletin* was limited to the ANAI membership, the group sought to reach a broader public by organizing exhibits, attempting to pursue pedagogical projects in schools, and engaging in public debates over the colonial legacy. Beginning in the mid-1980s, the ANAI curated exhibits with the support of the Army Information and Public Relations Service (SIRPA; Service d'information et de relations publiques de l'armée) and the Institute of Communication and Audiovisual Production of the Ministry of Defense (ECPAD; Établissement de communication et de production audiovisuelle de la Défense). Composed of mounted photos matched with explanatory panels, the exhibits addressed the colonial period as well as the various stages of the war. The section on the colonial period frequently extended back to the first contact between French missionaries and the inhabitants of the peninsula in the seventeenth century. In 2001 alone, according to its own records, ANAI exhibits were open for a total of fifty-two days across the country.[19]

The ANAI was also committed to gaining a greater foothold in schools, a practice common in France with veterans of the First World War, Holocaust survivors, and former members of the Resistance. Its attempt to reach out to the younger generation is clear from the expansion of its membership, and there is a frequent emphasis in the *Bulletin* on including schoolchildren in commemorative events. Accounts of the activities of regional branches refer occasionally to members, usually veterans, visiting their local schools to relate their experiences to the students. Given the perceived lack of interest on the part of youth, there is even an article from a 1990 issue that gives advice on how to make the Indochinese past interesting, which includes "using contemporary language."[20] The pedagogical goal, according to the *Bulletin,* is to "break the silence, provoke reflection, and above all create awareness in schoolchildren, conscious as we are of the vacuity of the history curriculum."[21] The allusions to the dire situation created by the "leftist tendencies" of the national education system are summarized in one editorial: "The rot has been setting in since 1945."[22]

THE POLITICS OF COMMEMORATION

The ANAI fought strenuously against what it perceived to be a general indifference on the part of the French public and government to those who fought the Indochina War.[23] The association maintained a strong memorial emphasis observing a series of commemorative dates of civilian and military importance in addition to lobbying for state-sponsored ceremonies and monuments. The commemorative dates honored within the organization reflect both the complexities of the process of decolonization from the Second World War through the French defeat at Dien Bien Phu, and the narrative of the war that the ANAI sought to entrench. The association's involvement in the three ceremonies and monuments organized by the state—the burial of the unknown soldier, the Memorial to the Indochina Wars, and the national day of homage—indicates not only the importance accorded to the group by the state but also the degree to which the ANAI's narrative of the war and interpretation of colonialism were reflected in official discourse.

The ANAI's origins as a primarily civilian organization meant that the foundational commemorative date is 9 March, to mark the Japanese takeover of the peninsula in 1945. As a result of this seizure of power French civilians were attacked, tortured, and killed or interned in camps. The ninth of March thus represents an obvious collective trauma, one that affected many ANAI members[24] (in 1985, at any rate; by 2001 General Simon's editorial recognized that most members had not been in Indochina at the time of the attack[25]). Beyond the obvious impact on civilians the association identified 9 March as setting the stage for the Indochina War,[26] since the strength of the Viet Minh grew noticeably after the Japanese were overthrown.[27] Ho Chi Minh declared Vietnamese independence on 2 September in the wake of the Japanese defeat of August 1945. Given the violence of the Japanese overthrow of the French, it is not surprising that the ANAI discourse surrounding 9 March emphasized the "glorious band of 'martyrs'"[28] that resisted the takeover to the best of its abilities, only to be forced into the "obscurity to which these days were relegated."[29] Speeches made at commemorative ceremonies as well as articles published in the ANAI *Bulletin* tended to evoke the heroic resistance of the French. The speech made by the president of the Basque section to commemorate the fortieth anniversary of 9 March is a good example of this rhetoric: "The French resisted heroically, but were outnumbered and were forced to yield. Our prisoners were chained, often tortured, and massacred with machine guns, bayonets, or knives. They demonstrated astounding courage; the Marseillaise was on their lips as they died."[30] The narrative of martyrdom and victimhood, though not unwarranted given the circumstances, provides a significant point of comparison with the ANAI's glorification of the soldiers killed during the course of the war. French (and colonial) troops, particularly those who fought at Dien Bien Phu, were presented as stoic heroes, whose sacrifice for the nation and the freedom of Indochina should be fully recognized.

The parallels between the two sets of victims carry over into a discourse of forgotten martyrs: both the survivors of the Japanese coup and the survivors of Dien Bien Phu, in particular those who survived the camps, are referred to in this language of neglected heroes. There is a common language of a collective trauma that has been ignored by the metropolitan public, and an emphasis on courage and resistance. This discourse was reinforced by the Boudarel affair and the resulting media coverage of the Viet Minh prisoner of war camps, in which mortality rates were exceptionally high due to extreme malnutrition and disease. No matter how public opinion viewed the objectives and tactics of the French expeditionary corps (CEFEO), the emaciated prisoners could hardly be seen as anything but victims. The discourse surrounding the camps identified the prisoners of war as the victims of communism just as those killed in the 9 March coup were the victims of the Japanese. In both cases the emphasis on victimhood serves to elide previous activities; in the case of the prisoners of war it allows their collective actions against civilians and enemy soldiers alike to be overlooked. This is of particular relevance given the CEFEO's use of torture on Viet Minh prisoners and its policy of targeting civilian populations under particular circumstances. With respect to the narrative of French civilians as victims one wonders whether the emphasis on the victims of the Japanese does not also serve to divert attention from, or compensate for, the allegiance to Vichy of French Indochina. An article published in the ANAI *Bulletin* on the Japanese takeover argues not only that these "martyrs" were not given the recognition they deserved but also that they frequently faced postwar purges and saw their careers compromised due to suspicions about their activities under Vichy.³¹ René Poujade, a member of the French resistance in Indochina, argues that there has been a persistent failure to recognize the victims of Vichy in Indochina. In fact, he contends, they are the only French victims of the Second World War to go unacknowledged.³² The ANAI's own discourse arguably contributed to this ignorance of the victims of Vichy (and therefore the perpetrators) by focusing attention on the victims of the Japanese after March 1945.

The amalgamation of the experiences of French settlers and soldiers into a common narrative of victimhood can also be seen as displacing the position of the colonized as victims, a process identified by the editors of *The Politics of War Memory and Commemoration*, who suggest that

> the privileging of veteran memory defines the "survivor" in a way which threatens to displace other kinds of war experience [...] . In addition, the effect of veteran narratives [...] is to leave the impact of violence on the colonized, not just during the "wars," but across the centuries of [...] colonial rule, outside the frame of understanding.³³

In the case of 9 March this process can arguably be extended to include civilian narratives of victimhood, which leave little room for the narratives of those who see themselves or are seen as victims of French colonialism. The diversity of the ANAI membership adds yet another dimension: how could the experiences of its Indochinese members be reconciled with these narratives of victimhood? While the *Bulletin* offers little in the way of a solution to this problem, I would argue that those members who had their roots in the colonized population found their place in the ANAI community primarily because of its anticommunist stance. Though information on such members is sparse, it would be perfectly understandable that Indochinese members of the ANAI sympathized with nationalist (anticommunist) forces. They were thus positioned in solidarity with the soldiers and others who fought the Viet Minh, simultaneously placing them in a community of victims of communism and reinforcing the image of age-old Franco-Indochinese partnership.

While 9 March continued to be a central date for the ANAI, there was a slow shift beginning in the mid-1980s to a greater focus on the anniversary of the fall of Dien Bien Phu (7 May) and later to the official day of homage to the war dead (8 June). The same period was also marked by the transition from the civilian presidency of Hélène Bastid to that of General Simon. The seventh of May was typically commemorated through articles in the *Bulletin* as well as through ceremonies sponsored by the national branch in Paris and by regional branches. There was, however, a recognition that commemorating the battle of Dien Bien Phu overshadowed the contributions of those who had fought in other battles; in 2003 Simon supported the government's plans for commemorative events to mark the fiftieth anniversary the following year but noted that 7 May was not an inclusive date and that "next year we will choose a date that brings them all together."[34] Ultimately 8 June was chosen as the official national day of homage to the dead of the Indochina War, which was celebrated for the first time in 2005.

In addition to 9 March and 7 May, the ANAI maintained a number of other core commemorative dates. These included 19 December, the date of the Viet Minh attacks on French forces in Hanoi in 1946, which the group identified as the beginning of the Indochina War. The second of September was commemorated as the date of the Japanese surrender in 1945. The second of November represented the legacy of the Souvenir Indochinois: it was a day to commemorate the sacrifice of Indochinese troops who fought for France during one of the major conflicts of the twentieth century. Each of these dates involved a ceremony in Paris and often smaller ceremonies in the cities and towns that are home to the departmental sections. There was little variation in the format; members gathered at a particular site, laid wreaths, and made speeches. Based on the accounts of such events in the *Bulletin,* they were generally attended primarily by veterans and thus did not have the same pedagogical role as other commemorative ceremonies in which the ANAI was involved.

The ANAI viewed commemorative ceremonies as public acts that not only created an awareness of the sacrifice of French troops in defending "freedom" in Indochina but also provided a forum to communicate the perceived merits of the colonial system.[35] In fact the "pedagogical value of commemorative ceremonies" was proposed as one of the ways to educate the public about the "realities of French colonialism in Indochina."[36] Since their own events were attended primarily by members, they lobbied for state-sponsored events intended for a broad public audience. The first truly state-sponsored commemorative event to honor the contributions of the veterans of the Indochina War was the burial of an unknown soldier in June 1980 at Notre-Dame-de-Lorette, the traditional resting place of the unknown soldiers of France's twentieth-century conflicts. While the degree of ANAI influence on the government is difficult to ascertain, the group was certainly active: a 1977 issue of the *Bulletin* makes reference to a second letter from Hélène Bastid to

Jean-Jacques Beucler, then minister of veterans' affairs, requesting that an unknown soldier be honored.[37] There is a further reference in a 1979 issue to a meeting between Bastid and the technical advisor to the Cabinet of the Head of State (Conseiller technique au Cabinet du Chef de l'État) the previous July, in which she pleaded for the repatriation of the ashes of an unknown soldier to be formally honored. This was followed by a second meeting in October. The *Bulletin* claimed in 1980 that "without boasting, we can say that the decision [to repatriate and honor an unknown soldier] was due to our President's appeals to the government."[38] Bastid herself referenced the "reiterated efforts and endless procedures" undertaken by the ANAI's executive.[39] While we might question the ANAI's representation of its own role in the process, it is clear that the government held the organization in high regard. Bastid received a personal telephone call from Maurice Plantier, Jean-Jacques Beucler's successor in Veterans' Affairs, to notify her of the impending arrival of the casket at the Roissy airport.[40] She also represented the ANAI at a small ceremony at the Invalides on 28 March to mark the arrival of the casket from Roissy; others in attendance included Anne-Aymone Giscard d'Estaing representing the head of state, Thérèse Leclerc de Hautecloque (wife of Marshal Leclerc), and the governor of the Invalides.[41]

When the official ceremony finally took place in June 1980 (over a period of three days), ANAI members were present at every step. Thirty of them acted as honor guards for the casket throughout the evening vigil on the sixth. Among the two thousand participants of the ceremony at the Invalides on the seventh, which was presided by Giscard d'Estaing, were Bastid and the members of the executive council of the ANAI. At least 190 ANAI members traveled to attend the actual burial at Notre-Dame-de-Lorette.[42] Much of the issue of the *Bulletin* published after these events was devoted to an account of the ceremonies. Overall the association was pleased that the ceremony had finally been organized; however, the author of the account did complain about the lack of overall media coverage, especially on television:

> One could ask—and we will—if it is a case of negligence on the part of the services in question, or whether it was a deliberate decision not to give national recognition to our sacrifices in Indochina. But we will continue our activities so that one day the French people will have knowledge of the Indochinese drama.[43]

The ANAI's efforts regarding the repatriation of war dead from Vietnam did not end with the return of the unknown soldier; rather, they closely followed the state of French military cemeteries that the Vietnamese government threatened to dismantle, and continued to lobby the French government to repatriate as many of the bodies interred there as possible. The *Bulletin* frequently published correspondence between the president of the association and the Ministry for Veterans' Affairs as a means of keeping members informed of the campaign and the progress achieved.

Shortly after the burial of the unknown soldier the ANAI became involved in the creation of a monument in the southern town of Fréjus to honor military and civilian victims in Indochina from 1939 to 1956. The monument, completed and inaugurated in 1983, was the first stage in the complex that is now known as the Memorial of the Indochina Wars, which includes a necropolis, a wall inscribed with the names of the dead, and a small museum. The project was spearheaded by two associations dedicated solely to the project, with the support of the municipality of Fréjus, the deputy of the Var, the Ministry of Defense, and the Ministry of Veterans' Affairs.[44] Once the plans were approved, a national committee was created to oversee the construction of the monument; the presidents of the most important associations of combatants in Indochina were all invited to participate.[45] Interestingly, and despite the association's commitment to commemorating the war, the archives reveal that the ANAI was initially unwilling to lend its support to the project. The source of this unwillingness is unclear particularly since the association was silent on the subject in the pages of the *Bulletin*. One source of displeasure apparently was the design of the bas-relief by Jean Souchon; a regional artist claimed that he had been approached by the vice president of the ANAI to create a new design "that might satisfy the members of the association."[46] While he did not identify the specific issues the ANAI had with the design, he did state that "I admit that this drawing is hardly a happy one. Given the position of the two characters, there is no doubt that the soldier and the Indochinese are going to break their backs against this dragon. Cruel memory!"[47] The bas-relief in question, remaining true to the original drawings, features a pair of soldiers, one French and one Vietnamese, struggling to hold up a map of Indochina with a dragon wrapped around it. The image reflects an emphasis common to the ANAI and most veterans of the war on the collaboration between French forces and the national Vietnamese army against the Viet Minh forces.

Correspondence between Hélène Bastid and Fréjus mayor François Léotard gives further indications of the ANAI's reticence to support the project. In a letter dated 16 November 1981, Léotard offered to meet with Bastid in order to "clear up any misunderstanding" given the "hesitation that [she had] indicated with respect to the project."[48] Nor did Bastid's belated decision to lend the support of the ANAI to the project in February 1982 appear to mollify the mayor's office:

> The ANAI, after having opposed the AEMNAI's project to build a monument in Fréjus, half-heartedly joining on 19 February 1982, and making a very modest financial contribution, now wants to make it a national affair involving the President of the Republic under its own oversight, and even wants to indirectly claim ownership.[49]

With or without the ANAI, the inauguration plans did in fact reach a "national" level. The schedule of events included a wide range of political representatives from all levels of government and an inaugural speech by Minister of Veterans' Affairs Jean Laurain. Interestingly there is nothing in the ANAI's own documentation to suggest that there was ever any kind of disagreement with the other parties involved in the planning. The *Bulletin* presented the association as one of several that had lobbied for a memorial to be built, and highlighted its role as consultant and fund-raiser. The municipality and the ANAI appear to have settled their differences by the time of the inauguration of the monument in March 1983, since Bastid was among those who laid wreaths during the ceremony. Furthermore the ANAI continued to be involved in the subsequent stages of the building of the memorial, maintaining a presence at the groundbreaking ceremony in 1988 and at the inauguration of the necropolis in 1993.

The ANAI was also involved in lobbying for the most recent commemorative project undertaken by the state: the institution in 2005 of a national day of homage to the war dead. The choice of date, 8 June, reflected the ANAI's own preoccupation with finding an anniversary that was both worth celebrating and representative of all combatants. The date corresponds to the burial of the unknown soldier in 1980 and appears to have been an acceptably neutral date for a number of organizations. The ANAI *Bulletin* made a number of references over the years to finding a date that represented *all* combatants of the Indochina War without symbolizing defeat. In 2003 the ANAI requested that President Chirac participate in a ceremony at the tomb of the unknown soldier as part of the fiftieth anniversary celebrations the following year; "June 8th will thereafter be the day of memory for the Indochina wars."[50] The association also claimed responsibility for having secured the president's agreement for the establishment of the day of homage in 2005.[51] Despite the lack of time to prepare (the decree was published on 27 May), the first commemoration of 8 June took place at the Invalides in the presence of a number of representatives of the government and 1,700 veterans, 950 of whom were members of the ANAI. Again the ANAI took credit for the majority of the organization of the event.[52]

The ANAI's commitment to lobbying for specific commemorative events was matched by its commitment to opposing those events it deemed to be inappropriate. In 1988–89 the group successfully led a campaign against UNESCO's proposal for a celebration of the centenary of Ho Chi Minh's birth planned for 1990; though the group acknowledged Ho as an "honest man" and a "patriot," they also viewed him as a perpetrator of crimes against humanity, against his own people, and against foreign troops.[53] The issue was taken up at the National Assembly by right-wing representative Eric Raoult (of the Union pour un mouvement populaire, or UMP, party), who presented it in virtually the same terms as the ANAI had.[54] He further argued that since the Assembly was in the midst of debating whether to establish the status of "prisoner of the Viet Minh," it seemed absurd to contemplate honoring the man responsible for the treatment of those same prisoners. Ultimately the French government decided against state-organized celebrations of the centenary. Reflecting on this victory, General Simon stated that "the ANAI has once again demonstrated the effectiveness of a national organization that is both strong in numbers and in unity."[55] Opposition to the centenary celebrations on the part of regional branches of the ANAI had similar results in Lyons and Marseilles.[56] Likewise the association spoke out against commemorations of the Geneva Accords organized by groups like the Association of Veterans and Victims of the Indochina War (ACVGI). Simon justified this opposition in the following terms:

> If the war had ended honorably, July 20th could have been suitable. However, on the one hand the ceasefire was not respected; many soldiers of the French Union fell after that date. On the other hand, and most importantly, it would be odious to celebrate the abandonment of the friends we fought to defend. Do we celebrate the annexation of Alsace and Lorraine in 1871, or the partition of France into three zones in 1940?[57]

Beyond the judgment of the date as undeserving of commemorative consideration Simon's comparison of Indochina's separation from France with the loss of Alsace-Lorraine and the German occupation goes beyond a common experience of territorial amputations to imply that Indochina was more than just a colony. One could even read into his statement a belief that Indochina had been an integral part of France, which disregards the fact that even at its colonial apogee Indochina had been a series of kingdoms, colonies, and protectorates where metropolitan law and rights never fully penetrated.

The commitment to promoting particular interpretations of the war while opposing events that were thought to undermine these interpretations is also evident in more subtle ways. A bibliography of recommended reading was included in the *Bulletin* since at least 1988, and it was assumed that works on the list were in line with the association's vision. In 1996, however, a further step was taken: in the first edition of the year a special note was included at the end of the bibliography asking whether members wanted to have a space dedicated to publications "deemed to be hostile to the memory that we want to maintain."[58] Several letters published in subsequent issues opposed the proposal, arguing that such censorship was too close to the totalitarian regimes that they had fought against, and the project was never pursued. It should be noted that this opposition was not extended to challenging the narrative of the war promoted by the association; rather, it was limited to critiquing the practice of censorship. Nonetheless, from its reading list to its coverage of the key commemorative dates the association used its bulletin to promote an interpretation of the war in which the French expeditionary corps and local troops had worked together to protect the Indochinese people from the threat of communism.

The Boudarel affair of 1991 (see chapter 6) was one of several galvanizing events for the ANAI, one that members felt highlighted the degree to which French society had ignored veterans of the Indochina War. While it was the ANAPI that took the lead as the representative of prisoners of the Viet Minh and as a party bringing civil action against the professor, the ANAI was nonetheless very vocal. It was also responsible for photocopying extra copies of an invitation to the event, which allowed Jean-Jacques Beucler and other veterans to access the conference in the Senate, where they interrupted Boudarel's paper and accused him of having caused the suffering of detained French soldiers.[59] Many of those with prominent roles in the affair were also members of the ANAI. Beucler was an honorary president of the association. General Yves de Sesmaisons was both a member of the ANAI and the acting president of the ANAPI; he published a number of updates in the ANAI *Bulletin* in order to keep members up to date on the legal proceedings. The association also promoted the sale of anti-Boudarel books such as former

POW Claude Baylé's memoirs and journalist Marc Charuel's *L'Affaire Boudarel*.[60]

THE "POSITIVE" ASPECTS OF COLONIALISM

The ANAI's second major mandate was to combat so-called disinformation about France's colonial past. This disinformation was generally understood as constituting attacks on the merits of colonialism primarily from the political left and extreme left. Charges that the French presence had no lasting benefits for its colonies, and worse, that it had perpetrated abuse and exploitation, were vehemently denied. There were rare instances in which some errors were acknowledged, but overall the focus was on the "progress" initiated by the French. The ANAI *Bulletin* was an obvious choice for promoting this view, and it often featured excerpts from works highlighting French contributions to progress in Indochina. These excerpts were frequently from colonial-era works although this was not usually immediately obvious as the publication dates were usually presented in small type at the end of the piece. One such excerpt from *Colonies Françaises* (*French Colonies*; 1932) outlines French contributions to progress in the areas of agriculture, public health, economic reform, and education, and ultimately concludes that "in Indochina, France has not failed in its role as mother and propagator of civilization."[61] There is no analysis of these documents; they are simply presented as evidence of the positive impact of the French presence. The *Bulletin* also printed accounts of trips to contemporary Vietnam as well as "Contemporary Indochina" sections, both of which tended to emphasize a plethora of problems, from infrastructure to political issues. While this appears to be merely a means of informing the readership of contemporary issues, it also functioned as a means of convincing readers that the region was better off under French tutelage.

The *Bulletin* was naturally not the sole means of communicating the ANAI's perception of the value of colonialism, and the association engaged in a number of public debates. These reached particularly volatile levels in 1984 in response to Henri de Turenne's six-part documentary series *Vietnam*, which was coproduced by Antenne 2. The first three episodes covered the French colonial period and the French war; the second three addressed the U.S.-Vietnam war. The coverage of the colonial period was quite critical of colonial authorities and policies, and Turenne presented the war as a valiant struggle for independence though he did also acknowledge the courage and sacrifice of French troops. The ANAI's immediate reaction was published in *Le Monde* and reprinted in the *Bulletin* under the heading "Falsified History." The author of the letter wrote: "On behalf of all veterans and settlers [*anciens*] of Indochina, I cannot accept that France's work in Indochina, nor the sacrifices she made, be so grossly distorted: it is an insult to both history and the nation."[62] Protest was not limited to letters to the editor, however; the ANAI was involved in demonstrations in front of the offending television network, a letter-writing campaign, and a televised confrontation between four representatives of various groups (including Jean-Jacques Beucler, a member and honorary president of the ANAI) and the producer of the documentary. The ANAI's goal was to "publicly unmask the parody of a trial [of colonialism] instituted by Henri de Turenne."[63] The four critics emphasized the positive contributions to Indochinese society which they felt had been ignored in the series; that is, education, public health, the preservation of cultural heritage, and the elimination of famine, among others. Furthermore they took issue with what they felt was the presentation of the war as one of national liberation from colonial domination, arguing that it was in fact a war between nationalists and communists. Turenne himself was given little time by the four critics to defend himself or his documentary.[64]

Not satisfied with the televised corrective to Turenne's documentary, the ANAI undertook the publication of a book entitled *Indochina: A Warning for History* advertised as "a warning against historical 'disinformation' hatched by a simplistic anticolonialism that is still predominant in France."[65] The foreword by former colonial administrator and prime minister Pierre Messmer states the objectives of the book quite simply:

> It is not a complete overview of the history of Indochina in the second half of the 19th century; neither is it a complete analysis of a century of French policies in Vietnam, Cambodia and Laos. [...] We chose to recall and describe a number of facts, of situations that the director of the film neglected to present, undoubtedly because they contradict the image that he sought to convey.[66]

The introduction, to which ANAI president Hélène Bastid contributed, stresses the importance of recognizing the benefits of the Franco-Indochinese partnership. The book itself is divided into sections on the history of the region; the structure of colonial administration; economic, cultural, and social development; and finally the Indochina War and peace process. The volume concludes with a study of the "historical and cultural convergences between France and Vietnam,"⁶⁷ which brings the theme of a long-standing partnership full circle. Echoing the statements of Turenne's critics during the debate on Antenne 2, the sections addressing the French colonial project focus on the "progress" in terms of protecting Indochinese cultural heritage (particularly through the French School of the Far East, or EFEO), promoting modern sanitary measures, and developing the education system. As a whole the volume interprets the colonial era as one of progress, protection, and propagation of the civilizing mission. An article by Alfred Sibert, a former journalist who spent considerable time in Indochina, makes the dubious claim that the interest and engagement of French settlers in Indochinese monuments and traditions prompted indigenous elites to take a greater interest in their own heritage. Furthermore this interest was made possible by the *pax gallica* that was part and parcel of the French presence.⁶⁸ In an attempt to redress perceptions of a colonial system based on inequality René Charbonneau's article maintains that although the Indochinese were subordinate to the French, particularly in terms of salaries, the difference in salaries corresponded to a difference in cost of living for the two groups: "Comparing the salaries of the Indochinese with those of French expatriates was to assume that all of Indochina had reached France's economic position in one fell swoop."⁶⁹ The sections addressing the war tend to focus on the role of Vietnamese members of the French forces and the territory that was to become South Vietnam; there is also a whole section devoted to the postwar situations of Cambodia and Laos. The range of contributing authors reflects the ANAI membership: there are former settlers, veterans, and people of Indochinese origin.

The emphasis on the positive aspects of colonialism naturally led the ANAI to be particularly critical of those who maintain an anticolonial position, including academics, journalists, and others. In a 1986 article outlining the history of France in Indochina, General Tessot counters an argument from "certain people" that the Indochinese could have "evolved" along a Japanese model without Western intervention.⁷⁰ He justifies the French presence by arguing that the Japanese elite had recognized as early as 1853 that following a Western model was essential to success, whereas the Indochinese elite refused to recognize the necessity of change. The implication is therefore that French intervention was needed to prompt this "modernization." Claims of the negative impact of colonialism are frequently countered with the "evidence" of the boat people and other refugees and immigrants, and not only within the ANAI. If not for a long-standing attachment between the inhabitants of the Indochinese peninsula and the French, it is argued, there would not be so many of them seeking refuge in France. This argument is further reinforced with the claim that there *were* no boat people until after the French presence had ended, suggesting that the French colonial system was better than the communist system that followed.[71] Rather than concentrate on "past blunders" or "exalt French failures while ignoring the successes," the association maintained that a more productive approach was to emphasize the shared Franco-Indochinese past.[72]

This commitment to promoting a positive view of the colonial legacy carried a particular resonance after 2005 when a controversial law was passed affirming the "positive" role of colonialism. Officially known as the law on the "Nation's recognition of the contributions made by repatriated French citizens," it was intended to acknowledge the contributions of French citizens to the colonial project as well as to acknowledge the difficulties faced by those repatriated to France, the sacrifices of those who fought alongside French forces, and the military and civilian victims of the "events associated with the process of independence."[73] The text also included a highly contentious article stating that school and university curricula were to acknowledge the positive aspects of colonialism. The law in general and this article in particular prompted heated debates among academics, special interest groups, and the general public. Supporters of the law emphasized the need to recognize those who had fought for France and been treated badly upon their "repatriation"; this argument was formulated in implicit acknowledgment of the *harkis,* who had fought alongside the French during the Algerian War. Others took a more extreme position arguing that it was time for the French to stop repenting for the "errors" of colonialism and focus on the "progress" initiated by the French presence in Asia, Africa, and elsewhere. Opponents argued that while recognition of the repatriates was long overdue, the law in effect represented a whitewashing of the history of the colonial period.[74] Unsurprisingly the ANAI viewed the law favorably.

THE ANAI AND STATE DISCOURSE

As has been demonstrated, the ANAI played a significant role in state-sponsored commemoration of the Indochina War and in several instances worked closely with government representatives. In light of this position of importance the association's interpretations of both the war and the colonial period are all the more relevant. While the official narrative does not reflect the ANAI's position exactly, there is considerable continuity between the two. Moreover the ANAI's tendency to use the pedagogical aspect of commemorative ceremonies to promote a positive view of colonialism is also reflected, though to a lesser degree, in official discourse. President Valéry Giscard d'Estaing's speech at the burial of the unknown soldier in 1980 emphasized "the contribution that France made to the progress of the people of this other half of the world."[75] This sentiment was echoed in a 1981 speech by the minister of veterans' affairs for the inauguration of a plaque to French dead in Indochina from 1858 to 1955, in which he reminded the audience that "the French presence was, for all those years, synonymous with peace and development."[76] The 1988 inauguration of the first phase of the Indochina War memorial site included speeches by Fréjus mayor François Léotard and Prime Minister Jacques Chirac. Both emphasized the forgotten Indochina War fought in the indifference of the French public. Both also, however, made reference to the colonial period as exemplifying a positive relationship between metropole and colony. Léotard did so less overtly than Chirac, who openly extended recognition to "all those—soldiers, missionaries and administrators—who put their heart and soul in the service of French glory, the expansion of its civilization and of peace."[77] A few years later, speaking at the inauguration of the Square of the Soldiers of Indochina in Paris (Square des combattants d'Indochine), Chirac stated that he believed the colonial relationship to have been "mutually beneficial for France and for those states of the Far East."[78] Although the ANAI was certainly more extreme than state representatives, its affirmation of colonialism as a positive force, and the parallels between the discourses of the two in combination with the evidence of the government's attention to the association, suggest that there is more than mere overlap.

. . .

The ANAI's narrative of the Indochina War, with its emphasis on the partnership between nationalist groups (primarily Vietnamese) and the French expeditionary corps in the struggle against communist forces threatening all three states of the Indochinese peninsula, sidelines the colonial dimension of the conflict. Although the ANAI recognized that the defeat at Dien Bien Phu marked the beginning of the end of French colonialism, it nonetheless viewed the primary outcome of the French defeat not as the independence of the three states that emerged from the former Indochina but rather as the abandonment of colonial "partners" to the communist threat. In this regard the ANAI is not alone: many other veterans' associations along with commentators from the political right and extreme right view the war in a similar light. Furthermore the group's emphasis on the positive role of colonialism ignores the grievances of those who were victimized by the colonial system and sought to overthrow it, whether they were communist or not. That one of the main "carriers" of the remembrance of the Indochina War maintained such an ambiguous relationship with the process of decolonization is indicative of the difficulties inherent in coming to terms with the multifaceted legacy of colonialism, a legacy which the 2005 law sought to address. The case of the ANAI also reveals the complexities inherent in the process of constructing and promoting particular narratives of events. ANAI members, feeling that their contributions to both the Indochinese development and the struggle against communist forces were actively ignored, sought to have these contributions legitimized through advocacy in political, educational, and public arenas. It is significant that this relatively small group had such an impact, primarily on commemorative practices surrounding the Indochina War but also on official discourse of the war and the colonial project.

While the ANAI was long one of the most vocal representatives of the veteran community, it did not represent the views of all veterans. A number of Indochina veterans have in fact positioned themselves in staunch opposition to the procolonial, prowar perspective of the ANAI. Among them are members of the Association of Veterans and Victims of the Indochina War (ACVGI), an organization with ties to the political left and far left, which commemorates the signing of the Geneva Accords in honor of the Vietnamese accession to independence and the return to peace. The ACVGI is just one of several voices that have contributed to the anticolonial narrative of the war; others include scholars and intellectuals, cultural organizations, and a community in the Paris suburbs.

THREE

From Activism to Remembrance

THE ANTICOLONIAL NARRATIVE

> The appeal from President Ho Chi Minh was heard by the entirety of the Vietnamese people, which rose up to defend its independence; the political and military provocations of French colonialism had blocked any possibility of peace, and prompted an atrocious war that would last close to eight years.[1]
>
> CHARLES FOURNIAU

THIS DESCRIPTION OF THE INDOCHINA WAR from historian Charles Fourniau's 1966 *Vietnam at War* illustrates several important themes of the anticolonial narrative: the emphasis on the colonial dimension of the conflict, its identification as a war of national liberation, and the characterization of French reconquest as illegitimate. Some proponents of this interpretation of the conflict overlook its Cold War context, while others engage with it directly. The anticolonial narrative is further characterized by an emphasis on the antiwar movement and even a celebration of it. Henri Martin and Raymonde Dien,[2] both antiwar activists who gained considerable public attention, are central figures. In fact their status in the anticolonial narrative is comparable to the reverence paid to Marcel Bigeard and Geneviève de Galard by proponents of the anticommunist narrative (see chapter 1). More broadly, adherents to the anticolonial narrative tend to emphasize the exploitative nature of colonialism and actively reject what they deem to be "colonial whitewash" promoted by some veterans' groups and elements of the political right. Ho Chi Minh is often evoked as a central figure through his depiction as a nationalist and anticolonial hero rather than as a communist. Several of the groups and individuals examined here are also supporters of the Democratic Republic of Vietnam (DRV) and its successor, the Socialist Republic of Vietnam (SRV), who often avoid critical evaluation of the communist agenda of these regimes. They are often fellow travelers of the French Communist Party (PCF), if not party members.

Those who have shaped the anticolonial narrative are quite disparate in their perspectives and their activities, unlike the proponents of the anticommunist narrative, who are united in their vision of the war and their commitment to commemorating it publicly. Among them are scholars and intellectuals who have shaped this interpretation of the war through their academic work and their activist engagements. Their interpretation is also reflected in the views of several veterans' and civilian organizations. In the former category are the Republican Veterans' Association (ARAC) and the Association of Veterans and Victims of the Indochina War (ACVGI). In the latter category is the Franco-Vietnamese Friendship Association (AAFV), a group that has actively sought to develop strong cultural, diplomatic, and economic ties between France and the DRV/SRV. Finally there is the city of Montreuil, an eastern suburb of Paris, unique in its relationship with Vietnam and its commitment to commemorating the war.

These groups have not only contributed to a shared narrative of colonialism and the Indochina War, but they also overlap in important ways.[3] The AAFV, for example, counts among its members a number of scholars and journalists with an interest in Vietnam and the former Indochina. The association is headquartered in Montreuil and has worked with city representatives on a variety of cultural and commemorative events. Representatives of the city and the AAFV have traditionally attended a ceremony each May to honor the anniversary of Ho Chi Minh's birth and also collaborated (along with the ARAC) on the events marking the fiftieth anniversary of the signature of the Geneva Accords in 2004. Perhaps the most significant connection between all of these groups is their relationship with the French Communist Party. Historically the ARAC has maintained close ties with the PCF as has the AAFV, which was created with party support. Like many Parisian suburbs of the "red belt," Montreuil was a Communist bastion from the 1930s through the turn of the century.[4] Several of the most prominent scholars of Vietnam and colonial Indochina have been members or fellow travelers of the party at one time or another, and some, like Charles Fourniau and Alain Ruscio, have been the motivating force behind the party's work on Vietnam.[5]

THE FRENCH COMMUNIST PARTY AND
THE REMEMBRANCE OF THE INDOCHINA WAR

As the only political party to explicitly denounce the Indochina War it is not surprising that the PCF has been instrumental in shaping the anticolonial narrative of the war. The party has a long history of anticolonial activism, which has been understood as part of the broader struggle against capitalism. Although it was far from being the only source of opposition to the war—there were Christian movements, pacifist organizations, and the editorial staffs of *Esprit, Témoignage chrétien,* and *Franc-Tireur,* among others—the PCF was by far the largest source of antiwar activism.[6] The major figures of the antiwar movement, including Henri Martin and Raymonde Dien, were members of the PCF. The largest demonstrations were led by the party. The most extensive antiwar strikes (including those of dockworkers in the Marseilles port) were initiated in workplaces with strong party and union ties. In spite of the party's active involvement in the antiwar movement and its celebration of Vietnamese victories (1954 and 1973) and reunification (1975–76), the PCF has not been particularly involved in commemorating the war. Martin and Dien remained active in the party after 1954 as did high-ranking party members with close connections to the leadership of the Democratic Republic of Vietnam,[7] yet this did not translate into an active memorial imperative.

The absence of a commemorative agenda where Indochina is concerned can be explained by numerous factors, including the PCF's negotiation of Cold War politics and alliances, its ambiguous position with respect to the Algerian War, and its staunch opposition to the American war in Vietnam. The party's commemorative projects tend to be ideologically inspired (the October 1917 Russian revolution) or related to party history (the founding of *L'Humanité* in 1904, the protests of February 1934, the liberation of France in 1944). This is not to say that the party neglects all commemoration of the Indochina War; in fact *L'Humanité* published one or more articles on the subject in all of the major anniversary years. These articles often share a common purpose: to remind readers that the PCF has always stood firmly in the anti-imperialist camp. In the absence of party-sponsored commemoration, the PCF has nonetheless supported the initiatives undertaken by affiliated (or at least like-minded) organizations such as the ARAC and the AAFV. Communist ideology is also reflected to varying degrees in the work of some French scholars of the colonial era and the Indochina War.

SCHOLARS AND THE CONSTRUCTION
OF THE ANTICOLONIAL NARRATIVE

Research on the Indochina War has been strongly influenced by ideological affiliations and scholars' stance for or against the conflict, which has colored their evaluations of both the war and the DRV.[8] The scholars examined here have all contributed to the anticolonial narrative, and though they represent diverse academic and ideological positions, their work comprises a number of common themes. They all engage with questions of the genesis of the war and the responsibility for its outbreak. They situate the war in its regional and international context, including global decolonization and the Cold War. Finally they all engage with the postcolonial trajectories of Laos, Cambodia, and Vietnam. Collectively their work offers a strong critique of colonialism, explores anticolonial and antiwar movements in metropole and colony, and emphasizes the war as one fought for Vietnamese independence. In spite of this common ground there is a clear division between those who have maintained an unwavering ideological understanding of the war, in which they side with the Democratic Republic of Vietnam against the French and American interventions, and those who have argued for a more nuanced, critical view that explores the ambiguities of French colonialism, the Indochina War, and the DRV.

The historiography of the colonial era and the Indochina War has been shaped by both French and non-French scholars,[9] but the focus here will be on a core group of French intellectuals. In addition to shaping the field, they have also contributed to the foundation of departments, institutes, and research groups that specialize in Southeast Asian studies in general and French Indochina in particular. Charles Fourniau, for example, helped found the Southeast Asian Research Institute (L'Institut de recherche sur le sud-est asiatique).[10] Jean Chesneaux, Pierre Brocheux, Daniel Hémery, and others were key players in the foundation of the Department of Geography and Social Sciences (GSS; Géographie et sciences de la société) of the University of Paris VII, which opened in 1970.[11] The concentration of historians of Vietnam and French Indochina along with the existence of a Department of East Asian Languages and Civilizations made Paris VII one of the top French centers for the study of the region.[12]

The participation of these scholars in a range of political, cultural, and activist organizations as well as their role in public debate and protest campaigns has enabled them to broadcast their perspectives to a wider audience.

A number of them were members of the PCF for some period of time, and several have also been strong supporters of the Communist regime in Hanoi. Despite these shared perspectives, however, there has been considerable ideological division among these scholars.[13] While some, like Charles Fourniau and Alain Ruscio, maintained a commitment to communist ideology if not to the French Communist Party, others, like Jean Chesneaux, Pierre Brocheux, and Daniel Hémery, shifted away from an earlier engagement with the radical left. Still others, like Paul Mus and Philippe Devillers, were not aligned with the left though they unequivocally supported the right of the Vietnamese to independence, even if under a Communist regime. The scholars examined here thus fall into two broad camps: those who have maintained commitment to an ideologically inspired approach to the study of the Indochina War, and those who have not.

Communist Scholars and Fellow Travelers

Scholars in this first category have been not only shaped by their communist ideology but deeply involved in the French Communist Party's work on Vietnam. In an approach that closely reflects the stance of the PCF (and the VCP, Vietnamese Communist Party), they reinforce the legitimacy of the DRV/SRV and emphasize the illegitimacy of French and American intervention in the peninsula.[14] If the proponents of the anticommunist narrative have a selective memory when it comes to the crimes and repression of the French colonial regime, some Communist scholars present a selective interpretation of the DRV and SRV, downplaying the impact of land reform, the repression of dissidents, and other state policies. Charles Fourniau and Alain Ruscio have both played a key role in shaping this version of the anticolonial narrative, though to different degrees. They have followed similar political and academic paths, and while their bodies of work diverge with respect to approach and methodology, their perspectives on colonialism and on the Indochina War are often similar. As will become apparent in later sections of this chapter, their perspectives are reflected in the discourses of both the ARAC (veterans' association) and the AAFV (cultural organization).

Charles Fourniau maintained a longtime commitment to both communist ideology and the DRV/SRV. Joining the PCF in 1951, he became the party's resident expert on Vietnam and even served as a correspondent for *L'Humanité* in the DRV from 1963 to 1965. Fourniau was also a widely respected scholar of the colonial period. His 1983 doctoral thesis focused on Franco-Vietnamese contact between 1858 and 1911 with a heavy emphasis on anticolonial resistance, and his subsequent scholarly monographs primarily addressed anticolonial and nationalist movements.[15] His activism in defense of Vietnamese independence began with membership in the Peace Movement (Mouvement de la paix), which played a significant role in the opposition to the war in Indochina. His commitment to antiwar activism and the defense of Vietnamese independence only increased during the period of the American war: he cofounded the Franco-Vietnamese Friendship Association (AAFV) in 1961 and joined the national committee of the Peace Movement in 1970.

Although Fourniau's academic work focused on the colonial era, it nonetheless informed his perspectives on the Indochina War. Yet it was through his associational and political activities that he made the most significant contributions to the anticolonial narrative of the war. In his introduction to a 1970 collection of reflections on Ho Chi Minh by prominent public figures and activists, Fourniau maintains that at the time of the March 1946 agreements France "had not given up on its objective of domination."[16] He also characterizes the French attack on Haiphong in November 1946 as a "monstrous provocation" that initiated the war.[17] He refers to the "brutal tactics" employed by those in the service of French imperialism, citing the use of napalm in particular. Despite the odds stacked against them, he states, the Vietnamese secured a "brilliant victory" in 1954 thanks to their "courage and intelligence" and the leadership of the Vietnamese Workers Party.[18] The emphasis on the war as being motivated by a French desire to reclaim control of Indochinese territory, and on the inhumane methods that were employed to do so, is in keeping with the general tenets of the anticolonial narrative. But his presentation of the reasons for Vietnamese victory, which echoes the VCP's own narrative, sets him apart from many of his colleagues examined here. Moreover, unlike several of his colleagues, Fourniau was unwilling to undertake any critique of the DRV, so much so that in his 1966 *Vietnam at War* he dismisses the significance of the "errors" of land reform, arguing that "one million seven hundred thousand peasants benefited" and that "Vietnamese society emerged profoundly transformed by this radical renovation of the production system" through which "formidable human energies were finally freed."[19] To be sure, Fourniau's later work does not reflect the same commitment to defending DRV policy evident here; however, he never publicly engaged in a critical examination of it either.

The AAFV *Bulletin* provided an important outlet for Fourniau's arguments against American intervention in Vietnam. He was consistent in his defense of socialist Vietnam and its fight for independence and international standing. Prior to 1975 he wrote pamphlets and articles that were intensely critical of the South Vietnamese regime, all while rejecting any criticism of the policies of the North.[20] He wrote articles commemorating the 1945 founding of the DRV and what he termed the "liberation" of South Vietnam in 1975;[21] in fact he had returned to Vietnam in 1975 to participate in the reunification celebrations. Furthermore he consistently defended the Communist regime of Vietnam after 1975: in 1992, for example, he published a critique of the "permanent malevolence" that "constantly perverts its image."[22] In his memoirs, he presents the August Revolution as a "national movement" that succeeded because

> it found, under the direction of the Party, the possibility of uniting the majority of the population, of all classes, against colonial domination, all the while offering to the peasantry and the nascent working class a vision of freedom from exploitation and misery, for the first time in the history of the country.[23]

Fourniau not only supported the successive Communist regimes of the DRV and SRV but also developed a good relationship with Ho Chi Minh, Pham Van Dong, and several of their successors. His work as a scholar and an activist was acknowledged in 2002 by the Vietnamese government, which inducted him into the Friendship Order (Huan chuong Huu nghi).[24]

Fourniau was a mentor to many younger scholars, but none followed his political and professional path as closely as Alain Ruscio. Like Fourniau, Ruscio was a PCF member who became a correspondent for *L'Humanité* in Vietnam from 1978 to 1980; he was one of very few Western journalists permitted to enter Cambodia in 1979 following the overthrow of the Khmer Rouge regime.[25] He earned his doctorate from the Sorbonne in 1984 and became a prolific historian of French colonialism. He has played a key role in the AAFV and has long served as president of its affiliated documentation center (CID-Vietnam; Centre d'information et de documentation sur le Vietnam); he has also maintained an ideological affinity with communism though he left the PCF in the early 1990s after a decade of increasing disenchantment with the party.[26] In spite of this break Ruscio has remained a defender of the former DRV; in a 2010 piece honoring Fourniau, who died nine days prior to the anniversary of the fall of Saigon, he commented that "we're not used to celebrating without you, Charles, what you, I, we, persisted in calling, come hell or high water, the Liberation of Vietnam."[27]

Like Fourniau, Ruscio has tended to focus on the manifold injustices of the colonial system on the one hand, and the legitimacy of the DRV's actions in demanding independence from foreign intervention on the other. Whereas Fourniau's academic work was primarily concerned with the colonial era, Ruscio has focused much more specifically on the Indochina War. His doctoral thesis, published in 1985, presents a thorough analysis of the wartime policies of the French Communist Party.[28] He has also published a study of the final years of the war and the battle of Dien Bien Phu, a history of the Indochina War, an extensive bibliography of sources on the war, and a book on the history and memory of the battle of Dien Bien Phu, cowritten with Serge Tignères.[29] Like Fourniau, Ruscio devotes considerable attention in his work to the anticolonial and antiwar movements; his history of the Indochina War, for example, covers public opinion and antiwar activism in far greater detail than most other studies.[30] However, he acknowledges the Cold War context of the conflict more directly than Fourniau, and he also engages with the darker side of the DRV. In his 1992 history of the war, for example, he refers to the "numerous blunders [*dérapages*]" of the land reform policy instituted in 1953 and the anger this inspired within the rural population.[31] He also addresses the difficult and often deadly conditions for soldiers detained in Viet Minh POW camps, including the forced labor and forced marches, though he is careful to contextualize these conditions within the broader phenomenon of chronic shortages of food and medicine in Viet Minh–controlled areas.[32]

Beyond his academic work he has also been involved in organizing museum exhibits on the colonial era and on the war, most notably at the Museum of Living History in Montreuil, and has been active in several protest campaigns. In late 2011, for example, he helped to organize opposition to Minister of Defense Gérard Longuet's proposal to transfer General Marcel Bigeard's ashes to the Pantheon. Together with journalist Rosa Moussaoui he drafted a petition that vehemently disagrees with the characterization of Bigeard as "a modern hero, a model of self-sacrifice and courage." The text of the petition argues that he was quite the opposite: an "unprincipled brawler [*baroudeur*] who often used vile methods."[33] The real heroes of the war, the petition states, were "those who, in the colonized countries, fought for freedom and independence; those who, in the metropole, had the foresight to denounce the colonial wars which were so obviously in violation of international law, of the right of self-determination, and of French national interests."[34] The Republican Veterans' Association (ARAC) and other organizations supported this campaign, and ultimately the minister's proposal was abandoned.[35] Bigeard was instead buried at the memorial in Fréjus alongside the other combatants of the Indochina War. This campaign is indicative not only of Ruscio's perspective on the Indochina War but also of his stance on colonialism more broadly. He has long been actively fighting what he describes as colonial revisionism; that is, a desire by some groups in French society to whitewash the violent and repressive facets of colonialism in favor of emphasizing its "benefits" for colonial subjects.[36]

In 2004 to mark the fiftieth anniversary of the end of the war, Ruscio coorganized a conference on antiwar resistance during the Indochina conflict, with a specific focus on Henri Martin.[37] The event was attended by some three hundred people, including Vietnamese ambassador to France Nguyen Dinh Bin, PCF national secretary Marie-George Buffet, and ARAC president Raphaël Vahé. Although it was not publicized as such, this conference served as a counterpoint to a series of conferences held in Paris, Hanoi, and Beijing between November 2003 and April 2004.[38] Ruscio's own role in the "memory wars" being waged over Indochina is evident in his preface to the published conference proceedings.[39] He presents the volume as "memory work" (*travail de mémoire*), which he defines as a more objective, critical study distinct from the "duty to remember" (*devoir de mémoire*).[40] The collection itself is divided into two parts: the first contains academic papers and personal testimonies presented at the conference, and a second part is devoted to contemporary primary source documents. The result is one of the most detailed examinations of the antiwar movement, though its contents and its orientation suggest it falls somewhat closer to a *devoir de mémoire* than Ruscio acknowledges.

In addition to celebrating the antiwar and anticolonial movements, the conference (and the resulting volume) drew explicit connections between these movements and the French Resistance. The focus on Henri Martin, who had fought with the Resistance prior to his engagement in the expeditionary corps, provided a natural opportunity to draw such a connection. The involvement of Raymond Aubrac, a well-known member of the Resistance, on the steering committee, reinforced the resistance credentials of the project. In a short preface to the published conference proceedings Aubrac describes Martin's "refusal to participate in a war against a people fighting for their independence" as evidence of his commitment to "what he had himself been: a French resister."[41] This vision of the antiwar movement as heir to the Resistance is a prominent feature of the anticolonial narrative of the war. Two collections of veterans' accounts of their involvement in the war further reinforce this connection: Marc Chervel's *From the Resistance to the Colonial Wars* and Claude Collin's *From the Resistance to the Indochina War*.[42] Each features accounts of soldiers whose careers spanned the Resistance and one or both of France's colonial wars and who expressed some degree of opposition to the latter. In his preface to Collin's collection Ruscio describes these accounts as redressing the balance in other veterans' accounts, which have in his opinion tended toward an "exaltation of the *good fight*, the *battle for freedom*" and a defense of colonialism.[43]

Noncommunist Intellectuals

The counterpoint to Fourniau's and Ruscio's ideologically inspired analysis of the French war, the colonial period that preceded it, and the American war that followed it is the work of scholars who have either distanced themselves from their engagement with the extreme left or never had any such connections. Among the latter group are Paul Mus and Philippe Devillers, who were also the first two French scholars to offer analyses of the Indochina War. Mus and Devillers shared the common goal of pushing the French state and public to acknowledge the nationalist objectives of Ho Chi Minh and the DRV as both legitimate and widely supported by the Vietnamese people. In their attempts to convince French authorities to negotiate a peace with the DRV both scholars downplayed (though by no means overlooked) the communist agenda of the regime.

Mus was a sociologist and member of the French School of the Far East (EFEO; École française d'Extrême-Orient), who would later become the director of the Colonial Academy (École administrative de la France d'outremer), which trained colonial administrators. Born in France but raised in Vietnam from the age of five, Mus was one of relatively few intellectuals to oppose the war from the outset,[44] a position that was particularly significant given his role in the colonial administration. Mobilized in Europe in 1939, he would later be trained by the Free French in India, who parachuted him into southern Laos in January 1945.[45] Part of his mission was to recruit support among the Vietnamese for the Free French, during which he witnessed the extent of Vietnamese nationalism firsthand; the outpouring of nationalism after the Japanese coup of 9 March 1945 only confirmed his impressions.[46] Christopher Goscha identifies Mus's wartime experience as a turning point in his perspective on colonialism and Vietnamese nationalism and of his evolution as a colonial humanist.⁴⁷ Once he returned to France, he became an adviser to General Leclerc and landed in Cochinchina with the first wave of French troops in September 1945. As the Indochina War got under way, he was convinced that the Vietnamese had the right to national independence, and sought to convince others that a peaceful decolonization was possible. He was subsequently called on for various diplomatic missions, including serving as envoy to Ho Chi Minh in the spring of 1947, by which time he was chair of Far East Civilizations at the prestigious Collège de France.⁴⁸ Beginning in 1949 he made waves with a series of articles in *Témoignage chrétien* critical of the French war effort.⁴⁹ He subsequently lost his position at the Colonial Academy, likely because of these articles.⁵⁰

Although his academic work focused primarily on Southeast Asian ethnological and cultural topics, Mus did publish his reflections on the outbreak of the Indochina War in his 1952 *Viet-Nam: Sociology of a War* with Éditions Seuil, then known for its position in favor of decolonization.⁵¹ Reading more like a collection of essays than a closely knit monograph, the study examines the factors that contributed to the outbreak of war, with a particular focus on the psychological makeup of each of the belligerents. His appreciation of the strength of Vietnamese nationalism and the flawed French understanding of the reality of the colonial situation after 1945 made the book a prescient commentary on current events. Powerful on its own, Mus's work arguably had an even greater impact due to its simultaneous publication with a second foundational work (also at Seuil) by Philippe Devillers, *History of Viet-Nam from 1940 to 1952*,⁵² which earned him a reputation as an authoritative commentator on Vietnam.

Devillers (né Mullender) arrived in Cochinchina in 1945 as a member of Leclerc's press service. He shared sleeping quarters with journalist Jean Lacouture during the trip, and the two became fast friends who would subsequently collaborate on a range of projects: they worked with the team of the *Paris-Saigon* newspaper from its foundation in late 1945 and cowrote several books on the Indochina wars.⁵³ Although he would gain recognition for his critique of the French management of the war, he did not arrive in Saigon with this mind-set. By his own admission Devillers was initially convinced of the legitimacy of the reimposition of French sovereignty.⁵⁴ His early columns for *Le Monde* questioned the ability of the Vietnamese to govern themselves without further education and lauded the positive contributions of the French to the peninsula. He describes his younger self as "a right-wing nationalist, Catholic, militarist, colonialist, imperialist, and even racist."⁵⁵ In his memoir Devillers claims that he was against the war from its origin and that although he wavered between supporting Ho Chi Minh and Bao Dai, his primary objective was "the unity and independence of Viet-Nam."[56] Confronted with the attitudes of many French settlers, the revelations of the use of torture by French forces, and the commitment of Vietnamese patriots to their independence, his perspective changed significantly, he maintains. This evolution can be traced through his newspaper columns as well as the publication of his *History of Viet-Nam,* in which he called for political negotiations leading toward peace, maintaining that the war was a "cancer" eating away at the French nation and, more controversially, that it could have been avoided.[57] Devillers also challenged the conventional notion that the Viet Minh was a relatively weak organization with little popular support; in this sense his work perfectly complemented that of Mus.[58] The book met with remarkable success, selling out its first two editions in four months.[59] His influence on the historiography of the war, begun with his 1952 study, was confirmed with his 1988 monograph *Paris-Saigon-Hanoi: The Archives of the War, 1944–1947.*[60] This study took up several of the arguments from his 1952 book, including French objectives of reestablishing colonial control and the degree of French responsibility for the escalation of the war, but with the added weight of newly accessible archives. He was also actively involved in the movement against the American war in Vietnam and was a longtime member of the AAFV.

A contemporary of Devillers and fellow critic of French and American engagement in Vietnam, Jean Chesneaux would likewise influence the anticolonial narrative. A China specialist and member of the PCF until 1969, Chesneaux published several works on modern Vietnam, including his 1955 *Contribution to the History of Vietnam.*[61] Like several of the scholars under study here, Chesneaux was heavily involved in the AAFV. He was also instrumental in shaping new institutional approaches to the teaching of history, cofounding the Department of Geography and Social Studies (GSS) at the University of Paris VII with Emmanuel Le Roy Ladurie.[62] In the late 1960s and early 1970s Chesneaux recruited three young scholars to join GSS who would all have a tremendous impact on the field of Vietnam and Indochina studies: Pierre Brocheux, Daniel Hémery, and Georges Boudarel.

The members of the GSS department at Paris VII were not only inclined toward activism outside of the confines of academia but also brought that spirit to their work.[63] They sought to redefine their discipline by moving away from the standard historical periodization of the curriculum and from its

Eurocentrism by developing a strong program in Chinese, Southeast Asian, and African studies as well as through their participation in a Third World studies research group.[64] That the formative period for this newly created department coincided with the peak period of the American war in Vietnam (1968–73) through Vietnamese reunification in 1975–76 certainly left an indelible mark on its members. Many French intellectuals were antiwar activists, and as Agathe Larcher-Goscha states, "it was natural that up and coming experts on Vietnam took a position that was consistent with their convictions."[65] Hémery and Chesneaux were members of the antiwar Inter-University Union Committee (Comité Syndical Inter-Universitaire) as well as the Indochina Solidarity Front (Front de Solidarité Indochine), to which Boudarel and Brocheux also belonged; the latter organization was linked to the Communist Revolutionary League (Ligue Communiste Révolutionnaire).[66] As discussed in chapter 6, virtually all of these scholars defended Georges Boudarel during the "affair" of the early 1990s, although most refused to condone his role in Camp 113.

Members of the so-called Chesneaux gang (*bande à Chesneaux*)[67] at Paris VII, Pierre Brocheux and Daniel Hémery established themselves as key figures of a second (post-1945) generation of scholars of the colonial era and the Indochina War, and as the mentors for a third generation of scholars.[68] Together with Georges Boudarel they often collaborated on both academic and nonacademic publications and followed a similar path from embracing communism to critiquing it. In 1980, for example, Brocheux and Hémery published a lengthy article in *Le Monde diplomatique* which highlighted the dire economic situation of Vietnam and the weaknesses of the regime as witnessed during a trip there the previous year.[69] The article not only garnered significant attention in France but also resulted in the suspension of visas for the two by the Vietnamese government for a period of seven years.[70] A few years later Boudarel edited a volume on bureaucracy in Vietnam, which offered a range of critiques of the DRV and SRV.[71] The introduction, cosigned by Boudarel, Hémery, and Brocheux, reveals an ongoing commitment to socialism combined with a critical evaluation of the Vietnamese regime:

> We want Vietnam to be a socialist state. But we think that in that context, everyone should be able to thrive—those who believe in socialism and those who do not—without feeling that their own horizons are limited by their beliefs. In the face of the power of the bureaucracy and the corruption, as well as the massive exodus of skills and knowledge that are exhausting the

country, we must ask ourselves what sort of political regime causes the departure of those it claims to make happy.[72]

In 1991, as communism was collapsing in the former Soviet bloc, Boudarel published a critical study of the violent purge of dissidents in the DRV during the 1954–56 land reform movement, entitled *One Hundred Blooming Flowers in the Vietnamese Night: Communism and Dissidence*.[73] Such willingness to actively critique the policies and actions of the Communist regimes of Vietnam, especially on the part of former members of the PCF (and in Boudarel's case, the VCP), while maintaining a commitment to other tenets of the anticolonial narrative, marks a clear distinction between these scholars on the one hand, and Charles Fourniau on the other.

Although only a relatively small share of their respective bodies of work has focused explicitly on the Indochina War itself, all three scholars have addressed issues related to the war and the rise of communism in the peninsula; all three have also made use of a range of archival sources, including French and Vietnamese materials. Hémery has published work on Vietnamese communism in the interwar period with a particular focus on the 1930s and the impact of the Popular Front; in a 1977 article he identified the failed policies of the short-lived government as one of the medium-term causes of the eventual war of decolonization.[74] Brocheux for his part has published a number of articles and essays on various aspects of the communist revolution and the Indochina War,[75] and he is one of few scholars to have explored issues of historical memory related thereto.[76] Brocheux and Hémery have also published three biographies of Ho Chi Minh between them.[77]

In 1994 Brocheux and Hémery published the first comprehensive study of colonial Indochina.[78] As suggested by its title, *Indochina: An Ambiguous Colonization*, the book elaborates on the complexities of the colonial project. The authors acknowledge the range of motivations for colonization, including the genuine belief that it would improve conditions for colonial subjects but all the while providing a detailed examination of the fundamental inequalities and abuses of the colonial system. On the question of the Indochina War they state unequivocally that the Vietnamese were fighting for their independence. However, they do question whether the characterization of the first phase of the war as one of colonial reconquest is completely accurate.[79] "Was it," they ask, "about colonial reconquest in the most literal sense?" They suggest that the stance of French officials was much more ambiguous than their Viet Minh counterparts and that they operated under the belief that a political solution to the situation in Indochina could only be achieved through military intervention.[80] If French objectives were somewhat ambiguously defined in the first phase of the war, they argue, those of the second were much clearer as the war reflected growing Cold War tensions.[81] Elsewhere Hémery has argued that the war in Indochina should be understood not as a colonial war "seeking to restore the colonial order" but rather as a neocolonial one.[82] The major difference, he argues, is that France's Gaullist government sought to create a new, neocolonial partnership with the elites of each of the constituent countries of French Indochina (a project that would eventually result in the French Union) rather than restore the prewar colonial system. Across their respective works Brocheux and Hémery, along with other scholars, have stressed the dual influence of the colonial and Cold War contexts.

The scholars examined here represent a range of generations, backgrounds, political and ideological alignments, areas of study, and public activities. Mus and Devillers's early characterizations of the war as a legitimate struggle for Vietnamese independence and their critiques of French policy and tactics set the groundwork for subsequent scholars. The second generation, which included Brocheux, Hémery, Boudarel, and Fourniau, became increasingly divided over their interpretations of colonialism and their willingness to critique successive Communist regimes in Vietnam. Alain Ruscio for his part has pursued a less stringently ideological approach to the war than his mentor Fourniau, and has published more work on the Indochina War than any of the other scholars studied here. Despite these vast differences these scholars have all made significant contributions to the anticolonial narrative, and their arguments have been taken up by numerous groups seeking to define the Indochina War as an illegitimate war of colonial reconquest. Among these groups are two veterans' associations—the ARAC and the ACVGI—and the civilian Franco-Vietnamese Friendship Association (AAFV).

"WAGING WAR AGAINST WAR": VETERANS AND THE ANTICOLONIAL NARRATIVE

While the ANAI (National Association of Veterans and Friends of Indochina) has been the most vocal organization representing veterans of the Indochina War, there are many within the wider veteran community who fundamentally disagree with its perspective. Some of them joined antiwar organizations during the war itself, and some went on to protest the Algerian War.[83] Many of them would join the Republican Veterans' Association (ARAC), which brings together veterans of all of France's twentieth-century conflicts. Later they would found an affiliated group, the Association of Veterans and Victims of the Indochina War (ACVGI). Through their shared anticolonial and antiwar stance both groups have played a prominent role in shaping the anticolonial narrative.

The ARAC was founded in 1917 by leftist intellectuals Raymond Lefebvre and Paul Vaillant-Couturier, metalworker Georges Bruyère, and Henri Barbusse, who had gained great recognition for his 1916 antiwar novel *Under Fire* (*Le feu*). All would join the PCF in the early 1920s. From its inception the ARAC has been committed to antimilitarism: one of the association's earliest and longest-lasting slogans is "Waging war against war" (*Faire la guerre à la guerre*), a refrain common to several pacifist and antiwar organizations. As Norman Ingram has demonstrated, however, the pacifism of the interwar period was a varied enterprise; while some organizations opposed all violent conflict, others opposed war but made exceptions for the proletarian revolution.[84] The ARAC fell into this latter category, though it occasionally set its antimilitarism aside, as during the campaigns against the extreme right in the 1920s and 1930s.[85] The ARAC leadership has also maintained close ties with the PCF; historically many of its executive members have also been party members.

Like the PCF, the ARAC sent regular delegations to the Soviet Union and the Eastern Bloc, and it continues to maintain ties with the Socialist Republic of Vietnam. By 1990 the ARAC—like the ANAI—was organizing trips to Vietnam;[86] unlike the ANAI's trips, ARAC's trips included meetings with government representatives. At the same time, it initiated a solidarity campaign to raise funds for humanitarian projects in Vietnam, including the development of the "Friendship Village," an international project to build a village with the necessary infrastructure to care for orphaned children and those with severe disabilities resulting from the war with the United States and in particular the effects of Agent Orange. Even as the organization distanced itself somewhat from the Soviet-style communism of the Eastern Bloc,[87] it has remained an essentially communist-oriented organization, which has frequently brought it into conflict with right-leaning veterans' groups and politicians.

The ARAC was very vocal in its opposition to both the Indochina and Algerian wars, on the basis of a general principle of pacifism as well as a specific opposition to the maintenance of French sovereignty over these regions. A 1953 article in the ARAC bulletin, *Le Réveil des combattants* (*The Soldiers' Awakening*), argued that "the Indochina War is ruining the nation: thousands of young Frenchmen are dying, or mutilated, or disabled through illness, and the gulf that separates the Vietnamese people from France is growing wider every day."[88] Moreover the war was described as a "bloody colonial expedition" that sought to deny "the political aspirations of a nation of 25 million people" in order to maintain the "privileges of the rubber and rice corporations and the Bank of Indochina."[89] The ARAC further denounced the reassignment of soldiers who had enlisted to fight the Japanese only to find themselves being used "against their wills to crush the young Republic of Viet-Nam."[90] Criticism of the treatment of French expeditionary corps (CEFEO) soldiers continued through the end of the war; shortly before the fall of Dien Bien Phu an article by Jean Bresson addressed the treatment of liberated CEFEO prisoners by French authorities. While in captivity, he argued, prisoners "had heard the Vietnamese, free in their own country, speak of their aspirations, explain why they were fighting against the expeditionary corps, and express the friendship they felt for [the French] people despite the suffering imposed on them by [the French] government." Upon liberation, he maintained, French military authorities deemed it necessary to "eradicate all of these evil things that were contributing to an 'intolerable poisoning' of the spirit," and essentially brainwashed them into believing that "what they had heard was false, that they had been mistreated, and that the Viet-Minh was nothing but a gang of pillagers."[91] The end of the war was met with relief by the ARAC, which expressed excitement for Vietnam's newfound independence.[92]

As was the case across French society, the ARAC paid little attention to the commemoration of the Indochina War during the Algerian and American-Vietnam wars. It was not until the mid-1980s that the association began to address the legacies of the conflict. The war is clearly defined in associational literature as a colonial conflict; more dramatic descriptions cast the French wartime military and political leadership as "the extremists of reconquest" (*les ultras de la reconquête*).[93] There is little engagement with the broader Cold War context or the impact of DRV policies on Vietnamese citizens. The advent of a more explicit focus on commemoration within the association in the late 1980s only accentuated the characterization of the war as a struggle for national independence from colonial rule. As opposed to groups like the ANAI, the ACVGI advocated remembering not only those who fought and died in combat but also "the repression in France of the men and women who fought for peace."[94] In other words the ACVGI sought justice for those who had actively protested French military engagement and who had been arrested, imprisoned, or fired from their jobs as a result. This had particular resonance given that it coincided with the campaign spearheaded by the ANAPI and the ANAI for the creation of the status of "prisoner of the Viet Minh" akin to the status granted to those who had been deported by the Nazis during the Second World War.

The ARAC's commitment to war remembrance was reinforced with the 1989 creation of a commission on civic duty, history, and memory. Among other things this resulted in a new "Civics and Memory" section to the monthly bulletin, which was expanded in 2008 with the publication of a special "memory" supplement (*Cahiers de mémoire*); the sixth such supplement was devoted to the Indochina War.[95] This special issue included an overview of the war by Alain Ruscio as well as reprints of excerpts from eyewitness accounts and commentaries of a range of militants, from striking dockworker Alfred Pacini to Raymond Aubrac's reflections on the outbreak of war. In his editorial Paul Markidès argued that French leaders "weren't capable of seizing the opportunities offered by the Vietnamese leadership for reaching an agreement, nor did they understand that colonialism had already been condemned."[96]

While the ARAC addresses the issues faced by veterans of multiple wars, the specific interests of veterans of the Indochina War led to the creation in 1987 of an affiliated group, the ACVGI (Association of Veterans and Victims of the Indochina War). The ARAC and the ACVGI share a common perspective on the legacies of the Indochina War and colonialism as well as significant crossover in both leadership and membership.[97] The ACVGI is a small organization even in comparison to groups like the ANAI, but its influence is bolstered by its affiliation with the ARAC. The founding objectives of the ACVGI focused first and foremost on the right to reparations "for physical, psychological, material and moral damage suffered by veterans, victims of the war, and those who fought for peace through negotiation."[98] Thus it was never intended to be simply a veterans' organization but also one that represents other "victims" of the war, including those who have been targeted for their antiwar activities. Like the ANAI, the ACVGI is also focused on informing the public and especially the younger generation about the Indochina War and the legacies of colonialism. The ACVGI leadership was also clearly responding to the agenda set by the ANAI, the ANAPI, and others responsible for the anticommunist narrative. In 1991 President Guy Lamothe described the founding of the association as a response to "the justification [*apologie*] of the war carried out in Indochina" and to the fact that the "'merits of French civilization' ha[d] been granted a prominent place." He further argued that "considerable liberties ha[d] been taken with respect to historical truth."[99] The ARAC, too, claimed to be pursuing "historical truth" by challenging "the nostalgics, politicians, brawlers [*baroudeurs*] and patent falsifiers" who seek to "exorcise reality in order to save the honor of the French army in Indochina."[100] This conviction led both groups not only to protest the 2005 law on the positive aspects of colonization but also to continue to challenge the attitudes associated with it long after its abrogation. In 2008 the ARAC executive argued that

> the main elements of the law remain. The role and impact of French colonialism are validated without taking into account the long series of wars and injustices it wrought over the course of several centuries. This law is not only the expression of attachment to French colonization, it also opens the door to neocolonial ideas, which threaten friendship and peace between peoples.[101]

Since 1988 the ACVGI has commemorated the signature of the Geneva Accords, a practice which has been met with considerably hostility. Every 20 July association members hold a ceremony at the Arc de Triomphe in recognition of "the victory of reason, of French national interests, of peace, and of fraternity and cooperation between peoples."[102] Representatives of the ARAC, the AAFV, and the PCF invariably participate. The ANAI for its part has repeatedly and vociferously denounced the practice.[103] This practice of commemorating 20 July echoes the far more contentious campaign waged by the ARAC and others for an official day of commemoration of the Algerian War on 19 March, the date of the ceasefire in 1962.

The bitter animosity between the ANAI and the ACVGI over the appropriate date for commemoration of the war is but one example of a larger conflict between the two groups. The ARAC has long been a target for politicians and veterans of the right and extreme right, but the ACVGI was confronted with a particularly vicious attack campaign a few years after its creation. It all began innocuously enough: in January 1990 the ACVGI submitted a request for membership in the French Union of Veterans' and War Victims' Associations (UFAC; Union française des associations de combattants et de victimes de guerre), an umbrella organization that at the time brought together over fifty veterans' associations. The request lay dormant for two years until it was brought to a vote in January 1992 and accepted. On 7 May 1992 Jean-Jacques Beucler, who had instigated the Boudarel affair just a year earlier, published an article in the conservative newspaper *Le Figaro* (entitled "Boudarel—The Sequel") denouncing the ACVGI as nothing less than "partisans of the Viet Minh."[104] He describes the association's membership as comprising those who "engaged in treason for the benefit of the Vietminh," including "the one who, in 1950, symbolized the sabotage of the expeditionary corps in Indochina" and "the one who preached desertion."[105] A week after Beucler's article the extreme-right-wing publication *Minute-La France* added to the sensationalization of the story with the following lede: "A mysterious organization of traitors who defected to the enemy during the Indochina War has secretly infiltrated veterans' groups. Its objective? To rehabilitate deserters and torturers."[106] The connections with the ARAC, described as "the ultra-official line of communication from the Communist Party," were also highlighted. The ANAI also entered the fray, informing its members of the objectives of the ACVGI, which it maintained were to advance the interests of

> the "spontaneous" protestors who impeded the departure of trains and ships transporting troops or materiel, those who tore off the bandages of the wounded aboard a train stopped at the Avignon station, the workers who sabotaged vehicles and armaments in munitions factories, deserters, mutineers, and communist activists in the army who remained more militant than military.[107]

These characterizations are extreme, but they are representative of a tendency by some on the political right and especially the extreme right to conflate those who disagreed with the war, those who protested it, and those who committed acts of sabotage, treason, and desertion: all are consigned to the category of traitors and saboteurs.

The executive of the UFAC faced considerable pressure to rescind the membership of the ACVGI,[108] which it refused to do, arguing that the UFAC was a pluralist, inclusive organization. In response to these accusations the ACVGI issued a press release and invoked its right to respond (*droit de réponse*) in several newspapers. The published responses all address similar points and at times are identical in their wording. In *Le Journal des combattants,* Robert Croenne not only responds to what he calls "offensive" accusations and "baseless rantings" but also presents a rectification of the depiction of the Indochina War:

History has shown that this war waged by France was a war of colonial reconquest, while for the Vietnamese, Lao and Cambodian people, it was a war of national liberation. The responsibility for the war, the dead, the wounded, the prisoners, and the invalids lies solely with the civilian and military authorities who initiated it, and the successive governments who accepted and pursued it blindly until defeat. They are the ones who acted against the interests of France.[109]

This brief statement captures the essence of the anticolonial narrative, which continues to be promoted by the ACVGI and the ARAC. In a 1995 critique of an exhibit on the Indochina War sponsored by an unnamed veterans' organization in Guéret (Creuse), ACVGI member Louis Gohin decried the glorification of the colonial project and the mischaracterization of the causes of the war ("not one word on the events at Hai Phong, of the bombing of civilians"[110]). He also devoted considerable space to the treatment of CEFEO prisoners of war, which was apparently a significant theme in the exhibit. While he openly acknowledges that soldiers, and POWs in particular, suffered during the war, he echoes Alain Ruscio's argument in *The French Indochina War* that the reason so many prisoners suffered was because of the shortage of food and medicine in Viet Minh areas rather than as the result of intentional deprivation. He concludes by asking, "Can we seriously accept that the high mortality rate among prisoners was due to the deliberate intentions of the Vietnamese?"[111] Nowhere in the article is there any mention of the Cold War context of the conflict, a common theme within both the ARAC and the ACVGI.

THE CIVILIAN DIMENSION: THE FRANCO-VIETNAMESE FRIENDSHIP ASSOCIATION

The characterization of the Indochina War as a colonial conflict intent on depriving the Indochinese of their right to independence and the celebration of the antiwar/anticolonial movement promoted by the ARAC and the ACVGI find their echo in the Franco-Vietnamese Friendship Association (AAFV), a civilian organization dedicated to promoting cultural ties with Vietnam. The AAFV was founded in 1961 just as the United States stepped up its involvement in Vietnam. Its founders had four major objectives: to educate the French public about Vietnamese culture, society, and current affairs; to develop and maintain friendly Franco-Vietnamese relations in the cultural, scientific, economic, and social spheres; to lobby the French government to take the necessary steps to ensuring peace in Vietnam as well as its reunification; and to eliminate the uneven treatment of the two Vietnamese states, notably by establishing diplomatic ties with the Democratic Republic of Vietnam.[112] As these objectives might suggest, the AAFV was a strong supporter of the DRV and the Provisional Revolutionary Government of South Vietnam, and later of the Socialist Republic of Vietnam. It was also a staunch opponent of both the Republic of Vietnam (South Vietnam) and American interventionism. Despite its pro-Hanoi stance, it is worth noting that not all members of the association have been members of the PCF or even fellow travelers. The AAFV was further motivated by the conviction that French interests were best served by an "open and cooperative attitude favorable to the spread of French culture," and expressed a commitment to nurturing the friendship established between the French and Vietnamese people over a century and a half.[113]

The founders of the AAFV—Alice Kahn, Elie Mignot, and Charles Fourniau—were members of the PCF, and the association has long enjoyed party support.[114] The three shared a keen interest in Vietnam for both personal and professional reasons. Kahn, who is credited with the idea of founding the association,[115] spent three years with her children and journalist husband in the DRV. Elie Mignot was a former delegate to the French Union as well as the director of the Asia section of the PCF's foreign policy section. Charles Fourniau, as discussed above, would become the PCF's resident expert on Vietnam as well as a Vietnam correspondent for *L'Humanité* shortly after the founding of the AAFV. The three founders were joined on the national committee by several other prominent academics, public figures, and PCF members associated with Vietnam, including Henri Martin and historian Jean Chesneaux. Over the decades association membership has included a number of other prominent academics and public figures associated with Vietnam.[116] Many of the early members of the association were "veterans of the battles for peace and against the French and American wars," but over the decades membership expanded to include

> younger members who hadn't known those heroic times but who want to understand the trajectory of [Vietnam's] development; others who are seeking to explain the connections between the two peoples, marked by the cruelty of colonialism, but also by the solidarity of French anticolonialists; and those who simply find the country beautiful and its inhabitants kind.[117]

The evolution of the AAFV falls into three distinct periods. Its first few years of existence were characterized by efforts to rebuild Franco-Vietnamese ties, which had been "condemned to disappear" after 1954.[118] The second major phase, from 1965 to 1975, was shaped by the American Vietnam war, during which the association "stood with Vietnam in the battle for its survival as an independent state."[119] Issues of the AAFV *Bulletin* from this period are redolent with anti-Americanism and scathing critiques of the Diem regime as well as its successors. The United States is presented as yet another imperialist aggressor that the Vietnamese had to drive out; the successive regimes of the South in turn are accused of perpetrating atrocious crimes against their own people.[120]

AAFV members were also involved in protest activities, and they published books and pamphlets on the use of chemical warfare in the South, American war crimes, and related topics.[121] The association's solidarity with those Vietnamese fighting against the United States led it to meet with the delegation representing the Provisional Revolutionary Government (PRG) attending the 1970 negotiations in Paris, and to send a delegation to the DRV in 1972 to report on the situation there. It also donated school supplies and funds for medical supplies to the PRG.[122] AAFV activities were not solely focused on the war and its ramifications, however; members were also committed to informing the French public of Vietnamese history, culture, and current events. In its early years the association sought to do this through dinner-debates and information sessions.[123] By the early 1970s the AAFV was preparing photo-based exhibits on the impact of the American war on the Vietnamese people as well as on Vietnamese culture and traditions.

With the fall of Saigon in 1975 and the political reunification of Vietnam in 1976 the AAFV reevaluated its priorities. The national committee reorganized its activities along the three central axes of information, cooperation, and solidarity. Each axis reflected existing areas of activity, but these were significantly expanded. In the realm of information, for example, members of the association created the Center for Information and Documentation on Vietnam (CID-Vietnam) in 1985. The CID-Vietnam maintains an extensive collection of scholarly work from around the world in addition to periodicals, specialized magazines, and personal collections of documents dating back to the 1950s. An agreement with the Hanoi National Library guarantees regular deliveries of Vietnamese periodicals, monographs, and other materials; CID-Vietnam now claims one of the most comprehensive collections of Vietnamese materials in Europe.[124] In addition to making these resources available to scholars, CID-Vietnam has partnered with other organizations, such as the Vietnamese Cultural Center, to stage events such as the 2014 exhibit and miniconference on "Combatants for Peace in Vietnam" (Combattants pour la paix au Vietnam).[125]

The axes of cooperation and solidarity were established as distinct spheres of activity, although there is often considerable overlap between the two. "Cooperation" was intended to focus on scientific, medical, social, and cultural partnerships between the two countries, while "solidarity" was to affirm economic support for reconstruction and development. The AAFV has worked with the Pasteur Institute in Ho Chi Minh City to develop a BCG lab,[126] and was solicited by the European Union to collaborate on a program to treat blindness at clinics in Hanoi and Ho Chi Minh City. One of the AAFV's major campaigns in recent years has been to lobby for greater research into the effects of Agent Orange and for compensation for its victims.

Although the AAFV is not mandated to commemorate the Indochina War in the way that groups like the ANAI are, it nonetheless contributes to the anticolonial narrative of the French conflict. In 2004 AAFV president Francis Gendreau stated that while the association

> did not yet exist at the time of the battle of Dien Bien Phu and the signature of the Geneva Accords in 1954, [its] battle against the "American war" and in favor of peace and unity in Vietnam was an extension of the struggles of the anticolonial movements that protested the "Indochina war."[127]

In fact the association traces its lineage back to the period prior to the Indochina War, and specifically to the 1933 Committee for the Amnesty and Defense of the Indochinese (Comité d'amnistie et de défense des Indochinois). Counting Romain Rolland, Henri Barbusse, Victor Margueritte, and Andrée Viollis in its ranks, the group brought together anticolonialists, pacifists, socialists, communists, and communist sympathizers to stand against the French treatment of Indochinese subjects.[128] The same anticolonial stance was central to the France-Viet Nam Association (AFV) established in 1946 in solidarity with Ho Chi Minh and the other Vietnamese delegates to the Fontainebleau conference. The group was short-lived, disbanding in late 1949, but is often cited in AAFV literature as its own direct antecedent. A third organization, founded in 1952, the National Research and Action Committee for the Peaceful Conclusion of the Vietnam War (Comité national d'étude et d'action pour le règlement pacifique de la guerre du Vietnam), also contributed to the ideological framework of the AAFV.[129] By claiming the legacy of these earlier organizations, the AAFV clearly positions itself within a tradition of protest and activism dedicated to Vietnamese independence.

The emphasis on anticolonialism and protest is conveyed through portraits of a variety of activists in the AAFV *Bulletin*. Justin Godart and Andrée Viollis are both the subject of biographical articles,[130] and other articles remind readers of the role of association members Henri Martin, Raymonde Dien, and Raymond Aubrac during the Indochina War. Furthermore controversial figures like Georges Boudarel receive sympathetic treatment.[131] In an article on Boudarel following his death in December 2003, Monique Chemillier-Gendreau describes him as "belonging in the category of the 'Righteous' [*les Justes*]" for his refusal to accept "the political project of colonialism, the mentalities it engendered, or the abandonment of principles it required."[132] She also qualified those who denounced Boudarel as seeking to "rehabilitate the colonial expedition and discredit the anticolonial struggle."[133] Boudarel's position is explicitly aligned with the AAFV's objectives, which is particularly interesting given that there was no such defense of Boudarel in the *Bulletin* at the time of the affair, and this despite the fact that he had at one time been a member of the association.[134] A biography of Albert Clavier on the occasion of his death in 2011 was similarly elegiac. A member of the expeditionary corps, Clavier deserted and joined the Viet Minh; he recounted his experiences in a 2008 memoir entitled *From Colonial Indochina to Independent Vietnam: I Regret Nothing*.[135] The AAFV article concludes with a reflection on the memoir's subtitle: "Indeed, what is there to regret? Those who remain will be inspired by his actions."[136]

Above and beyond the emphasis on anticolonialism, the association's commitment to upholding Vietnam's right to independence led it to give its unqualified support to Ho Chi Minh's regime as the legitimate representative of the Vietnamese people and the only possible guarantor of independence. While this support was motivated in large part by the context of the American Vietnam war, it is also consonant with a vision of the Indochina War as a "heroic battle for independence and national sovereignty."[137] Along with this support of the DRV is the absence of any critique of its policies during the war or after. Ho Chi Minh is celebrated for proclaiming and fighting to protect this independence; indeed he is almost exclusively referred to as a hero and a leader who made great sacrifices for his people.[138] Upon his death in 1969 the AAFV sent a letter expressing its condolences to the North Vietnamese delegation attending peace negotiations in Paris, which described him as having led a "long career dedicated to the Independence of Vietnam [and] the Happiness and Security of the Vietnamese people."[139] The association also undertook the publication of a special commemorative booklet (*plaquette souvenir*) with a photo, a short biography, and three poems from Ho's prison diaries. This celebration of Ho was eventually transformed into a memorial imperative within the association.

In 1990 the AAFV was involved in the events organized by UNESCO to celebrate the centenary of Ho Chi Minh's birth, though the *Bulletin* expressed dismay over the limited number and scope of events—limitations that the ANAI congratulated itself on having achieved (see chapter 1).[140] In a piece published in the AAFV *Bulletin* in preparation for the centenary events, Alain Ruscio addressed diverging French perspectives on the Vietnamese leader: "For some, his name will always be linked with the 'international communist' plot that chased 'us' from Indochina. For others, Ho Chi Minh was the standard-bearer of one of the most important—and most positive—movements of the century: the emancipation of formerly colonized peoples."[141] Unsurprisingly the AAFV is firmly committed to promoting the latter interpretation of Ho Chi Minh. Since the 2005 inauguration of a bust of Ho Chi Minh in Montreau Park in Montreuil, the AAFV has participated in a small annual ceremony commemorating Ho's date of birth, to which Vietnamese representatives are also invited. Nor has the group's support been limited to Ho Chi Minh: the association has continued to support the Vietnamese government since Ho's death in 1969.

As is the case with some communist scholarly analyses, the AAFV *Bulletin* is selective in its representation of events, even those addressed and debated by anticolonial scholars. The impact of land reform and the repression of dissidents in the 1950s are never mentioned, and at the height of the American war the Vietnamese are shown as remaining steadfast even in the face of the crimes of the regime in the South and the devastation wrought in the North by American bombs.[142] Following a trip to Vietnam in 1975, Fourniau assured AAFV members that "the PRG's promise to pursue a policy of national reconciliation has been fulfilled," maintaining that rather than severe punishment the PRG had imposed only short education programs on supporters of the Republic of Vietnam.[143] The ideological alignment evident in this AAFV article has obvious implications for the association's vision of the Indochina War and its combatants.

For the first four decades of its existence the association's commemorative activities were overwhelmingly focused on important dates in post-1945

Vietnamese history and the association's own milestones. However, the Indochina War came increasingly into focus in the last years of the twentieth century. This transition is apparent in the AAFV's collaboration with *Mémoires Vivantes* (Living memories)—a group dedicated to popularizing aspects of Marseilles's history—on an exhibit and a book highlighting the connection between Marseilles and Indochina. The book, entitled *Words for Xuan and Marius: Marseilles and Indochina,* addresses the Franco-Indochinese relationship from the beginning of the colonial era to the era of decolonization with a special focus on the city of Marseilles as a point of colonial exchange.[144] The book is framed as an explanation to Xuan, born in Ho Chi Minh City, and Marius, born in Marseilles, of the history that connects their two countries; according to the AAFV, the target audience was middle school students.[145] Among the topics covered are Marseilles's role in colonial trade; the exploitative nature of French colonialism in Indochina (supplemented with excerpts of Andrée Viollis's *Indochine SOS*); and opposition to the "dirty war" in Indochina with a specific focus on the striking dockworkers of Marseilles. Far from constituting a mere explanation of the historical connections between France and Vietnam to two imaginary adolescents, the book is thus an ideologically oriented exploration of anticolonialism and the antiwar movement.

The fiftieth anniversary of the end of the war prompted a flurry of activity in the pages of the AAFV *Bulletin.* In the January 2004 issue the war is described as both a "national independence movement" and as "just one stage in the painful process of national liberation."[146] Unlike accounts of the war that appeared in earlier issues the conflict is also acknowledged as having been a front of the Cold War.[147] The subsequent issue included several reflections on the defeat of the French forces at Dien Bien Phu and the role of this defeat in marking the beginning of the end of the colonial period. Charles Fourniau returned to Vietnam for the fiftieth anniversary and published an account that encompassed not only the official events but also his visit to Dien Bien Phu and Con Dao (formerly a prison island the French called Poulo Condore).[148] The choice of sites is revealing: the former is the site of a victory over colonialism, and the latter a symbol of colonialist oppression.

The antiwar movement has been another integral part of the AAFV commemorative agenda. In 2003 plans were developed to commemorate the fiftieth anniversary of the liberation of Henri Martin and the association supported a conference organized by member and historian Alain Ruscio on Martin and the antiwar movement. Ruscio's announcement of the one-day conference, published in the AAFV *Bulletin,* emphasized that the fiftieth anniversary of Martin's release provided the perfect opportunity to reflect on "the idea of engagement and the diverse manifestations of French anticolonialism."[149] In addition to supporting the conference, the AAFV was an active sponsor of the exhibit hosted by the Museum of Living History, and representatives attended the 20 July commemoration led by the ARAC and the ACVGI.[150] The AAFV and the ARAC also cosponsored a ceremony to honor the dead of the war in the Montreuil cemetery on 7 May.

MONTREUIL: A (COMMUNIST) FRANCO-VIETNAMESE CROSSROAD

While villages, towns, and even neighborhoods are often considered to be *sites* of memory, it is rare they are considered to be *agents* of memory. The city of Montreuil (Seine-Saint-Denis) is just such an agent: it has actively contributed to shaping the anticolonial narrative through political and cultural initiatives undertaken by the municipal government as well as through local sites and institutions. This predominantly working-class suburb of Paris was a Communist bastion for most of the twentieth century. With the exception of the era of the Occupation, the city leadership was Communist from 1935 until 1996, when mayor Jean-Pierre Brard broke with the PCF and joined the leftist Convention for a Progressive Alternative (Convention pour une alternative progressiste). In the last half century Montreuil has developed ever closer ties with the Socialist Republic of Vietnam, particularly under Brard's stewardship from 1984 to 2008. Virtually all Vietnamese delegations visit the city, and Montreuil has hosted several Franco-Vietnamese diplomatic and cultural meetings.[151] It also maintains a partnership with the Vietnamese province of Hai Duong. In 2010 a Hanoi-based publisher produced a bilingual reference work on the relationship between Montreuil and Vietnam entitled *Montreuil and Vietnam: Symbol of Franco-Vietnamese Friendship,*[152] which outlined key aspects of Vietnamese history, the historical and commemorative role of Montreuil in the Indochina War, as well as the economic and cultural partnerships between the city and Vietnam.[153]

Montreuil is also home to the Museum of Living History (MHV; Musée de l'histoire vivante), which has staged four exhibits on Vietnam since the late 1980s, including two that have focused in whole or in part on the colonial era and the Indochina War and one on Ho Chi Minh's time in Paris. Indeed as the museum noted in the press release for one of these exhibits, "the road that leads to Indochina passes through Montreuil."[154] The museum is also connected to two commemorative sites maintained by the city and dedicated to Ho Chi Minh: a replica of the room he rented during his stay in Paris in the 1920s and a bust of his likeness. The municipality has not always been active in commemorating the Indochina War, though it did coordinate a series of initiatives in 2004 to mark the fiftieth anniversary of the signature of the Geneva Accords. These initiatives included collaboration with the Museum of Living History, the ARAC, and the AAFV, whose headquarters are not far from city hall.

Historically the museum has maintained close ties with the PCF, although that relationship has waned somewhat since the early 1990s. In 1937 Jacques Duclos, a prominent member of the PCF leadership, founded the Society for the Museum of History. The society's primary objective was to open a museum dedicated to educating the public (and the working classes in particular) about France's history of popular struggle. The museum was opened two years later on 26 March 1939, though it was forced to close the following September with the outbreak of the Second World War. It reopened in 1946 and its permanent exhibit remained much the same until its closure and renovation in the 1980s. In her master's thesis on the museum Audrey Gay-Mazuel describes its objectives in the following terms:

> To introduce the visitor to popular struggle, from the French Revolution to the Resistance; to teach him the pages of his own history through original documents with the objective of presenting a new perspective on French history; but above all, to demonstrate the progress of history toward the victory of communism.[155]

In keeping with these objectives, exhibits tended to focus overwhelmingly on select themes, such as the French Revolution, the Commune, the Popular Front, and the liberation of Paris. The museum's collections have developed accordingly; in fact the MHV has quite significant holdings related to the French Revolution. The museum was in many ways comparable to the people's museums of Eastern Bloc and other Communist countries, and it was quite popular with visiting delegations from those countries. Throughout this period the ties between the museum, the municipality, and the PCF remained strong: the membership of the administrative council of the museum largely comprised current and former members of the mayor's office, who also tended to be party members.[156]

Despite the broad pedagogical objectives of the museum board, visitor numbers remained low. Moreover the majority of visitors were workers who were brought by their unions and other organizations; the general public did not visit the museum in great numbers.[157] In an attempt to deal with declining attendance the museum was closed in December 1981 for extensive renovation. Gay-Mazuel notes that the renovation was not just material; part of the plan for renewal was to move away from a Marxist interpretation of history and toward a more professional museological approach.[158] The museum continues to engage with social and labor histories. A popular 1992 exhibit on the Paris toy factory Jouets de Paris included sections on the experiences and working conditions of those who made the toys. However, the MHV has also expanded its collections and areas of interest to include colonialism, decolonization, and immigration.[159] Despite the fact that the museum was no longer strictly speaking the party's museum, the membership of the museum board initially changed very little and continued to represent municipal and party interests. Former Communist mayor Marcel Dufriche served as president of the museum board until 2000, and Jean-Pierre Brard also held several positions on the board during his mayoral terms. The extent of the ongoing involvement of the PCF is evident in the choice of Dufriche's successor in 2001, Frédérick Genevée, a trained historian who is also a member of the national party leadership. However, the staff of the museum has sought since the early 1990s to pursue a more critical approach to the exhibits they curate.[160]

Since the museum's reopening, Vietnam and its connections with France have become increasingly prominent topics of exploration. In 1990 the museum inaugurated an exhibit on Vietnam in honor of the centenary of Ho Chi Minh's birth, which would be the first of four exhibits to date on the subject of Vietnam, including a 2007 exhibit on Ho Chi Minh's time in Paris and most recently an exhibit entitled "Indochine—France—Vietnam." The museum also curated an exhibit in 2004 as part of Montreuil's fiftieth-anniversary commemorations, which is discussed below. This focus on Vietnam and on Ho Chi Minh in particular is echoed in the two commemorative sites adjoining the museum. The first is the Ho Chi Minh room, which is the odd result of an arrangement between the municipality and the museum: the room is located in the museum but is not part of the exhibition space. The room was originally created when the building Ho Chi Minh had lived in from 1921 to 1923 at 9 impasse Compoint (Seventeenth arrondissement) was slated for demolition.[161] The Vietnamese embassy intervened to claim various materials from Ho's former residence on the floor formerly used for maids' quarters (*chambre de bonne*). The floorboards, door, sink, street number, and various other small pieces were dismantled and removed from the site. Subsequently members of the MHV board agreed to create a space in the museum to put the items on display. The site was quite popular with visiting Vietnamese delegations, and when it was dismantled in the early 1990s the municipality faced diplomatic pressure to reinstall it.[162]

In 2000 the new Ho Chi Minh room was opened, though it bore little resemblance to the original: while the materials had been in storage, someone absconded with some of them, including the floorboards.[163] The current room features laminate floors, a wall painted to depict the bed area, and a small mezzanine. The only original pieces appear to be the small sink and the street number. Nonetheless virtually every visiting Vietnamese delegation makes a pilgrimage to the site, including President Tran Duc Luong in 2002.[164] Authenticity, it seems, is less important than the pilgrimage value of the site.[165] The room is decorated with a variety of gifts brought by visitors: portraits and photographs of Ho, books, and various small decorative objects. As former museum director Gérard Lefèvre once commented, "the Ho Chi Minh room is a diplomatic site, not a historical one."[166] The museum staff has sought to exclude the room from its more recent activities and exhibitions. For example, while the room was actually incorporated into the 2004 exhibit on the Indochina War, it was explicitly not included in the 2013 exhibit on France and Vietnam. Members of the public are not allowed to visit the space without special permission.

Montreuil's commitment to honoring Ho Chi Minh was reinforced in May 2005 with the inauguration of a bust of Ho Chi Minh in Montreau Park located just outside the Museum of Living History. A gift offered by the Vietnamese government, the bust is accompanied by a commemorative plaque that reads, "Hero of national liberation and eminent man of culture of Vietnam." The bust is now the site of the annual ceremony in honor of the anniversary of Ho's birth, which is regularly attended by representatives of the Vietnamese embassy, the AAFV, and representatives from the city of Montreuil.[167] The characterization of Ho Chi Minh imparted by the plaque, and the celebration of his birthday, have enraged many, including some members of the Franco-Vietnamese community.[168] In fact the bust has been vandalized with red paint more than once.[169]

The overlap between the ARAC, the AAFV, the city of Montreuil, and other like-minded groups and individuals reached its peak in 2004. The

FIGURE 1. Bust of Ho Chi Minh, Parc Montreau, Montreuil.

mayor's office sponsored a series of events in June and July to commemorate the fiftieth anniversary of the Geneva Accords as a reminder of "the long-standing solidarity of Montreuil with those who are struggling for their independence,"[170] and to introduce *Montreuillois* and visitors alike to Vietnamese culture and history. In a ceremony on 7 May to honor the dead of the war, which was attended by representatives of the ARAC and the AAFV, Montreuil mayor Jean-Pierre Brard emphasized that the objective was "not to rejoice in the defeat of [the] country, but to work tirelessly to remind people that this war was fought as much against the people of Vietnam as against [French] national interests."[171] Other events included programs designed to introduce people to Vietnamese culture and history as well as the connections between France and Vietnam since the seventeenth century.[172] Scholarly work was a prominent aspect of the programming. Individual scholars, including Stein Tønnesson, Michel Bodin, and Alain Ruscio, gave presentations on various aspects of the colonial era and the war. The city also cosponsored a roundtable with the CID-Vietnam, which was held at the Museum of Living History.[173]

Central to the city's programming was an exhibit curated by the museum entitled "From Indochina to Vietnam," which explored both the colonial era and the war. "A 'just war for freedom' for some, [and] a 'dirty war' for others," states the official press release, which also describes the conflict as "a long and painful confrontation."[174] The objectives of the exhibit were to explore the most important moments of the war, the impacts of the war on the Indochinese peoples, the reactions of the French public, and the information that was communicated to the latter, especially through the press. The exhibit itself placed a strong emphasis on nationalist and anticolonial movements as well as the antiwar movement that developed in France, devoting two of the seven rooms to these topics. This resonates with the AAFV's celebration of the antiwar movement; in fact the association solicited the loan of relevant documents and artifacts from its members. "From Indochina to Vietnam" distinguished itself from both ANAI-sponsored exhibits and the pedagogical center of the Memorial to the Indochina Wars (discussed in chapter 4) in its emphasis on the antiwar movement in France and on the legitimacy of the grievances of indigenous nationalist and anticolonial movements. Moreover unlike these other exhibits the French colonial period is not depicted as one of great progress and modernization but rather as a period of occupation and repression.

. . .

Each of the groups examined here—scholars, veterans' organizations, and civilian groups—has contributed to a narrative of the Indochina War that emphasizes its colonial dimension over its Cold War context; highlights the role of anticolonial and antiwar activism; and engages in a broader critique of the colonial system. However, none of the individuals or groups examined here contribute to this narrative in exactly the same way. Although they all share a belief in the exploitative nature of the colonial system and a right of the Indochinese to independence, they differ in their ideological positions, including their views of communism and the Communist regimes of Vietnam, Laos, and Cambodia. The study of these groups also reveals the complexities of the politics of remembrance concerning a conflict that was both a war of decolonization and a front of the Cold War. The two dominant narratives of the war—as a legitimate war of independence or as a struggle against communism—reflect colonial-era and Cold War ideologies and make it extraordinarily difficult for the proponents of the two sides to discuss the issues, let alone reach any kind of consensus. The ongoing relationship of groups like the ARAC and the AAFV with the Socialist Republic of Vietnam is anathema to right-wing organizations. Likewise the focus of the ANAI and others on the dark side of communism and the positive aspects of French colonialism is impossible to reconcile with those who claim the legacy of the antiwar and anticolonial movements. Though these disputes and conflicting narratives are less heated than those related to the "memory wars" related to the Vichy regime or the Algerian War, they nonetheless represent a high-stakes engagement for those who are most invested.

In spite of the often heated factional debates and in spite of the efforts of each side to promote its views widely, the terms and nature of these debates do not always reach the general public. Messages conveyed by the state, particularly through commemorative practices, do have the potential to reach a broader audience. As the next chapter demonstrates, the anticommunist narrative has generally had pride of place in state discourse however much official positions may have softened since the mid-1990s and the end of the Cold War.

FOUR

Morts pour la France?

OFFICIAL COMMEMORATION OF
THE INDOCHINA WAR

> In the presence of our troops gathered in the courtyard of the Invalides and our flag, the nation welcomes the Unknown Soldier from the Indochina War. He died for France![1]
>
> VALÉRY GISCARD D'ESTAING

ON 7 JUNE 1980, twenty-six years after the Geneva Accords, President Valéry Giscard d'Estaing honored an unknown soldier of the Indochina War in the main courtyard of the Invalides in the presence of some two thousand attendees. The ceremony, months in the making, had begun with the exhumation of an unidentified soldier from the Dong Hoi cemetery in Quang Binh province just north of the 17th parallel in December 1979. After being held at the Ba Huyen cemetery just outside of Hanoi, the remains were repatriated to France by air, arriving at Roissy on 28 March 1980. The casket was transferred from the airport to the crypt of Saint-Louis des Invalides in Paris where it would remain until the ceremonies began on the evening of 6 June. That evening a military vigil was held in the Saint-Louis chapel by representatives of various veterans' associations. Next to the flag-covered casket lay ledgers containing the names of the missing and dead. Rotating every quarter hour, honor guards, including thirty members of the ANAI, stood watch over the casket. The following morning a special mass was held in the chapel in the presence of the president, the minister of defense, and other dignitaries. A small cortege bearing the casket followed the president from the chapel to the center of the courtyard, where Giscard d'Estaing spoke to assembled veterans and dignitaries. Later that afternoon the casket was airlifted to Arras to be transported and buried at Notre-Dame-de-Lorette the following day. Upwards of ten thousand people attended the burial itself,[2] which was overseen by veterans' affairs minister Maurice Plantier and the head of the Army General Staff, General Lagarde. The ANAI's assessment of the events echoed the sentiments of many veterans: "These words [. . .] can only fill our hearts with joy, and erase the bitterness of having long been forgotten."[3] The ceremony was thus construed as righting a memorial wrong, filling a commemorative void, and healing an open wound.

The significance of the ceremony honoring the unknown soldier lies not only with the fact that it represented the state's recognition of the sacrifices made by those who fought the Indochina War, but also with the fact that this was the first major national state-sponsored commemoration of the conflict. It was followed in 1988 by the construction of the Memorial to the Indochina Wars, the last stage of which was completed in 1996. Pierre Brocheux has argued that the Memorial formed the basis for the state's rehabilitation of the veterans of the Indochina War, and that provided the institutional framework for an official memory of the war.[4] This institutional framework was confirmed in 2005 with the creation of a national day of homage to the dead of the war. Beyond these national events and sites, municipalities and veterans' groups have raised funds to install plaques, monuments, and stelae in many French departments.[5] In addition there are a number of commemorative sites in Paris, including a plaque in the Saint-Louis chapel at the Invalides and the Square of the Soldiers of Indochina in the Twelfth arrondissement, next to the Museum of Immigration (formerly the permanent pavilion for the 1931 Colonial Exhibition and later the Museum of African and Oceanic Art).[6]

State-sponsored commemorative sites and ceremonies are critical to shaping public remembrance of an event or period. While public remembrance may exist without state sponsorship, state commemoration serves to reinforce its presence in the public sphere as well as to reinforce an "official" narrative of the events and their significance.[7] The Indochina War, like the Algerian and American-Vietnam wars, raises the question of how to assimilate events into the national narrative that are "less than glorious and whose memory induces controversy instead of consensus."[8] The solution is frequently to emphasize the elements that are common to the more "glorious" wars: the honor, courage, and sacrifice of soldiers and the noble objectives of the army. In the case of Indochina the major state-sponsored commemorative sites and events have also promoted the idea of fraternity between the French soldiers and the Indochinese people, both civilians and military, and have frequently emphasized the positive contributions made by the French colonial state. The objective of the expeditionary corps is often defined in this narrative as defeating the communist Viet Minh in order to secure the freedom of the Vietnamese people from totalitarianism. Jacques Chirac's speech at the 1988 groundbreaking ceremony for the Fréjus memorial effectively illustrates this narrative:

> They fought, and many of them suffered to a degree that is difficult to imagine, so that the essential values of honor and liberty could survive. Very quickly, they made this faraway land that they were defending their own, and sympathized with the Vietnamese people who were threatened with losing their souls under the harsh yoke of a totalitarian ideology.[9]

This chapter is divided into two sections, the first of which provides a detailed discussion of the genesis of each of these major state-sponsored initiatives. This section also includes an overview of commemorative activities organized by the ANAI and other veterans' organizations,[10] which took place outside of the parameters of state-sponsored events. The second section examines the narratives promoted by the monuments and ceremonies, in particular the themes of heroism, colonial partnership, evaluations of the colonial project, and the vilification of the Communist regime(s). Additionally this section will consider the ways in which these memorial initiatives have been shaped by those undertaken for other wars, specifically the Algerian and American-Vietnam wars. All three conflicts were the source of national trauma characterized by political and social divisions, and all ultimately ended in defeat for the Western powers. Finally I will address the connections that are so frequently drawn between the Second World War and the Indochina War, which have resulted in a narrative of resistance that transcends the parameters of the two wars and draws upon the powerful Gaullist myth for legitimacy.

COMMEMORATIVE MONUMENTS AND CEREMONIES

Long before the ceremony for the unknown soldier a veterans' association gained parliamentary approval to install a plaque honoring the combatants of the Indochina War under the Arc de Triomphe. Though not a truly state-sponsored project, the plaque is nonetheless significant because of its location underneath Paris's war memorial par excellence. Commissioned by Napoleon following the French victory at Austerlitz and engraved with the name of the important leaders and battles from the period of the Revolution and empire, the Arc de Triomphe is also the site of the tomb of the unknown soldier of the First World War. Multiple commemorative plaques have been installed

FIGURE 2. Rolf Rodel's monument at Dien Bien Phu.

over the years, including a reproduction of de Gaulle's call to resistance of 18 June 1940 and a plaque to the combatants of the conflicts in North Africa. The 1955 plaque, bearing the simple inscription "To the soldiers of Indochina from a grateful nation," was unveiled in early April 1955 by the Association of Veterans of the Far East Expeditionary Corps and the French Forces of Indochina and Korea (Association des Anciens du Corps Expéditionnaire d'Extrême-Orient et des Forces Françaises d'Indochine et de Corée).[11] No dates are listed, no war mentioned. The choice of dates was a complex issue, and the absence thereof can be interpreted as an attempt to avoid controversy or merely to allow readers to interpret the inscription as they wish. The plaque, however, is the only national monument to the Indochina War without dates; from the tomb of the unknown soldier to the various stages of the memorial complex in Fréjus, the choice of dates was a hotly contested issue, which is examined in greater detail in the second section of this chapter.

The plaque is representative of the commitment of veterans' organizations to commemorate the Indochina War in the absence of any official honors. In May 1969 the National Association of the Combatants of Dien Bien Phu (Association nationale des combattants de Diên Biên Phu) held its first commemorative ceremony in Pau, thereby initiating a tradition that would continue until the fiftieth anniversary of the end of the war, after which point the organization disbanded.[12] Until 2006 veterans gathered each year on 7 May for a ceremony at the Arc de Triomphe or for a special service at the Saint-Louis chapel at the Invalides, to honor the war dead.[13] Veterans also raised funds to support a project initiated by Rolf Rodel to build a monument to the French forces on the battlegrounds at Dien Bien Phu.

After years of struggle the monument was completed in 1996 and inaugurated in 1999 in the presence of the minister of veterans' affairs and some three hundred veterans.[14] The cooperation between state and veterans evident in this undertaking reflects a relatively recent state of affairs and is indicative of the gradual rehabilitation of the soldiers who fought the Indochina War. The state's decision to acknowledge the contributions of those who had fought in Indochina—metropolitan French but also Indochinese and colonial troops from North Africa—met with approval and gratitude from veterans.

The Unknown Soldier

The practice of honoring an unknown soldier was established in the wake of the First World War though the concept was developed during the war itself, ostensibly in France in 1916.[15] In a speech at a commemorative ceremony in Rennes in November of that year, François Simon, president of Souvenir Français, queried, "Why would France not open the doors of the Pantheon to one of these ignored soldiers, who died so bravely for his country?"[16] He intended the unknown soldier to be a symbol for those who had remained missing or unidentified as well as a means to celebrate the entire French army. The idea gradually gained more popularity and in November 1918 Maurice Maunoury put forward the first bill. A second bill put forward in 1919 was successful, and on 28 January 1921 a ceremony honoring the unknown soldier was held at the Arc de Triomphe. Similar ceremonies were held in Britain and elsewhere, and the practice of honoring an unknown soldier became standard following the other major French wars of the twentieth century. The traditional resting place for these soldiers is Notre-Dame-de-Lorette

(Pas-de-Calais), a national necropolis established in 1920 to house the remains of those who died on the battlefields of the Artois. A small basilica is located in the center of a thirteen-hectare cemetery, which holds the remains of the unknown soldiers in its crypt. A soldier from the Second World War was buried there in 1950 and was joined in 1955 by the ashes of an unknown deportee, who represented all those who had been sent to camps in Germany and Eastern Europe, be they Jewish or resistors, whether they survived or not. In October 1977 an unknown soldier from North Africa was entombed to honor those who were killed in Algeria, Morocco, and Tunisia between 1952 and 1962. The unknown soldier of the Indochina War was not buried until 1980, representing the longest delay between the end of a war and the honoring of its combatants in this way. The decision to bury the unknown soldier from the Indochina War with the other unknowns at Notre-Dame-de-Lorette was significant not only as the first state recognition of the combatants of the war but also because it acknowledged the soldiers of the Indochina War as the equals of those who had fought in France's other major conflicts of the twentieth century. The burial of the unknown soldier of the Algerian War was important for much the same reasons; its soldiers had finally been recognized as the third military generation (*génération du feu*) of the twentieth century.[17]

In fact it was the burial of the unknown soldier of the Algerian War in 1977 that further fueled Indochina veterans' demands for a comparable honor. The ANAI, for one, contacted the minister of veterans' affairs a number of times between 1977 and 1979 requesting that such an honor be granted. There are two explanations for the significant delay in honoring an unknown soldier in a manner similar to those of the other major French conflicts of the twentieth century. The first is that of logistics. The French traditionally grouped the dead together in the area of combat, which meant that the remains of those who were unidentifiable or whose families had specifically not requested repatriation were maintained in a variety of cemeteries across Vietnamese territory. The French were occasionally forced to abandon certain cemeteries and consolidate the remains in other locations. The transfer of bodies out of the Democratic Republic of Vietnam (DRV) prior to 1975 and out of the Socialist Republic of Vietnam (SRV) after that date was a complicated process characterized by frequent interruptions of negotiations and refusals to cooperate.[18] France and the DRV signed protocol no. 24[19] on 1 February 1955 providing for the regrouping of bodies, creation of necropolises, and transfer of remains, but the Republic of Vietnam (South

Vietnam) refused to allow search teams from the DRV access to its territory on the grounds that it had not been a signatory to the protocol. The DRV then denied access to French search teams as of July 1955 in retaliation.[20]

The situation improved little in the years following the 1955 rupture as is evidenced by smaller-scale negotiations undertaken in 1959. On 14 December an agreement was signed by French representatives and the DRV agreeing to the repatriation of 213 bodies and the abandonment by France of three cemeteries in Bac Ninh province (in the North), the contents of which were to be transferred to a new necropolis at French expense.[21] Given that there were over 30,000 bodies to be grouped together and a total of 2,600 to be repatriated, the agreement was not well received, particularly by veterans.[22] This tension was exacerbated by the fact that the agreement did not require any commitment from the DRV to the eventual repatriation of all French dead. Moreover the head of the French war graves commission in Vietnam, Major Perros, had signed the agreement without specific instructions from the French government to do so.[23] This agreement, one of several between France and the DRV, highlights the difficulties that plagued negotiations over the repatriation of bodies well past 1975 and the reunification of Vietnam. Between 1954 and 1975 just under twelve thousand bodies had been repatriated to France, leaving well over thirty thousand in Vietnamese territory.[24] By 1980 the French government was finding it increasingly difficult to tend to the cemeteries from a distance, prompting it to begin negotiating in earnest for the repatriation of remains; this resulted in a signed agreement by 1986.[25]

Above and beyond the logistics of repatriating remains, which would naturally have delayed the process of selecting an unknown soldier, there is the critical issue of the actual interest in commemorating the Indochina War. A major contributing factor is the difference in status between the combatants of the Indochina War and these other conflicts. The two world wars were fought with conscripts in addition to the professional army (though in the case of the Second World War a motley assortment of resisters also claimed veterans' rights after 1944), as was the Algerian War. The Indochina War, however, was fought exclusively by the expeditionary corps, which included members of the foreign legion and colonial troops as well as local auxiliaries. The long delay in honoring an unknown soldier from Indochina is also undoubtedly due to the relatively low level of public interest in the war; that veterans self-identify as "those forgotten by history" (*les oubliés de l'histoire*) is perhaps not unwarranted.

According to Serge Tignères the years from 1979 to 1981 were marked by a new commemorative impetus influenced by the American process of introspection regarding its own war in Vietnam.[26] This new commemorative focus was expressed in part in the burial of the unknown soldier. While the event was extremely important in terms of the state's recognition of the parity of the soldiers of the Indochina War with those who fought in the other major wars, it was nonetheless limited in its public impact. Media coverage in particular was sorely lacking. Leftist publications essentially ignored the event, and *Le Monde*'s sole article on the subject was limited to reprinting excerpts from Giscard d'Estaing's speech and providing basic information on the ceremonies. Major right-wing dailies, in particular *Le Figaro* and *France-Soir*, did publish coverage of the events on 7, 8, and 9 June, applauding the decision to honor the soldier, who "finally gives [...] his comrades (who have been excluded for too long), both dead and living, their rightful place at the heart of the army and the nation."[27] Radio coverage was hardly more forthcoming: there was a single interview on France-Inter with the general secretary of the Association of the Combatants of the French Union (ACUF; Association des Combattants de l'Union Française).[28] Television archives reveal nothing in the way of news footage of the events, an oversight that was bitterly resented by members of the ANAI and presumably by other veterans.

Media coverage of and public interest in the Indochina War increased over the course of the 1980s. The plight of refugees from Vietnam and Cambodia, the American process of reconciliation and commemoration of the Vietnam War, the politicization of immigration and the rise of the extreme right, and the publication of Marguerite Duras's Goncourt Prize–winning *L'Amant:* all contributed to a heightened awareness of Southeast Asia and France's colonial connection.[29] Following on the heels of the inauguration of the American Vietnam Veterans Memorial in Washington, the Monument to the Dead of Indochina (Monument aux morts d'Indochine) was inaugurated in 1983; it was the first element of what would eventually become the Memorial to the Indochina Wars (Mémorial aux guerres en Indochine). The 1986 protocol, which provided for the repatriation to France of some twenty-five thousand bodies,[30] necessitated the construction of a necropolis in France to hold them; Fréjus mayor François Léotard offered the site adjacent to the existing monument.[31] Construction began in 1988 and was completed in early 1993. It was followed soon after by the addition of a wall bearing the names of those with the status of *morts pour la France* whose bodies had not been repatriated, which was completed in 1996.[32] The finished

FIGURE 3. Bas-relief on the Monument to the Dead of Indochina (1983), Fréjus.

memorial complex is unquestionably, as Robert Aldrich has argued, a colonial site of memory and as such must be examined in its form and content as well as in its planning and execution.[33]

The Monument to the Dead of Indochina

The initial monument, built in 1983, is a simple stone wall with a bas-relief in the center and a plaque on the ground at its base dedicated "To the Dead of Indochina 1939–1956." The bas-relief, designed by Jean Souchon and sculpted by local artist Jean-Marie Luccerini, features two soldiers—one French, one Vietnamese—struggling to hold a map of Indochina encircled by a dragon.[34]

The choice of dates and the bas-relief were both sources of great debate, the significance of which is explored in the second section of this chapter. Indeed the construction of the initial 1983 monument is a prime example of the difficulty in building consensus, even when the parties involved have the same interests and objectives. The monument was the result of a long campaign on the part of several frequently competing associations. Two groups were created to campaign for the construction of a monument: the Association for the Construction of a National Monument to the *Anciens* of Indochina, Combatants and Victims of War (AEMNAI; Association pour l'érection d'un monument national des anciens d'Indochine, combattants et victimes de guerre),[35] founded in September 1980 under the direction of Félix Aumiphin; and the Association for the Construction of a Memorial to the Soldiers of Indochina and the Victims of War (AEMSI; Association pour l'érection d'un mémorial aux soldats d'Indochine et victimes de guerre), founded in July 1979 and presided over by Jean Le Bras.

Although the two organizations had the same goal—the construction of a memorial to military and civilian dead in Indochina—there was little cooperation between them. The AEMNAI was ultimately given control of the project in collaboration with the municipality of Fréjus, although a board was created to oversee the construction, which included the presidents of the most prominent associations connected with the Indochina War. The often bitter disagreements between the two groups are evident in their respective correspondence with Fréjus mayor François Léotard. A 1982 AEMNAI memo with news of the advances in the construction of the monument states that "the AEMNAI has no legal or moral connections with the AEMSI," further specifying that this decision was voted "unanimously" by the administrative council.[36] In a letter to François Léotard, Jean Le Bras complained that Jean Pascal (then AEMNAI president) refused to collaborate with the AEMSI, and this despite the fact that Le Bras had "seniority over the Memorial project."[37] He further contended that the AEMNAI "may well put a wrench in the works" with respect to his ongoing negotiations with the government to secure funding for the monument.[38] The AEMSI and the AEMNAI both ran subscription campaigns, and a number of veterans' associations (such as the ANAI) also sought donations from their members. In addition to the subscriptions, postcards were sold, and Jean Le Bras of the AEMSI generated further revenue from the sale of a special-issue record entitled "March of the Indochina Veterans" (Marche des anciens d'Indochine).[39]

After considerable lobbying, first from Le Bras and later from the AEMNAI, the Ministry of Defense agreed to a subsidy.

The rivalry between the two groups was further exacerbated by other veterans' organizations: for example, Colonel André Rottier of Citadels and Maquis of Indochina (Citadelles et maquis d'Indochine) wrote to Pascal in January 1982 expressing the support of his organization for the monument but making a firm request that Le Bras's efforts not be ignored. He further suggested that the AEMNAI and AEMSI collaborate to complete the project by pooling their resources and sharing the administrative duties.[40] The ANAI was also a supporter of Le Bras (at least initially), and its reticence to get involved in the project at the outset may well be connected to his isolation by the AEMNAI. The end result is that the history of the monument has been edited to exclude this lack of consensus: the booklet from the 1988 groundbreaking ceremony for the necropolis ignores Le Bras and the AEMSI altogether, acknowledging only the role of the AEMNAI.[41]

Logistically speaking, the construction of the monument was relatively straightforward. The municipality of Fréjus granted the AEMNAI a small area on the side of National Route 7, bordering the area that had once been the Gallieni military training ground.[42] Colonial troops, particularly those who fought in the First World War, arrived in Fréjus and were trained there before moving to the front; they were also often sent there during their breaks, as it was thought that the climate most closely approximated that of their homelands.[43] Metropolitan troops on their way to the colonies frequently passed through Fréjus as well. It thus seemed a natural choice for a memorial site with colonial ties. The town's colonial connections are features of the landscape: there is a Buddhist pagoda built by Vietnamese soldiers during the First World War, a "Sudanese" mosque,[44] and many of the roundabouts and major roadways have been given colonial military names. In addition to the Memorial to the Indochina Wars there is a museum to the marine corps (Musée des Troupes de marine).

The inauguration of the monument, presided over by Minister of Veterans' Affairs Jean Laurain, was held on 4 June 1983. While the ceremony was well attended—there were approximately five thousand participants[45]—and well received, the organizers did contend with a few disappointments. As was the case for the burial of the unknown soldier, media coverage was minimal. The AEMNAI's final report states that it was "too limited at the local level" and "non-existent at the national level."[46] The blame for this oversight was assigned to the municipal government, which was responsible for organizing media contacts. Worse, the municipality had also failed to ensure that the inauguration plaque would be ready in time for the ceremony.

The Memorial to the Indochina Wars

Following the signature of the 1986 protocol on the mass repatriation of the remains of CEFEO (French Expeditionary Corps of the Far East) soldiers, the commemorative site in Fréjus was significantly expanded to accommodate a new memorial complex. The scale of the repatriation operation necessitated the building of a necropolis in which to house the remains of those who were not claimed by their families for private burial. The process targeted three major cemeteries in Vietnam: Tan Son Nhut and Vung Tau in the south and Ba Huyen in the north. The exhumation and repatriation of bodies began on 1 October. The first bodies arrived in France on the tenth, where they were met by Prime Minister Jacques Chirac; a ceremony honoring the dead at the Invalides, presided over by François Mitterrand, was held on the eleventh. The entire repatriation process took just over a year.

On 19 January 1988, a little over a year after the last bodies had been repatriated, ground was broken on the site adjacent to the 1983 monument. The ceremony was presided over by Chirac and was attended by a host of military dignitaries, including the wives of Marshals de Lattre and Leclerc, Marcel Bigeard, Geneviève de Galard, Jean-Jacques Beucler, and approximately twenty thousand others.[47] Contrary to the ceremonies for the unknown soldier and the inauguration of the 1983 monument, media coverage of the groundbreaking ceremony was fairly comprehensive. No doubt this was due to a number of factors, not least of which was Chirac's recent announcement of his candidacy for the upcoming presidential elections. However, public and government awareness of the Indochina War had also been increasing in recent years, in particular since the thirtieth anniversary of the fall of Dien Bien Phu in 1984 and the release of Henri de Turenne's televised documentary *Vietnam* that same year.[48] Robert Bonnafous's doctoral thesis on the experiences of French prisoners of the Viet Minh was published in 1985, and the campaign for a special status for those prisoners was being waged in the National Assembly. The increasing commemorative trend of the late 1980s is apparent in the addresses of both politicians, pervaded by a discourse of "memory" and "amnesia." Léotard opened his speech at the groundbreaking ceremony with a reflection on the arrival of the first bodies the previous October, describing its impact as "a memory wound." It was not, he qualified, "resentment over thirty years of

FIGURE 4. Memorial to the Indochina Wars, Fréjus.

being forgotten" but rather "a sadness about the amount of time it has taken our people to turn and face those who expected so much of it."[49] Chirac for his part spoke of the indifference of public opinion during the war. A *Nice-Matin* article of 20 January entitled "Indochina: Chirac Corrects an Injustice" echoed the sentiments of many veterans.[50]

The Memorial housing the necropolis was completed in April 1992 and inaugurated in February 1993. The elevated, circular structure (110 meters diameter) is built on a slight hill oriented toward the Mediterranean, where troops had embarked on the *Pasteur* and other ships destined for Indochina. The military ossuaries are divided according to the provenance of the bodies: those originating in the north of Vietnam are separate from those from the south, and the remains of sixty-two soldiers transferred from a necropolis in Luynes were interred separately. A special dispensation was granted so that a civilian ossuary could be included in the military necropolis. On the lower level of the complex is a place of worship in which Judaism, Christianity, Islam, and Buddhism are all represented, a reflection of the multicultural makeup of the French forces who fought the war. At the entrance to the structure is a small pedagogical center outlining the French colonial presence and the evolution of the Indochina War.

The commitment to commemorating an event is traditionally translated into the very architecture and design of memorial sites and monuments. These formal sites are intended to be durable so as to educate and inform future generations about their history.[51] There are exceptions to the rule, such as the sinking "Monument against Fascism" in Hamburg,[52] but generally monuments are intended to have a certain permanence. Architect Bernard Desmoulins, whose design was selected for the necropolis, conceptualized the project in a completely different manner. In a radio interview with France-Culture in 1996, he described his vision in the following terms:

> I imagined that in 50 years no one would know what the Indochina War was, but the site would still exist. […] In 50 years, when the site is completely overrun by nature, even the idea of death will have completely disappeared. It will be a different site, a little unusual, but that will maintain its mystery. And as for the Indochina War, it's true that it will be present through a few barely legible names on plaques.[53]

This commitment to have nature overtake the Memorial is shared with Maya Lin, the architect of the American Vietnam Veterans Memorial, who saw her monument as "an initial violence that in time would heal" as the grass grew up to the surface of the wall.[54] In the American case, the "healing" of nature was intended to symbolize the national healing power of the memorial.[55] In the French case, however, the motivation for the monument was not about national reconciliation as much as it was about recognizing the contributions of the soldiers to the nation. For this reason the emphasis on the monument—and therefore this recognition—fading into the natural landscape is fundamentally at odds with the intended role of the Memorial.

The site was inaugurated in February 1993 by François Mitterrand following a controversial trip to Vietnam and Cambodia, the first by a French head of state since the end of the war.[56] Though he was accompanied to Southeast Asia by high-profile veteran and filmmaker Pierre Schoendoerffer, not all veterans supported the president's trip. Geneviève de Galard spoke openly about her opposition to the visit, stating that Vietnam was still living under a totalitarian government and that she would only consider returning if there was a liberalization of the regime.[57] Many veterans held similar positions and not only with respect to state visits; some also condemned their fellow veterans who returned to Vietnam as tourists. De Galard expressed further shock at Mitterrand's characterization of the war: "I was appalled to hear François Mitterrand speak of a colonial war. As Marshal de Lattre said, it wasn't a colonial war, but a war against communism to defend the free world."⁵⁸ She along with Jean-Jacques Beucler decried the timing of the state visit, arguing that veterans had been forced to wait much longer than the original projected completion date for the Memorial to be inaugurated, and that the trip should have been postponed until after the ceremony. The Boudarel affair, which had so recently rocked the French public, still loomed large for many veterans, who equated the Vietnamese whom Mitterrand was visiting with their tormentors (*bourreaux*).

During his trip to Southeast Asia, Mitterrand met with General Vo Nguyen Giap, the victor of Dien Bien Phu, and traveled to the site of the final French defeat to pay his respects to those who had fought and died there. The trip to Dien Bien Phu was also intended, in Mitterrand's words, to "close a painful chapter."⁵⁹ The press covered the trip with enthusiasm, though the focus alternated between the trip itself and the scandal it had provoked. Reporters traveled to cover the story, and interviews with General Giap were featured on several news programs. He spoke eloquently in elegant French of the "feelings of deep affection" felt by the Vietnamese toward the French and asserted that "now is the time for reconciliation, [. . .] we have turned over a new leaf."⁶⁰ The impact of Mitterrand's statements regarding the nature of the Indochina War and his travel to Vietnam on the inauguration of the Memorial mark a clear departure from earlier state discourse of the conflict. It is facile to reduce this shift to the division between the political left and right, although it is certainly the case that the politicians of the right (Chirac, Léotard) promoted a different version of the official narrative than did Mitterrand.

The final addition to the memorial complex was a wall, inscribed with the names of the roughly thirty-four thousand dead with the attribution "*mort pour la France*" whose bodies were not contained in the necropolis either because they had not been repatriated or because they had been returned to their families.⁶¹ Inspired by Maya Lin's Vietnam Veterans Memorial in Washington, it features the same glossy surface, although in the French case this is due to a clear Plexiglas overlay on which the names are engraved. Furthermore the wall is white marble, matching the tone of the necropolis structure surrounding it, unlike Lin's granite monument dubbed the "black gash" by critics.⁶² As discussed earlier, despite the similarities in design, the objectives of each monument differ greatly. The interactive focus of the American monument, which encourages people to make rubbings of the names and to leave objects at the site, is absent from the French monument. Moreover, whereas many of those behind the Vietnam Veterans Memorial sought an end to the domestic divisions of the war period through

FIGURE 5. Memorial wall (1996), Fréjus.

national reconciliation, the French sought to reintegrate the Indochina veterans (and fallen soldiers) into the national narrative. The Indochina War was divisive for the metropole, though this division is rarely mentioned with respect to commemorative events. It is alluded to with the occasional reference to the "hostility" faced by some returning soldiers, but the official narrative rarely proceeds beyond that point. The Americans have also been much quicker to face the legacy of the Vietnam War than the French have that of the Indochina War, though this could be attributed to the additional factor of the loss of a colony. The Vietnam War is also arguably *the* American national trauma of the twentieth century, while the French have had to contend with several dark periods.

The National Day of Homage

The most recent state-sponsored commemorative initiative is the national day of homage to the dead of the Indochina War, to be celebrated on 8 June. Created by decree in May 2005,[63] it was celebrated for the first time a month later. Despite the short notice, veterans' associations like the ANAI organized small-scale events. The decree states that a ceremony is to be held each year in Paris as well as in each department and in the overseas departments and territories. This was the ultimate step in the rehabilitation of the soldiers who had fought in Indochina, a process that was really begun in 1988 with the initiation of the necropolis. While the choice of date—the anniversary of the burial of the unknown soldier—may have been confusing to some, it was as we have seen a commonly suggested date for commemorative celebrations. The idea for a national day of homage was not a new one; Jean Le Bras wrote to the minister of veterans' affairs in 1982 suggesting that a national day be instituted to honor the memory of the "victims of the Indochina campaign."[64] He proposed the relatively obscure date of 14 November, which marked the beginning of Operation *Castor* and the establishment of the fortified camp at Dien Bien Phu. The choice of 8 June reflected a desire to find a neutral date: 7 May was deemed unacceptable by many because it symbolized defeat, and 20 July represented for many veterans the ultimate abandonment of the Indochinese to totalitarian regimes. The ANAI, which had long held commemorative events on 7 May, argued that this was an unacceptable date for a national day of remembrance because it favored the combatants of Dien Bien Phu over those of other battles. Not only was the anniversary of the burial of the unknown soldier an acceptably neutral date, but it also symbolized the beginning of the long process of state recognition and rehabilitation of those who had fought in the Indochina War.

The process was similar to that for the national day to commemorate the Algerian War, which was established in 2003.[65] The issue of a government-sanctioned national day had been debated in the National Assembly for several decades before it was formally created. The largest veterans' organization for those who had fought in Algeria, the National Federation of Veterans of Algeria, Morocco and Tunisia (FNACA), had been holding commemorative ceremonies on 19 March since the 1960s to mark the promulgation of the Evian accords. Veterans not belonging to the leftist FNACA were vehemently opposed to celebrating the date on which France had "abandoned" her Algerian territory. They were also opposed to the date on the grounds that a large number of *harkis* were massacred following the signing of the accords; to set 19 March as the national day was to effectively remove them from the community of soldiers being honored. For the *pieds-noirs* forced to leave Algeria, 19 March was also a dark day. Given the prominence of the *pied-noir* community in France, the attention (eventually) paid to the *harkis*, and the overall place of the Algerian War in the French consciousness, the decision over the date of the national day was arguably even more divisive than in the case of the Indochina War. The result of the search for a neutral date to commemorate the Algerian War mirrors the process for the Indochina War: it is the anniversary of the inauguration of the memorial to the war on the Quai Branly in Paris on 5 December 2002.[66]

The first celebration of 8 June was held in the courtyard of the Invalides in 2005. Minister of Defense Michèle Alliot-Marie presided and was accompanied by Minister of Veterans' Affairs Hamlaoui Mékachéra. Though the planning was rushed, this first celebration of the national day featured an unexpected event. Days earlier the bodies of twelve French soldiers had arrived in France after being discovered in Dien Bien Phu. Only one was unidentified and was given special honors at the Invalides. Alliot-Marie's address emphasized the courage and heroism of the combatants, French and foreign, in their fight for the principles of "liberty, justice and democracy."[67] She referred to the prisoner of war camps as well as to the indifference and even hostility of public opinion facing soldiers when they returned. According to the ANAI, which also took credit for much of the organization of the event, there were 1,700 veterans in attendance, of which 950 were from their own ranks.[68] Outside of Paris small ceremonies were organized by the presidents of the departmental sections of the ANAI and a special ceremony was held at the Memorial in Fréjus. The 2006 celebration, which had the advantage of advance planning, took place at the Arc de Triomphe. After a procession of four hundred people down the Champs-Élysées, there was a small military ceremony led by Mékachéra, and the flame at the tomb of the unknown soldier of the First World War was lit; this was to become a central element of future celebrations of the national day. The ANAI placed more emphasis on events organized by its regional sections, and the reports from each section attest to the fact that they were more widespread and better attended than the previous year.[69]

COMMON THEMES AND NARRATIVES

Each of these state-sponsored commemorative events and sites reveals the construction of a broader official narrative of the Indochina War, its combatants, its objectives, and its context. From the burial of the unknown soldier in 1980 to the celebration of the first national day of homage in 2005, certain key themes have emerged through the speeches of state representatives and local dignitaries as well as through the choice of inscriptions, images, and dates. The most prominent themes are familiar to us: the courage and sacrifice of the French forces; the vilification of the communist enemy; the celebration of the partnership between the French forces and their Indochinese brothers-in-arms; and an appreciation of the positive aspects of the colonial presence. In many instances the war has also been characterized as being intimately connected with the events of the Second World War in Southeast Asia.

Giscard d'Estaing's speech honoring the unknown soldier paid homage to the military achievements and valor of the French troops and identified the unknown soldier as the successor to a long line of soldiers and sailors who from the era of conquest to the war had brought their "courage" and "faith" to the peninsula and had stood by their "Indochinese brothers."[70] Minister of Veterans' Affairs Maurice Plantier sought to rehabilitate the soldiers, reminding his audience that "the French army in Indochina showed itself to be worthy of the traditions of its predecessors, and that it has nothing to be ashamed of: neither the way in which it fought, nor of the reasons for combat."[71] He also spoke of the "affection" that French soldiers had had for the people of the Indochinese peninsula, whom they sought to protect from "the totalitarianism that threatened them."[72] Three years later Léotard's speech at the inauguration of the Monument to the Dead of Indochina praised the courage and sacrifice of the soldiers, referring specifically to the battle of Dien Bien Phu. He framed the conflict in terms of a battle for the liberty of the Indochinese people, evoking the contemporary plight of the boat people to justify the objectives of the French forces decades earlier. This was followed by barely veiled criticism of those who had objected to the war, those whose "pacifist campaigns" were characterized by a "renunciation, an abandonment." This abandonment, which he compared to "the spirit of Munich" and characterized as "the cowardly pursuit of peace at all costs," guaranteed that those abandoned would be forced into servitude.[73] Léotard did not limit his speech to military affairs, however; he also addressed the legacy of the French presence abroad, which he described as a "presence of civilization" of which France should be proud.

The response to Léotard's words was overwhelmingly positive; even Jean Gardes (ACUF), who had initially been opposed to the Memorial project, wrote to express his gratitude on behalf of the veterans who "have so often felt forgotten by the metropole" and who "particularly appreciated the words that you spoke in their honor."[74] Amid all of the congratulations there were also several letters disparaging the "hopeless" situation faced by the soldiers in Indochina and criticizing the Socialist government of the day, as in the following letter to Léotard:

> Under this luminous *provençal* sky which has accompanied so many of us as we left for Overseas France, your words, high-minded and even mystical, have evoked the crusaders' spirit that filled the troops fighting in the Far East against the communist totalitarianism that now subjugates the people of Laos, Cambodia, and Vietnam, with whom we have such a special connection. Alas, our struggle was a lost cause, for we were rejected by part of the Nation that had already given up, and betrayed and besmirched by those who now govern us.[75]

Similar themes were raised by Marcel Robert, secretary of the Isère chapter of the ACUF, who thanked Léotard for demonstrating his "love of the truth," which he had "bellowed with passion and courage before the representative of the current regime." He went on to argue that there was an imperative to continue the struggle against the same enemy they had during the war, in the East and in France proper, and he pledged his association's support for this struggle.[76] As demonstrated in chapter 2, this committed anticommunism was characteristic of many veterans and it lasted long after the collapse of the Eastern Bloc in 1989.

In 1988 the speeches delivered by Prime Minister Jacques Chirac and Fréjus mayor François Léotard—both of right-wing political parties—at the groundbreaking ceremony for the Memorial to the Indochina Wars reiterated many of the themes already discussed. However, both speeches were also shaped by issues that had recently been thrust into the spotlight, such as the experiences of prisoners of the Viet Minh and the exodus of the boat people in the mid- to late 1970s. Léotard reinforced the narrative of the war as a struggle for freedom, claiming that "only after forty years did we fully understand, in the haggard gaze of the 'boat people' or the silence of the 400,000 drowned in the China Sea, the real meaning of [the French Union soldiers'] commitment and the real significance of their struggle."[77] As noted above, Chirac spoke of the battle against the "harsh yoke of a totalitarian ideology" as the motivating force of the war. He reinforced this criticism of the Vietnamese regime through several references to the horrendous conditions of the Viet Minh prisoner of war camps. This was no doubt an effort to both recognize the suffering of the survivors publicly and offer support to the ongoing campaign for a special status of "prisoner of the Viet Minh." Members of the ANAPI were in attendance at the ceremony, holding a banner reading "The survivors of Indochina" as a means of drawing public (and political) attention to this campaign. Chirac's recognition of the contributions and sacrifices of the French forces extended to its non-French members as well: he praised the "brotherhood of arms" between soldiers of all nationalities—Cambodian, Lao, Vietnamese, African, and Malagasy, all fighting for France. The emphasis on the Franco-Indochinese partnership in particular was reminiscent of Giscard d'Estaing's 1980 speech for the unknown soldier, in which he evoked the "heartbreak of having to fight alongside them, and against those among them who had refused France's outstretched hand."[78] This close relationship was presented as having been part of France's "great adventure,"[79] with the burial of the unknown signaling the closure of "a glorious page of our history."[80] He further reflected on this "glorious" history, suggesting that "once calmer times prevail, History will be able to judge the work of those who accomplished a great task in Indochina, and measure the contribution that France made to the progress of these peoples of the other half of the world."[81]

The themes of colonial partnership and the positive legacy of the French presence in Indochina featured prominently in discussions and debates over the 1983 Monument to the Dead of Indochina. Although the various parties ultimately settled on the dates of 1939 to 1956 for the inscription, this was far from a simple process. Citadels and Maquis of Indochina had reservations about including any dates at all, arguing that despite France's sacrifices in Indochina the "extensive work that she accomplished" should also be honored.[82] For this reason, he continued, "the inscription should evoke the broader charitable work of France, as well as her dead."[83] The Indochina War was thus conflated with a colonial influence that could be understood as going back to the reign of Louis XVI. The group also took issue with the image of the two soldiers, whom Léotard described as "united in their struggle, their acts driven by solidarity and desperation."[84] They argued that it was unconscionable to privilege one of the three states of Indochina (Vietnam) over the others, even if it was only done symbolically. As discussed in chapter 2, the ANAI also opposed the design although their reasons are less explicit. The disagreements between the various factions obviously took a toll on the mayor's office, which was quite involved in the construction process. The previously cited letter from a local artist regarding the ANAI's opinions of the planned bas-relief[85] has a handwritten note attached, presumably from the mayor, stating, "We can't get caught up in this mess," and advising that the letter be forwarded to the AEMNAI.

While various parties took issue with the design, it seems that the root concern was the fair representation of all regions that Indochina had comprised. The spirit of the design—a partnership between the French forces and the Indochinese people, both soldiers and civilians—was in tune with the narrative of the war promoted by a majority of veterans. As we have seen, it was also a theme invoked by both Giscard d'Estaing and Plantier at the burial of the unknown soldier three years earlier. The "desperate" nature of the fight highlighted the fact that the odds were stacked against success, with the French trying to roll back the clock after Vietnam declared independence in 1945. The emphasis here on solidarity between the French forces and the Indochinese and the inclusion of the colonial other in the design was reflected in the composition of the national committee that was to oversee the construction: in 1982 Colonel Félix (ANAI) requested that "members of the Indochinese community" be invited to join.[86] Finally, by featuring the French and Vietnamese soldiers working together to save Indochina from communism, the monument denies the colonial dimension of the war—after all, France could not have been waging a war of reconquest if it was also working with the Indochinese.

The emphasis on partnership is in fact indicative of much more than just a Franco-Vietnamese cooperation to fight communism. It also reflects a desire on the part of many proponents of the anticommunist narrative to honor the French colonial project and the civilians who helped build it. In their speeches for the 1988 inauguration of the groundbreaking ceremony for the new Memorial, both Léotard and Chirac elaborated on the positive legacy of colonialism to a greater degree than had been the practice at previous commemorative events. Chirac spoke of the "great work of Overseas France,"[87] though he did also recognize that the colonial project was not without its "grey areas."[88] Overall, however, he praised all those who had contributed to the development of Greater France as well as those from the colonies who had fought to defend the metropole in the two world wars. Léotard for his part focused on the more tangible French accomplishments: "We left behind us roads and hospitals, schools and dispensaries, high schools and canals; we left urban and rural areas in which the French language maintains the hope of a freedom that is yet to be established."[89] This emphasis on the positive legacy of colonialism was reinforced by a three-day exhibit on Indochina, cosponsored by the Ministry of Veterans' Affairs, veterans and former settlers, and the municipality of Fréjus. The exhibit was divided into two sections: the first covered three centuries of the French presence in

Indochina, and the second, the period 1939–54. As a testament to the suffering of the Indochinese after the French departure from the peninsula, a fishing boat used by refugees fleeing Communist Vietnam was included as part of the exhibit.[90]

While the official narrative of the war and the colonial era represented by the speeches of Chirac and Léotard echoes that upheld by a majority of veterans, the tone of the 1993 inauguration of the completed necropolis was markedly different. François Mitterrand's speech gave due recognition to the sacrifices of French soldiers, including the prisoners of the Viet Minh, who faced "atrocious conditions" and were then forced to "wait forty years to be granted the status they deserve."[91] He also acknowledged the range of soldiers who died for the French cause: metropolitans but also legionnaires, Africans, North Africans, and Vietnamese. However, he refused to identify the specific objectives of the French forces, instead referring rather obliquely to the "mission confided in them by the government of the Republic."[92] Nor did he address France's contributions to its former colonies; in fact he did not refer to the colonial era at all, save a vague reference to "tasks left unfinished because the progression of time cannot be reversed."[93] Although the speech itself was not particularly controversial, it was overshadowed by the controversy over his recent trip to Vietnam and Cambodia.

The original pedagogical exhibit in the Memorial's information center dedicated a significant section to the colonial era through displays on "The Land and Its People" and "A Long Common History." These sections established the narrative of a long-standing Franco-Indochinese partnership, which drifts into rather crude Orientalist descriptions of these partners: the Vietnamese are "clever and active," while the Cambodians are "religious and refined" and the Lao "affable and hospitable." The French colonial presence was depicted as having had an overwhelmingly positive impact on the peninsula by driving away the Chinese and roving bands of pirates and bringing peace and prosperity to the region. The many achievements of the French colonizers were represented, from railways to education. This introduction framed the rest of the exhibit, implying that the Viet Minh threatened all that France and its colonial protégés had accomplished, in addition to justifying the war as necessary to ensuring the freedom of those colonial subjects. The explanations of the war itself were overly simplistic—in the words of Robert Aldrich visitors were presented with a war fought by "benevolent Frenchmen and willing allies facing nameless enemies who refused to obey the rules of war."[94] Indeed there was no mention of the longer history of

FIGURE 6. Permanent exhibit of the Memorial.

Vietnamese nationalism or of rising anticolonial movements in the first half of the twentieth century. In addition to this problematic presentation of French colonialism and the elision of the colonial dimension of the war, the exhibit reinforced a characterization of soldiers and veterans as victims. This was clear from the first panel visitors encountered, which identified the memorial site as one "of memory, of unrecognized sacrifices, of ignored heroism, and of forgotten suffering."

In 2010 a newly renovated exhibit was inaugurated by Secretary of State for Veterans' Affairs Hubert Falco. The new exhibit is organized into seven sections, each of which is introduced with an interactive video booth.[95] Visitors can select one of several categories on each touch screen; the first screen, for example, offers the options of learning more about the geography and people of the peninsula, the French conquest, the colonial administration and its accomplishments, and the rise of indigenous nationalisms. The video stations are separated from one another with panels featuring archival images. While the narrative imparted by the renovated exhibit is essentially the same as its first iteration, there are important modifications as well. The French colonial project is still celebrated, but this praise is tempered by an acknowledgment that economic development did not always benefit the peasantry and that this contributed to the rise of nationalism and anti-French sentiment. The video also acknowledges the harsh treatment of dissidents, including beheadings and imprisonment at Poulo Condore. However, even this rectification is ultimately undermined by other statements, such as that "despite its successes" France long faced resistance. This is followed by a characterization of Vietnamese nationalist Phan Boi Chau as having "launched the first terrorist attacks" against the French colonial state.

The sections on the Indochina War predictably depict the Viet Minh as the "bad guys": in the section on the first battles and Viet Minh zones are described as rife with violence, executions, and hostage takings; while this description is not entirely without merit, there is no comparable evaluation of the zones under French control, leading the viewer to believe that no such abuses existed there. In a further reproach to the DRV, the creation of the State of Vietnam under the leadership of Bao Dai is presented as an example of independence reached through negotiation rather than through armed conflict; this ignores the fact that this state was not completely independent but rather an Associated State within the French Union. Unlike the original exhibit the renovated version does acknowledge—at least in passing—that the war was more than a front of the Cold War, although it is presented as also being a war waged for the "maintenance of the French Union" rather than an outright war of colonial reconquest. The emphasis on the suffering of the soldiers is still present through footage of liberated prisoners and statistics on the survival rates in the Viet Minh camps, and is extended to the suffering of those abandoned to the Communist regime. The final section of the exhibit addresses the exodus of Catholics and others from the North to the South, who are described as the "first boat people."

While the textual content of memorial sites is central to the construction of historical narrative, the choice of dates (for inscriptions and events alike) is equally important. As we have seen, there were extensive debates over an appropriate date for the day of homage to the dead of the war. It was in fact not the first time that 8 June was chosen as a significant but neutral date. For the inauguration of the 1983 monument the date ultimately chosen was 4 June because it coincided with the "commemorative period" of the burial of the unknown soldier three years prior[96] (it was likely held on the fourth because it was a Saturday). The other option for the inaugural date was 9 March in reference to the Japanese attack of 1945. There was at least one opponent to this option, who argued that commemorating a French defeat was undesirable,[97] but the proposal hints at the critical place occupied by 9 March in the French narrative.

The Japanese coup of 9 March 1945 stands out in veteran and settler narratives as a key date for the French experience in Indochina, first and foremost because it was a particularly violent and traumatic event that targeted the

French military and civilians alike. The French colonial authorities (representatives of the Vichy regime) had been forced to establish a power-sharing agreement with the Japanese in 1940, but by 1945 the latter put into motion a plan to knock the French out of power altogether. Civilians and soldiers were attacked and imprisoned. Many veterans and other commentators understand the Indochina War as emerging directly from the circumstances created by the Japanese takeover, given that the Viet Minh gained support and popularity as a result. Moreover the Japanese defeat in early August created a power vacuum. This in turn paved the way for Ho Chi Minh's declaration of independence and establishment of a Communist state in northern Vietnam, and in the eyes of many veterans it was this communist threat that prompted the French to increase their military commitment to the peninsula.

The ninth of March is far less central to the state narrative of the war, but it has occasionally been featured in commemorative addresses. At the burial of the unknown soldier at Notre-Dame-de-Lorette on 8 June 1980, for example, Minister of Veterans' Affairs Maurice Plantier referred to the coup and drew strong links between the Second World War and the subsequent conflict: "On March 9, 1945, the Japanese attacked the French troops. Faced with their tenacious resistance, they did not treat their prisoners honorably, but delivered them to the executioner or imprisoned them in veritable death camps. It was to rescue them that the combatants of 1939–1945 came."[98] The centrality of 9 March is further reinforced by the fact that it was suggested as an appropriate date for the inauguration of the Monument to the Dead of Indochina in 1983. According to available archival evidence, this met with widespread approval; the reason it was not selected was because of a conflict with the elections and not because it was deemed to be inappropriate to hold the inauguration on the date of a French defeat. The choice of a date that was symbolic for both military and civilian groups indicates a desire to be inclusive of both communities, which is reflected in the 1983 monument's inscription, "To the Dead of Indochina" (*Aux morts d'Indochine*), conforming to a common formula for war memorials since the First World War but also acknowledging the sacrifices of civilians and soldiers alike. ANAI president Hélène Bastid's interpretation of this symbolic community included civilians, the military, and the Second World War–era resistance, "whether they fought as legionnaires, colonial troops, cavalrymen, sailors, pilots, parachutists, whether they were part of the expeditionary corps or the former maquis of Indochina."[99] The heterogeneous community identified by Bastid was reinforced in the later stages of the memorial complex, which houses the bodies of 3,630 civilians[100] and features commemorative plaques to civilian groups, such as the rubber plantation owners as well as military platoons and battalions.

The memorial complex in Fréjus (including the 1983 monument, the Memorial, and the necropolis) provides a more detailed case study of the issues surrounding choices of dates and the perception of a continuum uniting the Second World War and the Indochina War. The archives suggest that most of those involved in the planning and execution of the 1983 monument felt it was natural to include the years of the Second World War on the inscription. After some discussion it was decided that the dates on the monument would be 1939 to 1956. The original inscription was also to include the politically charged phrase "For a Common Ideal" (*Pour un idéal commun*), but this was ultimately dropped. The dates 1939–1954 are inscribed on the crypt in the Memorial, while the end dates inscribed on the wall of names unveiled in 1996 are the same as the monument. The choice of dates, which represents the period of the Second World War (in Europe) through the withdrawal of the last French troops from Vietnam in 1956, is intriguing. While the latter date is understandable given that French soldiers continued to be killed after the formal end of the Indochina War (until their withdrawal in 1956), the choice of 1939 is somewhat perplexing. It represents the beginning of the Second World War in Europe but has little significance in the East Asian theater, where the war was well underway by 1937. Nor does the date hold any significance in the Indochinese context; the Japanese occupation began in the north in 1940 and subsequently encompassed the southern regions. A possible explanation is that the engagement of France in the Second World War necessarily committed its empire to the conflict, and thus while there was no fighting in Indochina in 1939 the region was nonetheless involved in the war effort.

What is to be made of this periodization and the fact that it went virtually unchallenged? Does it represent a desire to submerge the Indochina War by placing it in a continuum with the Second World War, as Panivong Norindr has argued?[101] Norindr posits that this periodization effectively erases "the not-so-heroic vision of France's historical involvement in Southeast Asia from the collective memory."[102] More than this, I would argue, the choice of dates effectively ignores the colonial dimension of the war by establishing a continuum of French resistance: first to the Japanese and later to the Viet Minh. Many soldiers who went to Indochina in 1945 understood their mission as liberating "Greater France," just as the metropole had been liberated from the Nazi occupier. The French mission to liberate the Indochinese from the Japanese is then seen as the precursor to a second liberation mission, this time from the Communists. In this view any motivation for colonial reconquest on the part of the French state and military can be conveniently elided. Furthermore the narrative of resistance allows the Vichy years in Indochina to be "forgotten" in favor of a "resistancialist myth," echoing metropolitan remembrance of the Occupation.

. . .

Despite the apparent overlaps between the official narrative of the war and that of veterans, as illustrated in chapter 2, it was not until 1994 that government representatives took part in the commemorative ceremonies in Pau organized by veterans themselves. In honor of the fortieth anniversary of the end of the war, Minister of Defense François Léotard attended the events in Pau. By 2004 it was the president of the Republic, Jacques Chirac, who was the guest of honor. The state's active acknowledgment of the veterans, beginning in 1980 and culminating with the creation of the national day of homage in 2005, certainly contributed to facilitating this cooperation. On 4 June 2006, days before the second celebration of the national day of homage, at least one television station took advantage of the renewed attention to the combatants of the Indochina War to air a news segment on another "forgotten" group with a connection to the Indochina War: the residents of the Reception Center for the French of Indochina (CAFI; Centre d'accueil des Français d'Indochine) in Sainte-Livrade (Lot-et-Garonne), the oldest of whom had arrived in 1956 following the withdrawal of the last French troops from Vietnam.[103] They and their children and grandchildren had in the previous decade sought to gain official recognition for the CAFI from the government as a site of memory. This "unofficial" site of memory reveals a different perspective on the remembrance of the war and of decolonization.

FIVE

"The Forgotten of Vietnam-sur-Lot"

REPATRIATE CAMPS AS SITES OF COLONIAL
MEMORY

> We know all too well that something is in the process of collapsing. The memory of what created us—colonial history—is being progressively erased. Those who were the witnesses and the actors will soon disappear. Our mothers and our fathers are dead, or very elderly, and it's only a question of years before Indochina sinks back into oblivion. It will be nothing more than a word.[1]
>
> DOMINIQUE ROLLAND

IN MID-APRIL 1956 some 1,200 French so-called repatriates[2] (*rapatriés*) from Indochina arrived at their new homes just outside of the small community of Sainte-Livrade-sur-Lot, in the southwestern department of the Lot-et-Garonne. Experiencing considerable disorientation and exhausted after weeks of travel, first by boat to Marseilles, then by train to Agen, and finally by bus to the reception center, these repatriates began what was to be perhaps the most difficult part of their journey: adjusting to life in metropolitan France and reconciling the promises of colonial officials in their homeland with the realities they faced. Their homes, provided by the state, were military barracks (thirty-nine of them, all measuring fifty meters in length) converted to single-family housing. The largest apartments featured four small rooms, with toilets located in enclosed buildings in the laneways between the barracks. Each family was provided with basic furniture and household items. Among the new arrivals was Joséphine Le Crenn, who remembers her four-year-old son asking, "*This* is France?"[3]

The site that was to become home for Le Crenn and hundreds of other repatriates was called the Reception Center for the Repatriates from Indochina, later renamed the Reception Center for the French of Indochina (CAFI; Centre d'accueil des Français d'Indochine). It was one of several sites sought out and converted in the early 1950s to accommodate the influx of French citizens from the colonies who did not have the means or the support networks in France to establish themselves on their own. In addition to the CAFI in Sainte-Livrade (and its annex in nearby Bias), centers were established in Noyant (Allier), Le Vigeant (Vienne), and Saint-Laurent-d'Ars[4] (Gironde); there were also housing and support facilities in Marseilles and Paris. Intended to serve as temporary residences, some of the centers developed into permanent communities; the CAFI outside of Sainte-Livrade continued to exist into the twenty-first century, though most of the buildings have since been demolished in order to make room for a new division of subsidized housing. While the process of transporting these French citizens from the colonies to the metropole was referred to as one of "repatriation," it should be noted that most experienced it as a process of immigration rather than repatriation.[5] Repatriates were treated much like refugees in terms of the housing, subsidies, and support that they received. They were also subject to pressures similar to those exerted on immigrants and refugees to "assimilate" into French society. It is thus perhaps more accurate to refer to their arrival in France as a "repatriation-immigration."[6]

Given the longevity of several of these camps and the central role they have played in the repatriate experience, they have become important sites of memory for the community. Though many within the repatriate community hope that the sites might gain status as "formal" memorial sites, they currently operate as unofficial memorial sites. My analysis of the camps focuses on the contexts of war remembrance and the legacies of colonialism, yet it also contributes to the history of immigration to France. Studies of immigration from the former Indochina to France, which are far from numerous, have tended to focus heavily on the wave of arrivals after 1975. Le Huu Khoa and Trinh Van Thao were long the only scholars to have examined the post-1954 wave of arrivals from the peninsula; this chapter builds on their work, particularly since greater archival access has been granted since their publications.[7]

In addition to chronicling the process of repatriation and the structure of the camp system, this chapter engages with the discourse and policies of assimilation and integration within the camps and the means by which they were implemented and evaluated. The discourse of assimilation is particularly significant given that the repatriates were already French citizens and some families had been for generations. Of further interest are the perceptions of nationality and citizenship. The repatriates had expectations of being treated as full French citizens (*Français à part entière*) but instead were treated much like refugees while in the camps: access to medical attention, financial subsidies, and primary education was mediated by the camp administration. The integration of the repatriates into the local population was described as "failed" for at least a decade and a half after their arrival, but the perception of the process by the 1980s and 1990s is one of absolute success. Moreover many locals remember the arrival of the repatriates with fondness; the archival record, in contrast, reveals a history of tension and conflict. This contradiction raises interesting questions about the perceptions of immigrants based on their place of origin; the *harkis,* who experienced a similar process of repatriation following the Algerian War, have not experienced the same softening of opinion.[8] Asian immigration to France is often perceived as more successful in terms of integration, while immigrants from North Africa (and particularly Algeria) are viewed more negatively and are frequently the targets of hostility. The positive view of Asian immigration extends to a celebration of cultural difference in this period, which itself raises interesting questions about changing models of integration in France.

The final section examines the camps as sites of memory along the lines of those documented by Pierre Nora; that is, as sites that reflect and shape what it means to be French.[9] As many scholars of colonial and postcolonial France have observed, Nora himself largely ignored colonial sites, an oversight that has since been remedied by Robert Aldrich and others.[10] The repatriate camp represents the intersection of memories: first and foremost, it is a site of memory for the experiences of the repatriates, themselves a consequence of decolonization. Second, although it does not have a direct connection to the Indochina War except through the presence of a few veteran residents, it is intimately connected with this conflict. In this sense it constitutes a foil for the memorial complex in Fréjus, which commemorates the dead of the Indochina War: whereas the Memorial represents soldiers' sacrifices, the camps represent the unintended fallout of the war. As a result of these particularities and in spite of their clear function as sites of memory, the repatriate camps do not easily fit into the framework of the two competing narratives of the war. Some residents of the camps were the victims of the Viet Minh and the DRV, directly or indirectly, and as a result express an antipathy toward communism. However, much more prominent is their anger at their mistreatment by the French state, which has been articulated as having reduced them to the second-class status of colonial subjects.

Several associations of current and former residents have promoted the memorial significance of the centers, including the Eurasian Association of

Paris-CAFI (CEP-CAFI; Coordination des Eurasiens de Paris-CAFI) and the Association of Residents and Friends of the CAFI (ARAC; Association des résidents et amis du CAFI; not to be confused with the veterans' organization with the same acronym). The fiftieth anniversary of the arrival of the first repatriates validated these memorial efforts: the Sainte-Livrade municipal library held an exhibit on life at the CAFI; a number of regional and national publications published special articles and issues; and documentaries on the repatriate experience were screened publicly. Although these initiatives succeeded in drawing greater attention to the history of the repatriates, it remains to be seen whether the camps will actually retain a place in the broader public consciousness.

MIGRATION AND REPATRIATION

With the fall of the French position at Dien Bien Phu in May 1954 came the southward evacuation of French soldiers and civilians along with Vietnamese soldiers and functionaries who had worked with the colonial authorities. The families of soldiers who had fought with the Far East Ground Force (FTEO; Force terrestre d'Extrême-Orient), of civilian employees of the North Vietnam Ground Force (FTNV; Force terrestre du Nord Vietnam), and of personnel of civilian industries that had been requisitioned by the military were all to be transported to the South at the army's expense.[11] Between 21 July, the date of the ratification of the Geneva Accords, and 10 October French authorities transported just over two hundred thousand people to the South.[12] Overall approximately one million people migrated south, among them some seven hundred thousand Catholics fearing persecution.[13] The journey began with the flight from Viet Minh–controlled areas to Hanoi or Haiphong. Refugees faced frequent obstacles: unreliable transportation, separation from family members, pirates, and Viet Minh attacks. Complaints and testimonials filed with the joint general staff attest to the hardships of those seeking to reach the South. Among them was an account written by N.T.L., who was separated from her husband as they tried to get their family to Hanoi:

> Because of the difficulties we face, our family must emigrate. We are leaving with our two children but, at Phat Diem, V[iet] M[inh] agents prohibited the use of boats to transport émigrés. We therefore had to rent a dinghy

to go as far as Nam Dinh. Once we arrived at Nam Dinh, on 11.9.54, we spent the night at the parish of Nam Dinh. The next day we had to walk because the V.M. had forbidden the rickshaws [*cyclos*], trucks and boats to transport the émigrés.

I respectfully request that the Commission of Control intervene in this matter, so that our family can finally be reunited and so that we can know the fate of my husband, who may have been killed and robbed by pirates.

En route, at night, the migrants were mistreated and insulted by the V.M. agents, who abducted their children, hit the elderly, and moreover blasphemed against our religion.[14]

Refugees arriving in Hanoi and Haiphong were housed in hastily organized centers. For example, the Redemptorist order housed some fifteen thousand people in Hanoi, while others sought shelter in schools and theaters. In Haiphong a further ten thousand were housed in tents along the coast in proximity to the harbor.[15] Many were transported to the South by the French navy, while others traveled by air.

Following this mass exodus south, many of those eligible for "repatriation" to France, whether they originated from the North or the South, were housed in temporary camps in and around Saigon-Cholon prior to departure.[16] Estimates of the total number of repatriates transported to France after 1954 range from thirty to forty-five thousand,[17] not including the tens of thousands of French and colonial troops. It was by no means a homogeneous group: among them were a majority of Eurasians[18] (primarily of mixed European and Vietnamese origins, although Lao, Cambodian, Indian, Maghrebi, and other origins were also represented); naturalized Indochinese (primarily from the southern Vietnamese region of Cochinchina); citizens from the "old colonies" of both European and indigenous extraction; and a small number of European men, who were repatriated with their indigenous or Eurasian wives and children. There were also a significant number of single mothers with numerous children; some were widows while others had been abandoned by the French men who had fathered their children. The majority already had French citizenship, and it was offered prior to departure or en route to those that did not (these were usually indigenous women with children by French men, and particularly soldiers).[19] A complicating factor for French citizens of Vietnamese or mixed background was the August 1955 Nationality Convention (Convention sur la nationalité), which forced those who had acquired French citizenship prior to 1949 to choose (by 15 February

1956) whether to maintain it or revert to their Vietnamese citizenship; those born after 1949 reverted automatically to Vietnamese citizenship. The socioeconomic background of these repatriates was as varied as their ethnic background. Some were low or mid-level functionaries in the colonial administration; others were veterans of the French forces and the Vietnamese national army; still others were significantly less financially stable, especially those who had been forced to abandon whatever possessions they once had. Eurasians who had held well-respected positions in the colony experienced a substantial transformation in their status upon their arrival in France. As Le Huu Khoa posits, they had been treated favorably, as French, while in Indochina and had enjoyed a comfortable standard of living. Once in France, however, they were treated as indigenous colonial subjects.[20] While the treatment of Eurasians by colonial society was certainly more nuanced than Khoa indicates, not to mention their treatment by Vietnamese, Cambodians, and Laos, the change in status was nonetheless significant.

Most of this first wave was "repatriated" to France by boat, a journey which could take anywhere from three to four weeks. Upon their arrival in Marseilles repatriates without the means to support themselves were handled by Social Services.[21] They were housed temporarily in the city, after which point they were directed to centers in the departments of the Lot-et-Garonne, the Allier, the Vienne, and elsewhere.[22] Most of the Europeans and the naturalized citizens had the wherewithal to support themselves upon arrival in France and so had no need for prolonged support or housing. The minutes of the meetings of the Interministerial Commission for the Repatriates from Indochina indicate that between the fall of 1955 and the fall of 1958 some 9,000 repatriates had been assisted by Social Services; as of October 1958, 3,300 of them still resided in the centers.[23] Because of the high proportion of non-Europeans in this group of repatriates, it is often considered to be the first wave of post-1954 immigration from the Indochinese peninsula. The second major wave was initiated in 1975 by those fleeing newly established Communist regimes in Vietnam, Laos, and Cambodia, a phenomenon commonly associated with the iconic image of the boat people.[24] The first wave of arrivals from the Indochinese peninsula was largely ignored by both French and Vietnamese public opinion,[25] in direct contrast to the second wave of immigration. Not only was the second wave significantly larger—some 142,000, nearly four times the size of the first wave—but it benefited from considerable media coverage in France and around the world.[26]

THE RECEPTION CENTERS: STRUCTURE, ADMINISTRATION, AND POLICIES

Anticipating the potential issue of housing French citizens repatriated from the colonies, the French government began seeking sites for temporary centers at least as early as 1950.[27] Initially little thought appeared to be given to the location of these centers with respect to employment opportunities or the social and psychological impacts of isolation; essentially authorities appeared to be satisfied with any site that could be transferred to the state and which could be converted to house upwards of several hundred people. Requests for suggestions were sent to departmental and municipal authorities. Minutes from the meetings of the Interministerial Commission reveal that the choice of locations was constrained by a number of factors, including available funds for acquiring and refurbishing the sites, and the small number of suitable locations. The minutes also reveal that the members of the commission, if not other government representatives, did try to look for sites with employment possibilities—for example, they believed that Noyant would provide more job opportunities than Sainte-Livrade, and were surprised to discover that by July 1956 the opposite was actually true.[28]

Ultimately most of the sites chosen were located in rural areas outside of small communities whose populations were matched or exceeded by the repatriate population.[29] The type of housing provided varied significantly from center to center: at the CAFI in Sainte-Livrade and its annex site in Bias, the housing consisted of converted military barracks, whereas the site in Noyant was a subdivision of former miners' housing (*corons*). The site at Le Vigeant was a former detention center for prisoners of war and common criminals (*criminels de droit commun*). Interestingly the two largest sites—Sainte-Livrade/Bias and Noyant—had long-standing connections with foreign populations: from the end of the First World War until 1949 the mines in and around Noyant employed a majority of Polish workers, and the barracks at the CAFI had housed Spanish Republicans and colonial workers. In all cases the housing had been virtually abandoned for years before being converted for the repatriates, and the units were in varying states of disrepair. The difference in housing also led to different atmospheres in the centers. With their military arrangement of barracks the CAFI and Bias sites had a strong camplike atmosphere, whereas the houses in Noyant led to something closer to a community atmosphere. However, this community was still segregated from the local Noyant population; as Jeanne Cressanges describes in

FIGURE 7. Entrance to the Reception Center for the French of Indochina (CAFI).

FIGURE 8. Barracks and water tower at the CAFI.

her novel *The Betel Leaf,* "Yellow and White live[d] on either side of the cemetery."[30]

The housing conditions imposed on the repatriates were certainly inadequate, but other factors should nonetheless be taken into consideration. The housing at Sainte-Livrade and Bias was clearly not intended to be long term; the administrative archives reveal as much. Residents were intended to stay only long enough to be retrained for new jobs and then were to establish themselves elsewhere. Furthermore France in the mid-1950s was experiencing a population boom and a shortage of housing and so was in a poor position to come up with additional housing for overseas citizens.[31] Finally there is the issue of how significant the repatriate problem was deemed to be; Trinh Van Thao points to the fact that the influx of these citizens was not large enough in scale and was not sufficiently politically charged to warrant the kind of budgetary sacrifices made to accommodate the French from Algeria upon their arrival in 1962.

Though intended to be temporary housing centers, it was soon clear that the communities were likely to become permanent. Over time the camps grew into something resembling self-sustaining, insular communities. Schools were built to accommodate the disproportionate number of children, and chapels and pagodas were established in order to meet the spiritual needs of residents. At the CAFI a former missionary who had spent considerable time in Indochina tended to the Catholic flock in a small chapel. A building was also converted to serve as a pagoda for the Buddhist residents. In Noyant a separate pagoda was built with an adjacent building that serves as a community center, and the surrounding property is marked by large statues of the Buddha. Today the municipality of Noyant promotes the pagoda as part of its tourism marketing program. The CAFI long boasted two grocery stores selling Asian products, one of which doubled as a restaurant serving Vietnamese dishes; these were rebuilt as part of an urban renewal project that demolished most of the original buildings.

Administratively speaking, the camps fell under the purview of a succession of ministries over the decades, including defense, foreign affairs, and the interior.[32] All of the sites had been closed by the early to mid-1960s with the exception of the CAFI in Sainte-Livrade (the center in Bias was reassigned to *harkis* after 1962 along with Le Vigeant and Saint-Laurent-d'Ars). Noyant stopped admitting new residents as of 1964, and existing residents were given the option to purchase their homes as of 1966. Many families thus continued to reside in the community, but the administrative structure of the camp was removed. The CAFI continued to change ministerial hands until 1981 when the municipality purchased the property. The longevity of the CAFI is due in large part to its increased identification as the camp for those "unfit" for work (*inaptes*, also referred to as *incasables*). This aspect of the camp was reinforced by the transfer of *inaptes* from other repatriate camps as they closed down; when the housing units at Noyant were put up for individual sale, several families "without sufficient means to support themselves" were sent to the CAFI in Sainte-Livrade.[33]

The administration of the camps was entrusted to men who had experience in the colonies as soldiers or civilian functionaries, with a preference for those who had lived in Indochina. Medical personnel were also frequently chosen for their colonial background, and many of the teaching staff had some kind of colonial experience, primarily in North Africa.[34] In his sociological study of the community in Noyant, Pierre-Jean Simon points to the obvious implications of this policy: it resulted in the transfer of colonial attitudes, prejudices, and conflict. Frequently, he argues, functionaries' knowledge of colonial subjects was barely above "the level of [...] comfortable stereotypes."[35] This judgment is borne out in at least one case: in 1964 the director of Noyant (formerly the director of the CAFI) wrote a letter to the director of the service in charge of repatriates from Indochina and North Africa to protest electoral candidates making promises of various kinds to voters residing in the camp. Citing twenty-five years of experience with Asians in general and Vietnamese in particular, he contends that they have "no political maturity whatsoever,"[36] and that they would (naively) expect candidates to make good on their promises. Warning of the potential consequences of inciting residents by playing to the problems they face in the camps, he reminds the prefect that the repatriates have the potential to be like the Viet Cong, who are not real communists but rather "malcontents who have become rabid sheep."[37]

Many camp residents certainly felt that colonial structures had been transferred to the metropole: one resident featured in a France-Culture radio documentary on the CAFI commented that "at first, the heads of the camp colonized us, because they [...] couldn't continue to colonize the indigenous people of Indochina. They considered us second-class citizens."[38] The replication of the colonial system of authority was not unique to the repatriate camps for those arriving from Indochina; it would also be instituted after 1962 in the camps that housed the families of *harkis,* Algerians who had fought on the side of the French during the Algerian War.[39] Because the *harkis* were all veterans, however, the camp structure was much more military in nature than that of the Indochina repatriates, who were primarily civilians. In both cases the camps were heavily bureaucratized. Medical care was provided on site, with no option of seeking alternative treatment; financial subsidies for each family were handled by the camp administration; and there was a curfew imposed on all residents. The comparison goes beyond *harki* and repatriate camps, however; there is of course a much longer history of camps in France and in the colonies.[40] Housing for colonial workers in the metropole, which doubled as a means of surveillance and segregation, was commonplace beginning with the First World War. Resettlement camps were established during the Algerian War in order to separate civilians from "rebels" and empty problem areas of inhabitants. Camps were also established to detain Europeans fighting on the side of the FLN.[41]

Most of the repatriates arrived at the camps with few possessions and virtually no financial resources. There was a variety of social and family subsidy programs as well as special subsidies from the state that were granted for the first year after arrival. The paternalism inherent in the camp structure is evident in the fact that these subsidies, even those coming from institutions that served all inhabitants of the region, were disbursed by the camp director to the residents rather than passing from the institution straight to the recipients. The housing was rent-free and depending on the camp, so too were heat, electricity, and medical care. Children were provided with school supplies as well as whatever additional items were required by boarding schools, for those who attended them. While this network of social assistance allowed families to maintain a basic standard of living (albeit a very basic one in some cases), it also resulted in policies that served to create barriers to moving beyond that standard of living. For example, a ban was instituted by government decree in May 1959 on anything that qualified as "visible signs of wealth" (*signes extérieurs de richesse*), such as televisions, washing machines, or cars.[42] It was argued that anyone relying so heavily on government subsidies should not be seen as profiting from them. Residents could be asked to leave the camp if they were found to be in possession of an "illegal" item.[43] This policy was also tied to the objective of encouraging families to leave the camps once they had adjusted to life in France and found work.[44]

The education of children and job training for adults were a priority. Most adults were unable to find work that corresponded to their previous employment but were frequently offered retraining possibilities, particularly in manual labor. A December 1957 spreadsheet indicating the reclassification (*reclassement*) status of male heads of households in Noyant demonstrates that most of those capable of working were oriented toward employment as painters, locksmiths, and laborers, among others.[45] Some worked far from the camps, leaving their families there, while others worked in the region. Many also worked under the table for local farmers, frequently for lower than average wages; for former residents of the CAFI in Sainte-Livrade, picking green beans for local farmers is recalled with a certain degree of bitterness. The unemployed between the ages of seventeen and twenty-five were often encouraged to participate in a professional training program (FPA; Formation professionnelle pour adultes). During the program, participants were granted room and board at a modest price and also received a subsidy comparable to minimum wage.[46] In 1966 attempts to create employment for residents of the CAFI and Sainte-Livrade resulted in the opening of a branch of the Miramont shoe factory within the camp. By 1973 the factory employed eighty-five people, roughly half of whom were camp residents, but it closed only three years later.[47]

Children too were at a disadvantage. Having faced years of war, they were frequently years behind in their educations. Providing schooling for so many children was no mean feat: between April and November 1956, 650 of the 1,200 new arrivals at the CAFI were under the age of fourteen.[48] Local schools were in no position to take in that many new students, and so schools were hastily put together on site at the camps. The first classes at the CAFI were held on 8 October 1956 for 356 school-aged children;[49] Bias followed in November, opening eight classes for 300 children.[50] At Noyant too the capacity of the local school (with only four classrooms) was soon exceeded and new classrooms had to be arranged, but in contrast to the CAFI and Bias the children of the repatriates shared classes with metropolitan children. By August 1957 some 1,500 children from the reception centers were attending schools, many of them on site.[51] Although administrators and teachers tried to accommodate older students as much as possible, many reached the age for beginning middle school or vocational school without having earned the primary education certificate, and were too old to continue to attend the municipal primary schools. Exceptions were made where possible, but administrators often sought to enroll these adolescents in trade apprenticeships and other training programs, such as plumbing, carpentry, and sewing, hoping to provide them with some means of supporting themselves in the future. Like the adults, children and adolescents were evaluated according to aptitude tests to determine appropriate career paths.

CONFLICT BETWEEN THE RESIDENTS
AND THE ADMINISTRATION

The rigid structure of the camps combined with the attitudes of the administration and the residents' reactions to their living conditions led to considerable tension between the two parties, which at times escalated into serious confrontations. The earliest incident resulting from disagreements between residents and administration involved the resignation of Bernard Dutrait, director of the Saint-Hilaire annex of Noyant, less than a year after the arrival of the first repatriates. His resignation letter makes his position clear: "I believe that I have done enough for the repatriates in my Center without having to withstand being insulted and assaulted by a few black sheep who live there, and who cannot be evicted by Social Services because their families are too large."[52] Other clashes followed, including anonymous letters addressed to the administration of Noyant in 1957, widespread graffiti on CAFI buildings, and threatening messages targeting the administration in 1959, as well as clashes between camp residents, local residents (*Livradais*), and the administration in the late 1960s. Rather than chronicle each of these incidents, it is perhaps more useful to explore a single event and the responses of the administration, camp residents, and local authorities.

In December 1958 tensions between CAFI residents and the administration erupted, leading to threats of violence and the establishment of a police detachment on the premises. On 16 December an argument broke out between a resident of the camp at Bias and one of the groundskeepers, which escalated into a demonstration by fifty residents outside the administrative building.[53] There was little local press coverage of these "few episodes of internal unrest,"[54] which indicates a lack of appreciation of the seriousness of the incidents. Two days later another incident between a resident and the assistant director led to shots being fired; that same day residents protested by occupying the director's office.[55] The police were called, order was restored, and six police officers were assigned to maintain surveillance at the camp for a period of eight days beginning on 19 December.[56] The causes of the incidents were, unsurprisingly, perceived very differently by the administration and the residents. Administrative reports focus on the perception that morale at the camp had never been particularly good, despite the efforts of the administration to improve conditions, and they attribute much of the blame to a small number of troublemakers who fomented discontent among the others; the recommendation was that these residents be expelled. The director of the Bias center claimed that he, his family, and his subordinates were facing very real threats to their lives and that he "was personally convinced that [the camp residents] would not back down even in the event of a bloody incident."[57] He identified several residents as "troublemakers"; these people also formed the nucleus of a residents' association (*amicale*) within the camp. They were encouraged, the director argued, by a person external to the camp who maintained close ties with the *amicale*. There may also have been other external factors at work; a 1964 letter from the director of Noyant, who had previously been the director of the CAFI, refers to the impact of "electoral propaganda" in 1958 as a motivating factor of residents' actions.[58] However, there is no mention of this aspect in any of the other archives consulted.

Residents' reactions were mixed. Some clearly felt uneasy with the truce between demonstrators and the administration, as witnessed by the submission of a petition on 22 December signed by over seventy residents requesting that the police presence be maintained beyond the initial eight-day period. A report was also submitted to the commissioner for the Repatriates of Indochina by a member of the *amicale*, who was among those recommended for expulsion by the camp director. In it the author identifies two primary reasons for the administration's "failure," which caused the recent "protest movements."[59] The first of these was the lack of a coherent housing policy. The fact that the CAFI, like the other centers, was initially intended to serve only as temporary homes was reflected in the housing policy. The problem, the author contends, is that the policy was not revised when it became apparent that few families were actually able to leave the camp due to the high numbers of those deemed "unfit" for work. The second major error on the part of the administration, the report claims, was the absence of deadlines for subsidies. Although it was initially appropriate to offer residents free housing, electricity, coal, unemployment subsidies, and medical care, these should have been offered with limitations to the scale of the subsidies and the period of time they were to be available. Another no less important dimension of this faulty subsidy policy is the fact that the administration had used its absolute control of the distribution of these subsidies to try and force departures from the camp by reducing or eliminating residents' access to them.

Significantly the solutions proposed by the report are framed in terms of permitting the residents to exercise their full rights as French citizens and to be treated as such by authorities. The report's proposals range from repatriate representation at the local, departmental, and national levels to revising the policies concerning subsidies. It also recommends removing the administrative framework of the camp altogether and allowing residents to rent or buy their homes. The question of housing, the report contends, is the largest factor in ensuring that camp residents are not treated like full French citizens. The report summarizes the positions of residents as follows:

> Effectively, at any point, eviction is possible, legally speaking. The Administration is all-powerful in this area. There is not a single French person, a single French citizen, who is in a similar situation. Even a young couple with children living in a hotel has laws to protect it, the equivalent of which does not exist with respect to the housing attributed to the repatriates.[60]

It is fair to assume that this report reflected the opinions of at least the other members of the *amicale,* of which the author was a leading member, if not the entire camp community. However, there is little in the way of archival evidence that offer any further insight into the reactions of the residents.

The responses of the administration and some residents seem to reinforce each side blaming the other for the problems facing the camps. While outside perspectives are not available for all of the incidents recorded in the archives, in this particular case we do have access to the reaction of departmental deputy and mayor of Villeneuve, Jacques Raphaël-Leygues. With experience as a representative on state missions to Indochina and as a representative to the assembly of the French Union, Raphaël-Leygues manifested a keen interest in the repatriates. In response to the events of December 1958 he wrote directly to the minister of the interior, who was scheduled to take over responsibility for the camps on 1 January 1959. His letter states that the administration of both camps (CAFI and Bias) had over the previous three years "not only demonstrated their incompetence, but at Bias tolerated, and sometimes encouraged, inadmissible practices."[61] With respect to the outbreak of hostilities he places the blame squarely on the administration, claiming that they were the result of "provocations on the part of the functionaries [. . .] who act as though they want to see the situation get worse, leading to tragic consequences."[62] He concludes by stressing that the replacement of the directors and assistant directors of both camps was absolutely necessary, without which there were sure to be worse (and bloodier) incidents. In fact the director of the CAFI and both the director and assistant director of the Bias center resigned, although it is not clear whether these were forced resignations. What is clear, however, is that the director of the CAFI was not deemed to have been so unsuccessful as to warrant being removed from the system entirely; in fact he was transferred to Noyant.

While the housing proposals put forward by this report were never implemented, there is evidence that the administrations of both the CAFI and Noyant sought to make changes that would at least superficially address the desire of residents to be treated as full citizens. For example, in 1959 the oversight of the camps was transferred to the Ministry of the Interior; among the changes at the CAFI prompted by this transition was the transfer of responsibility for overseeing health-care access from camp social workers to the Sainte-Livrade town hall. While camp residents would continue to be treated by camp medical staff, their records and subsidies would be governed by the municipality, just like other local residents.[63] Another example, albeit of a more trivial nature, is that of Emmanuel Bretonnière de Chèque's request to allow residents to keep their televisions without penalty.[64] He argued that enforcing this regulation would surely raise opposition from residents on the grounds that they were not being treated like other French citizens, and he was eventually successful in securing the right to own a television for the residents.[65]

INTEGRATION, ASSIMILATION, AND CITIZENSHIP

Central to immigration policy in France as elsewhere are the issues of integration and assimilation. The term "assimilation" was increasingly avoided in the postcolonial era, precisely because of its ties to colonial policy, in favor of the term "integration." However, as Gérard Noiriel and Stéphane Beaud have shown, the two terms were frequently used interchangeably, and this until the 1980s.[66] According to this policy of assimilation-integration, repatriates from Indochina, like immigrants from other parts of the world, were to leave their distinct cultural practices at the door and take on French values, culture, and practices. In the context of the repatriate camps efforts to promote integration targeted both adults and children. Adults were expected to "assimilate" first in the workplace and later by moving their families out of the camps altogether. Trinh Van Thao argues that the FPA was a success in terms of integration, if not in terms of professional training, because during this period "the repatriate learned to speak French and, thanks to the boarding house, to meet other metropolitans and to make his first social contacts since his arrival in France."[67] Nonetheless there was considerable doubt on the part of authorities that the adult repatriates would actually successfully adapt to metropolitan life, and efforts were therefore to be concentrated on the younger generation.[68]

As the site where all children learn a common history, heritage, and the rights and responsibilities of citizenship, the school was the natural place for the children of the camp to learn how to "be French."[69] In the words of the director of Noyant in 1957, the objective of the school was to "make our little Eurasians into good, honest French people."[70]

Ideally integration was to be facilitated not only by the curriculum but more importantly through interaction with metropolitan children. The possibility of this interaction was, however, hampered by the fact that the schools were located within the camps and thus attended solely (or predominantly) by the children who resided there. Moreover, in addition to the educational delays experienced by many students, mastery of the French language was a significant barrier to overcome. Many of the camp residents spoke a language other than French, usually Vietnamese, at home. Some spoke no French at all when they arrived.[71] As the French General Delegate to South Vietnam observed in 1955, many of those scheduled for departure for France were Vietnamese women with Vietnamese or Eurasian children, who "regardless of their race and nationality, do not speak French and have been raised in the Vietnamese way."[72] In a 1959 report the director of the girls' school at the CAFI states that the children's lack of language acquisition was a "serious handicap" and that no amount of punishment or threats could dissuade them from speaking Vietnamese at recess, and even in the classroom. This was exacerbated, she continues, by the persistent use of Vietnamese in the home. The situation could be remedied, she implies, by placing children in boarding schools.[73] Bernard Dutrait (who oversaw the Noyant annex of Saint-Hilaire) comes to a similar conclusion in a letter about three teenaged girls who were to be admitted to an apprenticeship program: "The boarding school would have the advantage of freeing them from the family atmosphere, where they unfortunately continue to speak in their mother tongue and to follow Asian customs."[74] This discourse of making "good" citizens out of children of mixed parentage has a strong resonance with established Church practices but also with colonial discourse, especially that of the 1930s. As Emmanuelle Saada and Christina Firpo have demonstrated, aid societies in Indochina sought to remove children who had been abandoned by their European fathers, in order to place them in French-run orphanages and boarding schools to educate them to be good French citizens.[75] It was believed that these children could not live up to their full "French" potential while in the care of their indigenous mothers.[76] The goals of the camp administrators and teachers clearly differed from those of French colonial authorities, whose "rescue" of Eurasian children was predicated on making them French and therefore useful tools of the colonial state. Nonetheless there is a common logic regarding who is most fit to oversee the education of a child and their integration into French society.[77]

The integration rate of children and adults alike was the subject of constant concern on the part of camp administrations and local authorities. After only two years a bleak report on camp morale stated that all of those who could be expected to integrate had already left the camp and that those who remained were far from integrated, a situation that was exacerbated by marriages and growing families within the camp. Reports also emphasized that the subsidies that residents relied on were creating a culture of dependence that made it easier for people to stay than to leave; such arguments came not only from the administration but also from the resident who sent the report on the realities of the camp to the departmental prefect.[78] Even in 1973 the CAFI was deemed to represent the "story of a failed integration."[79]

The evaluation of success in the integration of the repatriates naturally calls into question the relationship between them and the established local population. Initial contact seems to have been one of both curiosity and suspicion. In the case of the CAFI, residents of Sainte-Livrade were given little notice of the impending arrival of the repatriates, and the few newspaper articles announcing their arrival gave little in the way of actual information about their backgrounds or the situation that had prompted their departure from the Indochinese peninsula. Reactions to the arrival of the repatriates was also likely shaped by locals' previous experience with Indochinese subjects living in their midst. The military barracks of the CAFI and Bias sites had been used during and following the Second World War to house some 2,500 soldiers from Southeast Asia. They were under close surveillance, as were the reactions of the local population. According to intelligence reports, the latter were not thrilled with the presence of the Indochinese by the spring of 1946: "The sympathy that existed a few months ago between the population and the Indochinese troops has completely disappeared. It has been replaced by suspicion."[80] In 1948 the municipal council of Sainte-Livrade got wind of a potential plan to use the Moulin-du-Lot site to house workers from Indochina and immediately passed a motion to oppose the project. The mayor and all members of the council informed the departmental authorities that they would resign en masse if the project were approved.[81] Pierre-Jean Simon's sociological study of the repatriate experience in Noyant identifies three phases in intercommunity relations. Prior to arrival there was, a priori, sympathy for the repatriates. The first phase of contact was marked by a reciprocal curiosity, which he contends lasted until the early 1960s. From that point forward the relationship was characterized by a lack of understanding of cultural differences, and irritation with repatriates' habits. Finally he describes the third stage as one of "acclimatization to an environment of permanent hostility."[82]

Beyond mutual misunderstandings and suspicion a number of altercations between camp residents and locals can be registered. The summer of 1968 was particularly marked by conflict, beginning with an argument between young people at a local dance on the evening of 23 June, ostensibly prompted by a relationship between a young man from the CAFI and a young woman from Sainte-Livrade. The young man in question was the target of insults from other *Livradais* youth, and he got into a fistfight with one of them. The following night toward eleven o'clock a group of youth from the CAFI and a group of *Livradais* squared off in the town center; police were alerted by a passerby who stated that a fight had broken out between "Europeans" and "Eurasians." According to witnesses, some thirty to fifty youth from the CAFI had marched to the site of the festivities. One *Livradais* witness, who was injured in the mêlée, described the youth, who, "armed with axe handles, and even one carrying an axe, arrived from a small street and came toward the entrance to the dance. Shirtless and brandishing their clubs, they screamed like 'Indians.'"[83] The young man from the CAFI for his part described returning to the dance hall on the twenty-fourth to seek out the *Livradais* who had punched one of his friends the night before; he admitted to being shirtless and to carrying a small axe. However, according to him the first blows were thrown by the *Livradais* and he was hit several times in the head with a chair until his face was bloodied.

This violent confrontation prompted further incidents in the days following it; on the twenty-sixth and twenty-seventh, *pétanque* players in the town square were harassed by CAFI youth throwing pebbles, and an employee of the shoe manufactory was allegedly attacked by several youth at the camp. The confrontations culminated in a demonstration of some three hundred *Livradais* in front of the town hall on 27 June. They were apparently looking to take revenge on six CAFI youth, who were meeting with the mayor and six *Livradais* youth in an attempt to bring an end to the hostilities. According to the police captain who filed the report, "It is certain that if the crowd gathered in front of the town hall had gotten their hands on the young Eurasians, the latter would have suffered a real lynching."[84] The police reports and witness testimony tend to put much of the blame on youth from the

CAFI, although the real responsibility is attributed to only seven of them, identified as "troublemakers." The press reinforced this perception, referring to the aggressors "of Indochinese origin" as "sowing terror at the dances."[85] The article goes on to validate the actions of *Livradais:* "Really, (and we completely understand), the *Livradais* population had had enough of tolerating the 'savagery' of these youth with their revolutionary spirit."[86] The archives reveal no attempts on the part of the municipal authorities or camp administration to explore the underlying reasons for the conflict and violence; rather, the solution was to send the seven instigators out of the community (and the department). The director of the camp was also replaced. According to a report dated 11 September, these two solutions calmed tensions considerably.[87]

The events of the summer of 1968 provided evidence for many of the growing difficulties associated with the burgeoning adolescent population of the CAFI.[88] Those who had arrived at the camp as young children in the mid- to late 1950s had since become teenagers with few education or employment options. Clashes between some of these youth and authorities, as well as youth from Sainte-Livrade proper, were on the rise from the mid-1960s on. The atmosphere of protest and rebellion across the country in the spring and summer of 1968 undoubtedly contributed to the tense atmosphere as well. Representatives of the Inter-Organizational Committee in Support of Evacuees (CIMADE; Comité inter-mouvements auprès des évacués), a nongovernmental organization founded in 1939 to assist displaced persons, among others, arrived in 1966. By the summer of 1967, it was decided that a youth center would be of benefit, and the Youth and Cultural Center (Maison des jeunes et de la culture) was created. Initially the new director worked with three CIMADE representatives who were already established at the camp. A report by the new director of the center links youth delinquency with the "degradation of social relationships and morals"[89] created by the closed world of the camp. He contends that the repatriates were living as "*assistés*" (dependent on government subsidies) and had never been required to take on the same duties and responsibilities as their compatriots. Young people, who made up the vast majority of the camp population, suffered not only from this lack of civic engagement but also from an absence of structure and authority. The author contends that the only means by which these youth could succeed was through integration into the national way of life (*intégration dans la vie nationale*), which left them with two choices: "rapidly becoming French, with the same rights and responsibilities as other French citizens, or spending the rest of their lives as asocials, searching in vain for a sense of balance in a universe that will have remained foreign to them."[90] The goals of the center were thus to provide structure for the youth of the camp and to encourage their integration.

The vision of a failed integration, which prompted the measures described above, has experienced a fascinating evolution in the period since the mid-1970s. In spite of clashes with local residents and the perceptions of a failed integration in the first two decades following the creation of the camps, by the 1980s people of the region remembered the arrival and eventual integration of the repatriates with fondness. Writing in 1991, a local newspaper columnist claimed that *"Livradais* today have the impression of a successful integration."[91] Another newspaper claimed that "the Vietnamese community has integrated itself perfectly for close to a half century."[92] This shift is evident in individual experiences as well: a former resident of the CAFI, quoted in a 2004 *Libération* article, claimed that "we didn't dare bring school friends [to the camp],"[93] while a *Livradais* fondly remembers that "we got into the habit of walking them home to the camp [...]. I remember that at the time, we spent more time in the camp than in Sainte-Livrade!"[94] The shift in expectations of immigrants in the realm of integration and assimilation are also clear; in the late 1980s a local newspaper could claim that "cultural identity has never been an obstacle to integration."[95] The question of cultural identity is an interesting one, given that the pagodas, Vietnamese restaurants, and specialty grocery stores are now part of the local experience in Noyant and Sainte-Livrade and are even used as selling points to attract tourists. These same aspects of cultural identity were considered impediments to integration decades earlier. For example, in 1964 the director of the Noyant camp worried that public events with an Indochinese flavor hosted by the youth center drew people in solely on the promise of "exoticism," thereby promoting "a certain distinctive identity detrimental to integration."[96]

This celebration of cultural difference can be understood in a variety of ways. It may be indicative of a shift in certain circles from expecting assimilation in the form of conformity to French norms to greater acceptance of multiculturalism. However, it is also possible that the acceptance of cultural practices is related to the perception of Asian immigration to France as being "successful," which is further reflected by the rosy view maintained by locals of the arrival of the repatriates. This idea of a "successful" immigration emerged in the late 1970s and particularly in the 1980s and later, and is frequently contrasted with the perceived "problematic" immigration from

North Africa. While no substantial academic study of this phenomenon has been undertaken, many scholars agree that it is more than simply hearsay. A 1984 poll of French perceptions of the relative success of minority ethnic groups found that 47 percent of respondents believed that Asian immigrants were well integrated, while only 33 percent and 21 percent said the same of Moroccans and Algerians respectively.[97] Alec Hargreaves explains this "relatively favourable evaluation of Asians" by connecting it with widespread public sympathy for the refugees who arrived after 1975.[98] A study published in 1990 comparing the degree to which immigrants from the Maghreb and Southeast Asia were perceived as fulfilling the French "ideal" found that the former were criticized in each category of evaluation, while Southeast Asians were seen as "exemplary citizens, even more so than 'most French people.'"[99] Although there is an absence of in-depth scholarly studies of the positive view of Southeast Asian immigrants in France, anecdotal evidence can provide some insight into the phenomenon. For his study of Vietnamese immigration to France, Jean Hugues conducted interviews with a number of Vietnamese repatriates and immigrants as well as those who had frequent contact with them (schoolteachers, classmates, work colleagues, neighborhood residents). The principal of the Collège Victor Hugo in Paris commented that students from Southeast Asia

> are reserved but active: they are the heads of the class, with a very low rate of failure. [. . .] They have such a will to integrate that they gallicize their names when they can. They look to blend in at school, in class, through their clothing in particular. They are methodical, perfectionists: their silence is often due to a desire to speak perfectly.[100]

Residents of the Thirteenth arrondissement of Paris spoke of the fact that "since the arrival of the Asians, we can take the dogs out as late as eleven o'clock, without worrying."[101]

The relatively positive view of Southeast Asian integration contrasted with the far more negative view of Maghrebi integration is not a recent dichotomy. In fact the case of the CAFI highlights the different perceptions of Indochina repatriates and the Algerian *harkis*. In 1967 a proposal was put forward to create an outdoor center in Sainte-Livrade for the children of the *harki* camp in Bias. This proposal came in reaction to an earlier attempt to send these children to the outdoor center in Villeneuve, which the children of the CAFI had attended. Parents in Villeneuve balked at the idea purportedly because they "[did] not appreciate having their children be in the presence of so many little Muslims."[102] A 1973 article in *Le Point* quotes a resident on the subject of the repatriates: "When they came, we quite liked them. Much more than the Arabs."[103] Even the repatriates themselves have identified the difference in perceptions and treatment. One interviewee reported to Le Huu Khoa that "we are not treated like Arabs and Blacks in France."[104] Likewise one of Jean Hugues's interviewees stated that "people see us as nice [*gentils*]."[105] The narrative of a successful Asian immigration as one that has resulted in a high degree of assimilation, as compared to the perception of a problematic North African, predominantly Muslim immigration, is one that continues to resonate today.

The question of integration is particularly critical in the case of the repatriates precisely because they were French citizens and not immigrants or refugees. The imposition of a policy of assimilation was experienced by some as an attack on their very nationality. After a visit to the CAFI, a veteran and self-described Eurasian wrote a report to local and regional authorities denouncing the policy of assimilation: "Assimilate who? Them? But they have been French for generations."[106] Residents' demands, whether it be for televisions, access to medical services outside of the camp, or an end to the administrative structure, were framed by the question of citizenship and the desire to be treated as full French citizens. Relatively early on, residents were permitted to vote in municipal elections, but it took much longer for them to have access to subsidies directly from the agencies involved or to seek medical care outside of the camp doctor's office if they chose to. The administrative structure lasted the longest at the CAFI, but this is primarily due to the fact that the CAFI outlasted all of the other sites.

THE REPATRIATE CAMPS AS SITES OF MEMORY

Not only were the sites of the repatriate camps home for a number of repatriates, but they long served as physical reminders of the history and experiences of the residents as well. They straddled the line between the history of immigration and the legacy of decolonization. However, outside of the communities neighboring the camps there is little awareness of their existence, which makes it very difficult to ascribe to them the status of "sites of memory" that many repatriates and their descendants would like to see awarded. In fact when the camps are the subject of any kind of attention, it is frequently in the context of commenting on their "forgotten" nature. The media have expressed interest in them very sporadically; in the realm of television, between 1972 and 2006 only a dozen news stories on the topic had aired on the major French networks.[107] Moreover the image in the media of the camps and their residents has been overwhelmingly static. In 1959 an article on the CAFI in *France observateur* referred to the residents as "forgotten."[108] In 1972 Antenne 2 aired a short documentary on Noyant entitled *The Forgotten of Indochina*.[109] By 2004 France 2 and France 3 were collaborating with a Hanoi television station to produce *The Camp of the Forgotten,* hailed by the regional newspaper *Sud-Ouest* as having "filled a gap in national memory."[110] While this praise is perhaps overstated given that the camps have yet to emerge from their relative obscurity into the spotlight of national awareness, it is true that media coverage has increased, relatively speaking, since 2000. While national media coverage generally continues to be limited, local media coverage has been on the rise. In the realm of film and investigative journalism the camp has been the subject of at least ten documentaries.[111]

Faced with a public oblivious to the history of the repatriates, and undoubtedly guided by an increased memorial imperative beginning in the early 1990s, current and former residents of the camps created a number of associations to lobby for official recognition and to write the repatriate experience back into national history. Among them are the Eurasian Association of Paris-CAFI (CEP-CAFI); Memory of Indochina (Mémoire d'Indochine); the Association of Residents and Friends of the CAFI (ARAC; not to be confused with the veterans' association with the same acronym); and the Association of Repatriates of Noyant d'Allier (ARINA; Association des rapatriés de Noyant d'Allier). All have sought to foster a greater awareness of the camps and the experiences of the repatriates, and the CEP-CAFI and Mémoire d'Indochine in particular have also sought state recognition akin to that granted to the *harkis* in 2005.

In 2006 the CEP-CAFI identified its two primary objectives as the defense of the CAFI as a historical and cultural site, and the "moral and material recognition" of the repatriates.[112] The group originally envisioned a commemorative space of four hundred square meters with an information center, library, and rotating exhibits; an "exotic garden" would also be maintained, to be tended by residents. CEP-CAFI president Daniel Frêche remains adamant that the site be one of "living memory."[113] Securing agreements regarding the construction of such a memorial seems like a small task in comparison with the second major goal of the organization. The CEP-CAFI maintains that while "moral recognition" of the contributions of the

French of Indochina to the colonial state, as well as of their experience upon their arrival in France, is critical, the association will continue to push for financial compensation. Although the French government has passed a series of legislation since the era of decolonization granting indemnities to repatriated populations, the French of Indochina have not benefited from them.

The experiences and treatment of the repatriates have often been compared to those of the *harkis,* predominantly by the repatriates themselves. This tactic has become increasingly prevalent in the past decade as associations like the CEP-CAFI and Mémoire d'Indochine lobby for indemnities and recognition. Comparison with the fallout of Algerian independence has a long history with the repatriates: in Trinh Van Thao's 1966 doctoral thesis, a sociological study of a sample group of repatriates living in Paris, he highlights the bitterness expressed by many repatriates comparing the (perceived) "surge of solidarity [...] that welcomed the Pieds-noirs" as opposed to the "detached indifference" that the same population had shown them upon their arrival.[114] The comparison with the *harkis* is equally valid despite the fact that they were soldiers while the Indochina repatriates were primarily civilians. There were strong similarities in the treatment of the two groups through the process of "repatriation" and their respective experiences of the camps, which were occasionally the same sites (as in the case of Bias and Saint-Hilaire). Nonetheless the comparison has taken on particular currency in recent years as the *harkis* have gained increasing public attention. Yet as Bruno Icher wrote in *Libération,* "If the scandal of the *harkis* returns regularly to the spotlight, that of the Indochina repatriates is glaring in its absence from the debates."[115] At the time of writing, the repatriates had been granted no significant indemnities by the state despite the arguments of Réunion senator Anne-Marie Payet during the Senate debates over the drafting of the legislation,[116] as well as the efforts of Yves Simon (deputy of the Allier) to have the legislation amended after the fact.

While the struggle to acquire legal recognition of their status is ongoing, the memorial efforts of the CEP, Mémoire d'Indochine, and the ARAC were validated by the events of the fiftieth anniversary of the arrival of the first repatriates. Both Noyant and the CAFI have been the subjects of commemorative projects, but it is the CAFI that has been a focal point for repatriate remembrance, in part because it maintained camp status for the longest period of time. As former resident Émile Lejeune argues, "In all of France, it's the only area that marks the repatriation of the French of Indochina."[117] It is not only residents, however, that confer a special status on the CAFI; in

1992 the camp was chosen for an advanced screening of his major release *Diên Biên Phu,* which chronicled the end of the Indochina War and of the French presence in the region. Events and ceremonies were held in both Noyant and Sainte-Livrade, although the latter was the center of activity.

The focal point of the fiftieth anniversary events was an exhibit running from 29 April to 17 September entitled "CAFI 1956–2006 ... De Saïgon à Sainte-Livrade," hosted by the Sainte-Livrade municipal library. Showcasing archival documents, photos, testimony, household objects, clothing, and other items, the exhibit illustrated various aspects of life at the CAFI over the years. Visitors were provided with carefully prepared documentation on various aspects of the center, including the history of the "Moulin-du-Lot" site, colonial Indochina, the migration of the repatriates, religious life, and important Vietnamese celebrations like Têt. Sharing the history of the CAFI was also expanded beyond the museum exhibit: visitors were also offered the opportunity to take a guided tour of the site during the summer months, including one apartment that had been redecorated as it would have been when the repatriates first arrived. Other stops on the tour included the pagoda, the chapel, the two grocery stores specializing in Asian products, and the garden of Asian vegetables grown from seeds originally brought from Vietnam. The ARAC also hosted a photo exhibit at their CAFI headquarters. In addition to the exhibit and the guided tours, the library put together a portable information kit on Vietnam, Indochina, and the experiences of the repatriates. A miniature version of the exhibit, it was used as a pedagogical tool to be circulated throughout libraries in the Lot-et-Garonne. For its part the CEP capitalized on the attention being paid to the CAFI to promote intellectual reflections on the camp experience. As part of the opening day events on 29 April, it hosted a roundtable featuring historians, sociologists, representatives of local authorities, and CAFI residents. In addition it arranged for multiple screenings of the documentary *The Camp of the Forgotten* in Sainte-Livrade and Paris. In the case of the latter, screenings were followed by commentary from scholars Gilles Manceron, Charles Fourniau, and Alain Ruscio. The interest in the fiftieth anniversary was also shared by regional and national publications; *Ancrage,* a periodical on the culture and history of the Lot-et-Garonne, dedicated a special issue to the CAFI.[118] *Carnets du Viêt Nam* published profiles of the camps of Noyant and Sainte-Livrade,[119] and even the national press published cursory coverage of the events. Finally the anniversary events maintained the connection between the camps and the Indochina War by incorporating a ceremony to honor the war dead on 8 June.

The memorial imperative associated with the fiftieth anniversary of the camps was bolstered by the retabling of a plan to demolish the existing structures of the CAFI. The proposal called for the demolition of the existing buildings to be replaced with subsidized housing. Those who still had legitimate claims to housing would have the right to move into this new housing, but they would be joined by other local residents. Projects had been tabled since the mid-1970s but had been delayed or abandoned, frequently under the pressure of residents and their families. By 2006 there were fewer than one hundred residents who had the right to housing at the CAFI (*ayants-droits*); these *ayants-droits* were those who had been adults at the time of arrival. Of these were a number of quite elderly women known simply as the *mamies* (grannies) or the *tatas* (aunties). Most of them rejected the idea of moving, even if it were to better housing. While their experience in the camp had been a difficult one, they had come to think of it as home, with their gardens, grocery stores, and friends all close by. There was also concern that a move might prove to be too much for the elderly residents, some of whom were over ninety. In addition to logistical concerns over the renovation of the site there was a feeling that despite the quality of the housing and the sometimes bitter history associated with the camp, the site was nonetheless home to a small community, one that expands exponentially during holidays and festivals. Each year during Têt and the CAFI celebration of 15 August families of residents and former residents flock to the camp to visit and reconnect.

For those already concerned with the relegation of repatriate history to obscurity, the physical elimination of the site was tantamount to erasing it completely. Léon Nguyen, then president of the CEP, interpreted the demolition plans as a desire to eliminate the shame associated with the Indochina War: "The state says something must be done; razing the residual and recurring shame of the Indochina War. This is the cost of forgetting and erasing this indelible stain that is the Indochina War, this stain which consists of the survival of the older generation that is still around."[120] Not all repatriates saw the same motivations on the part of the state or the municipality, but the majority agreed that to demolish the camp in its entirety was to erase part of France's history, one that was already struggling to be heard.

Demolition of the first buildings began in 2008. Rather than clearing the whole site to make way for new construction, groups of buildings were torn down and replaced one after the other. The disappearance of the barracks has motivated the CEP-CAFI and other organizations representing former residents to move forward with proposals for commemorative and pedagogical spaces on site.¹²¹ Four of the buildings were preserved for a future memorial and/or pedagogical site, including the pagoda and chapel spaces; these buildings have actually been granted protected status as historical monuments.¹²²

Among these projects has been the renovation of the pagoda, completed in 2015, which is described by *La Dépêche du Midi* as "a religious site, but also—and more importantly—a site of memory for residents."¹²³ Dominique Rolland, an anthropologist who is close to the CAFI community,¹²⁴ has proposed a "bricks of memory" project, which would consist of bricks featuring the names of CAFI families or individuals, embedded around the site. Ideally, she states, these would be accompanied by an online database of information and photos.¹²⁵ In fact in the absence of a fully developed memorial on site, the CEP-CAFI has developed a virtual "site of memory." At rapatriés-vietnam.org, former residents and the public at large can view archival photos of the site and its residents, articles from the press, and a forum for those associated with the community to keep in touch and be informed of major developments.¹²⁶

. . .

The repatriate camps of Noyant and Sainte-Livrade represent a tangible legacy of decolonization and the repatriation-immigration of French citizens to a homeland they had never seen. For residents the camps also represent personal memories of a childhood spent in rural isolation, of working under the table for local farmers, but also of celebrating Têt with an extensive network of family and friends. The process of seeking state recognition, both moral and financial, thus operates on a personal as well as collective level. In addition to providing financial compensation to individuals, such recognition has the potential to reinforce the place of the repatriate experience in the national narrative.

In the final two chapters I turn to the cultural manifestations of war remembrance. Although the topics are very different—the first examines the Georges Boudarel affair, while the second explores cinematic representations of the war—each chapter highlights the influence of the anticommunist and anticolonial narratives. In the case of the Boudarel affair proponents of the two narratives were brought into a direct and very public conflict waged through the media, the court of public opinion, and the legal system. Likewise the study of feature films and documentaries about the Indochina

War reveals the influence of the two narratives. Nor is the significance of these films limited to their depictions of the war; several of these productions have played a key role in contributing to either the anticommunist or anticolonial narratives. Finally analysis of the reception by critics and members of the public alike is a further indication of the lack of consensus over how best to represent the war.

SIX

"La Sale Affaire"

COLLABORATION, RESISTANCE, AND THE GEORGES BOUDAREL AFFAIR

And so there is a "Boudarel affair." One of these Franco-French affairs in which one finds, once again, a mix of anger and disgust, sorrow and pity, regret and forgetting. A small, greying man, practically on the brink of retirement, has suddenly unleashed a new debate on "revisionism" and forced the French to face their fractured history. But what is it really all about?[1]

YVES CUAU, *L'Express*

ON 13 FEBRUARY 1991, just as he was about to present his paper at a conference on Vietnamese current affairs at the Senate in Paris, Professor Georges Boudarel was interrupted by a member of the audience who introduced himself as Jean-Jacques Beucler, a former prisoner of war and a government minister under Valéry Giscard d'Estaing. Accompanied by a small group of veterans who had all gained access to the conference armed with fake invitations provided by the National Association of Veterans and Friends of Indochina (ANAI),[2] Beucler described a letter he had received in 1986 from a certain Colonel Mitjaville, another former prisoner of the Viet Minh. Mitjaville claimed that he had recently discovered that the French political commissar who had abused him and other prisoners was living in France, and he asked Beucler to track him down. Mitjaville had died soon after from complications related to his internment, and Beucler had vowed to fulfill his promise to find the "torturer." He reminded the stunned audience that the death rates of the Viet Minh camps had been proportionally higher than the Nazi deportation camps,[3] and then spoke directly to Boudarel, interrogating him on his activities during the Indochina War: "Were you in Indochina between 1950 and 1954? Did you desert and join the Viet Minh? Were you the tormentor of Camp 122?"[4] Boudarel readily acknowledged that he had been a political instructor in a Viet Minh camp and went so far as to correct the number of the camp: it had been Camp 113, not 122. The accuser barreled on, charging the professor with having "blood on his hands"[5] given the high rates of mortality in the camp. The accusations sparked what one politician dubbed a "media lynching"[6] that lasted several months and more importantly led to a trial for crimes against humanity, a charge that was ultimately dismissed.

The "Boudarel affair," as it came to be known, reveals a great deal about the remembrance of the Indochina War as well as the relationship of the French with their colonial past. The affair was both indicative of a slowly reemerging interest in the colonial period as well as the wars of decolonization, and the source of a renewed debate over the underlying objectives of the Indochina War. Though it garnered considerable attention, the affair should be viewed as a "flashpoint" of collective remembrance rather than a turning point, given that it did not contribute to a major shift in awareness or interpretations of the war comparable to the "breaking of the mirror" of the so-called Vichy syndrome.[7] The affair's presence in the public eye did however provoke considerable debate about broader issues of collaboration, treason, and the collective remembrance of war and decolonization. Analysis of the affair must address a number of elements: first and foremost it must address the ensuing debates over the nature of the Indochina War as well as the debates over the merits of the colonial project. As I demonstrate, pro- and anti-Boudarel groups frequently understood the war in different terms, which inhibited any productive dialogue from taking place. Disagreements over whether the war was primarily a war of colonial reconquest or a struggle against communism were also inherently tied to varied interpretations of the French colonial system in Indochina. Second, the affair must be examined within the context of the renewed commitment in the late 1980s and early 1990s to the "duty to remember." This memorial emphasis meant that the affair acted as a catalyst for discussions of France's "forgotten" colonial wars and became yet another example for commentators of a French inability to face the national past. Furthermore the timing of the affair, which coincided roughly with the arrest and trials of several Vichy collaborators accused of having committed crimes against humanity, ensured that Boudarel's actions would be compared to and even conflated with the actions of the collaborators. The collapse of the Soviet bloc encouraged a desire for some to stage a thorough assessment of the communist system through a "Nuremberg trial of communism," and Boudarel provided a timely target. Marxism had remained a fairly powerful force from the 1950s through the 1990s, one that was much maligned by the extreme right in particular. The affair then was not simply a matter of one man's actions toward his compatriots during an unpopular and far-off war but represented far greater divisions in French society.

The discourse of collaboration and resistance, which has dominated discussions of the Vichy period, provides a fascinating framework for discussion of the Boudarel affair. Boudarel was alternately identified as a *collabo* (collaborator) and *kapo* (a prisoner in Nazi concentration camps who oversaw other prisoners) or as a resistant who opposed an oppressive colonial system. This discourse of collaboration and resistance is certainly not new in the context of the Indochina War: following so closely on the heels of the Second World War, the colonial conflict was frequently described in similar terms.[8] The mantle of the Resistance was variously attributed to the French soldiers who were ostensibly fighting to liberate the colonies (in this case from the Japanese and then the Viet Minh), or to anticolonial forces. In the latter case the Viet Minh was frequently compared to the Resistance and the French military and colonial authorities to the Nazi occupier. The spectrum between collaboration and resistance, with its inherent shades of grey, was thus further complicated by the colonial context. The debates over the legitimacy of the colonial system, which led wartime commentators to view one side or the other as the heirs to the Resistance, had an obvious impact on reactions to the Boudarel affair. For some Boudarel's decision to join the Viet Minh was clearly a case of collaboration with the enemy; for others (including Boudarel himself) he had acted out of resistance to an unjust colonial system. Although not widespread during the Indochina War, this kind of resistance would gain in popularity during the Algerian War; those who fought on the side of the National Liberation Front (FLN) were known as "suitcase carriers" (*porteurs de valise*).[9]

This chapter considers numerous facets of the Boudarel affair, beginning with an examination of the immediate reaction of the press, politicians, and the public. Not only was there a stark division between Boudarel's supporters and opponents, but there was a fundamental disjuncture in their arguments, which reflected the complexity of the war as both a colonial war and a hot spot of the Cold War. His supporters argued from an anticolonialist point of view, claiming not only that he had been justified in his opposition to colonialism but that the war had inherently been a "dirty" one. His critics for their part took an anticommunist stance, arguing that the war had been legitimate in its opposition to the Communist Viet Minh, who had perpetrated unspeakable horrors during the war and since. They also placed

Boudarel's actions within a broad narrative of collaboration and treason. In addition to analyzing the ramifications of the Boudarel affair within the framework of remembrance of the Indochina War, I expand the scope of the discussion to include its impact on provoking debates over French "memory troubles" in general.

GEORGES BOUDAREL DURING THE YEARS 1948 TO 1991

Eager to experience life in the colonies, and following an unsuccessful bid to find a position in Madagascar, a young Georges Boudarel boarded the *Pasteur* in April 1948 bound for Saigon. A member of the French Communist Party, he had been advised by the party to leave his membership card in France, though he was given contact information for members of the Marxist Cultural Group (GCM; Groupe culturel marxiste) in Saigon.[10] He took up teaching positions, first in Laos and later in Saigon, but quickly became disenchanted with colonial society. His autobiography describes the colonial society that he encountered in Dalat in 1948 as "living off the backs of the natives without making any attempt to listen to them."[11] The settlers he describes are snobbish and arrogant and either misunderstand the Vietnamese language and culture completely or are overtly hostile to elements of the so-called civilizing mission, such as the education of the indigenous population. Emphasizing the exploitative nature of the colonial system, Boudarel argues that it was based on "pillaging, contempt and annexation under the pretext of the civilizing mission."[12]

His fundamental opposition to a society based on such inequalities was so strong that he made contact with representatives of the Viet Minh and arranged to cross into their territory. In mid-November 1949 he was summoned to a meeting with Nguyen Tho Chan, the secretary of the Communist Party in Saigon; shortly thereafter, the date of his passage was fixed. On 17 December 1950 a taxi driven by a man sympathetic to the Viet Minh drove Boudarel out of central Saigon to the Lai Thieu district just north of the city. After switching vehicles in a small village, Boudarel was driven to a house outside of the community; the last leg of the journey was accomplished on foot through the paddy to the unoccupied zone, only a short distance from a French border post. A group of Viet Minh members were waiting for him and escorted him to the command post of the local company of the Lai Thieu subdistrict. Boudarel was initially assigned to work for the French-language radio broadcast "The Voice of Free Saigon-Cholon" (La Voix de Saigon-Cholon libre). In early 1953 he received orders to travel north to the Viet Bac region to take up the position of propaganda instruction in a prisoner of war camp, Camp 113, where he remained until 1954. Boudarel's responsibilities, as he recounts, consisted of leading political education sessions with the camp inmates, which were designed to convince them of the importance of peace and the withdrawal of the expeditionary corps from Vietnamese territory. According to former prisoners, Boudarel also played a role in deciding who was eligible for release and supporting a food reward system according to which those who performed best in the education sessions would be given larger rations. All parties agree that the death rate in Camp 113, as in most of the camps, was exceptionally high and was due in large part to malnutrition and a plethora of tropical diseases for which there was little to no medical treatment; the medical reports on the state of liberated prisoners certainly confirm the appalling condition of survivors.[13] However, Boudarel contested the statistics claimed by veterans of between 270 and 280 deaths out of 340 prisoners in the year 1953, contending that these figures were exaggerated. He further argued that there had been a lack of proper medication and food not just for the prisoners but also for the soldiers in the Vietnamese military.

Boudarel left Camp 113 before the battle of Dien Bien Phu, and following the French defeat he moved to Hanoi. By his own account Boudarel grew increasingly disillusioned with the Vietnamese communist system, to the point where he was viewed with considerable suspicion by the regime. Though he makes only a few allusions in his autobiography to the "bloody mistakes"[14] of the Vietnamese Communist Party, his *Cent fleurs écloses dans la nuit du Vietnam* (*One Hundred Flowers Blooming in the Vietnamese Night*), published in the same year, is far more revealing of his criticisms of the regime. *Cents fleurs* chronicles the evolution of the party through the 1954–56 period, and although the focus is on the work of several literary dissidents and their treatment by the regime, his critique extends to the violent implementation of agrarian reform and the party purges. His autobiography makes it clear that his questioning of state policy led him to be viewed with increasing suspicion by the regime after the war's conclusion.[15]

Boudarel left Hanoi for Prague in 1964, where he stayed until a French amnesty law was passed on 18 June 1966. Initially intended to cover crimes committed during the Algerian War, the text was expanded, on the proposal of Communist deputies Robert Ballanger and Guy Ducoloné, to include "all crimes or offences committed in relation to the events following the

Vietnamese insurrection and prior to the 1st of October 1957."[16] Boudarel's decision to wait for amnesty before returning to France could be read as an admission of wrongdoing and certainly has been by the National Association of Former Prisoners and Internees in Indochina (ANAPI);[17] however, Boudarel's status was complicated by a conviction for failing to present himself for his compulsory military service (*insoumission*) in March 1950. He also would likely have been found guilty of treason had he returned to France without amnesty, as had been the case for a group of deserters (*ralliés*) who had returned in 1962, even though he was a civilian and not a member of the French forces. He returned to France in January 1967 along with "Cassius" and "Ribera," the only other two deserters who benefited from the amnesty.[18] While the amnesty in effect covered treason and his conviction for *insoumission*, there remained the question of his fulfillment of mandatory military service. It was quietly decided that he would not be forced to complete the latter. Boudarel earned his doctorate at the National Center of Scientific Research (CNRS; Centre national de la recherche scientifique) under the supervision of Jean Chesneaux, and in 1971 was offered a position at the newly created Université Paris VII (Jussieu). By the time the controversy erupted in 1991, he had gained a solid academic reputation as an authority on Vietnam whose work frequently focused on Vietnamese dissidents and critiques of the Communist regime.

The public uproar surrounding the case took on a legal dimension on 3 April 1991 when lawyer Jean-Marc Varaut filed a charge of crimes against humanity against Boudarel on behalf of former prisoner Wladislaw Sobanski, with the ANAPI taking civil action (*constituer partie civile*). Although the *parquet* opposed pursuing the case on 23 May, the presence of a party taking civil action meant that Judge Lucie LeHoux was within her rights to override this opposition and recommend moving ahead with the case, which she did on 13 September. The case was brought to a close on 20 December when the court decided not to pursue Boudarel for crimes against humanity on the basis of the 1966 amnesty. The very possibility for pursuing the charge of crimes against humanity had considerable implications for the legal system, which is discussed in greater detail shortly. Finally, while Boudarel faced no legal consequences for his past, he was forced into early retirement. Contrary to standard practice, according to which a university professor could expect to work the full academic session the year he or she turned sixty-five, Boudarel was informed on 27 November 1991 that his term of employment would be terminated as of his sixty-fifth birthday (December 1991).[19]

REACTIONS AND CONTROVERSY

While reactions to the revelation of Boudarel's past did reach a high level of intensity, there was very little in the way of immediate response in the press. The first article published about the incident was Beucler's own account in the *Figaro* of 19 February, six days after his denunciation, but the media did not swing into high gear until early March. Close to three hundred articles on the affair were published in the Paris-based press between February and May 1991 supplemented by numerous television news clips and interviews. Among them was a special episode of *Le Droit de savoir* (*The Right to Know*), hosted by Patrick Poivre d'Arvor, which ostensibly sought to clarify the details of Camp 113 by moderating a discussion between Boudarel and Beucler. The first special issue dedicated to the affair was published the week of 6–12 March by *Minute-La France,* which latched on to the affair, devoting two subsequent issues to Boudarel.[20] By the end of March both *Politis* and *L'Express* had also published special issues, and practically every major national newspaper had provided some degree of coverage for its readers.

The most extensive press coverage was that of the right and extreme right, particularly the *Figaro* and *Minute-La France*. Anti-Boudarel articles, interviews with veterans and former prisoners, and indignant letters to the editor were published on a frequent basis. *Paris Match* ran a photo spread in early April depicting emaciated prisoners of war, entitled "Boudarel, Here Are Your Victims."[21] In addition to publishing the first article by anyone connected to the affair, that of Beucler on 19 February, the *Figaro* devoted considerable space to the affair throughout its peak. Readers were evidently also very engaged by the affair—the newspaper published letters to the editor on the subject on a near weekly basis through March and April, most of which supported Beucler's denunciation and accused Boudarel of being a traitor and a torturer. While a number of these letters were from veterans, many were from ordinary citizens, suggesting that at least part of the general public saw great significance in the affair.

The extreme right was predictably more aggressive in its denunciation of the "tormentor" (*bourreau*) of Camp 113. *Minute-La France, National-Hebdo,* and *Présent* used the affair not only to launch vicious attacks on Boudarel but also to attack Communists in France and abroad. *Minute* presented a series of testimonies from former prisoners with sensationalist headlines like "Boudarel Inflicted a Slow Death on Us"[22] and "How I Almost Died."[23] Communism and the French Communist Party were also repeatedly indicted: an article by Serge de Beketch in the issue of 20–26 March was entitled "These Communists, Professionals of All Forms of Treason."[24] *Présent* columnist Alain Sanders sought to go one step further than Beucler to "unmask" the network that helped the "torturer" reenter France, identifying Pierre Vidal-Naquet, Jean Chesneaux, and Jean-Marie Domenach as responsible parties.[25] While the attacks from the extreme right can certainly be explained by the radical nature of the publications and their unabashed anticommunism, a number of commentators maintained that this was a tactic to divert attention away from Jean-Marie Le Pen's controversial support of Saddam Hussein during the recent Gulf War, which had prompted considerable internal divisions for the National Front.[26]

Newspapers from the center and the left, from *Le Monde* and *L'Express* to *L'Humanité* and *Libération,* covered the affair with somewhat less regularity. Interestingly though perhaps not surprisingly the left was divided over whether to support or condemn Boudarel. The majority of columnists and commentators supported Boudarel's anticolonialism but condemned his role in Camp 113. *L'Humanité* gave the least coverage to the affair, publishing very little in the way of commentary on the affair save to denounce the "suspicious tenacity"[27] of the extreme right. Editorialists also seized the opportunity to remind readers that the Indochina War had been a "dirty" one and that the French Communist Party had a strong history of anticolonialism and antiwar protest. The closest the publication came to taking a position on the affair was in an editorial of 18 March, which applauded Boudarel's anticolonialism without explicitly supporting him: "At the time, true patriotism and courage consisted of taking a stand against colonialism. The French Communist Party is proud not to have failed in this respect. Mr. Boudarel's political path is far from our own, but his refusal of the Indochina War was inspired by such courage."[28] *Libération* was far more supportive and gave more coverage to the affair as it unfolded, including several exposé pieces on Boudarel and the greater implications of the affair for the French remembrance of the colonial wars. *Politis* and *L'Express* both featured special issues devoted to the affair, though their positions varied: *Politis* was the most supportive of Boudarel, while *L'Express* featured a mix of support and criticism. The *Nouvel observateur* was the most critical of the publications of the center-left, including a singularly unforgiving article by Marie-France Etchegoin,[29] though it only published a handful of articles on the topic.

Much of the firsthand testimony describing the camp conditions was provided by interviews with veterans who had spent time in Camp 113. In addition two relevant memoirs were published in the spring and fall of 1991: Claude Baylé's *Prisoner of Camp 113: Boudarel's Camp* (published in May) and Thomas Capitaine's *Captives of the Viet Minh: Boudarel's Victims Speak Out* (published in November).[30] Both had been penned in the early 1970s, but neither had found a publisher prior to the affair breaking. Each also featured a preface by Jean-Jacques Beucler, the "hero of the hour." The memoirs echo the bleak pictures of the abysmal living conditions of the camp painted by the veterans interviewed by the press, and neither is at all forgiving of Boudarel, who is identified as the cause of their suffering. Not all former prisoners of 113 were critical of Boudarel's role, however. Jean Robert, who contacted Boudarel to offer his support after seeing a televised news clip on the affair, appeared with him on *Le Droit de savoir* and attempted to counter the images of the camp propagated by Baylé, Sobanski, and others. Marcel Croenne, though not a supporter of Boudarel, claimed in an interview that he had no reason to complain about Boudarel and that he had never witnessed or heard of Boudarel striking or torturing prisoners.[31] The only other book published in the wake of the affair, aside from Boudarel's autobiography, was Marc Charuel's *L'Affaire Boudarel,* another highly critical piece of journalism.

While the affair certainly divided the French into two camps, they were clearly not defined along strict political lines. The right and extreme right were almost exclusively in the anti-Boudarel camp, yet it was a right-wing minister, François Léotard, who denounced the "lynch mob" attitudes of many critics. Likewise it was the Socialist minister of education Lionel Jospin who accused Boudarel of having acted as a "*kapo.*" Despite the lack of clear divisions along political lines the press of both ends of the political spectrum engaged in vicious attacks against each other. The press of the left accused that of the right and particularly the extreme right of being "nostalgic for French empire"[32] and of engaging in both a "fantasmatic reconquest of Indochina"[33] and a revision of colonial history. Conversely the press of the right and extreme right frequently charged those who supported Boudarel of ignoring the horrors perpetrated by the communist system, or worse, of supporting them.

The arguments put forward by Boudarel's supporters were overwhelmingly characterized by two predominant beliefs: that the colonial dimension of the Indochina War could not be overlooked, and that the war itself had been a "dirty war." References to the conflict as a "colonialist war"[34] or a "war of reconquest"[35] were common in the press of the center and the left. Many, like

Dominique Le Guilledoux of *Le Monde*, argued that while the crimes committed during the conflict should undoubtedly be investigated, both sides deserved equal scrutiny.[36] A secret report by General de Beaufort dated 11 March 1955 was among the pieces of evidence marshaled by Boudarel and his supporters to demonstrate that French treatment of Vietnamese prisoners was also problematic. The report essentially advises the cessation of attempts to determine the fate of missing French prisoners of war, as they were bound to provoke similar demands from the Vietnamese side. This was problematic, Beaufort states, given that an estimated nine thousand Vietnamese prisoners who had been captives of the French had died or been executed in captivity.[37] There were also outright references in the press to the use of torture by the French military: Gabriel-Xavier Culioli, while unsympathetic to Boudarel's role in Camp 113, argues in *Politis* that if Boudarel were to be judged for war crimes then innumerable soldiers would have to be judged for "the combing of villages, the rape and murder of civilians, the use of napalm by the French air force."[38] Likewise a flyer attributed to a committee in support of Boudarel about the affair and the Indochina War included excerpts from wartime accounts published in *Témoignage chrétien* of torture and summary executions committed by French troops.[39] Finally Pierre Vidal-Naquet emphasized the importance of putting the horror of the Viet Minh camps within the context of the violence associated with the colonial state, directing readers to Andrée Viollis's exposé *Indochine SOS* (1935). "After all," he argues, "this horror is part of a context that was itself horrible. One cannot separate this horror from all that surrounding it."[40]

Boudarel himself emphasized his actions as having been rooted in anticolonialism. His adamancy that he had no regrets about joining the Viet Minh did not evoke much sympathy, but he insisted that he "was right to join the Vietnamese for their independence."[41] He did also, however, admit that his memories of his time at Camp 113 were "tragic" and "painful,"[42] and that he regretted his communist commitment "100 percent."[43] He countered charges that he was a traitor to the nation by arguing that if anything he had been a "traitor to colonialism"—the original title, in fact, of his autobiography.[44] His primary defense was that he was both a prisoner of ideology and of a hierarchical system, and that it was impossible for him to do more than he did for the prisoners given the nature of the system and the lack of food and medicine.[45] In a letter to the *Nouvel observateur*, responding to Etchegoin's highly critical article, Boudarel actually shifts the blame for the lack of available supplies to the expeditionary corps and French political authorities, who had given orders for a variety of blockades to be established.[46]

While Boudarel's supporters focused on the colonial dimension of the war and called for an evaluation of the war in its entirety, his critics (veterans in particular) either refused to engage with the colonial dimension of the war or argued that French military objectives had nothing to do with colonialism. Colonel Déodat Puy-Montbrun, for example, stated in *Le Figaro* that "we did not conduct, gentlemen, a colonial campaign in Indochina. The 'colony' was long gone."[47] Déodat goes on to argue that the Viet Minh were not fighting a national war for Vietnam but rather a communist war against the "three states of Indochina."[48] Jean-Jacques Beucler maintains a similar position in his autobiography, citing the agreements signed in Halong Bay with Bao Dai in 1948 as proof that France was fighting alongside an independent Vietnam rather than pursuing a war of reconquest.[49] There was much support for this position, which identified the primary objective of the war as the defeat of the Communist Viet Minh in order for the newly independent Vietnam to flourish. The suffering of prisoners in Viet Minh camps is thus inscribed in a larger context of anticommunism. In this way the crimes committed in these camps became the crimes of communism and a trial of these crimes provided a stage for a trial of the communist system writ large. Commentators on the extreme right certainly saw it as such; columnists writing in *Aspects de la France, Minute-La France,* and even the far less radical *Figaro Magazine* called for a trial of communism through the prosecution of Boudarel. Yves Daoudal of *Présent* and *National-Hebdo* reflected a decade after the affair first broke that it was nothing short of an "impossible trial of communism."[50]

Though most of Boudarel's critics avoided addressing the colonial dimension, there were a few who maintained that the colonial project had had certain merits. Jean-Jacques Beucler, who took advantage of the public's attention to publish his memoirs (October 1991, with the subtitle *The Man Who Unmasked Boudarel*), was among those who defended the idea that "the balance sheet is eminently positive" and that "France could and should be proud of its work in Indochina,"[51] though he did not make such statements publicly with reference to the Boudarel affair. When he was interviewed about the affair by *Présent,* veteran Pierre Guillaume, however, implied the merits of colonialism when he stated that "during the French colonial period, there were never any boat people who fled," and this despite the availability of unsupervised fishing boats.[52]

Reactions to the affair were naturally not limited to the press. In the anti-Boudarel camp, extreme right-wing organizations were particularly active:

Action Française and the National Combatants' Circle (CNC; Cercle national des combattants) staged a march from the Odéon intersection to the Jussieu campus on 27 March, where they were met with riot police (CRS). This was not the first such demonstration; the press reported several earlier (and somewhat smaller) demonstrations. The student branch of Action Française distributed flyers depicting an emaciated prisoner of war and calling for Boudarel's resignation. The Front National de la Jeunesse (the youth component of the National Front) held a protest at the Arc de Triomphe on 18 March, unfurling a banner reading "Boudarel traitor, Jospin accomplice" from the monument. The extreme right-wing publication *Présent* also bragged about the activities of Action Française in language eerily reminiscent of that used to describe military operations in Indochina and Algeria. It reported that "cleanup commandos" (*commandos de nettoyage*) had made several incursions into the Jussieu campus to erase all of the "graffiti, tags, spray-painted slogans or posters in support of the traitor Boudarel."[53] The CNC also laid a wreath to the "combatants of Indochina and the dead of the Viet Minh camps" in front of the statue of Marshal Lyautey, a conqueror of Tonkin in the late nineteenth century, and created a Committee for the Dismissal of Georges Boudarel (Comité pour la révocation de Georges Boudarel). Given the CNC's ties with the National Front, it is not surprising that a number of highly placed party members, including party leader Jean-Marie Le Pen, were members of the committee. Boudarel also received threatening messages on his answering machine,[54] and his apartment building was the target of graffiti and even gunshots.

Boudarel's supporters reacted to the attacks by creating a support committee and publishing a number of statements and petitions. The university council released a statement on 20 March 1991 maintaining that Boudarel "must be protected, like any other academic, from arbitrary media attention" and strongly condemned "the violence perpetrated on campus by outside elements."[55] A petition signed by forty well-known intellectuals including Pierre Vidal-Naquet, Félix Guattari, and Laurent Schwartz was released in early March expressing solidarity with Boudarel and lauding his "courageous choice [and] his refusal of the 'dirty war,' of the colonial situation, of racist contempt."[56] The petition also accuses Boudarel's attackers of being those "for whom the victories of decolonization amounted to personal defeats."[57] This petition was matched by a second one signed by seventeen scholars specializing in Asian studies, who urged the public to recognize Boudarel's contributions to a better understanding of Vietnam in France and abroad, despite his activities during the Indochina War. In addition a number of Jussieu students posted pro-Boudarel posters and flyers intended not only to defend his actions but also to inform passersby of the "real" nature of the Indochina War.[58] Among the posters and slogans was one notice signed by the Anti-Authoritarian Collective (Collectif anti-autoritaire) that emphasized the colonial nature of the war, justified Boudarel's choice to join the Viet Minh, and charged his critics with wanting to rewrite colonial history:

> What was the Indochina War? A colonial war against an entire people. Populations were terrorized, villages destroyed, civilians tortured ... by the "glorious French army." [...] A hundred French people—"traitors to the nation" [...]—were condemned to death—and amnestied—for having chosen to side with the oppressed, in this case the Vietnamese people. We stand in solidarity with all of the deserters of the period—and thus with Georges Boudarel—without ignoring a system that generated "political re-educators." Boudarel is the victim of a slanderous campaign [...] led by nationalist and militarist groups who want to rewrite the history of the colonial wars.[59]

The connections between the Boudarel affair and the legacy of colonialism were drawn most explicitly by Jean-Luc Einaudi, well known for his work on controversial periods of French history, a decade after the affair first broke. The project that became *Viêt-Nam! The Indochina War, 1945–1954* began with a phone call from Boudarel, who Einaudi claims was seeking to pull himself out of "the historical garbage can."[60] Though the first chapter opens with this mise-en-scène, the subsequent chapters that constitute the first half of the book are devoted not to the affair but rather to the abuses inherent in the colonial system and the ubiquity of illness and malnutrition in prisoner of war camps on *both* sides of the conflict. Though the connections are not explicit, the reader is led to believe that any judgment of Boudarel's actions must take into account the impact of rampant tropical disease and the chronic lack of supplies in the peninsula as well as the violence of the colonial system.

With the dismissal of the charges of crimes against humanity against Boudarel, Wladislaw Sobanski lost his opportunity to confront Boudarel in a court of law.[61] He did, however, have the opportunity to confront him on an episode of TF1's *Le Droit de savoir (The Right to Know)*. Whether or not it was deliberately structured as such, the show had the distinct feel of a trial being staged on a studio television set. The format echoed that of an earlier television "trial": that of Henri de Turenne in 1984. The two confrontations even shared a prosecutor in the person of Jean-Jacques Beucler.⁶² Hosted by Patrick Poivre d'Arvor, the one-hour show opened with a brief documentary entitled "The Death Camps: The Boudarel Affair" and was followed by a discussion pitting Boudarel against Sobanski. Each was allowed to bring a guest for support: Boudarel was accompanied by Jean Robert, another former prisoner of Camp 113, while Sobanski was supported by Beucler. The two parties sat facing each other on either side of the set, with Poivre d'Arvor positioned as judge/moderator in the center. The goal of the show was ostensibly to establish "the facts" about Camp 113 and Boudarel's role within it, but it quickly turned to outright accusations on the part of Sobanski and Beucler with very little in the way of effective mediation from Poivre d'Arvor.

The charged atmosphere was dominated by an emotional Sobanski, who could hardly contain his rage: "I have lived through thirty-seven nightmarish years, and I'm not the only one. [. . . Boudarel] killed us, [. . .] invaded our consciences."⁶³ While Poivre d'Arvor attempted to establish a question and answer format, the discussion was in fact dominated by Sobanski and Beucler's attacks on Boudarel and Robert's attempts to "state the real facts."⁶⁴ It was a full eight minutes before Boudarel finally intervened to defend himself. He commanded little sympathy, however, with his statements that he had "a clear conscience"⁶⁵ and his correction of what he deemed to be "factual" errors such as his position within the camp (adjunct of the camp chief in charge of political education, and not political commissar), the camp number, and the death rates. Beucler raised the issue of Mitjaville's letter, which Boudarel challenged him to produce. This letter, which had ostensibly been the motivating factor in Beucler's denunciation, had in fact never been reproduced in the press nor shown to Boudarel. Moreover he maintained that he had no idea what the conditions in the camp would be: "No one told me—and they knew at the time—'you're going to a prisoner-of-war camp and in two months they are all going to get sick and you won't have anything [to help them with].' If I had known, I never would have gone."⁶⁶ Boudarel further emphasized the need to place his actions within the "context of the period," and that he had broken with the past by renouncing his communist ideals. Implying that his own actions had been guided by his communist beliefs, he accused Beucler of having "defended colonization and colonialism."⁶⁷

Boudarel felt that he had been grossly mistreated by the show's producers and host. He later claimed that show representatives had assured him that he would be part of a historical debate with equal speaking time for each participant, but that instead it "was quickly revealed to be a premeditated attack."[68] Despite Beucler's assertions that he and others were not seeking a witch hunt, he accused Boudarel of being a "vile character," a "real criminal" who "knew all too well [...] how to kill people without laying a hand on them."[69] The opening documentary and Poivre d'Arvor's approach to the interview were visibly biased in favor of Beucler, Sobanski, and the other veterans they represented. Boudarel did very little to counteract this bias; his interruptions of the host, his refusal to formally apologize, and his focus on correcting details cast him in an unsympathetic light and marred even his attempts to demonstrate regret for having been involved with the deaths of so many. Insofar as it was an "informal trial," Boudarel certainly did not emerge with any new supporters.

LEGAL IMPLICATIONS OF THE AFFAIR

Leaving aside the court of public opinion, the affair carried with it significant legal implications. Theoretically the charges of crimes against humanity against Boudarel represented an opportunity for an expansion of the Nuremberg statute, already modified within the scope of French law by the Cour de cassation on 20 December 1985 to include

> inhumane acts and persecutions that are committed in a systematic manner, in the name of a state practicing a hegemonic political ideology, not only on the basis of membership in a particular racial or religious group, but also against those who oppose this policy, regardless of the nature of their opposition.[70]

Had Boudarel been convicted of crimes against humanity, a precedent would have been established for the recognition of a Communist group or state as pursuing "ideological hegemony" along the same lines as National Socialism, and would also have been the first successful application in France of the definition of crimes against humanity to a context unrelated to the Second World War and the Axis powers.

Jacques Vergès, who was not directly involved in the prosecution of the case but is well known for his controversial attempts to force a trial of colonialism through a number of other cases, addressed the colonial dimensions of the war in terms of the definition of crimes against humanity in an article in the controversial left-wing weekly *L'Idiot international*.[71] The additions to the Nuremberg statute served a critical role in the charges laid by Sobanski and the ANAPI, who argued that this definition could also be applied to French prisoners of war subjected to persecution and political indoctrination in Viet Minh camps. A successful application of the statute to their case would have been based on the recognition of an independent Vietnamese state that maintained a hegemonic ideology. This was problematic because while Ho Chi Minh had declared independence for the Democratic Republic of Vietnam in August 1945, the French never fully recognized the nascent state. The agreements signed between Ho Chi Minh and Jean Sainteny in March 1946 recognized an independent Vietnam within the context of the French Union. This was complicated by the Halong Bay accords signed in June 1948, which granted nominal independence to a unified (noncommunist) State of Vietnam under the leadership of Bao Dai. In effect to apply the modification of the Nuremberg code implied the recognition of North Vietnam as an independent state when its status during the war was far from definitive. Moreover Vergès argued that to apply the statute to the case of the former prisoners was in effect to accept that those who had fought to maintain Indochina "under the colonial heel"[72] were resisters and that the Vietnamese "patriots" fighting for their nation's independence were the tenants of a hegemonic ideology. In reality, he argued, it was colonial ideology that was hegemonic, and so not only did the actions of the Viet Minh not qualify as crimes against humanity, but crimes committed under the auspices of colonialism did qualify as such.

After the Boudarel affair, though not as a direct result of it, French law regarding crimes against humanity was changed. In 1994 a new penal code was introduced, in which the definition of crimes against humanity was extended to include periods and contexts not related to the Second World War. With respect to crimes committed during colonial wars, a law was passed on 17 June 2003 stipulating that French soldiers who had fought during the Algerian War could not be tried for crimes against humanity for actions taken against civilians. While this decision does not have a direct correlation with the Boudarel affair in that it addresses military actions against civilians, it does nonetheless have significant implications for the prosecution of crimes committed during the wars of decolonization.

The question arises as to why, given that Boudarel returned to France in 1967, the scandal only broke in 1991. Although Boudarel had not publicized his role in the Viet Minh, he had not hidden his past completely. He had not used a pseudonym, and he was relatively well known within the field of

Vietnamese studies. It was known that he had spent time in Indochina during the war, and he had been identified by name in a 1954 *Paris Match* article on the prisoners liberated from the Viet Minh camps.[73] In 1973 journalist Jacques Doyon published *Ho Chi Minh's White Soldiers* (*Les soldats blancs de Hô Chi Minh*), which recounted the experiences of a number of deserters, among them Boudarel (under the pseudonym Boris). Boudarel had also been a member of several groups like the Indochina Solidarity Front (Front solidarité Indochine) that opposed the American war in Vietnam, and he had even allegedly signed texts written during the turmoil of May 1968 with the title "former French cadre of the Viet Minh."[74] He had ostensibly been the target of similar accusations in 1986, and he had been receiving anonymous letters since 1988.[75] Why then did it take so long for Boudarel to be "unmasked"? Scholars and commentators have offered a variety of theories. Among them is the context of renewed focus on Franco-Vietnamese relations. Vietnam underwent a series of economic reforms beginning in 1986 known as *doi moi*, which encouraged a general opening of society to the West; 1990 was declared the year of tourism. Renewed connections with France followed, and negotiations had begun almost immediately to repatriate the bodies of French war dead that had not been returned following the reunification of Vietnam in 1975. A second factor was the fall of the Soviet bloc, which provided an opportunity for its critics to engage in a thorough assessment of the communist system; for many of them this would ideally have resembled the denazification process following the Second World War. Both Pierre Vidal-Naquet and Annie Kriegel, writing in support of and in opposition to Boudarel, respectively, cite the end of the Gulf War as another key factor. For Kriegel the conclusion of the war brought an end to the "climate of patriotic union"[76] and a return to petty politics. Vidal-Naquet speculated that while the Gulf War could not be considered a colonial conflict, "we can ask ourselves whether the fact that several tens of thousands of Arabs were killed doesn't lend support to new colonial ideologies,"[77] implying that such a context would encourage a revisiting of France's colonial past.

The broader memorial context is also crucial to understanding the intensity of the affair; both the Algerian War and the Vichy period were the objects of new or renewed memorial projects, though the latter appears to have played a greater role in the Boudarel affair. Former head of Vichy's Militia (Milice) Paul Touvier had been arrested in 1989 and was on trial for crimes against humanity during the course of the Boudarel affair, and Vichy functionary René Bousquet faced similar charges in 1991. The press unanimously made frequent allusions to these cases as well as that of Klaus Barbie, former head of the Gestapo in Lyons found guilty of crimes against humanity in 1988 for his role in the deportation of Jews and members of the Resistance from the Lyons area during the Second World War. Headlines like "Boudarel-Bousquet: The Same Struggle?"[78] and "Boudarel Like Touvier"[79] were common, as were comparisons between the cases. Boudarel himself bitterly acknowledged that according to the press, "I walk in lockstep, sometimes with Touvier, sometimes with Bousquet."[80] He was, however, deeply offended by such comparisons: "I have absolutely nothing in common with those men, who were racist, antisemites, Nazis. I said some stupid things that Stalinists were known to say in the fifties. I never behaved like a brute or a bastard with anyone."[81] Many commentators from the left argued that such comparisons were the product of a desire to match the "criminals of the right" with comparable "criminals of the left." Annie Kriegel's call in *Figaro* to use the affair as an opportunity to try not a single man but a system was echoed by other commentators from the right and the extreme right.[82] Jean-Marc Varaut, legal counsel representing Sobanski, saw the potential for the "first trial of communism" if the Boudarel case was to be prosecuted.[83] The trials also contributed to a memorial imperative, which naturally influenced the presentation of the affair in the press. The Algerian War too was used as a point of reference, albeit less frequently. Boudarel was compared to former members of the OAS (Organisation armée secrète, or Secret Army Organization) because of his amnesty and subsequent professional success, as well as to the "suitcase carriers" because of his decision to fight on the side of the colonized.[84]

The parallels drawn between Boudarel and the Vichy collaborators were also extended to the victims of each. Discussion of the Viet Minh camps was often prefaced, as Beucler had done in the Senate, with the claim that the death rate was proportionally higher than in Nazi camps. Witnesses and commentators alike compared the emaciated prisoners of war with their counterparts in the Nazi camps. Claude Baylé writes of his first impression of the inmates of Camp 113 in the following terms: "Yes, yes, these are the photos and newsreels that were shown in France when the striped pajama-clad deportees returned from the Nazi camps. [. . .] In an instant, I understand that we are on the road to extermination."[85] A number of commentators, particularly former prisoners, referred to the "Vietnamese Dachau"[86] or the "yellow gulag."[87] Éric Weinberger, a former prisoner of both the Nazis and the Viet Minh, is frequently cited to support the argument that the Viet Minh camps were actually *worse* than the Nazi camps.[88] Yves Daoudal, the director of the National Front's newspaper *National-Hebdo*, described Camp 113 as "a Marxist extermination camp, where the process of slow death was aggravated by communist propaganda, which made it worse in some ways than the Nazi camps since in the German concentration camps no one forced the prisoners to suffer through constant brainwashing or sing Hitler's praises."[89] Faced with the failure of the crimes against humanity charges, critics frequently argued that the lack of prosecution implied a hierarchy of victims—in which victims of the Nazis were more worthy of justice than those of the Viet Minh—and a system of "double standards."[90] While this line of argument was generally employed in support of prosecuting Boudarel just as Touvier and others were being prosecuted, it was used by Jean-Christophe Buisson in *Aspects de la France* to argue the contrary: if Boudarel was to be exonerated, then Touvier should be treated likewise.[91]

Undoubtedly encouraged by the spirit of national introspection prompted by the Touvier and Bousquet affairs, the press of both the left and right addressed the affair in terms of the "forgotten" Indochina War. Both *L'Express* and *Figaro Magazine* addressed the "collective repression" of the Indochina War, though what exactly was being concealed differs. For much of the press of the left what had been forgotten was the motivation for the war and the tactics used by the French forces; for the right it was the sacrifice of the soldiers who fought for France that had been overlooked. Alain Griotteray, writing in *Figaro Magazine*, gives voice to the grievances of many veterans by arguing that the war dead died twice—physically in Indochina, and a second time "in the consciousness of their contemporaries."[92] This lack of awareness applied equally to the soldiers who survived and returned home.

While the impact of the memorial project associated with Vichy, the fall of communism, and the opening of Vietnam to the West all influenced the course of the affair, Pierre Brocheux has rightly emphasized that it was also a product of the evolution of the remembrance of the war maintained by veterans.[93] Henri de Turenne's series *Vietnam* had prompted considerable debate when it aired in 1984, particularly from veterans, and this was followed by the first major study, academic or otherwise, to be undertaken on the experience of French soldiers in Viet Minh camps. Robert Bonnafous's doctoral dissertation, published in 1985 under the title *Prisoners of War from the French Far East Expeditionary Corps in the Viet Minh Camps (1945–1954)*, was born of his "disappointment with the French government's voluntary concealment of the story of the prisoners of war in Indochina."[94] The project was based on extensive use of the French military archives as well as a series of interviews with veterans, many of whom also completed questionnaires on their experiences. Construction of the Memorial to the Indochina Wars was initiated in 1988, which provided an institutional framework for remembrance of the war. This heightened awareness of the Indochina War and the experiences of former soldiers was further reinforced with the passing of a law in December 1989 that created the status of "prisoner of the Viet Minh," which granted certain benefits (medical and otherwise) to those who had been detained for three months or more. These shows of support for veterans undoubtedly encourage them to speak more openly about their experiences, making a public denunciation possible. Following on the heels of this succession of events, the Boudarel affair can be understood as being a partial product of a reawakening of interest in the Indochina War, and in fact of colonial Indochina more broadly speaking, particularly in the arts. Three films on the subject were in production at the time the affair broke—*Indochine, Diên Biên Phu*, and *L'Amant*—and a little-known film about the Marseilles dockworkers' opposition to the war, shot in 1953 by Paul Carpita and almost immediately banned by censors, had been screened publicly for the first time after being "found" in 1988 in the film archives. The war and the deserters in particular were also the subject of an award-winning graphic novel published in 1990–91 entitled *Les oubliés d'Annam (The Forgotten of Indochina)*.[95] Unbeknownst to its author, Frank Giroud, one of the characters was actually loosely based on Boudarel—Giroud had based the character on Doyon's "Boris."

Despite the discussions centered on the "memory" of the war and the reevaluation of the colonial project, some felt that there had been a failure to capitalize on the opportunity for a true evaluation of the past. Alain Léger spoke of the absence of a "collective trial of colonialism";[96] Gilles Bataillon and Jean-Philippe Béja called for greater access to colonial archives for historians.[97] Directing attention specifically to the Indochina War, Jean Chesneaux argued that the focus on Camp 113 and Viet Minh tactics overshadowed the greater context of the war and the questionable tactics applied by the French.[98]

The impact of the confluence of circumstances surrounding Beucler's denunciation of Boudarel is perhaps most obvious when one compares the case to that of "Robert Vignon"[99] in the early 1960s. In 1962 agreements between the French and North Vietnamese governments facilitated the return of thirty-nine deserters to France;[100] many of these men were eager to return, having faced declining conditions since the end of the war. The DRV viewed their continued presence as problematic and were all too happy to see them go. The group was flown to the Marignane airstrip just outside of Marseilles on the night of 23 November. There were approximately 120 people in total, since the majority of the men had brought their families with them. Of the thirty-nine, twenty-seven were amnestied by the army for their "sentimental desertion." The other twelve, who had committed far more serious acts determined to constitute "a violation of common law, treason, demoralization of the army: in sum, anything that threatens state security,"[101] faced a variety of charges. Among them was Vignon, a soldier who had deserted the French army in 1950 to join the Viet Minh and who, like Boudarel, had eventually become a political instructor in a prisoner of war camp. Vignon was ultimately sentenced to five years in prison. Pierre Vidal-Naquet headed a small campaign of support, and eventually Vignon's sentence was suspended, resulting in an early release.

While the return of the deserters caused a bit of a stir in the Marseilles press, there was very little coverage on a national level. Despite the similarities in the two cases, the Vignon affair did not garner nearly as much attention as the Boudarel affair. This is undoubtedly due in part to Boudarel's position as an intellectual and an academic. The connections between his past as a "political re-educator" and his present as a university teacher formed the basis for his opponents to question the substance of his courses and challenge what they saw as the heavy leftist influences on the universities.[102] However, given the similarities of the two cases—from the common role as political instructor in a prisoner of war camp to the formation of committees of support by certain intellectuals[103]—the difference in the reaction of the public serves to highlight the gradual development of awareness of the war and the veterans who survived it, as well as the evolution of the perceived importance of collective memorial projects.

. . .

The Boudarel affair then was both indicative of and contributive to a changing awareness of the Indochina War in French national consciousness, limited as it may have been. It was one of very few "flashpoints" that provoked heated public debate over the meaning and impact of the conflict. It revealed old political divisions as well as new attempts to come to terms with dark periods of the past. For anticolonialists and others it represented an opportunity to publicly reevaluate the nation's colonial past. For the anticommunist right it provided an opportunity to demand a trial of the so-called criminals of the left. And for the veterans, finally, the affair was an opportunity to remind the public of their sacrifices and horrific experiences as prisoners of war, which they felt had long been ignored.[104]

In the next chapter we turn to a very different cultural manifestation of war remembrance: film, both narrative and documentary. As demonstrated in this chapter, the attention to the Boudarel affair was driven at least partially by a renewed interest in the colonial period, evident in the release of three blockbuster films set in French Indochina. These films represent a high point of cinematic engagement with the conflict, which has been the subject of relatively few productions since 1954. Nonetheless these films constitute an important dimension of war remembrance in that they reflect the two dominant narratives of the war as well as the diverging perspectives on the colonial era. Moreover several of them have prompted extensive public debate, revealing the deep cleavages between the proponents of each narrative.

SEVEN

Missing in Action: The Indochina War and French Film

From *L'Amant* to *Indochine,* a certain kind of French cinema is truly occupying Viêt-nam. But even if it's clearly using more peaceful means, it certainly isn't the first time that this French occupation has established itself on Vietnamese territory. What is troubling and awful is that this cinema of occupation is starting over exactly as if it was the first time. [...] These three films [...] are all screaming the same thing: oh yes, I remember, now that you've said it, now that you've shown it, it was exactly like that. [...] In short, the good old days of the colonies.[1]

GÉRARD LEFORT

THE RELEASE OF THREE MAJOR motion pictures set in colonial Indochina—*L'Amant* (*The Lover*), *Diên Biên Phu,* and *Indochine*—in the first months of 1992 caught the attention of the French public and the media, who rushed to cover this cinematic "reconquest" of the former colony.[2] The release of these films in such a short period of time was deemed to be indicative of a return of the subject of the colony and of the Indochina War within the French film industry and within public consciousness. However, the notion of a "return" of Indochina as a cinematic subject implies an earlier period of interest, when in actuality neither the colony nor the war has ever been a particularly popular setting for filmmakers. Film (both fiction and documentary) naturally plays a significant memorial role as a means by which to process painful periods of the past and challenge contemporary interpretations of them, as has been the case in France with memories of the Occupation (*The Sorrow and the Pity/Le chagrin et la pitié,* Marcel Ophüls, 1969) and the Algerian War (*The War without a Name/La guerre sans nom,* Bertrand Tavernier, 1992). The United States too worked through its "Vietnam syndrome" through film: *Apocalypse Now, Platoon,* and

Full Metal Jacket not only performed well at the box office but also brought new perspectives to the experiences of a generation of American conscripts and volunteers. The Indochina War, however, has not been the subject of a similar cinematic reckoning with the past. As Delphine Robic-Diaz and Benjamin Stora have argued, the considerable cinematic production addressing the Algerian and Vietnam wars masks a neglect of the Indochina War.[3] Yet in spite of the limited number of films depicting the Indochina War, a number of them have nonetheless commanded significant attention; a case in point is the uproar caused by Henri de Turenne's 1984 documentary series *Vietnam*.

This chapter examines a range of key films and outlines the overall trends in representations of the war and the colonial period; it is not intended to be a comprehensive analysis of all films referencing the war.[4] The primary focus is on two films released in 1957 (*Patrouille de choc* and *Mort en fraude*), the productions of veterans-turned-filmmakers Pierre Schoendoerffer and Claude Bernard-Aubert, Henri de Turenne's documentary, and the three aforementioned films released in 1992. With few exceptions these films fall into two categories: those directed by people with intimate connections with Indochina (as soldiers, the children of veterans, or journalists), and those based on novels whose authors had firsthand experiences of the colony. In addition to this body of work, the chapter considers the unique case of Paul Carpita's *Rendez-vous des quais* (loosely translated as *Protest on the Docks*), filmed in 1953, completed in 1955, and seized by censors during one of its earliest screenings. The film was thought to be destroyed or lost for decades before making a miraculous appearance at the film archives in 1987. It was screened publicly for the first time after the discovery in 1989. *Rendez-vous* is a significant case not only because of this censorship but also because of the language used to describe it in the media and elsewhere: it was a "lost" film that represented a "repressed collective memory" of the war. As Marc Vernet demonstrates, however, the realities of the film's trajectory and treatment are far more complex and nuanced.[5] Given that few of the films that fall into this corpus are considered to be cinematically groundbreaking, the objective of the chapter is to engage with depictions of the war and the colonial era and the reactions of critics, veterans, and the general public to these works. Although these reactions do not always fall neatly into the anticolonial and anticommunist narratives, the assumptions and perspectives associated with each are quite evident in the vast majority of public commentary.

THE FIRST FILMS: *PATROUILLE DE CHOC* AND *MORT EN FRAUDE*

The immediate postwar years were characterized by a paucity of films that directly addressed the conflict: until the early 1960s, nearly a decade after the Geneva Accords, only three such films had been released.[6] In addition René Clément's *Un barrage contre le Pacifique* (*The Sea Wall*, 1956), set in 1930s Indochina, was released in this period; this was the first of several filmic adaptations of the work of Marguerite Duras. Marcel Camus's *Mort en fraude* (*Fugitive in Saigon*) and Claude Bernard-Aubert's *Patrouille de choc* (*Shock Patrol*) were released a few months apart in 1957; although both had respectable ticket sales, neither was among the 136 films that sold over 125,000 tickets in 1957 as listed by *Le Film français*.[7] Paul Carpita's *Rendez-vous des quais*, which was actually shot during the war, was released in 1955 and was seized by censors shortly thereafter. Given its limited exposure at the time of its seizure, particularly in comparison to the considerable attention it received when it was "found" in the late 1980s, it is addressed later in the chapter.

Filmed in South Vietnam, *Patrouille de choc* tells the story of a small, isolated French military post which is harassed and eventually attacked by Viet Minh forces. The film opens with a newsreel, which lends an air of documentary realism to the film. The first film to deal explicitly with the subject of the Indochina War, *Patrouille de choc* was Bernard-Aubert's attempt to create a "real film about the real Indochina War" that would be "dedicated to the French soldiers who fought well and hard."[8] *La Cinématographie française* dubbed it an "homage to the abandoned heroes of Indochina,"[9] a description that would later be applied to the work of Pierre Schoendoerffer. The opening voiceover, which plays over images of a convoy of trucks driving on a dirt road through a rural area, is a raw tribute to those who fought:

> They have a message for you. Their throats are hot. It smells of gunpowder, damp leather, cold pipes, burned rubber and the fog over the paddy field. It smells of blood, too. No one has ever listened to them; their war silenced them. Their voices were so weak amidst the din, and besides, *you* try to make yourself heard 12,000 kilometres away. Yet there were 200,000 of them who had something to say. Not counting those who could no longer speak.[10]

In addition to paying homage to those who fought, Bernard-Aubert sought to depict the "unfathomable absurdity"[11] of the war, which the metropole was voluntarily ignoring. The story is that of an isolated French military outpost at Luc Dao, which houses French Union soldiers and local auxiliaries. After the personnel of a neighboring outpost at Thuong Mai are massacred, the soldiers at Luc Dao seek to reinforce their position. The commanding officer, Lieutenant Perrin, presents the village notables with an ultimatum designed to strengthen protection for the military post: side with the French within twenty-four hours or be treated as enemies. The notables agree and concede to French demands for labor and supplies; in exchange, however, the French are to oversee the building of a school, an infirmary, and a bridge. Despite the increased security measures, the post is increasingly harassed by the Viet Minh and ultimately succumbs to a full-out attack. In many ways *Patrouille de choc* was the first film to use what would become a well-established formula: the story of a lone outpost or platoon fighting heroically against a shadowy Viet Minh and featuring a strong sense of solidarity between metropolitan French soldiers and colonial troops or local villagers. Films that conform to this model, like Schoendoerffer's *317ème section* (*The 317th Platoon*), Léo Joannon's *Fort du fou* (*Outpost in Indochina*), and even Bernard-Aubert's later works, often feature the sacrifices of the soldiers faced with the inevitability of defeat as a central theme.

Indeed *Patrouille de choc* is marked by a strong sense of defeat and despair, a tone which was captured by the film's original title, *Patrouille sans espoir* (*Patrol of Despair*). This emphasis on despair was highly problematic for censors: the censorship report issued by the Ministry of Defense and made public by a journalist states that "hope is the fundamental idea that must guide the transformation of this film."[12] The attempt to infuse the story with a sense of hope was encapsulated primarily by changing the title and the ending of the film. The revised ending features reinforcements arriving just in time to prevent complete defeat, and a postscript that announces that the five French soldiers surrounded by Viet Minh in the last scene did in fact survive. Frédéric Delmeulle argues that this censorship indicates the unwillingness of authorities to accept the depiction of French defeat;[13] he does not, however, acknowledge the probable impact of the ongoing war in Algeria on this censorship.

Bernard-Aubert has much in common with Pierre Schoendoerffer, who has become synonymous with the cinema of the Indochina War. Both experienced the war as young cameramen in the French forces, though Bernard-Aubert was there for considerably longer (1949 to 1954, as opposed to Schoendoerffer's tour from 1952 to 1954). Beyond the obvious impact that this experience has had on their respective choices of subject matter, they have both sought to maintain a focus on the experience of the average soldier, avoiding the broader subjects of political and military leadership and decision making. Bernard-Aubert experienced some success with *Patrouille de choc*, the first of his three films set during the war, but his later films would be plagued by constant and frequently unfavorable comparisons to Schoendoerffer.

Where Bernard-Aubert differs sharply from Schoendoerffer and indeed from many veterans is in his depiction of France's civilizing mission. While film scholar Catherine Gaston-Mathé perceives "a 'civilizing' France attempting to fraternize with the indigenous people while facing a destructive Viet Minh and an inevitable decolonization,"[14] *Patrouille*'s message about French colonization appears to be more nuanced. Although the soldiers are shown working and celebrating alongside the villagers, the classroom scenes present a much more critical view of the French civilizing mission. The only West African soldier in the group becomes the schoolteacher and is interrupted by Lieutenant Perrin during a lesson in which he has the children repeating, "Our ancestors, the Gauls, had blond hair and blue eyes. They had big mustaches." Perrin chides him that the Gauls were not all blond-haired and blue-eyed and that it would be better "to leave the ancestors alone and worry a bit more about the 26 letters of the alphabet." Later a reference to colonial financial mismanagement is made when a soldier is seen reading an article on the scandal surrounding the trafficking of piastres.[15] This is a relatively mild condemnation of the French colonial project, but it nonetheless distinguishes Bernard-Aubert's work from much of the rest of the corpus of veteran film and literature. Interestingly the film managed to appeal to critics and commentators from both ends of the political spectrum. Those on the right approved of its "authenticity" and the depiction of the loyalty and heroism of French soldiers and their allies,[16] while those on the left applauded Bernard-Aubert's depiction of the "absurdity" of the war.[17]

While the war is front and center in *Patrouille de choc*, it is little more than a backdrop in *Mort en fraude* (*Fugitive in Saigon*). Based on Jean Hougron's 1953 book by the same name, *Mort en fraude* is the story of a French civilian grappling with the impact of French colonialism and the threat of the Viet Minh.[18] The protagonist, Paul Horcier (Daniel Gélin), arrives in Indochina in 1950 to take up a low-level post with a large company. He is asked to transport a package containing a significant amount of money with him, which is stolen en route. Upon his arrival in Saigon his story of the theft leaves the intended recipients unconvinced, and their threats soon escalate into a citywide manhunt. Horcier seeks refuge in the room of a young Eurasian woman, Anh (Anh Méchard, also credited as Anne Méchard), who agrees to take him to her native village for a substantial fee. The village of Vinh Bao is located in a no-man's-land coveted by both French forces and the Viet Minh, next to a dam built by the French that has radically decreased fish stocks and the villagers' abilities to sustain themselves. It is here that Horcier grapples with his own stereotyped perceptions of the Vietnamese and falls in love with Anh. The villagers are hardly welcoming at first, fearing Viet Minh reprisals, but a symbiotic relationship eventually develops. Horcier lets go of his contempt and contributes to the village by buying medicine and rice and sharing in communal work. His ultimate sacrifice is to blow up the dam—literally destroying the work of French colonial authorities—which results in his being fired on by the French and the Viet Minh. As he and Anh make their escape in a canoe, they are stopped by French soldiers, who shoot Paul.

Camus's sympathies lie above all with the Vietnamese civilians. The villagers of Vinh Bao are depicted as merely trying to live according to traditional patterns, which have been disrupted primarily by the French. They stand in sharp contrast to the urbanized indigenous residents of Saigon, who are shown as being at the beck and call of Europeans; the goal is clearly to illustrate the corrupting effect of the French presence.[19] Those living in close proximity to the French are depicted as base creatures, while the villagers, who have managed to maintain a certain distance from them, are eminently nobler. Thus while Horcier is met upon his arrival in Saigon by a variety of men eager to transport his belongings or offering to do odd jobs for little pay, Anh's father is a wise and dignified village elder.

French soldiers and civilians on the one hand, and the Viet Minh on the other, are depicted in equally negative light. The former are presented as racist, oppressive, and corrupt; the latter as cruel and violent. Camus did not conceal his criticism of the colonial project, stating that "historically, the French have brought nothing constructive or positive to the Indochinese peoples, and have only degraded and debased their culture."[20] Corruption is accentuated in the depiction of the man who asks Horcier to carry the suspicious package and the gangsters who hunt him down for it, while the police in Saigon are characterized by incompetence. The company representative who meets Horcier at the ship to escort him to his quarters immediately reminds him that "we are at home here, don't you forget it," and advises him that when dealing with the natives, "there is only one approach . . . you have to keep them under control." Finally he tells Horcier: "Don't let yourself be disturbed by the poverty. They all look like they're dying of hunger, but in this country it's typical, it's part of the local color."[21] Camus's depiction of French settlers does not improve over the course of Horcier's first night in Saigon; after escaping the gangsters, he asks a passing French couple directions to get back to the street where he's staying. They advise him to take a rickshaw; after all, says the wife, "they are there for that." The husband warns him that "they're all thieves" and that if they ask for ten piastres for the trip, they should be given three. The discrimination inherent in the colonial system is highlighted with Anh's explanation to Horcier that she cannot visit her village without a pass. In response to Horcier's protestations that surely she has the right to see her family, she remarks bitterly: "The right . . . for a French woman, perhaps. You forget that I'm Eurasian." Much later when the two of them try to get a hotel room en route from Vinh Bao, they are turned away from a French hotel on the premise that *"congaïs"*[22] are not allowed. Two men in white suits and colonial hats accuse Horcier as being just another *encongayé*,[23] the kind of person "who screws up the prestige we once had in this country."[24]

In contrast Camus indicts the Viet Minh not for its actions against the French but for the attacks and reprisals against its compatriots. The experiences of the residents of Vinh Bao highlight the destructive aspects of both sides: they live in fear of the Viet Minh, and they have maintained a certain nobility and "traditional" way of life in the absence of contact with the French. Camus's commitment to a critique of colonialism is evident in the loose nature of his adaptation of Hougron's novel.[25] Hougron's Horcier seeks to liberate the villagers of Vinh Bao from the Viet Minh alone. Most strikingly his death in the novel is considerably less heroic: he is shot by the gangsters who had been searching for him since his arrival. Hougron's own body of work on Indochina reveals a critical evaluation of the French presence there,[26] but his characters, including Horcier, are considerably more flawed than those depicted in Camus's film.

Overall critics were overwhelming positive in their appraisals of the film, though several did have more mixed reactions particularly with respect to Camus's ability to render the complexities of Hougron's story effectively. In his review for *L'Humanité*, Samuel Lachize applauds Camus's evident anticolonialism as well as his pacifism. Camus, he writes, hates war and shows it.[27] Furthermore he "accurately identifies the responsibilities of the colonial system (and those who profit from it) in this war."[28] The lesson learned from the film, he adds, is that "one does not conquer the hearts of the people by sowing death, but by helping them to plant rice."²⁹ Lachize's support of this anticolonial and antiwar message was echoed by other critics as well, though primarily in publications connected with the political left or with the antiwar movement. Roger Fressoz of *Témoignage chrétien,* for example, lauded Camus's attempt to show the chaos of war and the conditions facing Vietnamese civilians "degraded by misery, fear, denunciations, the perpetual anguish caused by alternating reprisals."³⁰ Historian, writer, and member of the Vietnamese Communist Party Nguyen Khac Vien was much more critical than most on the left: in a letter to the Communist-funded *Les Lettres françaises* responding to the coverage of *Mort en fraude,* he takes issue with the depiction of villagers as being "outside of the war." On the contrary, he maintains, "the Vietnamese people weren't at all passive during this war; they led it, this war of liberation, with all of their might and all of their soul." The absence of this "spirit of the Resistance" undermined the authenticity of the film, he concludes.³¹

Undoubtedly due in part to its critical portrayal of French *colons*, *Mort en fraude* was banned in France's overseas territories. This, however, was not the first obstacle to the adaptation of Hougron's story: Henri-Georges Clouzot had sought to bring the story to the big screen in the latter years of the war but had faced significant obstacles to doing so. In an article in *L'Express* in December 1953, he states that he faced considerable opposition on the grounds that his "perspective of events in Africa and Asia does not strictly conform to official doctrine."³² While this undoubtedly played a role for censorship authorities, two other factors were surely as important: first and foremost, the war was ongoing, and it was thus unlikely that a film depicting resistance against the French was going to be approved. Second, Clouzot had hardly emerged from the period of the Occupation unscathed. He had released *Le Corbeau (The Crow)* in 1943, which depicted a small town beset by a poison pen letter writer. The theme of the French turning against and denouncing one another was not popular with Vichy authorities or the postwar regime, and the fact that the film had been produced by the German company Continental-Films only made matters worse. In 1944 Clouzot was banned from the film industry in perpetuity, a sentence that was later commuted to two years. Although the film proposal was made eight years after the end of the Second World War, following the release of a number of his films including the popular *Quai des Orfèvres,* his reputation with respect to "sensitive" subjects was undoubtedly a factor in the censors' decision.

VETERAN FILMMAKERS: THE DIVERGING PATHS OF PIERRE SCHOENDOERFFER AND CLAUDE BERNARD-AUBERT

The 1960s were marked by a slight increase in the number of films depicting the war. These were characterized for the most part by an emphasis on the heroism of French troops, the military values of courage and comradeship, and in some cases the plight of the victims of the Viet Minh. Léo Joannon's 1963 *Le Fort du fou* (*Outpost in Indochina*) depicts both heroic French soldiers and the plight of Vietnamese Catholics fleeing from Viet Minh forces. In 1964 Henri Decoin's *Les Parias de la gloire* (*Outcasts of Glory*), based on veteran Roger Delpey's novel of the same name, depicted the friendship that develops between a former member of the French Resistance, whose brother was killed by a German officer during the liberation of Alsace in 1944 and who subsequently enlists to serve in Indochina, and a German plantation owner. Thrown together by circumstance in the Cochinchinese delta after the German's plane makes an emergency landing close to a French military post, the two join forces to combat their common enemy.

Arguably the most significant film released in the 1960s on the subject of the war was Pierre Schoendoerffer's *La 317ème section* (*The 317th Platoon*), which became *the* film of the Indochina War and catapulted its director to a position of authority on the war. As the first film on the Indochina War to gain considerable attention and praise, *La 317ème section* clearly marks a turning point in the cinematic remembrance of the war. In fact Bénédicte Chéron argues in her DEA thesis that forty years after the fact, *La 317ème section* is understood as having "shaped a part of national memory."[33] Schoendoerffer himself would have appreciated the comment, as he conceived of his work as an expression of the "duty to remember" (*devoir de mémoire*);[34] indeed Schoendoerffer played a key role in defining the anticommunist narrative through his novels, films, and public commentary.

Like Claude Bernard-Aubert, Schoendoerffer volunteered as a cinematographer with the French forces (the Service presse information) and was taken prisoner at Dien Bien Phu. Although he had filmed combat during the siege, he had destroyed his reels rather than allow them to fall into the hands of the Viet Minh. He remained in captivity for four months and after his release stayed on as a press correspondent. His wartime experiences strongly colored his subsequent filmmaking. One of his earliest films, *Ramuntcho* (1959), alluded to the war, but it was not until 1964, a full decade after the French defeat and the signature of the Geneva Accords, that he delved fully into the subject with *La 317ème section,* based on his novel of the same name.[35] The film won the prize for best screenplay at Cannes in 1965, a success that would be matched over a decade later with the release of *Le Crabe-tambour (Drummer-Crab)*, another adaptation of his own novel, which itself won the grand prize from the Académie Française. Even those films that are not set in Indochina maintain a connection with it: the title character of *Le Crabe-tambour*, a veteran of the Algerian War, is the brother of Sergeant Willsdorf of *La 317ème section*, and 1982's *L'Honneur d'un capitaine* features flashbacks to Indochina. Schoendoerffer made a full return to the Indochina War in 1992 with the release of *Diên Biên Phu* and again in 2004 with *Là-haut, un roi au-dessus des nuages (Above the Clouds)*. Each of these films, and especially *Diên Biên Phu*, reinforces a narrative of war featuring heroic soldiers, abandoned by the metropolitan government and public, making a last stand against an overwhelming enemy.

La 317ème section opens with an aerial view of the Cambodian jungle, eventually transitioning to a shot of soldiers lowering a French flag at the Luong Ba military outpost.[36] It is 4 May 1954, and the 317th platoon has been ordered to abandon its post and retreat south. The platoon is composed primarily of indigenous auxiliaries,[37] led by a handful of French officers. Of these, Lieutenant Torrens (Jacques Perrin) and Sergeant Willsdorf (Bruno Cremer) play central roles in the development of the narrative. The former is a freshly minted graduate of Saint-Cyr, while the latter is a career soldier from Alsace who had been forcibly drafted into the German Wehrmacht during the Second World War and had been sent to fight on the Eastern Front. He later joins the French Foreign Legion and following the end of the Indochina War moves on to Algeria, where he is killed during a skirmish. The entire film takes place over the span of seven days, during which time the platoon is slowly decimated as they are stalked by the Viet Minh while forging their way through the jungle, stumbling on villages from time to time. The audience is informed at the end of the film that "the 317th platoon no longer exists."

Like *Patrouille de choc*, *La 317ème section* privileges the experience of a platoon of soldiers over the analysis of the causes and responsibilities for the war and the eventual French defeat, an approach that also characterizes Schoendoerffer's 1992 film *Diên Biên Phu*. Throughout the trials faced by the platoon the camaraderie of its members is highlighted. The soldiers are committed to helping one another, French and Lao alike. The choice of an indigenous auxiliary unit is not insignificant; in fact it serves to reinforce a narrative of colonial partnership common to many veteran narratives of the war. On the level of production the idea of a colonial partnership extending into the postcolonial period is reinforced by virtue of the film being shot in Cambodia with the assent of Norodom Sihanouk, whose support is recognized in the opening credits, and with the collaboration of the royal Khmer forces. Two scenes from the film itself serve to illustrate the commitment of French soldiers to anticommunist indigenous troops. The first is a scene in which a wounded French soldier tries to comfort a wounded Lao soldier, who is on the verge of death. The second is a much more lighthearted depiction of the friendship between the French and the Lao, in which two soldiers play a game with a stick to pass the time. As if to reinforce the theme of partnership and perhaps to implicitly absolve the French colonial state of wrongdoing, the villagers encountered by the platoon are never shown to be unhappy with the colonial situation. Rather, they either assist the members of the platoon or ask them to move on out of fear of Viet Minh reprisals. In one case a village chief asks the soldiers to leave, as the Viet Minh have already been there and if they return and discover that the villagers have sheltered French troops, the villagers will be massacred. The soldiers encounter a similar reaction in another village, the residents of which desert their homes in the middle of the night while the soldiers are sleeping. The chief leaves a note, in which he apologizes for leaving but claims that they have lived through the Japanese presence and they are not prepared to live with the Viet Minh. Thus the Japanese occupation and the treatment of civilians by the Viet Minh are both indicted by the villagers, but the French colonial presence is never questioned.

The self-sacrifice and courage of the soldiers is a second central theme and is illustrated primarily by the obstacles that they face. The jungle is an oppressive force and difficult to navigate. This is exacerbated by the ominous sense that the Viet Minh are always near but impossible to locate. In fact Viet Minh soldiers are rarely seen on-screen. In one of the few such scenes the platoon spots a Viet Minh commando group transporting supplies by bicycle and engages them in a small skirmish before retreating. Later, voices can be heard encouraging the Lao troops to leave the French and join their ranks, followed by threats of death should they refuse. One member of the platoon scans the surrounding hills with binoculars but is unable to locate the source of the voice. A similar scene is repeated later when the platoon finally gets a response on the radio and requests that supplies be parachuted in to them; the voice of a Viet Minh soldier comes across the radio informing them that all is lost and demanding their surrender. Despite this emphasis on the heroism of the French forces, however, Schoendoerffer is careful not to depict the soldiers as being entirely beyond reproach, and includes scenes of soldiers pillaging villages.

La 317ème section was the first French film about the Indochina War to gain widespread recognition and appreciation from critics and the public; historian Jacques Dalloz deems it to be nothing short of "the best film devoted to the conflict."[38] Indeed the film was acknowledged as the gold standard for Indochina War cinema; Claude Bernard-Aubert's second and third films on the war would both be unfavorably compared with *La 317ème section*.[39] It was popular with audiences as well: over its eleven-week run in Paris as a new release it sold 232,865 tickets, putting it in eleventh place for 1965 ticket sales.[40] In addition to the success at Cannes it won the favor of film critics across the political spectrum. *Minute* deemed it "the most beautiful French war film,"[41] although the reviewer doubted that it would have much commercial success. The reviewer from the *Nouvel observateur* called it a "masterpiece" and the "first real film on the war."[42] Even *L'Humanité*'s resident film critic Samuel Lachize praised the film as being "worthy of the best American productions of the kind."[43] Common to all of these reviewers and others was an appreciation of the film's realism. The *Nouvel observateur* reviewer argued that Schoendoerffer's film was distinct from the hundreds of others about "another platoon decimated in another war" precisely because "it is authentic." All of the gestures, the words, the looks, the voices, the sounds—all were "authentic," as if the camera had disappeared.[44] Writing in *Le Monde,* Jean de Baroncelli praised the film for "hitting a rare note of authenticity."[45] This authenticity is however understood differently by different reviewers: Lachize, for example, implies that the mark of authenticity is found in the fact that the characters do not know why they are fighting, only that they are paid to kill or be killed.[46] Although his review is essentially positive, Lachize does find fault with Schoendoerffer's avoidance of the "bigger picture" of the war. The filmmaker, he maintains, shows us the anguish and suffering of the soldiers but fails to condemn the war that they were waging. Moreover, he continues, the people against whom war was being waged are absent from the film with the exception of the auxiliaries, who are described as the "collaborators of the occupying army." Finally Lachize accuses Schoendoerffer of depicting a well-organized and virtually invincible Viet Minh without acknowledging the secret of its strength, which he identifies as the "virtually unanimous support of the population."[47]

The timing of the release of the film likely contributed to its reception as well. The tenth anniversary of the end of the war was the first to be granted any kind of public attention. There was a marked increase in media attention to the war from 1959, the year of the fifth anniversary of the war's end, to the tenth in 1964. Articles appeared in newspapers ranging from *Minute* and *Le Figaro* to *Le Monde* and *Combat*. *Cinq colonnes à la une* aired a special episode on 8 May 1964 featuring interviews with Schoendoerffer and Marcel Bigeard, which focused primarily on their experiences of the defeat at Dien Bien Phu and their reactions to footage of the battle that was presented as having been filmed by the Viet Minh.[48] This renewed attention to the Indochina War can also be attributed to the expansion of the American involvement in Vietnam in 1963–64. Under the Kennedy administration the number of American troops in South Vietnam had increased from 800 to 16,700.[49] By the late summer of 1964 Congress had approved more drastic measures, including the bombing of North Vietnam. With this resolution the Johnson administration had fully committed itself to war. The press certainly drew connections between the two conflicts,[50] and Schoendoerffer himself embodied a cinematic link between the conflicts. Sent by *Cinq colonnes à la une* to film the American war, he released the documentary *La section Anderson* (*The Anderson Platoon*) in 1967, which won both an Oscar and an Emmy. The American Vietnam War was naturally not the only point of reference for the audience: the Algerian War had drawn to a close only two years earlier. The connections between the two conflicts are drawn implicitly and explicitly. The heroism of soldiers combating an elusive rebel force is evocative of both conflicts, and Schoendoerffer even slips in a reference to the *gégène*, a form of torture that was pioneered in Indochina but that has primarily been associated with the Algerian War.[51] The transition from one colonial war to the next is also made explicitly in the epilogue, in which the narrator states that Willsdorf went on to fight in Algeria, where he was killed.

Two years after the release of *La 317ème section,* Claude Bernard-Aubert returned to the topic of the war with *Le facteur s'en va-t-en-guerre* (*The Postman Goes to War*), a tragicomedy loosely based on a semiautobiographical novel by Gaston-Jean Gautier.[52] Starring Charles Aznavour, the film tells the tale of a naive mailman named Thibon who enlists in the hopes of experiencing the colonial good life. Thibon is sent to an isolated military post, where he adjusts to the realities of war. Just when he has settled in, those stationed at the post receive orders to leave and head to Dien Bien Phu. They are attacked by the Viet Minh en route and imprisoned in a POW camp, where they spend the remainder of the film concocting scheme after scheme to escape. Despite its comedic style the film maintains at its core a number of the themes from *Patrouille de choc:* the commitment of the soldiers to see the war through to its conclusion, the camaraderie between French soldiers and locals, and the inevitability of defeat.

The response to *Le facteur* was mixed and like the reaction to *Patrouille de choc* seemed to depend on how critics interpreted the filmmaker's objectives. Reviewers from *L'Humanité* and *Les Lettres françaises* understood it to be promoting an anticolonial message, though neither felt it succeeded in this respect; Jean-Pierre Léonardini called it an "indecent film in which the ostensible pacifist and anticolonial message was lost amidst a flood of farcical ambiguities."[53] On the other end of the spectrum the reviewer from *Le Figaro* thought it a commentary on the tragedy of the war and commended the film for presenting "an occasionally poetic, often profound, and always sensitive analysis of a country, two races, and twenty centurions."[54]

The divergence between Schoendoerffer and Bernard-Aubert would become all the more entrenched with the latter's third and final film on the subject of the war, *Charlie Bravo* (1980). This last film marks a significant departure from his earlier work by engaging in a much more brutal critique of the war, particularly the decisions taken by military and political leaders and the actions of the soldiers who were waging it.[55] The influence of the American Vietnam War is clear, and in some ways the film presages later American films like *Platoon* (1986).[56] The soldiers of *Charlie Bravo* engage in horrific acts toward Vietnamese civilians and suspected enemy combatants, acts which Bernard-Aubert claims to have witnessed personally.[57] Troops are shown laughing as they burn down a village with flamethrowers, and torturing a suspect with the electrical current from a field radio. Although this is a stark indictment of the actions of French soldiers, Bernard-Aubert leaves room for some sympathy with the beleaguered platoon, which is decimated by the Viet Minh as it seeks to complete its mission of rescuing a French nurse (a Geneviève de Galard–like character) and bringing her back to safety. If *Patrouille de choc* was characterized by the inevitability of defeat, *Charlie Bravo* grimly asserts that the entire war was pointless, or at least that the last battles were. This message is delivered most poignantly by a journalist assigned to chronicle the platoon's mission, who acerbically identifies the objectives of the military and political authorities:

They want all of our positions to be the least bad possible—strategically speaking—at the time of the ceasefire, because Paris thinks it can negotiate. There you go. You massacred an entire village for nothing; you tortured, you killed, for nothing. Your buddies are dead for nothing, and we will also surely die for nothing. You don't get it. He [the commanding officer] had to save her, and I had to take the pictures. A new Joan of Arc for the press, to make people forget that we lost the war. We're nothing but pawns. Pawns, get it?[58]

Charlie Bravo fared little better than *Le facteur s'en va-t-en guerre* at the box office and was the target of considerable criticism, much of which stemmed from the depiction of torture and other atrocities.[59] Colonel Romain-Desfossés led a short-lived campaign in the press to counter the claims that the French army had engaged in such wanton destruction of life and property,[60] while the critic from the left-wing *La Vie ouvrière* praised the film for being the first to "denounce the colonial character" of the "dirty war" waged by the French.[61] The film did not provoke, however, the kind of explosive public debate that Henri de Turenne's series *Vietnam* would prompt just four years later.

FLASHPOINT: HENRI DE TURENNE'S *VIETNAM*

Le Figaro columnist Louis Chauvet's 1965 reaction to Schoendoerffer's *La 317ème section* was to wonder if the film had not come too late: "Have the French not gained the necessary spiritual fortitude in the meantime to free themselves from the bad memories of Indochina?"[62] Henri de Turenne's televised documentary series *Vietnam* would demonstrate that the French had most certainly *not* freed themselves from these bad memories, and that in fact they had barely begun to face them. The series aired in January and February 1984,[63] and is best understood as a flashpoint of collective remembrance akin to the Boudarel affair, though not of the same order or magnitude. The response to the series was unprecedented in France for a film dealing with the Indochina War. This was due in part to the fact that it was the first extended documentary on the war to be produced in France, but the impact of timing cannot be underestimated. The political context of the early to mid-1980s was characterized by the shift to the left of the government, the reaction of right-wingers to that shift, and the rise in popularity of the National Front. The result on the right and extreme right was renewed emphasis on traditional values, including military ones. Along with the recent state recognition of veterans of Indochina through the burial of the unknown soldier, and the impact of the heavily mediatized plight of the boat people, the atmosphere was such that veterans felt they could legitimately promote their narrative of the Indochina War with its emphasis on the evils of communism and the heroism of combatants. The year 1984 also marked the thirtieth anniversary of the end of the war, an event that was marked by unprecedented coverage in the press. Although there were no state-sponsored ceremonies and those organized in Pau by veterans' organizations were closed to the public, the year nonetheless marks a shift toward greater public discussion of the war.

Vietnam was the result of collaboration between Antenne 2 (France), Central Independent Television (United Kingdom), and PBS (United States).[64] There was considerable difference in the final products, however. Whereas the French series featured six episodes divided evenly between the French and American periods, the American series, entitled *Vietnam: A Television History,* featured thirteen episodes of which only two covered the French period. PBS actually began airing the series several months before Antenne 2, in October 1983. The producer of the French series, Henri de Turenne, was a career journalist. Shortly after the end of the Second World War he was hired by the Agence France-Presse (AFP) and sent to Berlin and Korea, where his reports for *Le Figaro* were awarded the Albert Londres prize in 1952. In June 1954 he accompanied Geneviève de Galard from Saigon to Paris and wrote a series of cover stories for *France-Soir* based on his interviews with the heroine of Dien Bien Phu.[65] Turenne had deep family ties with Algeria—his mother's family were *pieds-noirs* and his father had been posted at the garrison in Algiers for four years—and spent considerable time there in his youth. Reflecting on his childhood years later, he admitted that he had believed Algeria had legitimately been part of France.[66] He would later cover the Algerian War for *France-Soir.* In the late 1960s he turned to documentaries, gaining recognition for his *Grandes Batailles* (*Great Battles*) series. Over the span of his career he produced over a hundred documentaries, including *Vietnam.*

The first three episodes of the French version of *Vietnam* focused on the French colonial era with a brief survey of the precolonial era and the Indochina War. The final three episodes of the series were focused on the American war, but these prompted far less heated controversy. The depiction of the colonial period in the first episode was quite critical of both colonial authorities and policies, and Turenne presented the first Indochina War as a valiant struggle for independence though he acknowledged the courage and sacrifice of French troops as well. Although the series received only moderate coverage by the press of the center and left, reviews by Patrice de Beer of *Le Monde* and others were favorable. Veterans, however, were intensely critical of the series as were some members of the Franco-Vietnamese community and the right-wing press. Their criticisms stemmed from two major concerns. First, the representation of the colonial era showcased all of the negative aspects of colonialism without illustrating any of the French contributions to "progress" in Indochina. Second, they construed Turenne's portrayal of the war as a struggle for independence as outright support for communism. The reaction of the ANAI was particularly vehement; as discussed in chapter 2, the group engaged in a letter-writing campaign, contributed to the publication of *Indochina: A Warning for History*, and participated in a televised "trial" of Turenne.

The opening episode of *Vietnam* sets the tone for the rest of the series. Like a number of American historians of Vietnam, Turenne is interested in understanding how the Vietnamese succeeded in overthrowing a succession of occupying powers from the Chinese to the Americans. Early in the first episode the audience is presented with a bird's-eye view of Vietnamese history from the era of Chinese domination to the wars of the twentieth century. A voice-over specifies that the Vietnamese had over the course of several centuries perfected a system of defense against outside powers, in which the village played a critical role. Turenne also describes the consolidation of Vietnamese control over its current territory according to the standard narrative of a southward movement (*nam tien*). The French system is introduced in terms of its "original sin" and rigid system of control: "[Governor General] Sarraut controls everything, governs everything, regulates everything."[67] Evident throughout the episode, Turenne's opinion of the French colonial project is perhaps best illustrated in the juxtaposition of archival footage of Vietnamese workers in a coal mine, who are described by a narrator as volunteers receiving good pay, with Turenne's own evaluation of the dire situation of the workers. Contrary to the claims of the document's narrator, he states that these "volunteers" were in fact slaves recruited by force and paid little, whose workplace was closer to a penal colony (*bagne*). The second and third episodes tackle the "forgotten war" and the battle of Dien Bien Phu. The former begins in 1945–46 with the negotiations with Ho Chi Minh, which Turenne identifies as a missed opportunity for a peaceful resolution of the increasing tensions. France, he maintains, missed its chance to "invent" decolonization.⁶⁸ He attributes considerable responsibility to the French for sparking open conflict with the bombing of Haiphong in November 1946. Nonetheless his depiction of the French soldiers who fought what became a terribly long conflict is not ungenerous, emphasizing their heroism while targeting the general staff, who he claims consistently underestimated the enemy. The third episode on the French period deals exclusively with Dien Bien Phu. The most notable (and most criticized) scene is that of the French surrender. Turenne used footage shot by the Soviet filmmaker Roman Karmen, which was not of the actual French surrender but was rather a fictionalized reenactment using recently captured prisoners of war.⁶⁹ Turenne's critics were appalled by this inclusion because he had failed to acknowledge that the scenes were staged and were therefore not an accurate representation of the end of the battle, and because he was making use of what amounted to communist propaganda.

Media coverage of the series prior to and during the airing of the first two episodes was well within the range of what might be expected for a televised documentary. Antenne 2 aired a brief interview with Turenne during the midday news on 14 January,⁷⁰ and short articles introducing the series were published in leading dailies like *Le Monde, Le Figaro,* and *La Croix*. These early reviews were mixed: *Le Monde* reviewer Patrice de Beer applauded the series for not shying away from the "flip side of the 'civilizing mission.'"⁷¹ *L'Humanité* provided no weekly summaries but at the series's conclusion declared it "honest" and "balanced."⁷² *Libération* concluded that despite "fascinating" interviews and "amazing" archival footage, Turenne had produced "a series that was lazily chronological and without passion."⁷³ The position of *La Croix* was more nuanced. In addition to publishing an interview with historian Jean-Pierre Rioux on the subject of "submerged Vietnam" (*le Vietnam englouti*), the Catholic daily published a review by Noël Darbroz, in which he addresses the absence of a real examination of French cultural and missionary activities as well as what he terms the "negative, if not masochistic" tone of the series.⁷⁴ Antoine Keomanivong's summary in *Le Figaro* is more critical of Turenne's emphasis on the "errors and abuses of the colonial administration" and characterizes the series as "a panegyric to the Viet Minh and its struggle."⁷⁵

Reactions grew more heated as the series progressed. *France-Soir* and *Le Figaro* both published weekly summaries of each episode; in the case of the former the headlines went from a relatively benign "A Pamphlet against Colonialism" (episode 1) to the far more critical "Long Live Ho

Chi Minh!" (episode 2) and "Still the Same Disinformation" (episode 4).[76] By the time the third episode aired, which covered the battle of Dien Bien Phu, reactions from the right wing and veteran press had reached a fever pitch. Among the most immediate and vehement reactions in France was that of the ANAI, which published a letter to the editor of *Le Monde* (also cited in chapter 2). The author stated that "on behalf of all *anciens* of Indochina, I cannot accept that France's work in Indochina, nor the sacrifices she made, be so grossly distorted: it is an insult to both history and the nation."[77] This sentiment was echoed by other veterans, who denounced the series as "Soviet-Marxist propaganda that glorifies the heroes of the Viet Minh"[78] and charged Turenne with "intellectual dishonesty."[79] Jean-Jacques Beucler and Geneviève de Galard both published open letters to the filmmaker in the pages of *Le Figaro,* and Pierre Schoendoerffer published his reactions in both *Le Figaro* and *Paris Match.* Even Marcel Bigeard weighed in on the debate in an interview with Michel Laurillard of *Le Républicain Lorrain.*[80]

The reactions of these prominent veterans reflected the standard discourse: Turenne had ignored the "noble mission" of those fighting at Dien Bien Phu to protect the "free world," as well as the sacrifice of nationalist Vietnamese who fought to save their country from Communist oppression (de Galard); he had presented the war as a colonial one when it was anything but (Schoendoerffer); he had passed off enemy propaganda as "real" footage (de Galard and Beucler), and he was clearly in support of the Viet Minh. Beucler went so far as to say that Turenne should have saved himself the trouble of making the documentary and simply written "Long Live Ho Chi Minh!" on the screen instead.[81] That the film had been praised by at least one Vietnamese newspaper only reinforced the belief that Turenne was serving the cause of communism.[82] These reactions were reinforced by journalist Brigitte Friang, who referred to the series as a "caricature of history," and former colonial administrator Jacques Gandouin, who attempted to rectify what he saw as Turenne's omission of the positive French contributions to Indochina.[83] As a result of the controversy two requests for a formal rebuttal (*droit de réponse*) were made: the first was a request from Turenne to the editorial staff of *Le Figaro* that he be allowed to respond to the expansive critiques that had been published in the paper, and the second came to Antenne 2 from the ANAI.

Turenne's letter of response was published on 13 February and opened with a statement of his exasperation with *Le Figaro* columnists:

> I must protest. Enough is enough. For the last month, *Le Figaro* has taken up the vicious campaign unleashed against my television series. [. . .]. That my opinions and my talent are criticized, that my mistakes are identified—fine. I will keep quiet. But I refuse to allow my good intentions and my integrity to be undermined.[84]

He dismissed most of his critics' attacks as absurd but claimed that he was responding because he felt he owed an explanation to those victims of the Communists who had felt wounded or dismissed by his film; he specifically mentions Vietnamese refugees, who had been left "stateless," and soldiers "who were left to rot for eight years in the paddies of Indochina, without giving them the means to win a war that we were resigned to losing."[85] Turenne goes on to remind his readers of his original goal for the documentary—that is, to reflect on France's missed opportunity for a peaceful decolonization—and to address the more serious criticisms. To each he responds with references to the narrative text of the film and to time allocated to various issues. For example, he counters the claim that he overlooked the positive aspects of colonialism by citing the voice-over from the first episode:

> France should be proud. She built cities in the image of a miniature Paris at the ends of the world, like Hanoi with its theatre built in the style of the Garnier Opera. . . . [The companies] greatly increased rice production, and Indochina became the third-largest rice exporter in the world. They introduced the rubber tree, and rubber production that met French needs, never mind the superb tea and coffee plantations.[86]

To refute the second accusation that he granted more time for Vietnamese testimony about Dien Bien Phu than French, he points to the fact that French witnesses have nearly double the speaking time of their Vietnamese counterparts—8 minutes and 49 seconds as compared to 4 minutes and 28 seconds. These refutations were hardly going to convince his critics, however, and thus it is his reflection on the willingness of his compatriots to face the past that is of greatest interest in his rebuttal. "I thought," he writes, "that after thirty years—almost two generations—we could examine the events in Indochina with cold and detached eye. I was wrong." He ultimately concedes that he was wrong to have "thought highly enough of my compatriots to have believed that they were capable of looking the truth in the face. Apparently, some of them were not ready for this painful exercise."[87]

The second *droit de réponse,* this one emanating from the ANAI, was granted by Antenne 2, which agreed to air a debate between Turenne and his critics on 14 May.[88] Turenne made it clear that he welcomed the opportunity to respond to the criticisms and accusations leveled against him. Hosted by Philippe Labro, the debate featured Jacques Gandouin, Jean-Jacques Beucler, General René de Biré, and Professor Vu Quoc Thuc. Gandouin was the first to speak, and his comments encompassed virtually all of the criticisms of Turenne's detractors:

> Sir, as you know, your television series aroused [...] considerable indignation among all those who know Indochina, as well as among the Vietnamese who sought refuge in France. This indignation [...] is prompted by the fact that we believe that your series was a defense [*apologie*] of the Viet Minh—which is within your rights—but presented as a historical account of the facts. It was full of inaccuracies, errors, and omissions, voluntary or not; in a word, what is commonly referred to as disinformation.[89]

Beucler was much more vicious, accusing Turenne of using doctored footage and of brainwashing the audience; he went so far as to affirm that the filmmaker reminded him of the political commissars in the Viet Minh camps. The documentary, Beucler charged, presented the conflict as a long war of liberation on the part of the Viet Minh, when in fact France was there to protect the population and prepare the colony for independence. Moreover, he continued, the Viet Minh gained support only through the use of force and intimidation. Thuc, a professor at the University of Paris XII and a former government minister for Ngo Dinh Diem, was confronting Turenne on the air for the second time; the first had followed the airing of the final episode of the series in February. Thuc spoke on behalf of the Committee against the Falsification of Vietnamese History (Comité d'action contre la falsification de l'histoire du Vietnam) in that first discussion, and his statements during both interviews shared a similar focus: Turenne had wrongly cast the conflict as one of national liberation rather than a civil war between nationalists and communists. On some levels the televised exchange between Turenne and his critics is reminiscent of Boudarel's appearance on *Le Droit de savoir* seven years later. Both were, as Pierre Brocheux has argued, televised "trials" that pitted the accused against a panel of critics.[90] Boudarel was granted the right to bring an ally, though, while Turenne faced his judges alone. However, Boudarel's critics were undeniably more vicious than Turenne's, and Philippe Labro maintained a much calmer atmosphere as moderator than did Patrick Poivre-d'Arvor. Patrice de Beer, who had favorably reviewed the documentary in *Le Monde* of 8 January and 11 February, described the televised rebuttal as a "strange atmosphere" in which the journalist Turenne "appeared as the accused, alone against four."[91] He went on to criticize the television station for not having defended its programming or the filmmaker. Although he recognized that there were a few minor factual errors in the series, he took issue with Turenne's critics and Beucler in particular, whose comments he qualified as outright "abuse."[92] Citing their most stringent accusation—that Turenne did not celebrate the accomplishments of the French colonial state—de Beer questions whether they would have preferred that the filmmaker also "change the end of the film and make the 'good guys' win."[93]

The American version of the series elicited a much more mixed response from audiences and critics. It garnered high ratings and positive reviews from many mainstream media sources and won a variety of awards, including six Emmys, the Dupont/Columbia University Broadcast Journalism award, and the George Foster Peabody award. It was also used in classrooms to teach about the Vietnam War. *Focus on Asian Studies* published a special issue entitled "Vietnam: A Teacher's Guide" to provide additional support for educators, and chief correspondent for the film Stanley Karnow also published a companion book entitled *Vietnam: A History*.[94] The series was praised by the *New York Times* for its "meticulously researched and carefully balanced"[95] approach to the conflict.

However, the series also garnered considerable criticism. As in France the majority of critics were veterans and members of the Vietnamese diaspora, although the latter group was much more vocal in the United States than in France. Like their French counterparts American critics moved beyond the pages of the press to demand redress for what they perceived to be a heavily biased depiction of the conflict. While Antenne 2 had agreed to a televised response from a group of critics, PBS agreed to air a second, competing documentary by a group called Accuracy in Media (AIM), entitled *Television's Vietnam: The Real Story*. In addition to rectifying some of the "errors" of the PBS series, AIM sought to expose the ways in which media coverage of the war had led to distorted perceptions of American soldiers and strategies.[96] The collaborative publication *Indochina: A Warning for History* found its counterpart in James Banerian's *Losers Are Pirates*.[97] There were, however, significant differences in the objectives of these two publications: the former focuses exclusively on the merits of the French colonial project, while the latter presents an examination of the perceived errors of the series episode by episode.

THE "LOST" ANTIWAR FILM: PAUL CARPITA'S
LE RENDEZ-VOUS DES QUAIS

Five years after the Turenne debacle the screening of Paul Carpita's 1953 film *Le rendez-vous des quais* (loosely translated as *Protest on the Docks*) caused a stir in its own right. The film had ostensibly been lost for some thirty-five years following its seizure by police in 1955 and had only recently been discovered in the Bois d'Arcy film archives. It was restored and screened publicly in 1989, prompting considerable fascination from film scholars, who considered it a prime example of neorealism and the "missing link" of French film.[98] The PCF and other antiwar militants applauded its depiction of anticolonial activism, and the public was generally intrigued by this film that had been censored and "lost." The small-budget film by the first-time filmmaker had been shot in the Marseilles docks primarily in 1953 and was in production for two years after that. The production company, Procinex, received a favorable recommendation for a noncommercial license from the accreditation board (Commission d'agrément) in April 1955, which represents the first in a two-stage process of acquiring said license. However, when the request was forwarded to the regulatory board (Commission de contrôle) for approval in July 1955, the eventual response in August from the full committee was a denial of the license and of the right to export the film. As film scholar Marc Vernet emphasizes, a total prohibition of this sort was extremely rare.[99] By the time the film was screened publicly, then, it had been denied the license to do so. *Rendez-vous* was screened twice in 1955 for the workers who had supported and participated in the production process, before being seized by the police.[100] The official (and rather weak) reason given was that the film "contained scenes of violent resistance to police"[101] and as such constituted a threat to public order. This vague statement could refer to several sets of circumstances, including the recent dockworker strikes in Nantes and Saint-Nazaire as well as the more pressing context of the Algerian War.

The film's importance is twofold: first, it is one of very few that depicts opposition to the war in France and the only one to represent the antiwar militancy of the Marseilles dockworkers. In this respect it is the only film under study that truly represents the anticolonial narrative of the Indochina War maintained by the PCF and others. Indeed the newspaper of the left-wing Republican Veterans' Association (ARAC) capitalized on the re-release of the film to comment that "in France, the most clear-sighted members of the population had already offered their solidarity and committed themselves to bringing an end to this unjust, expensive, and harmful war."[102] Second, the film was subject to extensive censorship from the production period to its re-release in 1989. As a result of this censorship it was the story of the discovery of the censored and "lost" reels that captured public attention between 1989 and 1993, when the film aired on French television for the first time. However, at least one scholar has argued that this narrative is faulty; there is evidence, Marc Vernet argues, that the film was neither lost nor forgotten from 1955 until 1988.[103] All of this adds considerable complexity to the question of censorship and also raises questions about the public interest in "forgotten" eras of the past.

Featuring an interesting mix of fiction and documentary footage, *Le rendez-vous des quais* cast nonprofessional actors, primarily dockworkers. Filming antiwar scenes within the Marseilles port in 1953 was impossible,[104] so Carpita and André Abrias (who played Robert Fournier and who is also known as André Maufray) approached the authorities and explained that they were schoolteachers who wanted to shoot an educational film.[105] This gave them access to the port, although the heavy CRS (riot police) presence made it difficult to shoot. In order to maintain the illusion that the subject of their film was harmless, scenes were shot of the actors exchanging banal dialogue, which was later dubbed with the real dialogue in Marcel Pagnol's Victorine studios. In addition to the scenes filmed in the port and neighboring districts, Carpita incorporated footage of real events shot by Cinépax, a collective he cofounded which produced what members called *contre-actualités,* news clips that showed scenes and events that ran counter to the official reports. These "alternative news" clips were originally shown prior to union meetings. Carpita's self-professed goal, as the son of a dockworker, was to make a film that defended the dockworkers and brought them out of the humiliation they had suffered as a result of the repression of the mass strikes of 1950 and 1953.[106]

Initially entitled *The Springtime of Men* (*Le printemps des hommes*), the story itself is a simple one: a young couple struggles to make ends meet and find an apartment together while embroiled in union politics and strikes, all against the backdrop of the Indochina War. Robert comes from a long line of dockworkers, but work on the docks has been drying up; his fiancée Marcelle (Jeanine Moretti) works in a cookie factory. Early on in the film, Robert's brother Jean (Roger Manunta) reminisces about the work opportunities right after the Liberation:

It wasn't the work that was lacking after the Liberation. [. . .] Getting hired every morning was normal. There weren't enough tractors, cranes, arms for all of this work. It was hard, of course, but we hoped to be working towards something. It only lasted two years, despite our efforts. And then the work changed [*shot of sacks being loaded onto ships fades into the loading of cannons and tanks*]. And at the same time it became harder to get.[107]

Several short scenes later Jean makes an explicit connection between the decline in available work and the war: "There's only room for their tanks. Kilometers of dock for their dirty war. This morning, hundreds without work."[108] These antiwar sentiments are echoed by other characters, who take action. The actions depicted are, however, limited to a relatively peaceful strike and the painting of "Peace in Vietnam" on a pier in time for the impending arrival of the *Pasteur*, which is bringing home the dead and the wounded. Several of the women are also seen talking about events for the celebration of Bastille Day and encouraging the men to follow the example of a group of youths, who are planning on marching with pro-peace banners. This is followed by shots of a demonstration, which were actually "alternative news" footage shot by Cinépax.

While antiwar sentiments are common to the majority of the characters, at least one of Robert's friends is heard complaining about union politics and the war, which he claims "is none of our business."[109] A second scene in which several characters are discussing the war, the strikes, and the arrival of the *Pasteur* reveals that not all of the dockworkers are in agreement about the connection between the war and the lack of work. One character, Jo (Albert Manach), is overheard saying that "we stop working for the slightest things" and that "people want to explain everything by the Indochina War."[110] Jo's unwillingness to support antiwar activism and strikes becomes an increasingly significant obstacle for Jean, who is the leading activist of the group. While the others are on strike, Jo tells Robert that he is going back to work. While initially it appears that Carpita is allowing for divergent opinions within the dockworkers, it becomes clear that Jo is not merely a dissenting voice but that he is actually working for management against the strikers. In particular he puts considerable pressure on Robert to return to work and to oppose the strike organized by Jean, hoping to disrupt the latter's efforts; ultimately Robert discovers Jo's double game, slaps him, and heads off to join the strikers, who are facing off with the police. Thus the unanimous antiwar militancy of the dockworkers is maintained as a moral standard, one that has been upheld by the PCF in the decades since the release of the film.

Along with individual heroes like Henri Martin and Raymonde Dien, the dockworkers held a position of prominence in the anticolonial narrative of the party; by 1950, according to Jacques Dalloz, the dockworker had replaced the miner in the "communist Pantheon."[111] While there were several incidents involving dockworkers refusing to load war materiel, the strikes of 1950 in the port of Marseilles were the most significant, lasting some forty days. Former dockworker Alfred Pacini, who cowrote his memoirs with Dominique Pons, describes the scene:

> There were protests in the Canebière [the neighborhood around the port of Marseilles] and strikes everywhere—in the textile and chemical plants, at the SNCF [the French national railway], among the sailors. For example, they impeded the departure of the *Pasteur*, with 4,000 soldiers on board. [...] The sailors are walking off the job, everyone is walking off the job, coffins continued to arrive from Vietnam. At the CNASE, a munitions factory, the CRS charged at the workers, who were refusing to build Vampire bombers. There were 5 wounded, one of whom was in critical condition.[112]

Pacini also addresses other measures of antiwar protest undertaken by the dockworkers, and their reasons for doing so. He mentions distributing leaflets to soldiers boarding the *Pasteur* and other ships and even engaging them in conversations about the war and their role in it. While opposition to the war was the guiding principle, Pacini also frames his position as being in support of the soldiers to the degree that he believed that they were dying for an unjust cause and that those who returned in coffins were not given due reverence. He describes coffins being left wherever they ended up on the docks, "like ordinary merchandise," without so much as a proper military guard.[113] This image of the dockworkers as heroes has not gone unchallenged. The dockworkers, along with other antiwar militants in Marseilles in particular, have been much maligned by many veterans. The latter claim that they were the targets of verbal and sometimes physical abuse upon their return to France at the hands of the dockworkers and other protesters.

The support of the PCF, which supplied the film reels and the camera, seemed natural given the prominence of the dockworker in recent party mythology and the film's messages of anticolonialism and solidarity.[114] However, this backing vanished with the seizure of the reels. There was some support expressed by local party members but virtually nothing from Paris; interviewer Jean-Marie Cavada described it as a case of "abandonment."[115] Marc Vernet presents two possible factors for this lack of support: first, the potential impact of the film was significantly reduced due to the fact that the war was over. It was no longer current, in other words. Second, the anticolonial message of the film was perhaps somewhat awkward for the party given that its position on the Indochina War was significantly different from that on the Algerian War. He argues that while the party had unequivocally opposed the former, especially after 1947, it had initially favored a French Algeria, supporting independence only later. Thus, although the anticolonial message of the film clearly referred to Indochina, it made the PCF's position vis-à-vis the Algerian War somewhat uncomfortable. Both Claude Martino and Delphine Robic-Diaz have challenged this argument, though on different grounds. Martino claims that if the film was that out of line with PCF policy vis-à-vis the Algerian War in 1954, the party could have intervened to stop the production, which was still ongoing, but did not. Moreover the national party leadership did not step in to stop the application for release and distribution. Martino further argues that once the party withdrew support from Socialist prime minister Guy Mollet in January 1957, the film once again coincided with the party line, yet there was no call to lift the prohibition.[116] However, Martino's line of argument presupposes that the film was considered to be significant enough by the party to warrant either of these actions. For her part Robic-Diaz challenges Vernet's claim that the PCF's stance on the two wars was fundamentally different, stating that on the contrary in neither case did the party disagree with the government's stance in the early years; she is more inclined to agree with Vernet's first thesis, which is that the war was no longer current.[117] Indeed this seems the most likely explanation. Significantly the PCF glossed this lack of support when the film was re-released, which provided an opportunity to remind the public of its anticolonialism. One of the first screenings of the film in 1989 was sponsored by the PCF in the context of its Festival 89; prominent PCF member Guy Hermier took the opportunity to remind the audience that "with this screening, we simply want to demonstrate that the PCF contributed to the preservation of the original version of Carpita's film from the effects of time and censorship."[118]

Media coverage of the discovery of the film in 1988 and its public re-release in 1989 was characterized by the leitmotiv of memory and forgetting. *L'Express* described it as "the film no one was able to watch," which was finally "emerging from the shadows,"[119] while *L'Événement du jeudi* emphasized that it had been "a forbidden film for thirty-five years."[120] Its first public screening in February 1990 was thus a public resurrection both of the film itself and of the particular moment in working-class history that it represented.[121] Even five years after the discovery of the reels this tantalizing language of censorship and prohibition continued to characterize descriptions of the film. *L'Événement du jeudi* titled its synopsis of the film "Rendez-vous interdit" (literally "forbidden meeting" but also a play on the film title—"Forbidden *Rendez-vous*") when it aired on French television for the first time in 1993.[122] As titillating as this narrative of lost film is, it has been challenged by Marc Vernet in several ways. First, he has found evidence that two copies of the film were given to the film archives by the National Center of Cinematography (Centre national de la cinématographie) in 1968, which raises the question of where the second copy originated given that only one was seized in 1955. Moreover both film reels were some three hundred meters shorter than the version seized in 1955. The deposit of the negatives of the film reel in the film archives in 1979 by Procinex raises further questions about the role of the company in concealing the film. The final evidence marshaled by Vernet is the fact that Carpita had signed a deal in 1982 to buy back the rights to the film, suggesting that someone somewhere knew that the film had not been destroyed and might even have been aware of its location. So how can the path of this mysterious film be explained? Vernet argues that multiple degrees of censorship were at work: official censorship, of course, but also self-censorship on the part of Carpita and censorship on the part of the PCF, whose political line was ostensibly no longer reflected by the film it had initially supported.

Several years after Vernet's analysis was published, Claude Martino presented new information surrounding the film's seizure and disappearance. He clarifies that Carpita, far from thinking his film was lost for thirty-five years, had asked that the prohibition on the film be lifted in 1957, a request that was denied due to the circumstances of the Algerian War. In 1979 the negatives of the film were given to the film archives by Unicité, the PCF body responsible for film and audiovisual material. Between 1957 and 1979, however, Unicité had failed to tell Carpita that it had the negatives in its possession. In 1981–82 Carpita actually found the copy that had been seized in Marseilles at the film archives. Thus the film was actually not lost for the whole period from 1955 to 1989, although the idea that it had been certainly helped generate publicity upon its re-release. With respect to the length of the film and the missing segments (some twelve minutes of footage), Martino suggests that some of the editing was undertaken by Procinex in order to make it more suitable for screenings in Communist film clubs (*ciné-clubs*);

this included the deletion of a scene showing Robert working as a scab. Such a scene, Martino argues, would have been unthinkable for audiences who had paid dearly for their involvement in the strikes.[123] In addition he suggests that some of the editing took place with Carpita's knowledge between the screening of the original film for the authorities and the screening of an edited version that was seized in October.[124]

Despite these inconsistencies the myth surrounding the film has been maintained. Vernet's arguments, published in *Cinémathèque* and thus not destined for a broader audience, have not ultimately changed public perceptions. This fascination with the "forgotten" film is unsurprising given that the story was breaking at a time when interest in historical memory was gaining momentum. It is, however, interesting to note that the film did not prompt much in the way of discussions about the remembrance of the Indochina War itself, at least in the press. The focus was much more on the film as both an early example of neorealism and the "missing link" in French film, as well as on its "forbidden" status. It would take the trio of films released in 1992 to prompt public discussions about the colonial project and the Indochina War.

1992: *L'AMANT, DIÊN BIÊN PHU,* AND *INDOCHINE*

L'Amant, Diên Biên Phu, and *Indochine* were released in rapid succession between January and April 1992. Touted as the "return of the repressed"[125] and the French film industry's rediscovery of Indochina,[126] this cinematic trio can be considered to be a high point of filmic representations of the former colony and the war of decolonization. Film critic Anne Andreu argues:

> Our filmmakers did not appear to suffer from an Indochinese syndrome until last year, when the opening of the borders of Vietnam suddenly liberated collective memory. All at once, this led to the great return of the repressed in the profession; Indochina was in the air, and a number of directors were seized with the obsession of revisiting our Asian past on the grand airs of bad conscience or nostalgia.[127]

At the time, many columnists and film reviewers considered this to be the beginning of a new period of interest in Indochina; however, there have been few films devoted to the colonial era or the war since with the notable exceptions of Pierre Schoendoerffer's *Là-haut, un roi au dessus des nuages* (Above *the Clouds,* 2003) and Rithy Panh's remake of *Un barrage contre le Pacifique* (*The Sea Wall*, 2008). All three were big-budget films that performed well at the box office, though *Diên Biên Phu* rapidly trailed off by the fourth week in theaters.[128] All three also were nominated or won a variety of awards: the score of *Diên Biên Phu* was nominated for a César, while *Indochine* won multiple Césars as well as a Golden Globe and an Oscar for Best Foreign Film. *L'Amant* for its part won a César and was nominated for an Oscar.

Of the three only *Diên Biên Phu* addresses the war as a central theme; however, taken together the films are evidence of a nostalgia for empire and the exoticism of the "Far East." Filmed to showcase the height of empire, *L'Amant* and *Indochine* are most marked by this nostalgia. The press evoked the "monsoon of emotions"[129] and the "dream of empire"[130] prompted by these films. Though centered on the military defeat, *Diên Biên Phu* is also staged as the "end of a dream." Panivong Norindr emphasizes the characterization of the colonial relationship between France and Indochina as a "romance" or "love affair";[131] these affective bonds are celebrated in the 1992 films, particularly in *L'Amant* and *Indochine,* although Schoendoerffer also described his work as a "film of love."[132]

The three films have very little in common in terms of plot: *Diên Biên Phu* chronicles the battle and ultimate defeat of the French forces, while *L'Amant* chronicles the relationship between a (white) French adolescent girl and a wealthy Chinese businessman. *Indochine* is an epic tale of the relationship between a female French plantation owner and her adopted Vietnamese daughter set against the backdrop of economic crisis in the 1930s and the rapidly shifting dynamics between colonizer and colonized. What then do these films have in common? All three are set in Indochina between the 1920s and 1954, and in all cases the setting is much more than a backdrop. The landscape became a studio, enhancing the plots with lush jungles, rice paddies, and colonial architecture. As Andreu contends, the three filmmakers "found, through this return to Indochina, an endless source of dreams and adventures."[133] Moreover this "return" was not only artistic in nature but quite literally a return of the French to Vietnamese territory. Aside from Pierre Schoendoerffer (*La section Anderson* documentary, 1965) and Lam Lê (*Poussière d'empire,* 1984), no French filmmaker (or American filmmaker for that matter) had filmed on location in Vietnam since Bernard-Aubert's *Patrouille de choc* (1957).[134]

Each of these works is shaped by memory on both personal and collective levels. *Diên Biên Phu* is informed by Schoendoerffer's personal experiences during that battle,[135] but is also a requiem for a lost colony. *L'Amant,* based on Marguerite Duras's semiautobiographical novel of the same name, is clearly influenced by her own memories of the colony.[136] Finally *Indochine* is framed by the protagonist's narration of the plot through flashback as Éliane tells her grandson Étienne of his mother's life. The memorial aspect of these films goes beyond plot devices and framework to include an overwhelming sense of nostalgia. *L'Amant* and *Indochine* depict a bygone era permeated by exoticism, while *Diên Biên Phu*'s secondary storyline is essentially a farewell to empire.

The nostalgia of *L'Amant* and *Indochine* is intertwined with a fascination for the exotic and the erotic. The "exotic" settings were central to this fascination; Anne Andreu identified the two stars of *Indochine* as being Catherine Deneuve and the Vietnamese landscape.[137] Each film features familiar colonial sites: the Continental hotel, Catinat Street, Halong Bay, and the legionnaires' bar, where soldiers and others drink cognac-soda, *the* colonial cocktail. The nostalgia for these colonial sites is matched by a fascination with the "ancient" qualities of the people and their rituals. This fascination is a softer echo of colonial ideology, which viewed the societies of the colonized territory as being suspended in time and as therefore requiring French guidance in order to modernize. This is not to suggest that these films were promoting or justifying a civilizing mission, but there are certain similarities in the depiction of ancient tradition, in particular the royal funeral in *Indochine* and the Chinese marriage ceremony in *L'Amant*. These films arguably have more in common with the fantasies of colonial cinema than a postcolonial reevaluation of the colonial project.[138] At least two reviewers commented on the absence of any reevaluation of the past; filmmaker Danièle Rousselier wrote in the Franco-Vietnamese Friendship Association (AAFV) *Bulletin* that

> with these three films, French fiction film has once again demonstrated its inability to take stock of the darkest periods of national memory [. . .] . These films on colonial Indochina will certainly not weigh on anyone's conscience. In fact, there has been no debate, no controversy, no uproar surrounding their release. Just a flabby consensus. There has been no fundamental discussion on our responsibilities over there, in Indochina; no shame or remorse. Nothing on our mistakes, on our crimes.[139]

Rousselier's comments and those of other reviewers underscore the importance of considering the three films together, particularly given their close release dates. However, given their very different subject matter, it is equally important to analyze each film and its reception independently. As the only film to deal explicitly with the Indochina War, I will turn first to Pierre Schoendoerffer's *Diên Biên Phu,* which was his seventh feature film and his second on the subject of this war.

Schoendoerffer's objectives for *Diên Biên Phu* were twofold: to pay homage to his fallen comrades and to foster a renewal of ties between France and Vietnam. While the former is the same objective he claimed for *La 317ème section,* the latter was clearly new. He also suggested that the film was an exorcism of sorts—a "farewell to Indochina."[140] Although he was initially reticent to film on location, Schoendoerffer eventually sought and received permission from the Vietnamese government to film on-site in 1989, and the project later became a joint initiative with the support of the French Ministry of Defense and the participation of the French and Vietnamese militaries. In 1993 Schoendoerffer accompanied French president François Mitterrand to Dien Bien Phu as part of the latter's tour of Vietnam and Cambodia, the first for a French president (or Western head of state) since the end of the Indochina War. This was a landmark event by all accounts, and the fact that Schoendoerffer was permitted to accompany Mitterrand leads Norindr to conclude that his film was granted greater political legitimacy as a result.[141] On the contrary I would argue that Schoendoerffer's presence lent greater legitimacy to Mitterrand's presence at Dien Bien Phu, given his position as one of the most prominent authorities on the war.[142]

The film opens on 13 March 1954 on a hill overlooking the camp at Dien Bien Phu; two French soldiers are smoking a cigarette and discussing the military situation, thus introducing the primary storyline of the film. The secondary plot is revealed through the transition to a scene in Hanoi, where American writer Howard Simpson (Donald Pleasance) is on his way to the press headquarters. The rest of the film alternates between Dien Bien Phu and Hanoi, where the storyline centers on the arrival of a French violinist to play with the Hanoi symphony orchestra. The ebbs and flows of French success in the battle are reflected in a series of bets placed with a Chinese bookie.[143] The last days of the battle are paralleled by the orchestra's performance of George Delerue's *Farewell Concerto* (*Concerto de l'adieu*). Schoendoerffer's farewell to Indochina was thus not a subtle message; the French violinist was intended to represent the voice of France, and the orchestra that of Vietnam.[144]

Schoendoerffer's focus on the experiences of the common soldier is reminiscent of *La 317ème section*. Both films celebrate the heroism and courage of the French forces and their allies, though the latter have a stronger presence in the earlier film than in *Diên Biên Phu*. Moreover he explicitly opts not to engage fully with questions of political or military responsibility.[145] He does, however, make some pointed commentary through his characters. One soldier voices Schoendoerffer's criticism of the failure of the leadership: "A soldier hates to be sent to his death for nothing, because of stupidity, because of incompetence, because of spinelessness. It disgusts us."[146] This statement could be read as a criticism of the military leadership, the political leadership, or both. Toward the end of the battle, troops are ordered to destroy the artillery and drop back, leading to a more open criticism of the command as one soldier responds: "What a bunch of idiots. They think it's hopeless. Blow up my cannons? For the first time in my career as a soldier, I refuse to obey an order."[147] The most critical statements, however, are not made by a member of the French forces but by the Chinese bookie (speaking to Howard Simpson):

> See this guy Bigeard, he sends these people, his soldiers, to their deaths, and they're the only people he likes. [...] And for what? For who? People he doesn't like, people he hates, people he looks down on. Speculators, mediocre politicians, everyone, me, you, Mr. Simpson. It's a bizarre situation, really too strange. How do you say it? A paradox, that's it, a paradox.[148]

These scenes along with the majority of the battle scenes serve to reinforce the standard narrative of heroic soldiers abandoned by their country. Schoendoerffer's second goal, that of renewing ties with the Vietnamese people (though not with the government, of which he disapproved), was to be accomplished primarily through collaboration on the production of the film itself as well as through the fraternization between Vietnamese and French soldiers who played the roles of the Viet Minh and the expeditionary corps respectively. His attempt to restore ties between the two peoples is revealed through his script as well: a conversation between Howard Simpson and a Vietnamese newspaper editor by the name of Mr. Vinh leads the latter to state that "our struggle for national independence is not about resistance to French culture. [...] I like Victor Hugo, French philosophers, and I also like drinking red wine."[149] The military consultant for the film, Colonel Jacques Allaire, claimed that "there are great affinities between the Vietnamese and French people, an ancient and relatively similar history, a real complicity. The shooting of this film is contributing to reconciliation."[150]

This emphasis on the cooperation between colonizer and colonized (as well as between French and indigenous troops) is a particularly interesting one given that it is often reflected in the narrative of the war maintained by veterans and the political right. Schoendoerffer himself describes colonialism in Vietnam as being "an encounter between two ancient civilizations" rather than as "a colonial power in the midst of a desert."[151] The differences in perception of the relationship between French and indigenous soldiers is made glaringly apparent in a documentary based on footage shot during Schoendoerffer's return to Hanoi to present the finished film, where he was accompanied by eight other French veterans. In one scene a French veteran asks a local man what memories he has of the French presence:

> "What memories do you have of the French presence here? What lasting memories? [*Long pause as the man fumbles for a reply*]. But we were friends!"
> "You were the masters, and we were the servants."
> "Not masters, exactly..."
> "Yes, yes. But you did a lot for us."[152]

Reactions to the film from critics and the general public were mixed. *France-Soir*, *Le Figaro*, and *Figaro Magazine* were quite positive in their reaction, the latter deeming it a "masterpiece."[153] *Képi blanc*, the Foreign Legion's monthly magazine, initially gave a positive review of the "magisterial" way in which Schoendoerffer brought the sacrifices of the soldiers to life,[154] but a later article took issue with what it saw as the filmmaker's failure to take a definite stand on any of the critical issues: "We would have liked to have known his point of view, heard him decry France's abandonment of the people of Vietnam, the mistakes of the army general staff in Hanoi, or express a longing for the colonial paradise; in short, that he say something."[155] Other evaluations from the press ranged from deeming it a "semi-successful monument"[156] to "a very long monument to boredom."[157] The *Canard enchaîné* criticized the film for depicting the battle of Dien Bien Phu without telling the audience anything about the Indochina War.[158] Panivong Norindr takes this further, comparing *Diên Biên Phu* to American films about the Vietnam War such as *Apocalypse Now*. He argues that while the latter makes a point of revealing the absurdity of war, the former does not engage with this dimension of futility, nor does it address the motivations or responsibilities for it, an oversight for which it "should have been criticized severely."[159] In drawing these conclusions, however, Norindr overlooks Schoendoerffer's own interpretation of the war (as one that was perhaps badly managed but that was unquestionably a war that needed to be fought) and the fact that the explicit goal of the film was to depict the common soldier's experience.

The reaction from veterans was generally positive, but there was some debate prompted by the criticisms of a vocal minority in the pages of *Le Figaro*. The film premiered on 4 March, and by 10 March the second page of the newspaper was devoted to responses and letters to the editor. The letters to the editor covered a wide spectrum of reactions; some clarified what they saw as critical details such as the ostensible French recognition of Vietnamese independence in 1947–48 or the alleged treatment of the wounded arriving in Marseilles by communist protesters. Others praised Schoendoerffer for exposing viewers to the "real" "war without a name," a reference to the common characterization of the Algerian War. One reader questioned "what masochistic instinct pushes the French to celebrate their defeats and humiliations."[160] This proved to be only the beginning: the letters to the editor of 17 and 27 March were exclusively devoted to the debate over the film, and Max Clos gave considerable space to the topic in his weekly column.[161] The edition of 26 March featured a full page on "the great debate" over the film, which included testimony from four prominent veterans, including Marcel Bigeard and Geneviève de Galard.[162] The most prominent criticisms centered on the depiction of the soldiers and the military command. General Hervé Trapp's commentary, published in *Le Figaro* of 20 March, lambasted the film:

> [The soldiers] were not oafish gravediggers or clumsy stretcher-bearers, panicked and floundering, shamelessly manhandling the dying. [...] Contrary to what you imply, they were led by honorable commanders, [...] not left to their own devices or to the fantasy of a few vapid officers that you depict in your film.[163]

In addition to the coverage of reviews and reactions to the film, there was a considerable mobilization of print and television media around the topic of the war. Special issues of magazines and journals like *Historia* were published to coincide with the release of the film. A "televised offensive"[164] was aired during the month of March, including a special episode of *Bouillon de culture* featuring Schoendoerffer and Bigeard, Danièle Rousselier's two-part documentary *Vietnam, la première guerre* (*Vietnam, The First War*), Yves and Ada Rémy's *La mémoire et l'oubli* (*Memory and Forgetting*), and Patrick Jeudy's *Récits d'Indochine* (*Tales from Indochina*).[165]

In much the same way that *Diên Biên Phu* was an epic drama that ultimately reinforced the standard narrative of the war, *Indochine* and *L'Amant* were visually stunning films set in the colonial era that failed to challenge assumptions about colonialism itself. Of the two, *Indochine* was far more evocative of the colonial relationship. While the success of *L'Amant* was undoubtedly due in large part to the exotic setting, this setting was ultimately just a backdrop for the torrid love affair between the two protagonists. Much like the novel on which it is based, *L'Amant* is virtually devoid of Vietnamese or other indigenous characters except as servants, peddlers, and other background figures. *Indochine* in contrast features a broader array of characters and seeks to depict the colonial relationship between France and Vietnam through the lens of the familial relationship between French settler Éliane Devries (Catherine Deneuve) and her adopted Vietnamese daughter Camille (Linh Dan Pham). In a symbolic relationship akin to Schoendoerffer's symphony, Éliane represents France, Camille represents Vietnam, and the adoption is the metaphor for colonialism.[166] The casting of Catherine Deneuve is all the more apt given her role in the 1980s as the model for Marianne, symbol of the French Republic. Éliane is however a self-described "Asiate" and thus arguably embodies "French Indochina" more than France itself, a country she has never seen.[167] Joel David carries the metaphor to Étienne, Camille's son with the French naval officer Jean-Baptiste, arguing that he represents the part of Vietnam that the French brought home;[168] this is particularly appropriate given Étienne's mixed Franco-Vietnamese heritage.

It is to Étienne that Éliane tells the story that is the plot of the film, although the audience is not aware of this until close to the end. The opening scene is that of the royal funeral for Camille's parents, who are close friends of Éliane's. She adopts the child, raising her as her own. Éliane essentially runs her family's rubber plantation and faces considerable difficulties due to the economic crisis of the 1930s. Crisis soon strikes her personal life as well when she falls in love with a French naval officer, Jean-Baptiste, who later becomes the object of Camille's affections. Against the backdrop of growing Vietnamese nationalism and colonial instability, Camille sets off on a northward trek to find Jean-Baptiste. They are reunited but quickly become fugitives when Camille kills one of the French officers running a slave auction. Camille gives birth to their son while in hiding, and both fugitives are eventually caught. Camille is sent to the island penitentiary of Poulo Condore, and Jean-Baptiste entrusts the baby to Éliane before committing suicide. When Camille is released from prison as part of the Popular Front's amnesty program, she leaves her son with Éliane in order to commit herself fully to the Viet Minh. The closing scene is set in Geneva in 1954, where Éliane has brought Étienne to meet his mother, now a member of the Vietnamese delegation to the peace conference; he opts not to go through with it, telling Éliane, "You are my mother now."

Indochine was criticized for what was perceived by some to be a negative or at least problematic depiction of colonialism. However, the film reinforces more traditional depictions of colonialism than it undermines. The scenes in which Jean-Baptiste sets fire to a sampan he believes is transporting contraband, the slave auction intended to furnish southern plantation owners with workers, as well as Camille's experience on the prison island of Poulo Condore (which is alluded to though never depicted) are certainly not rosy visions of the colonial system. However, Éliane is depicted as a largely sympathetic character; indeed the audience is virtually forced to identify with her as the first voice and narrator of the film. She acts in the best interests of her daughter, subscribing to local custom and arranging a proper marriage for her to a young Vietnamese intellectual. She provides decent living and working conditions for "her" coolies. The destructive or corrupt actions of the French colonial regime are imputed to a few "bad" or ignorant characters, such as the chief of police Guy Asselin, rather than to her. Even when she is shown whipping one of the plantation workers, she asks him whether he "think[s] a mother likes beating her children."[169] The implication is that French actions, even when violent, were based in paternalism and a belief in the betterment of the colony. As Delphine Robic-Diaz states, it is a case of "responsible but not guilty"; at most the film criticizes the principle of an authoritarian colonial system, not those who participated in it.[170] Moreover the colonial relationship as a fundamentally affective one is reinforced by the depiction of France as a devoted mother.

The film's opening scene sets a tone similar to that of *Diên Biên Phu*'s theme of farewell to empire; the funeral is not only that of the royal couple but "a macabre apotheosis, a somber finale that mourns a world on the verge of disappearing."[171] Despite the negative aspects of colonialism that are depicted, the overall impression of the film is one of nostalgia for that era. Director Régis Wargnier and Deneuve both made comments in the media that are colored by nostalgia and echo colonial discourse about the static, unchanging nature of the ancient civilizations of conquered territories. Wargnier described Halong Bay with its fishermen and sampans as being straight out of the Middle Ages.[172] For her part Deneuve expressed her enchantment with Vietnam in these terms: "There is something so archaic and spiritual in this country; it's as if I had been in a virgin land."[173] Wargnier had a personal connection with the former colony through his father, who had served in the expeditionary corps, but denied that his characters were deliberately shaped by nostalgia.[174] Film critic Thierry Jousse takes the analysis of colonial nostalgia even further, contending that the most tangible impact of that nostalgia is that the film actually replicates the treatment of Indochina in film of forty years earlier—in other words it is "the exact replica of a style of film that they just don't make anymore."[175]

A number of viewers had the opposite reaction, however, taking issue with what they perceived to be an unfairly negative portrayal of colonialism. One letter to the editor of *Le Figaro* attacked the depiction of colonialism as "perfectly odious," arguing that it was no wonder that the Vietnamese government facilitated the shooting of the film given that "[the filmmakers] made the propaganda film that even they [the Vietnamese authorities] wouldn't have dreamed of!"[176] Unsurprisingly, similar opinions were expressed by veterans and former settlers, including one who acknowledged that while the colonial regime was not without its faults it nonetheless ensured "peace, order and security." Moreover, the author writes, "French Indochina was a rich and prosperous nation," while "Vietnam is one of the ten poorest countries in the world."[177] The ANAI also expressed its disapproval of certain aspects of the film. President Guy Simon claimed to have appreciated the homage paid to the landscape but refuted the message that he argued was emphasized over and over again: that the poor treatment of the Vietnamese by the French was bound to result in social unrest and the emergence of the Communist Party. He states that there are myriad problems with the film, but he deliberately focuses on a single scene: that of the slave market, which he describes as "intolerable." Though he responds to the scene through a series of unanswered questions—"Did the colonial authorities control the process? Did they consciously separate families?"—the answers are implied.[178] This criticism was seconded in a letter from a former recruiter for rubber plantations, who challenges the scene in its entirety.[179]

Of the three films *L'Amant* is the least engaged with depicting and interpreting periods of the French past; rather, director Jean-Jacques Annaud was concerned with conveying the essence of Duras's semiautobiographical novel in a visual form and thus with reincarnating the exoticism of late 1920s Saigon and surrounding areas. The storyline centers on the relationship between a French adolescent (Jane March) from a family of relatively poor settlers and her budding relationship with the wealthy son (Tony Leung) of a Chinese businessman, who is also considerably older than she is. The girl's widowed mother has been struggling to keep her creditors at bay and make something of her property, and her brother is continually in trouble. Her involvement with the Chinese man reflects a combination of adolescent curiosity, passion, enhanced social standing, and a desire for the gifts that result from the relationship. Annaud himself acknowledges that part of what prompted him to adapt the novel was his fascination with the element of the French colonial empire: "I have maintained a nostalgia for this period of French presence and greatness, even though I did not live through it."[180] This position is particularly interesting given Annaud's earlier film *La victoire en chantant (Black and White in Colour)*, which is quite critical of colonialism. Speaking to the nostalgic qualities of the film, Marcel Oms drew broader implications for the memories of former settlers: "Thus, idealized or not, fantasized or not, the affair between the young adolescent and the seductive Chinese man is of the same nature as the memories of Indochina maintained by former settlers, as well as the fascination with the Far East and its essence of opiate-induced eroticism."[181]

What is particularly significant about the nostalgic element of all three films is that their release in 1992 coincided with a critical revisiting and reevaluation of the Indochina War by historians, filmmakers, and other commentators. While Schoendoerffer was promoting a standard narrative of the Indochina War and Wargnier and Annaud were presenting audiences with a nostalgic view of the "good old days" of the colony, Bertrand Tavernier was challenging narratives of the Algerian War with his hard-hitting documentary *The War without a Name (La guerre sans nom)*. Francis Ramirez and Christian Rolot as well as Panivong Norindr have argued that the "return to the colonies" in the early 1990s resulted in a radically different treatment of Indochina and Algeria; the films dealing with Indochina, as has been demonstrated, tend toward a certain colonial exoticism, whereas this was completely lacking in Tavernier's film and in other productions.[182] Ramirez and Rolot maintain that this is due to the fact that Algeria was still too political and too sensitive as a topic, while Indochina had been "isolated [...] in a distant and mythical era,"[183] the result of a certain disconnect between contemporary Vietnam and the Indochina of the past. Although the evidence they provide to illustrate this Algeria-Indochina dichotomy is weak—they contrast the lack of support that Tavernier had from veterans with Schoendoerffer's considerable support from the same, without taking into account the vastly different goals of the two projects—the argument itself is credible.

. . .

Despite the relatively small corpus of films that address colonial Indochina or the war, particularly in comparison to the body of work on the Algerian and Vietnam wars, these films have clearly played a significant role in reinforcing the two dominant narratives. Lauded as *the* filmmaker of the Indochina War, Pierre Schoendoerffer's oeuvre has had a significant influence on how the public has perceived this conflict. His films reinforce the heroism of soldiers betrayed or abandoned by the metropolitan government, the public, or the military high command and emphasize Franco-Indochinese cooperation. This vision of the war is central to the anticommunist narrative promoted by the ANAI and other groups. Not all films produced by veterans fall so neatly into the same category. Despite early similarities between Claude Bernard-Aubert's work and that of Schoendoerffer, Bernard-Aubert had charted a very different course with the releases of *Le facteur s'en va-t-en guerre* and *Charlie Bravo*. If *Charlie Bravo*'s critique of French objectives and tactics aligns it with the anticolonial narrative, Paul Carpita's *Rendez-vous des quais* stands out as the only film to focus explicitly on the antiwar protest movement.

Films depicting the colonial era primarily from the 1920s through the end of the Indochina War have tended to reflect a certain nostalgia. A significant exception here is Marcel Camus, whose *Mort en fraude* is one of the only films set in the colony that challenges the premises of the civilizing mission, and does so more convincingly than did Régis Wargnier. Like *L'Amant* and *Indochine*, *Mort en fraude* centers on an interracial couple but without the attendant eroticism; in fact French discrimination against the Eurasian Anh is depicted on several occasions.[184] The fact that a French character is shown as single-handedly trying to "save" a Vietnamese village works at cross-purposes with this critique of colonialism, however, and ultimately casts Horcier as a character not unlike Éliane. While the "return to Indochina" of the early 1990s—itself undoubtedly shaped by the emerging interest in all things Indochina throughout the 1980s, as discussed in previous chapters—was certainly a remarkable period, it has yet to lead to a firm commitment to reevaluating the colonial past or the Indochina War.

This is evident in the release of *Là-haut* (2003; *Above the Clouds*) and *Un barrage contre le Pacifique* (2008; *The Sea Wall*), which have been the only two major releases on the subject since the 1992 "return."[185] Once again we have one film that is directed by a veteran, and one that is a literary adaptation. In the former Schoendoerffer returns to the device of the flashback to depict the war but maintains essentially the same narrative as in earlier films. In the latter Panh provides a more convincing critique of colonial society than did Wargnier, and although he maintains some of the eroticism of *L'Amant* he does not make it a focal point. Panh is perhaps the closest of all the filmmakers to challenging the status quo by giving far greater agency to the indigenous characters, but like Wargnier he tends to condemn the system without condemning those who participated in it. Overall the filmic representation of the Indochina War and the French colonial period reflects the broader trends with respect to public remembrance of the war: a majority of voices supporting the status quo and a few dissenting voices. There is little actual evolution or challenge to the dominant narratives. However, there is hope that Panh's most recent film will prove to be a starting point for a more critical examination of French Indochina, and from there possibly the war.

Conclusion

In 1994 Daniel Lindenberg wrote about France's so-called memory wars and the way in which the French relationship with memory provoked "particularly violent controversies."[1] He opened by tracing the phenomenon back to the French Revolution, before shifting his focus to several critical periods of the twentieth century: the First World War, the Vichy period, and the Algerian War. The Indochina War was omitted save for a brief discussion of the Boudarel affair contained within the rubric of "Communist memory, Anticommunist memory." A decade and a half later, Pascal Blanchard and Isabelle Veyrat-Masson published an edited volume on the subject of French memory wars, to which a great number of leading specialists contributed.[2] Again the Indochina War was ignored, while May 1968, the Holocaust, Vichy, Algeria, and colonialism were all featured. Trends in historical research of twentieth-century France have since the early 1990s revolved around the remembrance of traumatic events that have pitted the French against one another (*guerres franco-françaises*): collaboration and resistance, colonialism and decolonization, immigration and national identity. The Indochina War is inherently connected with each of these phenomena and yet has been understudied, as has the collective remembrance of the conflict.

It is evident that the Indochina War is far from being a "black hole" of French remembrance. On the contrary, uncompromising narratives of the war are fiercely defended and promoted by particular interest groups. The two most prevalent interpretations of the war—as a dirty war of colonial reconquest or as a war to contain communism—have clashed time and again, whether over the war's depiction in a documentary or over the controversial past of a Paris university professor. This conflict has only increased as veterans have grown ever more outspoken about their experiences and their opinions, and their pressure on the government has led to the initiation of a series of commemorative projects. It is also clear that evaluations of the colonial legacy are intertwined with the debates over the nature of the Indochina War. Moreover decolonization did not mark the end of the French connection with Indochina; rather the fallout of the war was repatriated to France with the soldiers, the settler community, and the French citizens of indigenous background. In a very real way they brought Indochina home with them, a phenomenon they referred to as *le mal jaune,* no different from a tropical disease contracted in Southeast Asia.[3] The repatriates in particular see themselves as embodying the legacy of colonialism and the state's failure to assume responsibility for that legacy. The sites of their repatriation to France commemorate a chapter in the history of French immigration, albeit a small one. There is also the question of the collective remembrance of the Cold War. Memories of the militancy and activism of the PCF during the war, of the staunch anticommunism of many soldiers and the political right, and the collapse of the Eastern Bloc have all left their mark on the events and processes described here, as have ongoing public debates over issues like the equality of pensions between French and colonial veterans.

The divisive nature of the Indochina War and the lack of consensus over its primary objectives has resulted in the creation of a divided memory. Even if, as we saw in chapter 1, the majority of public opinion was not consistently or heavily concerned with the war, there were nonetheless sharp divisions between political parties, between protestors and the military, and between supporters and opponents of colonialism. The experience of the Second World War dominated the perceptions of the Indochina War, leading both soldiers of the expeditionary corps and those who actively or passively supported the Viet Minh to claim the mantle of the Resistance. In the latter years of the conflict the politics of the Cold War came to define policy and perceptions, effectively substituting the tropes of one totalitarian system (Nazism) for another (Communism). The defeat of the French at Dien Bien Phu and the subsequent negotiations at Geneva confirmed the independence of the successor states of French Indochina and marked the beginning of a long and bloody process of decolonization of the French empire.

The opposition of the PCF and others to the war and to colonialism, which led to protests, strikes, and the heavily publicized Henri Martin affair, has formed the basis for the narrative of the "dirty war." In casting the war as one of colonial reconquest, this narrative emphasizes the abuses of the colonial system, the creation of a society based on the exploitation and oppression of the indigenous population, and the rights of a people to self-determination.[4] This narrative also privileges the nationalist and anticolonial aspects of Ho Chi Minh's rhetoric, leading to an emphasis on the war as one of liberation. The ANAI narrative, which is reflected in that of the political right and extreme right, rarely acknowledges the colonial dimension of the war. The war is reductively assimilated into the ideological conflict of the Cold War, in which Indochina (and more specifically Vietnam) became the site of a battle between international communism and the "free world." Far from waging war against the Vietnamese people, a majority of veterans saw themselves as fighting to protect the Vietnamese (as well as Laos and Cambodians) from the communist threat. This interpretation was reinforced after the Halong Bay accords of 1948, which are held up as proof positive that France was collaborating with an independent Vietnam, whose soldiers were partners of the French, fighting alongside the expeditionary corps. In this framework noncommunist Indochinese were the potential or actual victims of communism. To this community of victims are added all those who fought on the French side. The narrative not only highlights the heroism and sacrifice of the soldiers but also casts them as the victims of communism (through the experience of the prisoner of war camps) and as the victims of the ineptitude of the French government and the indifference of the French public. Virtually silent as a group for nearly two decades after the end of the war, veterans became increasingly vocal after 1975 and particularly as of the early 1980s. Their objective, echoed by the political right and extreme right, was to overcome their status as "forgotten" and to force the state to acknowledge their sacrifice during the war. In doing so they brought their interpretation of the war into public prominence. As a result of their lobbying efforts an unknown soldier was laid to rest along with the unknowns of the other major wars of the century; a memorial complex was built; special status was granted to former prisoners of the Viet Minh; and a national day of homage was created.

The close involvement of veterans, and more specifically of associations like the ANAI, with state-sponsored commemorative initiatives has meant that their narrative long characterized the official narrative of the war. This influence includes an emphasis on the heroism of the soldiers, whose mission is portrayed as having ultimately been a lost cause, as well as a strong emphasis on anticommunist objectives. The state narrative has since the mid-1990s shifted away from the overt anticommunism of earlier eras, at times even including references to the war's role in French decolonization. Only under François Mitterrand, however, was the colonial dimension of the conflict privileged over the Cold War context.

Inherent in these contrasting interpretations of the war are competing visions of the colonial period that preceded it. Indeed there are frequent instances of debates over the Indochina War spilling over into debates over colonialism; the Boudarel affair is the most prominent example. As has been discussed, those who understand the war as being motivated by colonial reconquest view the colonial project as flawed at best and destructive at worst. While many veterans refuse to make pronouncements on the colonial system, there are those who, like the ANAI, promote a positive interpretation of colonialism. In this view the French colonial system's achievements were set into stark relief by the abuses of the Communist regimes that succeeded it. Debates over France's colonial legacy have continued to shape public discourse, as evidenced by the lobbying for and subsequent outcry against the 2005 law on the positive aspects of colonialism.

The difficulties in commemorating defeat are apparent in veterans' long campaigns for moral and legal recognition and in the delays in establishing prominent national monuments and memorials. But what of the collective remembrance of the victors? In her review of a collection of Vietnamese veterans' memoirs, Carole Vann characterizes the conflict as a black hole in Vietnamese collective memory.[5] As is the case in France, the war has been subsumed by the subsequent American war but also by the larger project of unification and state building.[6] Moreover the war is the "intellectual and political property of the government," and so there is little variation on the official narrative that emphasizes the anticolonial struggle and roots the second and third Indochina wars firmly in the first.[7]

Although the Vietnamese landscape has become increasingly dotted with museums and monuments to the past,[8] commemorative sites and ceremonies connected with the French Indochina War are few and far between. Many museums, including the War Remnants Museum in Hanoi and the museum dedicated to the battle of Dien Bien Phu, do depict the abuses of the French colonial system and present the war as one of national liberation. Several of them include images of antiwar protestors in France and of Henri Martin in particular. Dien Bien Phu, which has grown into a city of well over one hundred thousand people, has maintained some of the war sites, though primarily for tourism purposes. The hill known to the Viet Minh as A1

FIGURE 9. Brigadier General de Castries's bunker, Dien Bien Phu.

and to the French expeditionary corps as Éliane has been maintained as a tourist site, trenches and all.[9] De Castries's bunker too has been preserved, and there are numerous pieces of decommissioned artillery dotting the landscape. Military cemeteries are impeccably maintained, and the small museum contains a few historical artifacts, weapons, and displays depicting battle scenes.

In 2004 the Vietnamese state undertook a number of commemorative initiatives in honor of the fiftieth anniversary of the end of the war. Events included a performance by thousands of dancers wearing different colored uniforms to create a mosaic effect depicting scenes from the battle.[10] A new Victory Memorial was installed in Dien Bien Phu, and the Museum of Ethnology in Hanoi curated a special exhibit on the battle. The Vietnamese

FIGURE 10. Military cemetery in Dien Bien Phu.

government collaborated with the French and Chinese governments to host one meeting of a three-part international conference series. It also published a collection of letters written by French prisoners of war (to Ho Chi Minh as well as to the French government and public) under the title *The Indochina War Told through the Voices of the French Expeditionary Corps*.[11] Since these letters were written under duress, the volume presents a blatantly biased view of the conflict. More recently a team of Vietnamese journalists undertook a project to record individual memories of the battle of Dien Bien Phu, interviewing veterans who fought the French and publishing their testimony in the aforementioned volume reviewed by Carole Vann.[12] This volume is in some sense the analogue to Pierre Journoud and Hugues Tertrais's *Voices from Dien Bien Phu* (2004).[13]

The events of 2004 in France and Vietnam represent a commemorative peak as far as the Indochina War is concerned. Although the French government's involvement in the events marking the fiftieth anniversary of the end of the war was significant, the sixtieth anniversary in 2014 was far more subdued; the commemorative ceremonies remain first and foremost the domain of the veterans. Despite their tireless campaigns to foster public interest in the war, it has remained a relatively ignored period of twentieth-century French history. The deaths of General Marcel Bigeard in 2010 and filmmaker Pierre Schoendoerffer in 2012, both prominent self-professed guardians of the memory of the Indochina War, remind us that as veterans age and die commemoration itself may disappear with its custodians.

NOTES

INSTITUTIONAL ABBREVIATIONS USED IN NOTES

ADA   *Archives départementales de l'Allier* (Moulins)
ADLG   *Archives départementales du Lot-et-Garonne* (Agen)
ADSSD   *Archives départementales de la Seine-Saint-Denis* (Bobigny)
AMF   *Archives municipales de Fréjus* (Fréjus)
AN   *Archives nationales, Centre d'archives contemporaines* (Fontainebleau)
ANOM   *Centre d'archives d'outre-mer* (Aix-en-Provence)
BDIC   *Bibliothèque de documentation internationale contemporaine* (Paris)
CADLC   *Centre d'archives diplomatiques de La Courneuve* (La Courneuve)
CADN   *Centre d'archives diplomatiques de Nantes* (Nantes)
CHT   *Centre d'histoire du travail* (Nantes)
IAO   *Institut d'Asie Orientale* (Lyons)
INA   *Institut national audiovisuel* (Paris)
SHD   *Service historique de la Défense* (Vincennes)

FRONTMATTER

Epigraph: Alain Ruscio, *Les communistes français et la guerre d'Indochine, 1944–1954* (Paris: L'Harmattan, 1985), 12.

INTRODUCTION

1. Robert Frank, "Les troubles de la mémoire française," in Jean-Pierre Rioux, ed., *La guerre d'Algérie et les Français* (Paris: Fayard, 1990), 604.

2. Nicola Cooper, "Heroes and Martyrs: The Changing Mythical Status of the French Army during the Indochinese War," in Valerie Holman and Debra Kelly, eds., *France at War in the Twentieth Century: Propaganda, Myth, and Metaphor* (New York: Berghahn Books, 2000), 126. It should be noted that the French term *occultée* implies an active process of silencing, whereas *overshadowed* implies a more passive process.

3. The total French population has been estimated at 23,700 in 1913, and between 34,000 and 39,000 in 1940. The population statistics of 23,700 and 34,000 are cited in Pierre Brocheux and Daniel Hémery, *Indochine: La colonisation ambigüe*, 2nd ed. (Paris: La Découverte, 2001), 178. David Marr estimates as many as 39,000 in *Vietnam, 1945: The Quest for Power* (Berkeley and Los Angeles: University of California Press, 1995), 73, while Eric Jennings cites 34,000 for 1940 in *Vichy in the Tropics: Pétain's National Revolution in Madagascar, Guadeloupe and Indochina* (Stanford: Stanford University Press, 2001), 136. To put these statistics in context, the total population in 1913 was 16 million, and in 1940 just under 23 million. In Algeria, by contrast, the settler population was close to 1 million for a total population of approximately 8 million.

4. Benjamin Stora addresses this comparison in *Imaginaires de guerre: Algérie-Viêtnam en France et aux États-Unis* (Paris: La Découverte, 1997), 28, 34.

5. Frank himself has since the publication of this essay engaged with aspects of the remembrance of the Indochina War. For example, he participated in a 2004 conference on the history and memory of the battle of Dien Bien Phu and wrote an introductory chapter for the published proceedings. See "Le dialogue nécessaire entre historiens et témoins," in Pierre Journoud and Hugues Tertrais, eds., *1954–2004: La bataille de Dien Bien Phu entre histoire et mémoire* (Paris and Saint-Denis: Société française d'histoire d'outre-mer, 2004).

6. Serge Tignères and Alain Ruscio, *Dien Bien Phu: Mythes et réalités, 1954–2004. Cinquante ans de passions françaises* (Paris: Les Indes savantes, 2005).

7. Alain Ruscio, "Dien Bien Phu: Du coup de génie à l'aberration. Ou, Comment les contemporains ont vécu l'ultime bataille de la guerre française d'Indochine," *Revue française d'histoire d'outre-mer* 72, no. 268 (1985), 335.

8. Hugues Tertrais and Pierre Journoud, *Paroles de Dien Bien Phu: Les survivants témoignent* (Paris: Tallandier, 2004), 13. Journoud argues in a separate piece that despite the single, unifying, heroic narrative that has been promoted about the battle, some veterans do not identify with it. See "Dien Bien Phu: Naissance et destin d'un mythe héroïque," in Claude d'Abzac-Épezy and Jean Martinant de Préneuf, eds., *Héros militaires, culture et société (XIXe-XXe siècles)*, "Histoire et littérature de l'Europe du Nord-Ouest" no. 52 (Villeneuve d'Ascq: IRHiS-Institute des Recherches Historiques du Septentrion, 2012), online only at http://hleno.revues.org/251.

9. Henry Rousso, *Le syndrome de Vichy (1944–198 . . .)* (Paris: Seuil, 1987).

10. Stephen Tyre has examined the ways in which veterans and the procolonial French right have shaped a particular memory of the battle of Dien Bien Phu in "The Memory of French Military Defeat at Dien Bien Phu and the Defence of French Algeria," in Jenny MacLeod, ed., *Defeat and Memory: Cultural Histories of Military Defeat in the Modern Era* (London: Palgrave Macmillan, 2008), 214–32.

11. Fredrik Logevall, *Embers of War: The Fall of an Empire and the Making of America's Vietnam* (New York: Random House, 2012), xvi.

12. Christopher Goscha and Christian Ostermann, "Introduction," in Goscha and Ostermann, eds., *Connecting Histories: Decolonization and the Cold War in Southeast Asia, 1945–1962* (Washington, DC, and Stanford: Woodrow Wilson Center Press and Stanford University Press, 2009), 2.

13. A recent exception is David Lowe and Tony Joel's *Remembering the Cold War: Global Contest and National Stories* (Hoboken: Taylor & Francis, 2013), though their study examines more than just Western Europe. A second edited collection of note is Jan-Werner Müller's *Memory and Power in Post-War Europe* (Cambridge: Cambridge University Press, 2002), in particular the introduction.

14. Stef Scagliola argues that the very nature of asymmetrical warfare with its arbitrary identification of victims and perpetrators, guerrilla tactics, and tactics that contravene modern rules of war makes commemoration of such conflicts particularly difficult. See "The Silences and Myths of a 'Dirty War': Coming to Terms with the Dutch-Indonesian Decolonisation War (1945–1949)," *European Review of History* 14, no. 2 (June 2007), 235–62.

15. For an application of the four-stage model of the evolution of memory (amnesty, amnesia, resurgence, hypermnesia/obsession) to the Algerian War, see Henry Rousso, *Les raisins verts de la guerre d'Algérie,* in Yves Michaud, ed., *La guerre d'Algérie (1954–1962)* (Paris: Odile Jacob, 2004), 127–51.

16. Efrat Ben-Ze'ev, Ruth Ginio, and Jay Winter, eds., *Shadows of War: A Social History of Silence in the Twentieth Century* (Cambridge: Cambridge University Press, 2010).

17. Despite the similarities between American and French remembrance—the existence of two interpretations of the war, one of which is characterized by a staunch anticommunism—there are considerable differences. American remembrance of Vietnam experienced a significant shift in the early 1980s with Ronald Reagan's characterization of the war as a "noble cause," with the controversy over the Vietnam Veterans' Memorial, and with a new wave of films.

18. These goals mirror those of Jenny MacLeod in *Defeat and Memory.* Those interested in a chronology of the evolution of the remembrance of the Indochina War should consult Serge Tignères's work, which relies heavily on quantitative analysis. See "La guerre d'Indochine et l'opinion publique française entre 1954 et 1994: Mémoire et histoire," PhD diss., Université de Toulouse-Le Mirail, 1999. Part of his dissertation was subsequently published in a volume cowritten with Alain

Ruscio entitled *Dien Bien Phu: Mythes et réalités, 1954–2004. Cinquante ans de passions françaises*.

19. These were French citizens with some Lao, Cambodian, and/or Vietnamese heritage. Many were of mixed French and indigenous heritage claiming citizenship through a French parent, while others were naturalized citizens. I use "Indochinese" in quotation marks here to indicate that the term is not an accurate reflection of an ethnic group. However, the term is frequently used by commentators and will be used without quotation marks in the rest of this study to reflect this usage.

20. Samuel Hynes, "Personal Narratives and Commemoration," in Jay Winter and Emmanuel Sivan, eds., *War and Remembrance in the Twentieth Century* (Cambridge: Cambridge University Press, 2000), 207.

21. Ibid., 207.

22. Although metropolitan French soldiers constituted less than half of those fighting with the expeditionary corps, they form the majority of members of veterans' associations and veteran lobbying groups in France. Veterans' organizations are not representative of the views of all or even a majority of veterans of the French forces who fought in Indochina. Nonetheless, these associations have the strongest voice on the public stage. There are some dissenting voices within the veteran community in France. For example, Pierre Journoud has demonstrated that not all veterans of the battle of Dien Bien Phu identify with the myth of a heroic, united French force; see "Dien Bien Phu: Naissance et destin d'un mythe héroïque." Moreover, there are dissenting voices among Indochina veterans affiliated with the Republican Veterans' Association, which is close to the French Communist Party.

23. Nicola Cooper addresses this aspect of French remembrance of the Indochina War as well as that of colonial nostalgia in "Dien Bien Phu—Fifty Years On," *Modern and Contemporary France* 12, no. 4 (2004), 445–46.

24. As Pierre Journoud argues, this image of solidarity among the members of the expeditionary corps is flawed, as is demonstrated most notably by the number of deserters (the so-called rats of the Nam Youn River) during the battle of Dien Bien Phu. See "Dien Bien Phu: Naissance et destin d'un mythe héroïque."

25. M.R., "Portrait de Geneviève de Galard: Des mots pour se souvenir," *Historia,* March 1992, 61.

26. Nicola Cooper has explored this phenomenon in the context of the war itself. Cooper, "Heroes and Martyrs," 126–41.

27. The image of American soldiers and veterans being spat upon by antiwar protestors is a fixture of American narratives of the Vietnam War. Jerry Lembcke challenges this image in *The Spitting Image: Myth, Memory, and the Legacy of Vietnam* (New York: New York University Press, 1998). Critiques of his study reveal the extent to which conflicting American narratives persist.

28. See, for example, the claims made by Jean-Marie Le Pen in "Le message de Léonidas," in *Chant funèbre pour Pnom Penh et Saïgon* (Paris: SPL, 1975), 206–13. He concludes that "in short, the Communists were waging war in France against France" (211). Several accounts of this treatment are also rendered in Amédée

Thévenet's *La guerre d'Indochine racontée par ceux qui l'ont vécue: Un devoir de mémoire assumé ensemble* (Paris: France-Empire, 2001), 571–78.

29. Erwan Bergot, *Les services secrètes en Indochine: Les héros oubliés* (Bagneux: Le Livre de Paris, 1979); Louis Stien, *Les soldats oubliés: De Cao Bang aux camps de rééducation du Viêt-minh* (Paris: Albin Michel, 1993); Alain Vincent, *Indochine: La guerre oubliée* (Paris: A. Sutton, 2007). Bergot and Stien are both veterans of the war.

30. Scagliola, "Silences and Myths of a 'Dirty War,'" 235.

31. Ibid., 241 and 244–45.

32. Early contributors to the anticolonial narrative, like Paul Mus, represent centrist or even conservative elements on the political spectrum. Mus was a graduate of the French Colonial School and a colonial administrator—a far cry from the activists of the French Communist Party—and yet was one of the first to offer a sustained critique of the French prosecution of the war. Likewise, anticolonial and antiwar positions were expressed by the editorial teams of *Esprit* and *Témoignage chrétien*, neither of which was a hardline left-wing publication.

33. Stéphane Courtois, ed., *Le livre noir du communisme: Crimes, terreur, répression* (Paris: Robert Laffont, 1997).

34. Ibid., 14. Among the critics were several of his collaborators on the volume, including Nicolas Werth and Jean-Louis Margolin, who claimed that Courtois had inflated the numbers they provided. See Nicolas Werth, "La Russie soviétique: Révolution, socialisme et dictature," *L'Histoire* no. 223 (July 1998), 8–21.

35. Jean-Jacques Becker makes this point very effectively in his review of the volume, published in *Vingtième siècle* no. 59 (1998), 177–79.

36. Daniel Lefeuvre, *Pour en finir avec la repentance coloniale* (Paris: Flammarion, 2006).

37. "Loi no. 2005-158 du 23 février 2005 portant reconnaissance de la Nation et contribution nationale en faveur des Français rapatriés," *Journal officiel de la République française*, 24 February 2005, 3128.

38. Laurent Greilsamer addresses this phenomenon in "Il y a 50 ans la légende de Geneviève de Galard," *Le Monde*, 13 July 2004. Former colonial administrator Edouard Axelrad's novel *Marie casse-croûte* includes a fictionalized account of a BMC at Dien Bien Phu (Paris: Jean-Claude Lattès, 1985).

39. This image of feminine caretaking is conveyed, for example, by Doctor Paul Grauwin's memoir of the battle of Dien Bien Phu: "Nothing can replace a young woman at the bedside of a wounded soldier, [. . .] especially at the front. Last year, when a wounded man arrived in my field hospital, anxious and worried, he saw two young women dressed in white leaning over him. That was it! No more anxiety, no more worries. He felt safe because he saw a young, calm, smiling woman." Paul Grauwin, *J'étais médecin à Dien Bien Phu* (Paris: France-Empire, 1954), 65–66. The gendered dimension of the battle is also evident in the choice of feminine names for the hills that the French sought to defend (Isabelle, Dominique, Huguette, etc.).

40. One of the first incarnations of this story was published in Lucien Bornert, *Les rescapés de l'enfer: Les héros de Dien Bien Phu* (Paris: Nouvelles Presses Mondiales, 1954), 53. It has since been published in her memoirs, *Une femme à Dien Bien*

Phu (Paris: Éditions des Arènes, 2003), 86. It has also been featured in several television and radio interviews over the years.

41. *Indochine, Diên Biên Phu,* and *L'Amant.*

CHAPTER 1: FRENCH INDOCHINA FROM CONQUEST TO COMMEMORATION

1. *Discours prononcé par M. Martial Merlin, Gouverneur Général de l'Indochine,* Conseil de gouvernement de l'Indochine, Session ordinaire de 1924 (Hanoi, 1924), 3.

2. Paul Doumer, *L'Indo-Chine française (Souvenirs)* (Paris: Vuibert et Nony, 1905), 33.

3. The war is more appropriately termed a Franco-Vietnamese or a Franco–Viet Minh war, as the bulk of combat took place on Vietnamese soil against the Viet Minh. However, there was some spillover into Lao and Cambodian territory and the inhabitants of these parts of Indochina were also implicated in the conflict as supporters and combatants on one side or the other.

4. French Jesuit missionary Alexandre de Rhodes first went to Hanoi in 1624, and representatives of the Paris Foreign Missions Society established themselves in the region in the early 1660s.

5. This connection has been emphasized both by French commentators who wish to trace a longer history of collaboration between the two countries as a means of legitimating the colonial period, and also by the Vietnamese state, which has often targeted Catholic communities as being "foreign" to Vietnamese society. For more on the history of Catholicism in Vietnam, see Charles Keith, *Catholic Vietnam: A Church from Empire to Nation* (Berkeley and Los Angeles: University of California Press, 2012).

6. The Nguyen dynasty had faced a serious challenge to its authority beginning with the Tay Son rebellion in 1777 and by the turn of the century was still trying to reclaim its former position of power in the south (the Trinh lords controlled the north at the time, though the Le dynasty technically ruled over the entirety of what was then known as Dai Viet).

7. The terms of the treaty were never implemented; however, as Agathe Larcher-Goscha argues, this agreement has nonetheless been "presented in 'origin-seeking' colonial quarters as the 'key charter of the Franco-Vietnamese community.'" Larcher-Goscha, "Prince Cuong Dê and the Franco-Vietnamese Competition for the Heritage of Gia Long," in Gisèle Bousquet and Pierre Brocheux, eds., *Viêt-Nam Exposé: French Scholarship on Twentieth Century Vietnamese Society* (Ann Arbor: University of Michigan Press, 2002), 206. She in turn cites Georges Taboulet, *La geste française en Indochine* (Paris: Adrien-Maisonneuve, 1955).

8. As Pierre Brocheux and Daniel Hémery emphasize in the introduction to *Indochina: An Ambiguous Colonization* (Berkeley and Los Angeles: University of California Press, 2009), resistance to French occupation ranged from fierce to

meager, depending on the region. Moreover resistance to the French was complicated by other domestic and geopolitical considerations; the Cambodian royal family sought a path toward modernization, and both Laos and Cambodia found themselves fending off Thai and Vietnamese threats to their territory. Brocheux and Hémery's book was originally published as *Indochine: La colonisation ambigüe* (Paris: La Découverte, 1994).

9. The administrative structure would be overhauled and centralized by Governor General Paul Doumer after 1897; see Brocheux and Hémery, *Indochina: An Ambiguous Colonization*, 80–82.

10. Ibid.

11. See, for example, the edited volume *Indochine, Alerte à l'histoire: Ni opprobre, ni oubli* (Paris: Académie des sciences d'outre-mer, 1985). The volume is discussed in chapter 2.

12. Nicola Cooper, *France in Indochina: Colonial Encounters* (Oxford and New York: Berg, 2001), 30.

13. Jacques Dalloz, *La guerre d'Indochine, 1945–1954* (Paris: Seuil, 1987), 19. Specifically he notes that infant mortality in Hanoi dropped from 44% in 1925 to 19% in 1938 (he in turn cites Philippe Devillers).

14. Brocheux and Hémery, *Indochina: An Ambiguous Colonization*, 219. The counterpoint to the number of schools is the kind of education that was provided; in her study of French colonial education Gail Kelly highlights the ways in which indigenous students in French Indochina were conditioned to see themselves as inferior to the French and to be grateful for the assistance the French were bringing them. Gail Kelly and David Kelly, *French Colonial Education: Essays on Vietnam and West Africa* (New York: AMS Press, 2000).

15. For more on the daily humiliations, see Brocheux and Hémery, *Indochina: An Ambiguous Colonization*, 192–97. For more on the colonial prison system and its impact, see Peter Zinoman, *The Colonial Bastille: A History of Imprisonment in Vietnam, 1862–1940* (Berkeley and Los Angeles: University of California Press, 1996).

16. Tran Tu Binh, *The Red Earth: A Vietnamese Memoir of Life on a Colonial Rubber Plantation*, trans. John Spragens Jr. (Athens: Ohio University Press, 1985), 15.

17. Stein Tønnesson clarifies that this was a confirmation of independence rather than a declaration; strictly speaking, Bao Dai had declared Vietnamese independence on 11 March 1945 and ceded that authority to the government of the DRV when he abdicated. *Vietnam 1946: How the War Began* (Berkeley and Los Angeles: University of California Press, 2010), 12. For more on the August Revolution, see David Marr, *Vietnam 1945: The Quest for Power* (Berkeley and Los Angeles: University of California Press, 1995).

18. Fredrik Logevall, *Embers of War: The Fall of an Empire and the Making of America's Vietnam* (New York: Random House, 2012), 113–15.

19. Excerpts of the statement can be found in Philippe Devillers, *Paris-Saïgon-Hanoï: Les archives de la guerre, 1944–1947* (Paris: Gallimard, 1988), 53–54.

20. While Lao king Sisavang Vong opted to work with the French, there was anything but consensus as to whether this was the correct course of action. Two movements committed to Lao independence emerged: the Lao Issara, created by Prince Phetsarath and other leaders, and the Pathet Lao, affiliated with the Viet Minh.

21. The DRV was to have control over its government, parliament, army, and finances, but its foreign policy was to remain under French control and it would be integrated into an economic union with the rest of the Indochinese Federation.

22. This thesis was first advanced by chief negotiator Jean Sainteny in his 1953 work *Histoire d'une paix manquée* (Paris: Amiot-Dumont).

23. What follows is a brief overview of the war intended to convey its general contours and character. For those interested in a more thorough account, please consult Fredrik Logevall's *Embers of War*, Alain Ruscio's *La guerre française d'Indochine, 1945–1954* (Paris: Complexe, 1992), or Jacques Dalloz' *La guerre d'Indochine 1945–1954* (Paris: Seuil, 1987), which is also available in English translation.

24. Ruscio, *La guerre française d'Indochine* (Complexe, 1992), 92.

25. Christopher Goscha, *Historical Dictionary of the Indochina War (1945–1954): An International and Interdisciplinary Approach* (Honolulu: University of Hawai'i Press, 2012), 198.

26. Michel Bodin, *Dictionnaire de la guerre d'Indochine, 1945–1954* (Paris: Commission française d'histoire militaire; Institut de stratégie comparée; Economica, 2004), 282.

27. Logevall, *Embers of War,* 115. Christopher Goscha states that "the war *for* Vietnam [began] in the South in September 1945," concluding only in April 1975. *Vietnam: Un état né de la guerre, 1945–1954* (Paris: Armand-Colin, 2011), 27.

28. *Journal officiel de la République française,* Débats de l'Assemblée nationale, 29 October 1990, 4504. The question was in reference to the wall of names that was to be added to the national Memorial to the Indochina Wars.

29. Philippe Devillers and Stein Tønnesson have both studied the archives extensively with respect to the events of 19 December, but neither is able to draw firm conclusions, although Devillers does argue that the Viet Minh were essentially manipulated and pressured by the French into war. Fredrick Logevall makes a similar argument in *Embers of War,* 163. The crux of the issue is whether the attack on the French was undertaken on orders of the Viet Minh leadership or whether it was launched by soldiers on the ground. See Devillers, *Paris-Saïgon-Hanoï;* and Tønnesson, *Vietnam 1946.*

30. It should be noted that not all historians and commentators periodize the war in the same way: among those who break the war into two phases, the dates for the first phase can vary from 1945 to 1946 as starting points and 1948, 1949, or 1950 as end points. Some choose to subdivide the war even further: Amédée Thévenet, for example, speaks of three phases (1945–47, 1948–50, and 1951–54); *La guerre d'Indochine racontée par ceux qui l'ont vécue* (Paris: France-Empire, 2001).

31. Martin Thomas has argued that the recommitment to empire was intrinsically connected with the reconstruction of a multiparty republican democracy in

the post-1945 period. "French Imperialist Reconstruction and the Development of the Indochina War, 1945–1950," in Mark Atwood Lawrence and Fredrik Logevall, eds., *The First Vietnam War: Colonial Conflict and Cold War Crisis* (Cambridge: Harvard University Press, 2007), 130–51.

32. Alain Ruscio addresses the tactics of search and destroy missions, the razing of villages, and the arrests and summary executions of "suspects"; *La guerre française d'Indochine* (Complexe, 1992), 161–64. Evidence of these tactics and others can be found in numerous newspaper accounts as well as testimonies of former soldiers like Jules Roy (*Mémoires barbares,* Paris: Albin Michel, 1989) and Philippe de Pirey (*Opération Gâchis,* Paris: La Table ronde, 1953). Fredrik Logevall also addresses the use of torture and other tactics by both sides in *Embers of War,* 177–78.

33. Fredrik Logevall rightly points out that by mid-1947 this truism was misleading since the Viet Minh controlled approximately half of Vietnamese territory; *Embers of War,* 175.

34. Many proponents of the anticommunist narrative use the 1948 Halong Bay agreements and/or the official creation of the State of Vietnam in 1949 as evidence that the French expeditionary corps was fighting to protect an independent Vietnam from the communist Viet Minh.

35. For an analysis of the Bao Dai solution in the context of the Cold War, see Mark Atwood Lawrence, "Recasting Vietnam: The Bao Dai Solution and the Outbreak of the Cold War in Southeast Asia," in Christopher Goscha and Christian Ostermann, eds., *Connecting Histories: Decolonization and the Cold War in Southeast Asia, 1945–1962* (Washington, DC, and Stanford: Woodrow Wilson Center Press and Stanford University Press, 2009), 15–38.

36. Logevall, *Embers of War,* 198.

37. Hugues Tertrais, *La piastre et le fusil: Le coût de la guerre d'Indochine, 1945–1954* (Comité pour l'histoire économique et financière de la France, 2002), 360.

38. Logevall, *Embers of War,* 261.

39. His perspective on the objectives of the French forces would convince many; see, for example, the quotes from Geneviève de Galard in the introduction and in chapter 4.

40. Logevall demonstrates that there were other considerations for the plan, including providing support for the Tai and Hmong partisans who had fought the Viet Minh in the region; *Embers of War,* 382–83.

41. *Le Figaro,* 15 April 1954, cited in Ruscio, *La guerre française d'Indochine* (Complexe, 1992), 197. As Pierre Journoud argues, the parallels drawn with the devastating First World War battle served to inscribe Dien Bien Phu in the "great tradition of just, patriotic wars fought by the nation to defend its territory and independence"; see "Dien Bien Phu: Naissance et destin d'un mythe héroïque."

42. Béatrice fell almost immediately; Gabrielle did so within a couple of days after an unsuccessful French counterattack.

43. Paul Grauwin, *J'étais médecin à Dien Bien Phu* (Paris: France Empire, 1954).

44. Goscha, *Historical Dictionary of the Indochina War,* 145.

45. Alain Ruscio, *Dien Bien Phu: La fin d'une illusion* (Paris: L'Harmattan, 1995), cited in Journoud, "Dien Bien Phu: Naissance et destin d'un mythe héroïque."

46. Bernard Fall, *Hell in a Very Small Place: The Siege of Dien Bien Phu* (Cambridge: Da Capo Press, 2002), 411.

47. Dalloz, *La guerre d'Indochine*, 232.

48. POW camps had not really been envisioned in the early phase of the war since relatively few soldiers were captured at any one time (and were typically executed rather than held). Following the major defeat of the French on the RC4 (Route coloniale 4), the Viet Minh had to come up with a detention system. More information on these camps is included in chapter 6.

49. Michel Bodin, *La France et ses soldats, Indochine, 1945–1954* (Paris: L'Harmattan, 1996), 7.

50. Official statistics released in 1955 cited a total of 92,800 dead on the French side; cited in Goscha, *Historical Dictionary of the Indochina War*, 9. Michel Bodin estimates a total of 112,032 in his *Dictionnaire de la guerre d'Indochine*, 214. Goscha notes that the reason for this discrepancy is Bodin's inclusion of those who died after the Geneva Accords of July 1954.

51. It is worth noting William Hitchcock's argument that the Fourth Republic was far more stable than historians and commentators have credited it. Indeed it is remarkable that in spite of instability domestically and in its foreign relations the political leaders of the Fourth Republic played an instrumental role in European integration, laying the foundations for the future European Union. Even he, however, acknowledges the general political instability of the period. Hitchcock, *France Restored: Cold War Diplomacy and the Quest for Leadership in Europe, 1944–1954* (Chapel Hill and London: University of North Carolina Press, 1998).

52. Philippe Devillers, Jean Lacouture, and Jérôme Kanapa, *La République est morte à Dien Bien Phu* (1974).

53. As Brocheux and Hémery note, this is undoubtedly an exaggeration but is nonetheless a formula that has stuck. *Indochina: An Ambiguous Colonization*, 372.

54. Dalloz, *La guerre d'Indochine*, 141; Ruscio, *La guerre française d'Indochine* (Complexe, 1992), 93–104; Alain Ruscio, "L'Opinion française et la guerre d'Indochine (1945–1954): Sondages et témoignages," *Vingtième siècle* no. 29 (1991), 35–45.

55. Statistics cited in Ruscio, *La guerre française d'Indochine* (Complexe, 1992), 102. The option to negotiate with the Viet Minh gained steady support over the course of the war: from 15% in September 1947 to 24% in October 1950, 35% in May 1953, and 42% in February 1954. Likewise the option to reestablish order and send reinforcements dropped from 37% in September 1947 to 19% in July 1949, back up to 27% in October 1950, then 15% in May 1953 and 7% in February 1954. The increase in October 1950 may be explained by the intensification of the Korean War, which brought renewed attention to the region as well as heightened fears of the spread of communism.

56. Ruscio, *La guerre française d'Indochine* (Complexe, 1992), 93.

57. Ibid., 94.

58. Dalloz, *La guerre d'Indochine*, 141.

59. Pierre Cenerelli, "Revisions of Empire: The French Media and the Indochina War, 1946–1954," PhD diss., Brandeis University, 2000, 24.

60. Ibid.

61. For more on the PCF and the war, see Alain Ruscio, *Les communistes français et la guerre d'Indochine, 1944–1954* (Paris: L'Harmattan, 1985).

62. See Sabine Rousseau, *La colombe et le napalm: Des chrétiens français contre les guerres d'Indochine et du Vietnam, 1945–1975* (Paris: CNRS, 2002).

63. *L'Humanité*, 12 February 1948, cited in Ruscio, *La guerre française d'Indochine* (Complexe, 1992), 100.

64. Among them were Jacques Chegaray's articles on the use of torture, which his own newspaper, *L'Aube*, refused to run, and Paul Mus's critiques of various aspects of the management and objectives of the war.

65. See, for example, Henri Alleg, *La question* (Paris: Éditions de Minuit, 1958); Pierre Vidal-Naquet, *La torture dans la République: Essais d'histoire et de politique contemporaine (1954–1962)* (Paris: Éditions de Minuit, 1972), and most recently, Raphaëlle Branche, *La torture et l'armée pendant la guerre d'Algérie: 1954–1962* (Paris: Gallimard, 2001).

66. Jules Roy, *Mémoires barbares* (Paris: Albin Michel, 1989), 13. His reflections in *La bataille de la rizière* (Paris: Gallimard, 1953), a book which was criticized by the left and the right, are also very informative.

67. Roy, *Mémoires barbares*, 396. The *gégène* involved using the current generated by machines like field radios to electrocute would-be informants.

68. Lyliane Veyrenc, *Opératrice de cinéma en Indochine* (Paris: Nouvelles Éditions Debresses, 1955), 59–61.

69. Ruscio, *Les communistes français et la guerre d'Indochine*, 237.

70. Ibid., 234.

71. The term first appeared in print in an article by Hubert Beuve-Méry in *Le Monde* on 17 January 1948.

72. Robert Bonnafous makes claims of sabotage in *Les prisonniers de guerre du corps expéditionnaire français en Extrême-Orient dans les camps Viet-minh (1945–1954)* (Montpellier: Centre d'histoire militaire et d'études de défense nationale, 1985), 121–23. Michel Bodin is careful to specify that there were many reports of sabotage and that veterans are certain that it contributed to their defeat, but that ultimately responsibility is nearly impossible to assign; *Dictionnaire de la guerre d'Indochine*, 238–40.

73. Law of 8 March 1950, cited in Dalloz, *La guerre d'Indochine*, 166.

74. *Regards*, special issue, "Henri Martin, marin de France," 20 October 1950; *Regards*, special issue, "Henri Martin, marin de la liberté," 22 February 1950, supplement to issue 340; *La Défense*, special issue, July 1952.

75. Jacques Prévert dedicated his poem "Entendez-vous, gens du Vietnam" to Martin, reprinted in Jean-Paul Sartre et al., *L'Affaire Henri Martin* (Paris: Gallimard, 1953); Raymond Lavigne published a book of twelve poems about the affair in *Poèmes pour Henri Martin* (Paris: Pierre Seghers, 1951); Serge Nigg and François

Monod wrote the "Cantate pour Henri Martin," cited in Ruscio, *Les communistes français et la guerre d'Indochine*, 279; and Maurice Morelly wrote the text for a song about Martin and Raymonde Dien, cited in Ruscio, *Les communistes français et la guerre d'Indochine*, 278.

76. Claude Martin and Henri Delmas, *Drame à Toulon*. According to Ted Freeman's foreword to a 1998 re-edition of the script, the play was performed some three hundred times to a total audience of one hundred thousand (Exeter: University of Exeter Press, 1998).

77. The committee was headed by André Marty and was involved in many of the aforementioned initiatives as well as publishing pamphlets, including the small booklet *Pour la libération d'Henri Martin* (Société nationale des entreprises de guerre, undated), BDIC O pièce 41398.

78. Jean-Paul Sartre et al., *L'Affaire Henri Martin* (Paris: Gallimard, 1953). Hélène Parmelin, a member of the PCF, also published *Matricule 2078: L'Affaire Henri Martin* (Paris: Les Éditeurs Français réunis) in 1953.

79. Alain Ruscio has suggested that Parmelin was heavily guided by the party while writing the book, and by André Marty in particular, who is widely acknowledged as having played a key role in promoting the affair; *Les communistes français et la guerre d'Indochine*, 271.

80. Those interested in a more detailed analysis of the chronology of remembrance should consult Serge Tignère's doctoral thesis. Serge Tignères, "La guerre d'Indochine et l'opinion publique française: Mémoire et histoire," PhD diss., Université de Toulouse-Le Mirail, 1999." Ruscio and Tignères also provide a very detailed periodization covering 1954 to 1995 in *Dien Bien Phu: Mythes et réalités, 1954–2004. Cinquante ans de passions françaises*.

81. This is not to say that commentary was limited to these three actors but rather that they became de facto representatives of the veteran community. Other veterans, including Pierre Langlais, Jacques Massu, and Raoul Salan, were also frequently quoted and interviewed, but the trio of Bigeard, Schoendoerffer, and de Galard was front and center.

82. As Pierre Journoud states, "public statements about Dien Bien Phu were monopolized, and in some ways confiscated, by political and military strategists who needed to justify their tragic decisions, and then later by the prominent figures of Dien Bien Phu, led by colonel Langlais and Bigeard." "Dien Bien Phu: Du témoignage à l'histoire," in Journoud and Hugues Tertrais, eds., *1954–2004: La bataille de Dien Bien Phu entre histoire et mémoire* (Paris and Saint-Denis: Société française d'histoire d'outre-mer, 2004), 213.

83. Henri Navarre, *Agonie de l'Indochine, 1953–1954* (Paris: Plon, 1956).

84. The piastre was set at seventeen francs following the end of the Second World War, but the going rate in Asia was between seven and ten francs. Transferring funds to the metropole thus allowed for tidy profits to be made on the exchange; since such transferals required permission, there was an unofficial system of "rewards" for certain people. This fraudulent system was not exposed until 1953 when a report was published attacking several high-ranking government officials.

85. The first volume of Delpey's first book, *Les soldats de la boue,* was actually published during the war itself in 1950. Bergot's *Deuxième classe à Dien Bien Phu* was published in 1964, the first of an extensive body of work that includes over a dozen books on Indochina alone.

86. *Cinq colonnes à la une,* Channel 1, 8 May 1964, INA.

87. See "Le toubib n'oublie pas Dien-Bien-Phu," *Minute,* 22 May 1964.

88. Geneviève de Galard, "Dien Bien Phu à la télévision: Lettre ouverte à Henri de Turenne," *Le Figaro,* 4–5 February 1984.

89. "Dix ans après Dien-Bien-Phu: La nouvelle guerre du Vietnam connaît une brusque accélération," *Le Monde,* 6 May 1964; "Dix ans après Dien-Bien-Phu...Le Vietcong se déchaine contre les Américains," *Combat,* 4 May 1964.

90. Among his works are *Street without Joy* (first published 1961) and *Viet-Nam Witness* (first published 1966).

91. Pierre Brocheux, "La mémoire contre l'histoire: L'Affaire Boudarel 1991–1997," paper presented at conference, "Decolonisations, Loyalties and Nations: Perspectives on the Wars of Independence in Vietnam, Indonesia, France and the Netherlands," Amsterdam, 2001.

92. *Journal officiel de la République française,* Débats de l'Assemblée nationale, 22 October 1986, 5116. This statement is reprinted nearly verbatim in his *De la brousse à la jungle* (Paris: Hachette, 1994), 223.

93. Jean-Yves Alquier et al., *Chant funèbre pour Pnom Penh et Saigon* (Paris: SPL, 1975).

94. Général d'Armée Bernard Lemattre, "Vers une réhabilitation des anciens combattants d'Indochine?" *L'Épaulette* no. 89 (1987), 7.

95. These included the election of Socialist François Mitterrand as president in 1981 and the subsequent reaction of the political right and extreme right, the rapid rise in popularity of the latter, and an attendant increase in emphasis on military and conservative values.

96. Ruscio and Tignères, *Dien Bien Phu: Mythes et réalités,* 325.

97. Robert Bonnafous, "Les prisonniers de guerre du corps expéditionnaire français en Extrême-Orient dans les camps Viet-minh (1945–1954)," PhD diss., Université Paul Valéry, 1985.

98. "Loi no. 89–1013 du 31 décembre 1989 portant création du statut de prisonnier du Viet-Minh," *Journal officiel de la République française,* 3 January 1990, 63. Transcripts of the debate in the National Assembly over the creation of this status are available in the *Journal officiel,* Débats de l'Assemblée nationale, 18 December 1989, 6762–71.

99. Some four hundred veterans visited Vietnam in 1993 alone. Journoud and Tertrais, *Paroles de Dien Bien Phu,* 274; they in turn cite *Le Figaro* of 7–8 May 1994.

100. The Institut d'histoire du temps présent did however hold a conference in 1995 on the Indochina wars from 1945 to 1975, the proceedings of which were edited by Charles-Robert Ageron and Philippe Devillers in *Les guerres d'Indochine de 1945 à 1975: Actes de la table ronde tenue à l'IHTP 6–7 février 1995* (Paris: IHTP, 1996). In honor of the fiftieth anniversary of the end of the war there was also a tripartite

conference in Paris, Beijing, and Hanoi as well as a day-long conference on the subject of "The Henri Martin Affair and the Struggle against the Indochina War."

101. Nicola Cooper, "Dien Bien Phu—Fifty Years On," *Modern and Contemporary France* 12, no. 4 (2004), 454.

102. Ibid., 453. The reference to the "shared memory" appears in Alain Barluet, "L'Asie bucolique a repris ses droits sur le champ de bataille," *Le Figaro,* 7 May 2004.

103. Barluet, "L'Asie bucolique a repris ses droits."

104. For more on Vietnamese commemoration, including the events of 2004, see the conclusion.

105. Decree no. 2005-547, 26 May 2005.

106. Pierre Schoendoerffer, *Là-haut, un roi au-dessus des nuages* (2004); and Rithy Panh, *Un barrage contre le Pacifique* (2006).

107. Mohammed Harbi and Benjamin Stora, *La guerre d'Algérie, 1954–2004: La fin de l'amnésie* (Paris: Robert Laffont, 2004); Amédée Thévenet, *La guerre d'Indochine racontée par ceux qui l'ont vécue: Un devoir de mémoire assumé ensemble* (Paris: France-Empire, 2001). The comparison of these two works cannot be taken too far given that the former is a scholarly publication while the latter is not.

108. Thévenet, *La guerre d'Indochine racontée par ceux qui l'ont vécue,* 17.

109. "Objet: Commémorations du 60e anniversaire de la fin de la guerre d'Indochine," *Maolen info* no. 107 (2014), 3.

110. "Indochine: Des territoires et des hommes, 1856–1956," Musée de l'armée, 16 October 2013 to 26 January 2014. An overview of the exhibit can be found online at www.musee-armee.fr/ExpoIndochine/index.html. An exhibit catalogue supplemented with scholarly articles on the era of French Indochina was published by Éditions Gallimard in 2013.

CHAPTER 2: REMEMBRANCE AND REHABILITATION

Parts of this chapter originally appeared in *Hagar: Studies in Culture, Polity, and Identities* 9, no. 2 (2010), 30–48.

1. Michel Bodin, *Le dictionnaire de la guerre d'Indochine, 1945–1954* (Paris: Commission française d'histoire militaire; Institut de stratégie comparée; Economica, 2004), 168–69.

2. See Antoine Prost, *Les anciens combattants et la société française, 1914–1939,* 3 vols. (Paris: Presses de la Fondation nationale des Sciences politiques, 1977).

3. The FNACA was originally created to compensate for the fact that veterans of the Algerian War were not eligible for membership in the formal veterans' organizations because of the status of the conflict as a police action rather than a war. Membership was later extended to veterans of the campaigns in Morocco and Tunisia. For more on the FNACA and the memory of the Algerian War, see Martin Evans, "Rehabilitating the Traumatized War Veteran: The Case of French Conscripts from the Algerian War, 1954–1962," in Evans and Ken Lunn, eds., *War and Memory in the Twentieth Century* (Oxford, NY: Berg, 1997), 73–85; Claude Liauzu,

"Le contingent entre silence et discours ancien combatant," in Jean-Pierre Rioux, ed., *La guerre d'Algérie et les Français* (Paris: Fayard, 1990), 509–16; and Frédéric Rouyard, "La bataille du 19 mars," in the same volume, 545–52.

4. The Amicale des anciens de Dien Bien Phu disbanded in 2004. The ANAPI, however, is still in existence; for more on its commemorative activities see Nicolas Séradin, "Les anciens prisonniers français de la guerre d'Indochine dans l'espace public: De l'affaire Boudarel à la reconnaissance mémorielle," *Modern and Contemporary France* 19, no. 1 (2011), 17–36. His doctoral thesis addresses the activism of Indochina veterans in greater detail. "Les anciens combattants de la guerre d'Indochine, sociabilités et écritures de l'histoire," Université de Rennes 2, 2015.

5. This distinction is shared with the ANAPI, founded in 1985 with the objective of gaining greater recognition of the experiences of former prisoners.

6. "Statuts de 1988," insert in *Bulletin de l'ANAI* no. 1 (1988), 1.

7. The complexity of the conflict is further illustrated by Ho Chi Minh's own combination of nationalist, communist, and anticolonial rhetoric. A nationalist who opposed the injustices of the colonial state, Ho's demands for reform in Indochina went unheeded by members of the French government, including Minister of Colonies Albert Sarraut. As a result he turned first to the French Socialist Party (SFIO) in 1919 and then to the French Communist Party (PCF) after its creation in 1920, drawn by the prominence of anticolonialism in party ideology. He went on to found the Indochinese Communist Party (ICP) in 1930, and the Communist-led Viet Minh in 1941, which also (initially) included noncommunists.

8. Guy Simon, "Éditorial: Drapeaux Rouges," *Bulletin de l'ANAI* no. 2 (2000), 3.

9. Neither the ANAI headquarters nor the National Library of France have the full run of the *Bulletin;* as a result I focus primarily on the period from 1977 to 2012. Given that commemorative activity centered on the Indochina War (and veterans' involvement in it) increased steadily after 1975 and the consolidation of communist control over Vietnam, the available publication run is more than sufficient to support the arguments made here.

10. This is according to President Hélène Bastid in "Allocution de la Présidente, Assemblée générale du 8 mars 1980," *Bulletin de l'ANAI* no. 2 (1980), 1.

11. Though still approximate, the best translation of the group's name is "Indochinese Remembrance."

12. His six years in Indochina were spent as a lieutenant with the twenty-second Régiment d'infanterie coloniale, and in Algeria he headed the Commando parachutiste d'Extrême-Orient.

13. Guy Simon, "Le dix millième adhérent de l'ANAI," *Bulletin de l'ANAI* no. 4 (1990), back cover. It experienced a decline from the mid-1990s: there were 9,000 members in 1995 and 6,700 in 2006. Statistics cited in the association's *Rapport d'activité 2006*.

14. "Historique et actualité de l'ANAI," information sheet distributed by the ANAI, personal copy, undated.

15. This is not uncommon for veterans' organizations; all of the First World War veterans' groups surveyed by Antoine Prost have similar articles in their constitutions,

though this does not exclude the groups having particular political leanings. Prost, *Les anciens combattants et la société française*.

16. Guy Simon, "Éditorial," *Bulletin de l'ANAI* no. 4 (2004), 3.

17. Guy Simon, "Éditorial: 9 mars–30 avril," *Bulletin de l'ANAI* no.1 (2001), 3. The numbers presented by Simon are difficult to confirm as is often the case with statistics on refugees and state-directed executions and internment. However, his statistics are comparable to other sources: see Marek Sliwinski, *Le génocide Khmer Rouge: Une analyse démographique* (Paris: L'Harmattan, 1995); and W. Courtland Robinson, *Terms of Refuge: The Indochinese Exodus and the International Response* (New York: Zed Books, 1998). The statistics of Vietnamese killed or imprisoned by the Communist regime are more difficult to ascertain; the least conservative estimate is that of Stéphane Courtois in the controversial *Livre noir du communisme: Crimes, terreur, répression* (Paris: Laffont, 1997): one million dead.

18. "Rapport d'activité 2005," *Bulletin de l'ANAI* no. 6 (2006), 5.

19. "Rapport d'activité 2001," *Bulletin de l'ANAI* no. 2 (2002), 21.

20. "Annexe au rapport d'activité," *Bulletin de l'ANAI* no. 2 (1990), 18.

21. Guy Simon, "Lettre aux anciens d'Indochine," *Bulletin de l'ANAI* no. 2 (1986), 2.

22. Guy Simon, "Éditorial: La place d'un homme," *Bulletin de l'ANAI* no. 5 (2006), 3. In an interview with the author (19 March 2007) Simon argued that the French Communists had been given an undue amount of influence over national education during the period of the provisional government following the Second World War, and that this had only encouraged leftist tendencies among teachers and educators.

23. Veterans of the Algerian War have pursued the same objective; see Evans, "Rehabilitating the Traumatized War Veteran," 76.

24. Hélène Bastid, "Allocution de la Présidente," *Bulletin de l'ANAI* no. 2 (1985), 1.

25. Guy Simon, "Éditorial," *Bulletin de l'ANAI* no.1 (2001), 3.

26. Bastid, "Allocution de la Présidente," 1.

27. For more on the Japanese takeover and its significance, see Pierre Brocheux and Daniel Hémery, *Indochina: An Ambiguous Colonization* (Berkeley and Los Angeles: University of California Press, 2009), 336–55. Chizuru Namba's *Français et japonais en Indochine (1940–1945)* (Paris: Karthala, 2012) presents an extended study of this period based on French and Japanese archives.

28. "Indochine d'hier et d'aujourd'hui," *Bulletin de l'ANAI* no.1 (1980), 6.

29. Ibid., 7.

30. "Cérémonies commémoratives du 9 mars 1945,"*Bulletin de l'ANAI* no. 1 (1985), 4.

31. "Indochine d'hier et d'aujourd'hui," *Bulletin de l'ANAI* no.1 (1980), 7.

32. René Poujade, *L'Indochine dans la sphère de coprospérité japonaise de 1940 à 1945* (Paris: L'Harmattan, 2007), 177.

33. T. G. Ashplant, Graham Dawson, and Michael Roper, eds., *The Politics of War Memory and Commemoration* (London and New York: Routledge, 2000), 51.

The focus here is on Portugal, but the concept is equally applicable to the politics of memory of the Indochina War.

34. Guy Simon, "Éditorial: Diên Biên Phu," *Bulletin de l'ANAI* no. 4 (2003), 3.

35. The emphasis on the pedagogical value of commemoration is obviously not unique to the ANAI; for more on the pedagogical value of military commemoration in France, see Prost, *Les anciens combattants et la société française*, vol. 3.

36. Simon, "Lettre aux anciens d'Indochine," 2.

37. "Inhumation d'un soldat inconnu d'Indochine au cimetière Notre Dame de Lorette," *Bulletin de l'ANAI* no. 20 (1977), 7.

38. "Rapport moral," *Bulletin de l'ANAI* no. 2 (1980), 8.

39. Hélène Bastid, "Le mot de la Présidente," *Bulletin de l'ANAI* no. 3 (1980), 1.

40. "Retour en France du corps du soldat inconnu d'Indochine," *Bulletin de l'ANAI* no. 2 (1980), 15. Attempts to locate archival records on the governmental end of this negotiation were fruitless.

41. The degree of significance accorded to the association by the government is further indicated by a 1981 letter from President Valéry Giscard-d'Estaing to Hélène Bastid agreeing to preside over a ceremony organized by the ANAI to honor the soldiers who died in Indochina between 1858 and 1955, and promising to work to repatriate bodies from eight cemeteries in Indochina. Letter dated 22 January 1981, reprinted in the *Bulletin de l'ANAI* no. 1 (1981), 3.

42. "Les cérémonies en l'honneur du Soldat Inconnu d'Indochine," *Bulletin de l'ANAI* no. 3 (1980), 12.

43. Ibid., 13.

44. For more on the construction of the various stages of the memorial as well as the numerous associations involved in its creation, please see chapter 4 on official commemoration.

45. Letter from François Léotard and Jean Pascal to General André Biard, 15 March 1982, AMF 87 W 3.

46. Letter from P.F. to François Léotard, 21 November 1981, AMF 87 W 3.

47. Ibid.

48. Letter from François Léotard to Hélène Bastid, 21 November 1981, AMF 87 W 3.

49. Unsigned; likely François Léotard. "Réflections sur la lettre de Mme Bastid," handwritten notes attached to letter dated 3 March 1983 from Léotard to Hélène Bastid, AMF 87 W 3.

50. Guy Simon, "Éditorial," *Bulletin de l'ANAI* no. 3 (2003), 3.

51. 8 juin 2006, *Bulletin de l'ANAI* no. 5 (2006), 33.

52. "Rapport d'activité 2005," 5.

53. Simon, "Éditorial," *Bulletin de l'ANAI* no. 3 (1989), 3.

54. "He was admittedly a Vietnamese patriot, but he was also responsible for a dictatorial regime that perpetrated crimes against humanity and for the horrors experienced by these prisoners of the Viet Minh whom we are talking about today." *Journal officiel de la République française*, 18 December 1989, 6762.

55. Guy Simon, "A propos du centenaire de H," *Bulletin de l'ANAI* no. 1 (1990), 10.

56. "Rapport d'activité 1990," *Bulletin de l'ANAI* no. 2 (1991), 7.

57. Simon, "Éditorial: 20 juillet, une date pour qui?" *Bulletin de l'ANAI* no. 3 (2003), 3.

58. "Bibliographie," *Bulletin de l'ANAI* no. 1 (1996), 24.

59. Interview with General Guy Simon, 19 March 2007.

60. Claude Baylé, *Prisonnier au camp 113: Le camp de Boudarel* (Paris: Perrin, 1991); Marc Charuel, *L'Affaire Boudarel* (Paris: Éditions du Rocher, 1991). Charuel was a journalist at the conservative *Valeurs actuelles* when he published the book.

61. Antoine Cabaton, "La France en Indochine," in *Colonies Françaises* (1932). In *Bulletin de l'ANAI* no. 4 (2000), 23.

62. J.F., "L'Histoire falsifiée," *Bulletin de l'ANAI* no. 1 (1984), 2.

63. "Activités de l'ANAI," *Bulletin de l'ANAI* no. 2 (1984), 2.

64. Further discussion of the reaction of the ANAI and others to Turenne's series can be found in chapter 7.

65. Advertisement for *Indochine: Alerte à l'histoire* in the *Bulletin de l'ANAI* no. 2 (1985), 13.

66. Académie des sciences d'outre-mer, Institut de l'Asie du sud-est, Association nationale des anciens d'Indochine, *Indochine: Alerte à l'histoire. Ni opprobre, ni oubli* (Paris: Académie des sciences d'outre-mer, 1985), 9.

67. Ibid., 373.

68. Alfred Sibert, "L'Évolution de l'encadrement politique et administratif de l'Indochine française," in *Indochine: Alerte à l'histoire*, 78.

69. René Charbonneau, "Le temps de méprises, mais non du mépris," in *Indochine: Alerte à l'histoire*, 84.

70. André Tessot, "La France en Indochine," *Bulletin de l'ANAI* no. 3 (1986), 8.

71. "Nécropole d'Indochine: Le programme de la journée," *Nice-Matin*, 19 January 1988.

72. "Indochine d'hier," special insert, *Bulletin de l'ANAI* no. 1 (1984), I.

73. "Loi no. 2005–158 du 23 février 2005 portant reconnaissance de la Nation et contribution nationale en faveur des Français rapatriés." Full text available at www.legifrance.gouv.fr.

74. For more on the controversies surrounding this law, see Romain Bertrand, *Mémoires d'empire: La controverse autour du "fait colonial"* (Paris: Éditions du Croquant, 2006).

75. "Les cérémonies en l'honneur du Soldat Inconnu d'Indochine," 6.

76. "Commémoration du 9 mars 1945," *Bulletin de l'ANAI* no. 2 (1981), 11.

77. "Discours de M. Jacques Chirac, Premier Ministre," *Bulletin de l'ANAI* no. 1 (1988), 13.

78. "Allocution de M. Jacques Chirac," *Bulletin de l'ANAI* no. 1 (1987), 5.

CHAPTER 3: FROM ACTIVISM TO REMEMBRANCE

1. Charles Fourniau, *Le Vietnam face à la guerre* (Paris: Éditions sociales, 1966), 32.

2. See chapter 1 for an overview of Martin and Dien's activism.

3. These connections are also highlighted by the ANAI in its attempt to depict a network promoting partisan misinformation. The ANAI published an attack on the ACVGI in 1992 linking it with the ARAC, with historians who propagate the idea that it was France that attacked the Viet Minh in 1945 and 1946 (several of whom are mentioned by name, including Philippe Devillers, Charles Fourniau, and Alain Ruscio), and with the AAFV, which the ANAI derides for its role in organizing events in Marseilles in honor of Ho Chi Minh in 1990. "L'UFAC et les porteurs de valises," *Bulletin de l'ANAI* no. 3 (1992), 17.

4. Longtime Communist mayor Jean-Pierre Brard (1984–2008) actually broke with the party in 1996 but continued to align himself with leftist coalitions.

5. This is not to suggest that these scholars were all reproducing the party line in their work but to acknowledge the impact of ideological and political affiliations on scholarly work.

6. For more on anticolonialism and antiwar activism, see the overview of the war in chapter 1.

7. Among them is Léo Figuères, then a member of the party's central committee and a journalist for *Avant-garde*, who went clandestinely to the DRV in early 1950 and met with Ho Chi Minh. He published a series of reports on the war and the climate in the DRV and upon his return published *Je reviens du Viet-Nam libre* (Paris: Éditions de la jeunesse, 1950), which demanded an end to the war.

8. Christopher Goscha makes the same argument in *Vietnam: Un état né de la guerre, 1945–1954* (Paris: Armand Colin, 2011), 13–14. The divide described here is similar to the cleavages within the American academic community on the subject of the Vietnam War.

9. Among the former are Jacques Dalloz, Bernard Fall, Jules Roy, Yves Gras, Michel Bodin, and Hugues Tertrais; among the latter, William Duiker, David Marr, Stein Tønnesson, Martin Shipway, Mark Atwood Lawrence, Eric Jennings, Christopher Goscha, and Fredrik Logevall.

10. In 2012 the IRSEA merged with another organization to become the Institut de Recherches Asiatiques (IrAsia).

11. Agathe Larcher-Goscha, "L'Enseignement et la recherche sur le Vietnam et l'Indochine à l'Université Denis Diderot-Paris VII: Expérience militante et militants d'expérience," unpublished article draft based on a paper given at a conference in honor of Charles Fourniau, "Hanoi-Paris-Aix-Hanoi: L'Itinéraire d'un historien français du Viêt-Nam," 24–25 October 2003. I am heavily indebted to Agathe Larcher-Goscha's work on the activist engagement of the scholars in question and to Christopher Goscha's biographies of them in his *Historical Dictionary of the Indochina War (1945–1954): An International and Interdisciplinary Approach* (Honolulu: University of Hawai'i Press, 2012), also available online at http://indochine.uqam.ca/.

12. These are far from the only programs and institutions: there is the National Institute for Asian Languages and Civilizations (INALCO; Institut national des langues et civilisations orientales); the Study Group on Contemporary Vietnam

(Groupe d'études sur le Vietnam contemporain) at the Paris Institute for Political Studies (Sciences Po); and the Institute for East Asian Studies (IAO; Institut d'Asie orientale), among others.

13. Jean Chesneaux specifically acknowledged this as early as 1971 in the introduction to *Tradition et révolution au Vietnam*, Jean Chesneaux, Georges Boudarel, and Daniel Hémery, eds. (Paris: Anthropos), 17. He states, "This volume brings together the work of authors who do not all subscribe to the same theoretical frameworks, or to the same ideology, and who do not necessarily share a common perspective on the relationship between intellectual life and social practices." Chesneaux, Daniel Hémery, Pierre Brocheux, Georges Boudarel, Philippe Devillers, Paul Mus, and Charles Fourniau all contributed to the volume.

14. Christopher Goscha addresses this theme in the introduction to *Vietnam: Un état né de la guerre*, 17–18.

15. Charles Fourniau, "Les contacts franco-vietnamiens de 1885 à 1896 en Annam et au Tonkin," PhD diss., Université de Provence, 1983. Part of this thesis was published as *Annam-Tonkin 1885–1896: Lettrés et paysans vietnamiens face à la conquête coloniale* (Paris: L'Harmattan, 1989). He pursued the theme of anticolonial resistance with *Vietnam: Domination coloniale et résistance nationale (1858–1914)* (Paris: Les Indes savantes, 2002).

16. Charles Fourniau, "Un patriote et un révolutionnaire exemplaire," in Léo Figuères, ed., *Ho Chi Minh, notre camarade: Souvenirs de militants français* (Paris: Éditions sociales, 1970), 77. Among the contributors to the volume were Henri Martin, Raymonde Dien, Madeleine Riffaud, and Jacques Duclos.

17. Ibid., 77.

18. Ibid., 79.

19. Fourniau, *Le Vietnam face à la guerre*, 57.

20. See, for example, "Faire tout notre possible," *Bulletin de l'AAFV* no. 23 (November 1969), 1–2; "Le trentième anniversaire de la fondation de la République démocratique du Vietnam," *Bulletin de l'AAFV* no. 15 (new series) (October 1975), 1–3. The association also published a supplement to the June 1973 issue (no. 7) on the conditions in the prisons in the South, which was heavily critical of the regime. It should be noted that the AAFV bulletin changed names several times (*Bulletin de l'AAFV, Bulletin intérieur de l'AAFV, Perspectives*); for the sake of simplicity I refer to it simply as the *Bulletin de l'AAFV*, or the *Bulletin*.

21. See, for example, Charles Fourniau, "Le trentième anniversaire de la fondation de la République Démocratique du Vietnam," *Bulletin intérieur de l'AAFV* no. 15 (1975), 1 and 3–7.

22. Charles Fourniau, "Journée d'information du 23 May 1992: Discours d'ouverture," *Bulletin de l'AAFV* no. 3 (June 1992), 4.

23. Charles Fourniau, *Le Vietnam que j'ai vu, 1960–2000* (Paris: Les Indes savantes, 2003), 242.

24. A number of other members of the AAFV have also received this honor, including Alain Ruscio, Hélène Luc, and Francis Gendreau as well as former Montreuil mayor Jean-Pierre Brard.

25. He has published an account of his time in Cambodia entitled *Cambodge, an I. Journal d'un témoin, 1979–1980* (Paris: Les Indes savantes, 2008). He has also refuted accusations that one had to be very close to the Vietnamese Communist Party in order to be granted such access—charges leveled at him by Olivier Todd in *L'Express* ("Génocides dans la joie")—in Alain Ruscio, *Nous et moi: Grandeurs et servitudes* (Paris: Tirésias, 2003), 240–41.

26. For his account of his relationship and break with the French Communist Party, see *Nous et moi*.

27. Alain Ruscio, "Merci, Charles," in *Charles Fourniau, 1921–2010: Un hommage* (AAFV, 2010), 26.

28. Alain Ruscio, *Les communistes français et la guerre d'Indochine, 1944–1954* (Paris: L'Harmattan, 1985). He addressed a similar subject in a two-part article cowritten with Charles Fourniau published in the *Cahiers d'histoire de l'Institut Maurice Thorez*. See "Le PCF et le déclenchement de la première guerre d'Indochine," no. 19 (1976) and no. 22 (1977).

29. *Dien Bien Phu: La fin d'une illusion* (Paris: L'Harmattan, 1986); *La guerre française d'Indochine* (Paris: Complexe, 1992); *La guerre "française" d'Indochine: Les sources de la connaissance. Bibliographie, filmographie, documents divers* (Paris: Les Indes savantes, 2002); with Serge Tignères, *Dien Bien Phu: Mythes et réalités, 1954–2004. Cinquante ans de passions françaises* (Paris: Les Indes savantes, 2005).

30. See Alain Ruscio, chapter 2, "La guerre impopulaire," *La guerre française d'Indochine* (Complexe, 1992), 93–132. Other work on public opinion and the antiwar movement includes "L'Opinion française et la guerre d'Indochine (1945–1954): Sondages et témoignages," *Vingtième siècle* no. 29 (January–March 1991), 35–45; "Dien Bien Phu: Du coup de génie à l'aberration, ou Comment les contemporains ont vécu l'ultime bataille de la Guerre française d'Indochine," in Pierre Lamant et al., eds., *La péninsule indochinoise et les Européens de la seconde moitié du XVIIIe siècle à 1954*. Issue of the *Revue française d'histoire d'outre-mer* 72, no. 268 (Paris: Société française d'histoire d'outre-mer, 1985); Alain Ruscio, ed., *L'Affaire Henri Martin et la lutte contre la guerre d'Indochine* (Paris: Le Temps des cerises, 2005).

31. Ruscio, *La guerre française d'Indochine* (Complexe, 1992), 175–76.

32. Ibid., 170.

33. "Appel: Non à Bigeard aux Invalides," nonabigeardauxinvalides.net (defunct website). It is available on Alain Ruscio's website, http://alain.ruscio.fr.

34. Ibid.

35. It should be noted that the proposal was delayed by the Sarkozy regime and then abandoned by the newly elected Hollande government.

36. He attacks this phenomenon directly in a volume coedited with Sébastien Jahan: *Histoire de la colonisation: Réhabilitations, falsifications et instrumentalisations* (Paris: Les Indes savantes, 2007).

37. The committee was presided over by Raymond Aubrac, Honorary Commissioner of the Republic, and Raphaël Vahé, ARAC president. Among the signatories of the original call for participants were Lucie Aubrac, Raymonde Dien, Madeleine

Riffaud, Henri Alleg, Léo Figuères, Albert Memmi, Daniel Hémery, and Pierre Vidal-Naquet.

38. The Paris conference was held on 21–22 November 2003, followed by Hanoi on 13–14 April 2004, and Beijing on 19–20 April. All three were primarily focused on the military and diplomatic aspects of the conflict, while Ruscio's conference focused on antiwar activism.

39. Ruscio, *L'Affaire Henri Martin et la lutte contre la guerre d'Indochine*.

40. He states that the "duty" to remember implies "a connotation of moralism, of quasi-mandatory respect," while memory work is focused on "advancing knowledge," which entails "a critical, even disrespectful, attitude." Ibid., 14.

41. Raymond Aubrac, "Préface: Désobéir, c'est le fait d'un homme libre . . . ," in Ruscio, *L'Affaire Henri Martin et la lutte contre la guerre d'Indochine*, 15. In addition to his role in the French Resistance, Aubrac played a minor but significant role in the Indochina War primarily as a political go-between. Among other things he hosted Ho Chi Minh at his home during the Fontainebleau negotiations.

42. Marc Chervel, *De la Résistance aux guerres coloniales* (Paris: L'Harmattan, 2001); Claude Collin, *De la Résistance à la guerre d'Indochine* (Paris: Les Indes savantes, 2011). Collin had previously produced a documentary entitled *Ralliés*, which chronicled the trajectories of three soldiers, including Albert Clavier, who abandoned the French Union forces to join the Viet Minh.

43. Alain Ruscio, "Une belle aventure humaine, un apport à l'histoire," in Collin, *De la Résistance à la guerre d'Indochine*, 8.

44. Goscha, *Historical Dictionary of the Indochina War*, 301.

45. It should be noted that Mus was also named director of education in French West Africa by the Vichy regime in the interim. As for the location of Mus's parachute drop Christopher Goscha claims it was southern Laos in his *Historical Dictionary of the Indochina War*, while Jacques Dalloz and Guy Moréchand state that it was Tonkin. Dalloz, *Dictionnaire de la guerre d'Indochine, 1945–1954* (Paris: Armand Colin, 2006), 165; Moréchand, "II. Paul Mus (1902–1969)," *Bulletin de l'Ecole française d'Extrême-Orient* no. 57 (1970), 26.

46. Christopher Goscha, "'So what did you learn from war?' Violent Decolonization and Paul Mus's Search for Humanity," *South East Asia Research* 20, no. 4 (December 2012), 580.

47. Ibid., 569–93.

48. He would subsequently receive a joint appointment with Yale University.

49. These articles include "Les Vietnamiens aussi sont des hommes: Il faut reprendre notre information à la base" of 11 November 1949, and "Un témoignage irrécusable sur l'Indochine: Non, pas ça!" of 12 August 1949. For more on Mus, his writings, and his stance during the Indochina War, see Christopher Goscha, "'Qu'as-tu appris à la guerre?' Paul Mus en quête de l'humain . . . ," in David Chandler and Christopher Goscha, eds., *L'Espace d'un regard: L'Asie de Paul Mus* (Paris: Les Indes savantes, 2006), 273–94.

50. David Chandler, "Paul Mus (1902–1969): A Biographical Sketch," *Journal of Vietnamese Studies* 4, no. 1 (Winter 2009), 175.

51. Paul Mus, *Viet-Nam: Sociologie d'une guerre* (Paris: Seuil, 1952).
52. Philippe Devillers, *Histoire du Viet-Nam de 1940 à 1952* (Paris: Seuil, 1952).
53. Philippe Devillers and Jean Lacouture, *La fin d'une guerre: Indochine 1954* (Paris: Seuil, 1960); and *Viet Nam: De la guerre française à la guerre américaine* (Paris: Seuil, 1969).
54. Philippe Devillers, *Vingt ans, et plus, avec le Viet-Nam: Souvenirs et écrits, 1945–1969* (Paris: Les Indes savantes, 2010), 35, 40, 45.
55. Ibid., 35.
56. Ibid., 8.
57. Devillers, *Histoire du Viêt-Nam de 1940 à 1952*.
58. In fact Bernard Fall states as much in his review of Mus's book. See *Pacific Affairs* 27, no. 2 (June 1954), 190–91.
59. Devillers, *Vingt ans, et plus, avec le Viet-Nam*, 315.
60. Philippe Devillers, *Paris-Saïgon-Hanoï: Les archives de la guerre, 1944–1947* (Paris: Gallimard, 1988).
61. Jean Chesneaux, *Contribution à l'histoire de la nation vietnamienne* (Paris: Éditions sociales, 1955).
62. The department would later add *History* to its title, becoming the department of *Géographie, Histoire, et Sciences de la société* (GHSS).
63. Larcher-Goscha, "L'Enseignement et la recherche sur le Vietnam et l'Indochine à l'Université Denis Diderot-Paris VII."
64. Ibid., 5.
65. Ibid., 10.
66. Ibid., 10. Other prominent intellectuals who were members of the Indochina Solidarity Front include Laurent Schwartz, Pierre Vidal-Naquet, and François Maspéro.
67. Agathe Larcher-Goscha uses the term in "L'Enseignement et la recherche sur le Vietnam et l'Indochine à l'Université Denis Diderot-Paris VII."
68. For an overview of the field of Vietnamese and Southeast Asian studies in France since 1990, see Christian Culas and Jean-François Klein, "Introduction: Vingt ans de recherches sur le Việt Nam (1990–2010)," *Moussons* nos. 13–14 (2009), 5–26.
69. Pierre Brocheux and Daniel Hémery, "Le Vietnam exsangue," *Le Monde diplomatique* (March 1980), 15–16.
70. Larcher-Goscha, "L'Enseignement et la recherche sur le Vietnam et l'Indochine à l'Université Denis Diderot-Pari VII."
71. Georges Boudarel, ed., *La bureaucratie au Vietnam* (Paris: L'Harmattan, 1983).
72. Georges Boudarel, Pierre Brocheux, Daniel Hémery, Nguyen Duc Nhuan, Nguyen Van Nguyen, Camille Scalabrino, François Thierry, Tran Van Xuan, and Trinh Van Thao, "Liminaire," in Boudarel, *La bureaucratie au Vietnam*, 7–8.
73. Georges Boudarel, *Cent fleurs écloses dans la nuit du Vietnam: Communisme et dissidence, 1954–1956* (Paris: Jacques Bertoin, 1991). A focal point of the study is the Nhan Van-Giai Pham affair, in which the state shut down two newspapers

calling for freedom of speech and other civil liberties, and exiled or executed those associated with the publications.

74. Daniel Hémery, "Aux origines des guerres d'indépendance vietnamiennes: Pouvoir colonial et phénomène communiste en Indochine avant la Seconde Guerre mondiale," *Le Mouvement social* no. 101 (October–December 1977), 3–35. He also published a monograph on the subject entitled *Révolutionnaires vietnamiens et pouvoir colonial en Indochine: Communistes, trotskistes, nationalistes à Saigon de 1932 à 1937* (Paris: François Maspéro, 1975).

75. See, for example, "Les communistes et les paysans dans la révolution vietnamienne," in Brocheux et al., eds., *L'Asie du Sud-Est: Révoltes, réformes, révolutions* (Lille: Presses universitaires de Lille, 1981), 247–69; "L'Économie de la Résistance vietnamienne, 1945–1954," in Charles-Robert Ageron, Philippe Devillers, et al., eds., *Les guerres d'Indochine de 1945 à 1975*, in *Les Cahiers de l'IHTP* no. 34 (1996), 77–92; and *Du conflit d'Indochine aux conflits indochinois* (Paris: Complexe, 2000).

76. Pierre Brocheux, "Retour sur l'Indochine, retour sur soi," *Revue française d'outre-mer* 80, no. 300 (1993), 479–87; "The Death and Resurrection of Indo-China in French Memory," *European Review* 8, no. 1 (2000), 59–64; "La mémoire contre l'histoire: L'Affaire Boudarel 1991–1997," paper presented at "Decolonisations, Loyalties, and Nations: Perspectives on the Wars of Independence in Vietnam, Indonesia, France, and the Netherlands," Amsterdam, 2001.

77. Daniel Hémery, *Ho Chi Minh, de l'Indochine au Vietnam* (Paris: Gallimard, 1990); Pierre Brocheux, *Ho Chi Minh* (Paris: Presses de Sciences Po, 2000); and *Ho Chi Minh: Du révolutionnaire à l'icône* (Paris: Payot, 2003).

78. Pierre Brocheux and Daniel Hémery, *Indochine: La colonisation ambigüe* (Paris: La Découverte, 1994). English translation by Ly Lan Dill Klein et al., *Indochina: An Ambiguous Colonization 1858–1954* (Berkeley and Los Angeles: University of California Press, 2009).

79. Although I refer to the arguments as belonging to both authors, Brocheux was primarily responsible for this chapter.

80. Brocheux and Hémery, *Indochina: An Ambiguous Colonization*, 361.

81. Brocheux proposes a similar argument in his more recent study of contemporary Vietnam. Pierre Brocheux, *Histoire du Vietnam contemporain: La nation résiliente* (Paris: Fayard, 2011). See in particular part 3, chapter 1, "L'Indépendance dans la douleur, la première guerre d'Indochine, 1945–1954," 139–53.

82. Daniel Hémery, "La guerre d'Indochine," in Claude Liauzu, ed., *Le dictionnaire de la colonisation française* (Paris: Larousse, 2007), 241. An essay published in 1995 examines this "neocolonial project" in greater detail and argues that this framework contributed more to the outbreak of the war than any unilateral decisions made on the ground by French political or military leaders. See Daniel Hémery, "Asie du Sud-Est, 1945: Vers un nouvel impérialisme colonial? Le projet indochinois de la France au lendemain de la Seconde Guerre mondiale," in Charles-Robert Ageron, ed., *Décolonisations européennes: Actes du Colloque international Décolonisations comparées, Aix-en-Provence, 30 septembre–3 octobre 1993* (Aix-en-Provence: Université de Provence, 1995), 65–84.

83. Such organizations included the Republican Veterans' Association (ARAC) and the National Association of Repatriates from Indochina (ANRI; Association nationale des rapatriés d'Indochine), which lobbied for negotiation with the Viet Minh and an end to the war. The counterpart of these organizations for soldiers and veterans of the Algerian War is the National Federation of Veterans of Algeria, Morocco and Tunisia (FNACA).

84. Norman Ingram, *The Politics of Dissent: Pacifism in France, 1919–1939* (New York: Oxford University Press, 1991); for a synopsis, see his entry on pacifism in Lawrence Kritzman, ed., *The Columbia History of Twentieth-Century French Thought* (New York: Columbia University Press, 2003), 76–78.

85. Georges Vidal, *La grande illusion? Le parti communiste français et la défense nationale à l'époque du Front populaire (1934–1939)* (Lyon: Presses universitaires de Lyon, 2006), 64. For more on the ARAC in the interwar period and particularly its paramilitary activities, see Chris Millington, "Communist Veterans and Paramilitarism in 1920s France: The *Association républicaine des anciens combattants*," *Journal of War and Culture Studies*, forthcoming.

86. This was made possible by the opening of the country to greater tourism as part of the *doi moi* reforms.

87. In an article honoring founders Henri Barbusse and Paul Vaillant-Couturier, ARAC president Georges Doussin argued that the collapsing Communist regimes of Eastern Europe were corrupt and did not reflect the same values as those maintained by the ARAC. "Hommage à Henri Barbusse et Paul Vaillant-Couturier au cimetière du Père-Lachaise à Paris," *Le Réveil des combattants* no. 552 (October 1991), 16–17. An undated history of the association states that the association opposed policies of foreign intervention at the time of the Prague Spring; "Bref résumé de l'histoire de l'ARAC," 8. CHT, Fonds ARAC, carton 17.

88. "Négocier avec ceux contre lesquels on se bat," *Le Réveil des combattants* no. 95 (September 1953).

89. Albert Duchesne, "Paix au Viet-Nam" (March–April 1947), cited in *L'ARAC 1917–2007: Combattants pour la vie, des voix pour l'espoir* (Paris: Le Temps des cerises, 2008), 200–201.

90. Albert Duchesne, "Arrêt du massacre: Reprise de pourparlers. Pour conserver l'Indochine à l'Union française" (January 1947), cited in *L'ARAC 1917–2007: Combattants pour la vie, des voix pour l'espoir*, 198–99.

91. Jean Bresson, "Un des aspects douloureux de la guerre au Viet-Nam," *Le Réveil des combattants* no. 102 (April 1954). Bresson was then the secretary general for the National Association of Repatriates from Indochina (ANRI)—see earlier note.

92. "Le cessez-le-feu en Indochine, victoire de la paix," *Le Réveil des combattants* (August 1954).

93. Roger Maria, "Vietnam," *Le Réveil des combattants* no. 427 (May 1981), 7.

94. Jean Marrane, "La guerre d'Indochine," *Le Réveil des combattants* no. 495 (January 1987), 11. Marrane had a personal connection with the topic as he was an envoy of the French Communist Party to the DRV from 1950 to 1953.

95. This was the supplement to the June–July 2009 issue. The first five supplements covered the First World War, the Algerian War, the Resistance (two issues), and the Spanish Civil War.

96. Paul Markidès, "Édito," *Le Réveil des combattants* no. 754 (June–July 2009), Cahier mémoire, "La guerre d'Indochine," 13.

97. Guy Lamothe, for example, served as both the president of the ACVGI and the national vice president of the ARAC in the late 1980s and early 1990s.

98. "Guerre d'Indochine (1945–1954): Une association est née," *Le Réveil des combattants* nos. 501–2 (July–August 1987), 7.

99. Guy Lamothe, "Indochine toujours présente," *Le Réveil des combattants* no. 543 (January 1991), 21–22.

100. Guy Lamothe, "Guerre d'Indochine: La route qui a conduit à Genève n'était pas une voie royale," *Le Réveil des combattants* nos. 659–60 (June–July 2001), 7.

101. "Colonialisme: Pour la vérité historique. Abrogation de la loi du 23 février 2005!" *Le Réveil des combattants* nos. 739–40 (February–March 2008).

102. "L'ACVGI rendra hommage au soldat inconnu le 20 Juillet à 11 H 30," *Le Réveil des combattants* no. 594 (July–August 1995), 6.

103. See chapter 2.

104. Jean-Jacques Beucler, "Boudarel: Suite," *Le Figaro*, 7 May 1992.

105. References to Henri Martin and Léo Figuères, respectively.

106. Arnaud Folch, "Comment le PC noyaute les anciens combattants d'Indochine," *Minute-La France*, 13–19 May 1992.

107. "L'UFAC et les porteurs de valises," *Bulletin de l'ANAI* no. 3 (1992), 17.

108. The ANAI was one group that opposed the admission of the ACVGI to the UFAC. See "L'UFAC et les porteurs de valises," *Bulletin de l'ANAI* no. 3 (1992), 17.

109. "Tempête à l'UFAC," *Le Journal des combattants*, 27 June 1992.

110. Louis Gohin, "Sur la guerre française au Viet-Nam (relativement à une exposition)," *Indochine vérité et droits* no. 6 (1995), 6–7. This is the ACVGI's bulletin.

111. Ibid., 7.

112. "Exposé des motifs discuté et adopté par l'Assemblée générale constitutive du 31 mai 1961," *Bulletin de l'AAFV* no. 1 (June 1961), 1.

113. Association d'amitié franco-vietnamienne, *Une histoire partagée: 40 ans de solidarité avec le peuple vietnamien, 1961–2001*, supplement to the *Bulletin de l'AAFV* no. 38 (June 2001), 5.

114. A 1960 report to the secretariat of the central committee clarifies the relationship between the party and the soon-to-be created AAFV:

> The PCF will actively support the activities of the France-Vietnam Friendship Association that is in the process of being created in France. [. . .] This Association must contribute to informing the public about the peaceful construction process undertaken by the DRV, to developing friendship between the French and Vietnamese people, to establishing a fruitful relationship between our two countries, and to defending peace in Southeast Asia and the rest of the world.

Élie Mignot, "Note au secrétariat du Comité central. Objet: Le Viet-Nam," 10 October 1960. ADSSD, Fonds PCF 264 J 7, fonds Gaston Plissonnier. The association itself also acknowledges that it has been "marked by the Left and [is] close to the Communist Party"; *Une histoire partagée: 40 ans de solidarité avec le peuple vietnamien: 1961–2001* (AAFV, June 2001), 37.

115. "Hommage à Alice Kahn," supplement to the *Bulletin de l'AAFV* nos. 22–23 (November 1997), 1.

116. Among them are historians Léon Vandermeersch, Philippe Devillers, and Alain Ruscio and public figures and activists Raymonde Dien, Madeleine Riffaud, and Raymond Aubrac.

117. Pierre Vermeulin, "L'AAFV, un chemin," *Bulletin de l'AAFV* no. 77 (April 2011), 24–25.

118. "25 ans de vie et de luttes au Vietnam, 25 ans d'activité de l'AAFV," *Bulletin de l'AAFV* no. 68 (June 1986), 4.

119. Ibid., 5.

120. "L'Horreur des prisons saïgonnaises," *Bulletin de l'AAFV* no. 28 (June 1971), 7; special issue on the conditions in South Vietnamese detention camps, supplement to the *Bulletin de l'AAFV* no. 7 (June 1973).

121. The AAFV investigated the use of chemical warfare, resulting in a dossier called "Chemical Warfare in the South" in 1963. A pamphlet entitled "The Franco-Vietnamese Friendship Association Accuses ... American Crimes in Vietnam" was published in 1970 and went through two print runs as the first thirty thousand copies were insufficient to meet demand. The association also contributed to a book entitled *The Black Book of American Crimes in Vietnam* (Fayard, 1970).

122. Report from the national committee, *Bulletin de l'AAFV* no. 26 (November 1970), 5–6.

123. The topics ranged from current events to Vietnamese culture. The dinner-debate held on 7 May 1963, for example, was a celebration of the 520th anniversary of the poet Nguyen Trai, while in July 1964 the topic was the tenth anniversary of the Geneva Accords. A list of themes is available in the AAFV booklet *Une histoire partagée: 40 ans de solidarité avec le peuple vietnamien*, 1961–2001; supplement to the *Bulletin de l'AAFV* no. 38 (June 2001), 50–51.

124. "Fonds documentaire," CID-Vietnam, www.cidvietnam.org.

125. Held at the Vietnamese Cultural Center 7–25 June 2014.

126. BCG, or Bacillus Calmette-Guérin, is a vaccine for tuberculosis.

127. Francis Gendreau, "Éditorial: De l'Indochine au Vietnam," *Bulletin de l'AAFV* no. 50 (July 2004), 2.

128. Romain Rolland was a writer, Nobel laureate, and renowned pacifist; Henri Barbusse, a First World War veteran, writer, pacifist, and cofounder of the ARAC; Victor Margueritte, a prominent writer and pacifist; and Andrée Viollis, a journalist and author of *SOS Indochine* (1935).

129. A number of the AAFV's founding members were in fact former members of the Action Committee, including Jean Chesneaux, Raymonde Dien, and Pastor

Maurice Voge. Information on all three groups taken from Alain Ruscio, "Des Français avec le Viêt Nam, avant 1961," *Bulletin de l'AAFV* no. 77 (April 2011), 8.

130. François Bilange, "Justin Godart et l'association France-Viêt-Nam" and "Justin Godart: Un homme dans son siècle," *Bulletin de l'AAFV* no. 38 (July 2001), 5–7; Léon Vandermeersch, "Andrée Viollis," *Bulletin de l'AAFV* no. 67 (October 2008), 19. Godart was a member of the Popular Front, who oversaw a commission of inquiry into the colonial system in Indochina, and a founding member of the AFV.

131. See chapter 6 on the Georges Boudarel affair.

132. Monique Chemillier-Gendreau, "Georges Boudarel ou l'esprit de résistance," *Bulletin de l'AAFV* no. 49 (April 2004), 22.

133. Ibid.

134. Boudarel is included on the membership list of the 1977 national committee. See *Bulletin de l'AAFV* no. 22 (October 1977), 12.

135. Albert Clavier, *De l'Indochine coloniale au Vietnam libre: Je ne regrette rien* (Paris: Les Indes savantes, 2008).

136. R.L., "Albert Clavier, une vie au singulier pluriel," *Bulletin de l'AAFV* no. 77 (April 2011), 31.

137. "Hommage au président Ho Chi Minh," *Bulletin de l'AAFV* no. 25 (June 1970), 3.

138. In a 1970 article, for example, Ho is referred to as "a great patriot who devoted his life to the independence of Vietnam, a leader loved by the Vietnamese people, whose highest virtues he embodied, and the brother of the French people." "Hommage au président Ho Chi Minh," *Bulletin de l'AAFV* no. 25 (June 1970), 3.

139. "Adieu au Président Ho Chi Minh," letter reprinted in the *Bulletin de l'AAFV* no. 23 (November 1969), 3.

140. "Centenaire du Président Ho Chi Minh," *Bulletin de l'AAFV* no. 87 (September 1990), 2.

141. "Centenaire du Président Ho Chi Minh: Ho Chi Minh et la France," *Bulletin de l'AAFV* no. 86 (April 1990), 2.

142. Charles Fourniau, "Faire notre possible," *Bulletin de l'AAFV* no. 23 (November 1969), 2. Additionally the DRV's efforts in the areas of industrial reconstruction, agricultural progress, and commitment to education are all highlighted.

143. Charles Fourniau, "Le trentième anniversaire de la fondation de la République démocratique du Vietnam," *Bulletin de l'AAFV* no. 15 (October 1975), 4.

144. Léo Lorenzi, *Paroles pour Xuan et Marius: Marseille et l'Indochine* (Mémoires Vivantes, 1999). The choice of *Marius* as the name of the French boy is no doubt a reference to Marcel Pagnol's working-class protagonist of that name; the choice of *Xuan* is less obvious but could be a reference to Trong Phung Vu's protagonist in *Dumb Luck*.

145. "Marseille et l'Indochine," *Bulletin de l'AAFV* no. 32 (January 2000), 3.

146. Untitled and unsigned article, *Bulletin de l'AAFV* no. 48 (January 2004), 16.

147. Ibid., 16.

148. Charles Fourniau, "Au Vietnam lors du cinquantième anniversaire de Diên Biên Phu," *Bulletin de l'AAFV* (July 2004), 2–3.

149. Alain Ruscio, "Journée d'étude. La guerre 'française' d'Indochine et l'affaire Henri Martin," *Bulletin de l'AAFV* no. 48 (January 2004), 17.

150. "La cérémonie de la flamme," *Indochine vérité et droits* no. 4 (1991), 11–12.

151. For example, in 2004 the municipality spearheaded Project Paddy, an initiative intended to foster cooperation between Vietnam and Mali to develop rice culture in the Yélimané region. In 2006 nine Vietnamese experts went to Mali to help implement a sustainable rice culture program. Information from Trinh Ngoc Thai, "Introduction," in Joëlle Cuvilliez, Trinh Ngoc Thai, Alain Ruscio, and Gilbert Schoon, eds., *Montreuil et le Viet Nam: Symbole de l'amitié franco-vietnamienne* (Hanoi: Nha xuat ban Chinh tri quoc gia, 2010), 11.

152. Ibid.

153. Deeply informative about the Montreuil-Vietnam connection, the publication is also indicative of the connections between various actors already discussed: Alain Ruscio was among the coeditors and several members of the AAFV contributed articles, including one on the AAFV in a section dedicated to the ongoing Franco-Vietnamese connections. See Hélène Luc, "L'Association d'amitié franco-vietnamienne: Des relations plus fortes entre Français et Vietnamiens," in Cuvilliez et al., *Montreuil et le Vietnam,* 88–95.

154. Musée de l'Histoire vivante, press release for the "From Indochina to Vietnam" exhibit. Personal copy.

155. Audrey Gay-Mazuel, "Le Musée de l'histoire vivante: Entre lieu de mémoire politique et d'histoire, un musée en quête d'identité," master's thesis, École du Louvre, 2003, 38. See also Éric Lafon, "Le musée de l'Histoire vivante de Montreuil," *Vingtième siècle* no. 106 (April–June 2010), 240.

156. For more on the connections between the museum and the PCF, see Gay-Mazuel's master's thesis; and Lafon, "Le musée de l'Histoire vivante de Montreuil," 239–42.

157. Gay-Mazuel, "Le Musée de l'histoire vivante," 30.

158. Ibid., 54.

159. Lafon, "Le musée de l'Histoire vivante de Montreuil," 241.

160. Éric Lafon, currently the director of research (*directeur scientifique*) at the museum, commented on this shift to a more critical museological approach in an interview with the author on 12 June 2012, and addresses the break with communist ideology in "Le musée de l'Histoire vivante de Montreuil," 239–42.

161. The date of the demolition is unclear, though an article published by the Vietnam Press Agency gives the year as 1986. "Célébration du 124e anniversaire du président Hô Chi Minh en France," *VietnamPlus* (online), 16 May 2014.

162. There is some disagreement as to when the room was dismantled and why. Éric Lafon maintains that it was done in 1992 to make room for the toy exhibit (interview of 12 June 2012). Former director Gérard Lefèvre states in his interview with Gay-Mazuel that it occurred in 1995 because of water leakage.

163. Interview with Éric Lafon, 12 June 2012.

164. For an account of the visit, see "Le président du Vietnam à Montreuil," in Cuvilliez et al., *Montreuil et le Vietnam*, 110–13.

165. For a discussion of the maintenance of material objects as part of a commemorative landscape, see Sarah Farmer, *Martyred Village: Commemorating the 1944 Massacre at Oradour-sur-Glane* (Berkeley and Los Angeles: University of California Press, 1999).

166. Interview with Gérard Lefèvre by Audrey Gay-Mazuel, 12 December 2002. In "Le Musée de l'histoire vivante," appendix no. 1, 5.

167. "Activités de l'AAFV," *Bulletin de l'AAFV* no. 70 (July 2009), 3.

168. Lafon in fact mentioned that there have been a number of attacks on the bust. It has been replaced once and has also been covered in red paint in a separate incident. Interview of 12 June 2012. The paint incidents are also mentioned by current director Gilbert Schoon in an article by Claire Fleury, "Montreuil Memories," *Le Nouvel observateur* (online), 13 July 2012.

169. Fleury, "Montreuil Memories."

170. "Ville de Montreuil-sous-Bois: Célébrations du cinquantième anniversaire des accords de paix de Genève," *Bulletin de l'AAFV* no. 49 (April 2004), insert.

171. Alain Ruscio, "Montreuil-Vietnam: Une longue amitié," *Bulletin de l'AAFV* no. 50 (July 2004), 22.

172. For an account of some of these events, see Joëlle Cuvilliez, "50ᵉ anniversaire des accords de paix en 2004: De l'Indochine au Vietnam," and "Des moments forts: Hô Chi Minh, entre commémorations et manifestations culturelles," in Cuvilliez et al., *Montreuil et le Vietnam*, 114–21.

173. "Guerre d'Indochine, témoins et historiens: Regards croisés," Musée de l'Histoire vivante de Montreuil, 19 June 2004.

174. Musée de l'Histoire vivante, press release for the "From Indochina to Vietnam" exhibit. Personal copy.

CHAPTER 4: *MORTS POUR LA FRANCE?*

1. Speech by Valérie Giscard d'Estaing in honor of the unknown soldier at the Invalides, 7 June 1980, 1, SHD 1 K 669, carton 44.

2. "Les cérémonies en l'honneur du Soldat Inconnu d'Indochine," *Bulletin de l'ANAI* no. 3 (1980), 11.

3. Ibid.

4. Pierre Brocheux, "La mémoire contre l'histoire: L'Affaire Boudarel 1991–1997," paper presented at conference "Decolonisations, Loyalties and Nations. Perspectives on the Wars of Independence in Vietnam, Indonesia, France and the Netherlands," Amsterdam, 2001.

5. A list of these sites can be found on the ANAI website, www.anai-asso.org.

6. Herman Lebovics examines French museums and the colonial connection in "The Dance of the Museums," in *Bringing the Empire Back Home: France in the Global Age* (Durham and London: Duke University Press, 2004).

7. See Daniel Sherman, *The Construction of Memory in Interwar France* (Chicago: University of Chicago Press, 1999). Although his focus is on the commemoration of the First World War, the theoretical underpinnings of his study are equally relevant here.

8. Robin Wagner-Pacifici and Barry Schwartz, "The Vietnam Veterans Memorial: Commemorating a Difficult Past," *American Journal of Psychology* 97, no. 2 (1991), 377.

9. "Discours du Premier ministre: Pose de la première pierre de la nécropole aux morts pour la France de la guerre d'Indochine," 19 January 1988, 1. AMF 87 W 21.

10. This excludes organizations such as the ARAC and the ACVGI, which are analyzed in the previous chapter.

11. Serge Tignères and Alain Ruscio, *Dien Bien Phu: Mythes et réalités, 1954–2004. Cinquante ans de passions françaises* (Paris: Les Indes savantes, 2005), 160. News footage of the ceremony can be viewed at the Institut national de l'audiovisuel (*Journal télévisé de 20h*, 4 April 1955). This association would later accept veterans of the Algerian War and North African campaigns into its ranks and change its name to the Association des Combattants de l'Union Française (ACUF; Association of the Combatants of the French Union).

12. The ceremonies were held every fifth year in Pau and in various locations around the country every other year.

13. See, for example, brief accounts in "La messe à l'intention des soldats tués à Dien-Bien-Phu," *Le Figaro*, 8 May 1957; "Deux anniversaires," *Le Monde*, 7 May 1958; "La cinquième anniversaire de Dien-Bien-Phu a été marqué par des cérémonies du souvenir," *Le Monde*, 9 May 1959.

14. Pierre Journoud and Hugues Tertrais, *Paroles de Dien Bien Phu: Les survivants témoignent* (Paris: Tallandier, 2004), 352.

15. The idea of honoring an unknown soldier has also been credited to at least two British men: Dean Ryle of Westminster Abbey and the Reverend D. Railton. See Thomas Laqueur, "Memory and Naming in the Great War," in John Gillis, ed., *Commemorations: The Politics of National Identity* (Princeton: Princeton University Press, 1994), 150–67.

16. Quoted in Jean-François Jagielski, *Le soldat inconnu: Invention et postérité d'un symbole* (Paris: Imago, 2005), 54.

17. The literal translation is "generation of fire." The term was first applied to the soldiers of the First World War, which made the soldiers of the Second World War the second generation. The state's acknowledgment of those who fought in Algeria was a validation of their position as the third generation. The term tends to refer to conscripts, and thus soldiers of the Indochina War are not usually referred to as constituting a generation, though many of them would go on to fight in Algeria.

18. The pressure from veterans to locate and repatriate the bodies of their fallen comrades, as well as the obstacles to doing so, are comparable to the much more politicized and contentious American campaigns to locate MIAs. See Thomas Hawley, *The Remains of War: Bodies, Politics, and the Search for American Soldiers Unaccounted for in Southeast Asia* (Durham and London: Duke University Press, 2005).

19. This protocol was drawn up with reference to article 23 of the Geneva Accords, which states that

> when the site of a burial ground is known, and the presence of graves has been established, the Commanders of the Forces of each Party will allow personnel from the war graves commission of the other Party to enter the region of Vietnamese territory under their military control to locate and remove the bodies of deceased soldiers of the other Party, including the bodies of deceased prisoners of war, within a time frame to be determined once the armistice Agreement has come into force.

The full text (in French) is available in the treaty database on the Foreign Affairs website, http://basedoc.diplomatie.gouv.fr.

20. This issue is addressed in a memo from the Ministry of Foreign Affairs, Direction Asie-Océanie, Cambodge-Laos-Vietnam, "Note au sujet des sépultures françaises au Nord Vietnam," 27 June 1960, CADLC, série Asie-Océanie, sous-série Vietnam-Nord, dossier 49, ff 40–43.

21. Ibid., 2.

22. Ministère des Affaires étrangères, Direction des Affaires Politiques, Asie-Océanie, "Note au sujet de l'accord franco-vietminh concernant les sépultures françaises au Nord-Vietnam," 2 February 1960, CADLC, série Asie-Océanie, sous-série Vietnam-Nord, dossier 49, ff 17–20, 2. The bodies in question were not just metropolitan French but included many non-French soldiers who fought for France, some of whom were eventually "repatriated" to France rather than to their home countries.

23. Ministère des Affaires étrangères, Direction Asie-Océanie, Cambodge-Laos-Vietnam, "Note au sujet des sépultures militaires françaises au Nord-Vietnam," CADLC, série Asie-Océanie, sous-série Vietnam-Nord, dossier 49, ff 178–183, 2.

24. Robert Aldrich, *Vestiges of the Colonial Empire in France: Monuments, Museums and Colonial Memories* (London: Palgrave Macmillan, 2005), 125. The actual number cited by Aldrich and the information pamphlet from the Memorial is 11,747.

25. This is identified as the motivating factor, along with "new Vietnamese demands," in the Memorial pamphlet. It should be noted that the *Bulletin de l'ANAI* published a number of columns expressing concern over the apparent threats of the Vietnamese regime to bulldoze the French cemeteries, which may not be an accurate reflection of the situation but certainly contributed to pressure on the French government from veterans.

26. Tignères and Ruscio, *Dien Bien Phu: Mythes et réalités*, 316.

27. Pierre Darcourt, "L'Hommage aux combattants d'Indochine," *Le Figaro*, 9 June 1980.

28. Portions of the interview are reproduced in the *Bulletin de l'ANAI* no. 3 (1980), 12–13, as well as in *Le Quotidien* of 9 June 1980.

29. Marguerite Duras, *L'Amant* (Paris: Les Éditions de Minuit, 1984).

30. The agreement was not a protocol signed by the two parties but rather an exchange of letters dated 10 and 23 September 1986. *Journal officiel de la République*

française, 25 April 1987, 4668–70. The number of repatriated bodies cited here is taken from an information dossier prepared by the Ministry of Veterans' Affairs for a meeting in Fréjus regarding the Memorial on 5 July 1989. Of the bodies repatriated, 17,830 were soldiers *morts pour la France;* 3,407 were soldiers without the status of *morts pour la France;* and 3,395 were civilians. Slightly different statistics are cited in the information booklet on the Memorial sponsored by the Ministry of Defense (a total of 27,239, of which 3,630 were civilians). Once again the numbers reflect not only soldiers of metropolitan origin but also colonial troops.

31. This protocol coincided with the Vietnamese period of economic reforms known as *doi moi,* which resulted in the opening up of Vietnam to the West and Japan.

32. The status of *mort pour la France* (killed in service to the nation) is not automatically attributed to those who died in combat; rather, it must be requested by the family of the dead soldier.

33. Aldrich, *Vestiges of the Colonial Empire in France,* 133.

34. They are indeed both soldiers, and not a French soldier and Vietnamese peasant, as is suggested by Robert Aldrich in *Vestiges of the Colonial Empire in France.* The Vietnamese figure, though wearing the *non* that is common to many peasants, is also wearing combat gear and boots that are very similar to those of the French soldier.

35. As noted in chapter 2, *ancien* is a term that in this context can refer to veterans, former settlers, or both.

36. "Nouvelles du Mémorial national aux morts d'Indochine," attached to a letter from Général H. Lapierre to François Léotard dated 17 May 1982, AMF 87 W 3.

37. Letter from Jean Le Bras to François Léotard, 12 January 1982, AMF 87 W 3.

38. Ibid.

39. Interestingly the record sleeve features the ANAI logo in large format though there is no mention of the ANAI anywhere. This was likely an arrangement with the ANAI, as correspondence between François Léotard and Jean Le Bras, and Léotard and ANAI president Hélène Bastid, indicates that the ANAI fully supported Le Bras and the AEMSI.

40. Letter from Colonel André Rottier, general secretary of the Citadelles et Maquis d'Indochine, to General Jean Pascal, 14 January 1982, AMF 87 W 3. A similar argument was presented by the ANAI *Bulletin* (issue no. 1, 1982, 8).

41. "Aux combattants tombés pour la France en Indochine," booklet published for the 1988 groundbreaking ceremony, Fréjus, AMF 87 W 21.

42. Joseph Gallieni had a long military and administrative career in the colonies, including Réunion, French Sudan, Indochina, and Madagascar.

43. For more on the use of Fréjus and nearby Saint-Raphaël for stationing colonial troops, see Gregory Mann, *Native Sons: West African Veterans and France in the Twentieth Century* (Durham: Duke University Press, 2006), especially 164–67.

44. "Sudanese" refers here to French Sudan (which included parts of present-day Niger and Mali) and not contemporary Sudan.

45. "Procès verbal de l'assemblée générale de l'Association pour l'érection d'un mémorial national aux anciens d'Indochine, combattants et victimes de guerre," 27 July 1983, AMF 87 W 3.

46. Ibid.

47. Such was the estimate given by Gabriel Jauffret in "Premier ministre le matin candidat l'après-midi!" *Var-Matin,* 20 January 1988.

48. See chapter 7 for an analysis of this series.

49. "Discours de M. François Léotard," 19 January 1988, AMF 87 W 21.

50. "Chirac répare une injustice," *Nice-Matin,* 20 January 1988.

51. Sarah Farmer has discussed the issues of the impact of natural decay altering commemorative landscapes in the case of Oradour-sur-Glane, a village destroyed by the Nazis in 1944, and the resulting shifts in attitudes toward the permanence of memorial sites. "Oradour-sur-Glane: Memory in a Preserved Landscape," *French Historical Studies* 19, no. 1 (Spring 1995), 27–47, especially 42–44.

52. See James E. Young, *The Texture of Memory: Holocaust Memorials and Meaning* (New Haven: Yale University Press, 1993).

53. "Les monuments aux morts," Lieux de mémoire, France-Culture, 14 November 1996, INA.

54. Maya Lin, quoted in Joel Swerdlow, "To Heal a Nation," *National Geographic,* May 1985, 557. Cited in Patrick Hagopian, *The Vietnam War in American Memory: Veterans, Memorials and the Politics of Healing* (Amherst: University of Massachusetts Press, 2009), 97.

55. Interestingly Lin's vision was not respected; there is now a concrete walkway along one side of the memorial.

56. To Vietnam, at any rate. De Gaulle did visit Phnom Penh in 1966.

57. Interview with Geneviève de Galard, *Le Soir,* France 3, 10 February 1993, INA.

58. "Quatre anciens d'Indochine réagissent," *France-Soir,* 11 February 1993.

59. Quoted in multiple newspapers, including Paul Guilbert, "Le retour de la France sur la scène indochinoise," *Le Figaro,* 10 February 1993.

60. *Journal de 20H,* France 2, 8 February 1993, INA.

61. While the practice of naming war dead dates back to the French Revolution, it was really the First World War that established the practice on a wide scale due in part to exponentially larger numbers. See Laqueur, "Memory and Naming in the Great War."

62. Wolf Von Eckardt, "Design: Storm over a Viet Nam Memorial," *Time,* 9 November 1981.

63. Decree no. 2005–547 of 26 May 2005, published in the *Journal officiel de la République française,* 27 May 2005, 9218.

64. Letter from Jean Le Bras to François Léotard, no. 22 BC/TL, 4 January 1982, AMF 87 W 3. In this letter Le Bras details all of his activities related to the commemoration of the war, including a letter he wrote to the minister of veterans' affairs regarding the institution of a national day on 14 November. The folder also contained a response from the minister's office acknowledging this request.

65. Decree no. 2003–925 of 26 September 2003, published in the *Journal officiel de la République française,* 28 September 2003, 16 584.

66. The choice of a commemorative date to remember slavery and its abolition (Journée commemorative du souvenir de l'esclavage et de son abolition) was made following similar principles. The date chosen was 10 May, the date on which the Taubira law, which recognizes slavery as a crime against humanity, was adopted in 2001.

67. "Discours de Madame Michèle Alliot-Marie, Ministre de la Défense, dans la cours d'honneur de l'hôtel national des Invalides le 8 juin 2005," *Bulletin de l'ANAI* no. 2 (2005), 35.

68. "Rapport d'activité 2005," *Bulletin de l'ANAI* no. 6 (2006), 5.

69. "Vie des sections," *Bulletin de l'ANAI* no. 6 (2006), 29–34.

70. Speech by Valérie Giscard d'Estaing in honor of the unknown soldier at the Invalides, 7 June 1980, 2, SHD 1 K 669, carton 44.

71. "Allocution de Monsieur Maurice Plantier, Secrétaire d'État aux Anciens Combattants pour l'inhumation à la nécropole nationale de Notre-Dame de Lorette du soldat inconnu mort pour la France en Indochine," 8 June 1980, 3, SHD 1 K 669, carton 44.

72. Ibid., 2.

73. "Mémorial de Fréjus," *Debout les para,* no. 89 (September–October 1983), AMF 87 W 3.

74. Letter from General Jean Gardes to François Léotard, 7 June 1983, AMF 87 W 3.

75. Letter from J.M. to François Léotard, 7 June 1983, AMF 87 W 3.

76. Letter from Marcel Robert to François Léotard, 5 June 1983, AMF 87 W 3.

77. "Discours de M. François Léotard," 19 January 1988. Excerpts of the speech are reproduced in François Léotard, *Place de la République* (Paris: Laffont, 1992), 208–11.

78. Speech by Valérie Giscard d'Estaing in honor of the unknown soldier at the Invalides, 7 June 1980, 5, SHD 1 K 669, carton 44.

79. Ibid., 6.

80. Ibid., 2.

81. Ibid., 3.

82. Letter from Colonel André Rottier, general secretary of the Citadelles et Maquis d'Indochine, to General Jean Pascal, 14 January 1982, AMF 87 W 3.

83. Ibid.

84. "Mémorial de Fréjus."

85. See chapter 2.

86. Letter from Colonel Félix to François Léotard, 20 February 1982, AMF 87 W 3.

87. "Discours du Premier ministre: Pose de la première pierre de la nécropole aux morts pour la France de la guerre d'Indochine," 19 January 1988, 7.

88. Ibid.

89. "Discours de M. François Léotard," AMF 87 W 21.

90. A brief description of the exhibit was included in the information booklet published for the groundbreaking ceremony, AMF 87 W 21. A photo and description of the boat that was located at the entrance was published on the cover of *Nice-Matin* on 19 January 1988.

91. François Mitterrand, "Déclaration lors de l'inauguration du Mémorial des guerres en Indochine," 16 February 1993. Accessed at www.vie-publique.fr/discours/.

92. Ibid.

93. Ibid.

94. Aldrich, *Vestiges of the Colonial Empire in France*, 131.

95. The seven sections: French Indochina from conquest to the Pearl of Empire; Indochina in the Second World War 1940–45; France's return 1945–46; The beginning of the Indochina War 1947–50; The war of movement 1951–53; The battle of Dien Bien Phu 1953–54; The Geneva conference and the consequences of the war.

96. General Jean Pascal and Mr. Cermolacce, "Procès verbal de la réunion du 24 Novembre 1982 pour l'organisation de l'inauguration du Mémorial aux Morts d'Indochine, 1, AMF 87 W 3.

97. Letter from M.B. to Félix Aumiphin, 26 January 1982, AMF 87 W 3.

98. "Allocution de Monsieur Maurice Plantier," 1–2.

99. Hélène Bastid, "Le mot de la Présidente: Inauguration du Mémorial des morts d'Indochine," *Bulletin de l'ANAI* no. 3 (1983), 1.

100. Information pamphlet from the Memorial to the Dead of the Indochina Wars, produced by the Ministry of Defense.

101. Panivong Norindr, *Phantasmatic Indochina: French Colonial Ideology in Architecture, Film and Literature* (Durham and London: Duke University Press, 1996), 152. Norindr is actually addressing the dates on the crypt inside the necropolis (1939–1954), but his general argument can be applied to the 1983 monument as well. Hee Ko has addressed the conflation of the Second World War and the Indochina War from a different angle, focusing on the rhetoric of the political left during the war itself, which reduced the complexity of the Indochina conflict to a mirror image of the Nazi occupiers and French Resistance, with the French in the role of the occupiers. "Trespass of Memory: The French-Indochina War as World War II," in Alec Hargreaves, ed., *Memory, Empire and Postcolonialism: Legacies of French Colonialism* (Oxford: Lexington Books, 2005), 98–111.

102. Norindr, *Phantasmatic Indochina*, 152.

103. Segment "Les oubliés," *19/20* (édition nationale), France 3, 4 June 2006, INA.

CHAPTER 5: "THE FORGOTTEN OF VIETNAM-SUR-LOT"

1. Dominique Rolland, *Petits Viêts-Nams: Histoires des camps de rapatriés français d'Indochine* (Bordeaux: Elytis, 2009), 32. The chapter title, a translation of "Les oubliés de Vietnam-sur-Lot," is taken from a radio documentary on the camps that aired on France-Culture's *La Fabrique de l'Histoire* on 26 March 2001.

2. The term "repatriates" will be used throughout in the interest of clarity; the term *Français d'Indochine* is also frequently used in the literature, but this can lead to some confusion as European settlers were also referred to in this way. Finally it should be noted that although "repatriate" is a problematic appellation for those of the second generation, it will be used nonetheless in the absence of a more suitable term.

3. Interview of Joséphine Le Crenn on the evening news program *20 Heures*, TF1, 22 May 2004, INA.

4. Archival and secondary sources give this spelling, but the name can also be spelled Saint-Laurent-d'Arce. The term "CAFI" refers specifically to the primary site at Sainte-Livrade, though occasionally also to its annex at Bias.

5. Le Huu Khoa, *Les Vietnamiens en France: Insertion et identité* (Paris: L'Harmattan, 1985), 115.

6. Although little work has been done on the arrival of European settlers from Indochina to France, there is a considerable body of work on the return of the *pieds-noirs* and *harkis* from Algeria. On the "return" of the *pieds-noirs*, see Todd Shepard, *The Invention of Decolonization: The Algerian War and the Remaking of France* (Ithaca: Cornell University Press, 2006); and Jean-Jacques Jordi, *1962: L'Arrivée des pieds-noirs* (Paris: Autrement, 2002). On the experience of the *harkis*, see Michel Roux, *Les harkis: Les oubliés de l'histoire, 1954–1991* (Paris: La Découverte, 1991), as well as the special issue of *Hommes et Migrations*, which includes an article on the Bias site after 1962; "Les harkis et leurs enfants," *Hommes et Migrations* no. 1135 (September 1990). Mohand Hamoumou, who has worked extensively on the question of the *harkis*, engages with the labels of "repatriate" and "refugee" in "Les Français-Musulmans: Rapatriés ou réfugiés?" *AWR Bulletin, Revue trimestrielle des problèmes des réfugiés* (1987), 185–201.

7. Several other scholars have published histories and studies of the reception centers (and the CAFI in particular), though they tend to focus specifically on the repatriate experience and not on its place in the broader context of immigration history; moreover they do not make extensive use of archival sources. Among them are Dominique Rolland's very engaging *Petits Viet-Nams* (Bordeaux: Élytis, 2009), which provides intimate portraits of camp residents. Pôleth Wadbled's study for the Ministry of Culture and Communication (see above) provides a general overview of the history of the sites and engages with the memorial dimension of the camps. Jean Delvert provides a more thorough account of the experiences and challenges of CAFI residents in "Les rapatriés d'Indochine en Lot-et-Garonne: Le CAFI de Sainte-Livrade," *Revue de l'Agenais* 132, no. 4 (2005), 1285–1311. Pierre-Jean Simon and Ida Simon-Barouh conducted sociological studies of the two centers in the 1970s, and each published a study as a result; Pierre-Jean Simon, *Rapatriés d'Indochine: Un village franco-indochinois en Bourbonnais. Aspects de la colonisation et de la décolonisation de l'Indochine orientale* (Paris: L'Harmattan/CNRS, 1981); Ida Simon-Barouh, *Rapatriés d'Indochine, deuxième génération: Les enfants indochinois à Noyant-d'Allier* (Paris: L'Harmattan, 1981).

8. Although they had very similar experiences, the Indochina repatriates and the *harkis* are not comparable on all levels—the repatriates with few exceptions had

French nationality prior to their arrival in France, while the *harkis* were given the option of acquiring French nationality shortly before their departure for France or within six months of their arrival.

9. Pierre Nora, *Les lieux de mémoire*, vols. 1–3 (Paris: Gallimard, 1984–92).

10. Robert Aldrich, *Vestiges of the Colonial Empire in France: Monuments, Museums and Colonial Memories* (New York: Palgrave Macmillan, 2005).

11. General René Cogny, "Note de service au sujet de l'évacuation de la population du Nord-Vietnam," Hanoi, 1954, SHD 10 H 3134.

12. Unsigned and undated report, "Exposé sur l'évacuation des réfugiés," SHD 10 H 248.

13. William Turley cites 928,152 civilian refugees total in *The Second Indochina War: A Concise Political and Military History*, 2nd ed. (Lanham, MD: Rowman & Littlefield, 2009), 75. He maintains that this is an estimate rather than an exact figure and cites Bui Van Luong, "The Role of Friendly Nations," in Richard A. Landholm, ed., *Vietnam: The First Five Years, An International Symposium* (East Lansing: Michigan State University Press, 1959), 49. Both Jacques Dalloz and Michel Bodin cite 700,000 as the number of Catholic refugees; Dalloz, *La guerre d'Indochine, 1945–1954* (Paris: Seuil, 1987), 256; Bodin, *Dictionnaire de la guerre d'Indochine, 1945–1954* (Paris: Economica, 2004), 54. Christopher Goscha cites 600,000; *Historical Dictionary of the Indochina War (1945–1954): An International and Interdisciplinary Approach* (Honolulu: University of Hawai'i Press, 2012), 91. It should also be noted that there was some migration from the South to the North, though the numbers were much smaller.

14. Appendix included with report of 3 October 1954 by General René Cogny, "Compte rendu hebdomadaire: Application des accords d'armistice au Nord Vietnam (Haiphong, 1954)," SHD 10 H 3134.

15. "Exposé sur l'évacuation des réfugiés."

16. The major camps (which overwhelmingly consisted of tent cities) were Lucien-Massard, de Gaulle, Lyautey, and Ba Quéo; some information on life in these sites can be gleaned from the minutes of the meetings of the Interministerial Commission for the Repatriates from Indochina, as well as from the transcript of the discussion about the repatriates in the Assembly of the French Union on 28 July 1955 (see the *Journal officiel* of 29 July 1955, 848–59).

17. Precise statistics on the total number of repatriates and the proportion of European and non-European French citizens are difficult to ascertain. Robert Boulin, then secrétaire d'État aux rapatriés, estimated in 1961 that 11,000 French citizens had been repatriated and that there remained 24,000 in Vietnam, Laos, and Cambodia; *Journal officiel de la République française*, Débats parlementaires, Sénat, 25 October 1961, 1225. Trinh Van Thao cites 35,000 total in "Le retour des rapatriés d'Indochine: L'Expérience des centres d'accueil (1954–1960)," in Jean-Jacques Jordi and Emile Temime, eds., *Marseille et le choc des décolonisations* (Aix-en-Provence: Edisud, 1996), 29. Colette Dubois also cites 35,000 in "La nation et les Français d'outre-mer: Rapatriés ou sinistrés de la décolonisation?" in Jean-Louis Miège and Collete Dubois, eds., *L'Europe retrouvée: Les migrations de la*

décolonisation (Paris: L'Harmattan, 1994), 75–101. Pierre-Jean Simon cites 30–35,000 in *Rapatriés d'Indochine: Un village franco-indochinois en Bourbonnais* (Paris: L'Harmattan, 1981), 5. Bouda Etemad estimates that between 1945 and 1990, 25–30,000 European French citizens and 10–15,000 non-European French citizens were repatriated to France, in *Possession du monde: Poids et mesures de la colonisation* (Paris: Complexe, 2000). Marcel-André Surleau, vice president of the Commission interministérielle pour les rapatriés d'Indochine, estimated in 1955 that there were 30,000 French citizens in South Vietnam ("Procès verbale de la réunion tenue le 19 septembre 1955," 10, SHD 1 R 238). In 1965 *Le Monde* estimated that 29,500 people had been repatriated from Indochina; "Bilan du septennat," *Le Monde,* 27 November 1965.

18. Though it is a problematic term and one that was challenged during the colonial era as well as since, "Eurasian" is the most common term used by scholars to describe those of mixed European and Asian heritage; many of the repatriates also self-identify as Eurasian.

19. It appears that this was the case for indigenous mothers of Eurasian children, for example.

20. Khoa, *Les Vietnamiens en France,* 115. "Les oubliés de Vietnam-sur-Lot," *La Fabrique de l'Histoire,* France-Culture, 26 March 2001.

21. Social Services here refers to the Service des affaires sociales de la France d'outre-mer et des États associés.

22. Other departments include the Indre, the Seine, and the Var.

23. Commission interministérielle pour les rapatriés d'Indochine, "Procès verbal de la réunion tenue le 2 octobre 1958," 3, CADN 590 PO A, carton 207. Once again the numbers are difficult to pin down. Of the few scholars who have studied some aspect of the repatriate question, not all cite population statistics. Trinh Van Thao states that of the 15,000 repatriates to arrive in France between 1954 and 1960, 12,000 went through the reception centers; he cites the Ministry of the Interior, but no source is provided; Thao, "Le retour des rapatriés d'Indochine," 33; also cited in Thao, "Essai sur une sociologie du rapatriement," *Ethno-psychologie* 28, no. 1 (1973), 64. Although this seems to be a little on the high end given that it would require 3,000 repatriates to have arrived between 1958 and 1960 (just when numbers were beginning to decline), it is not an unreasonable statistic. Pierre-Jean Simon states that 3,167 people lived in Noyant and its annex sites between October 1955 and January 1965, while 1,487 lived at the CAFI in Sainte-Livrade between June 1956 and August 1966, which seems on the low side given that these were the two largest reception centers; Simon, *Rapatriés d'Indochine,* 10.

24. An intermediate wave of immigrants from the peninsula between 1954 and 1975 was constituted primarily by students studying in France, most of whom later returned home.

25. Thao, "Le retour des rapatriés d'Indochine," 29.

26. Ibid.

27. Letter from the Minister of Reconstruction and Urbanism to the Prefect of the Allier, 20 October 1950, ADA 11 W 49.

28. Commission interministérielle pour les rapatriés d'Indochine, "Procès verbal de la réunion tenue le 31 juillet 1956," 4, SHD 1 R 238.

29. For example, the population of Noyant was just over one thousand in September 1955 (CIRI minutes of 19 September 1955, 4) when the *corons* were being prepared for the arrival of the repatriates, who numbered 960 by early 1957 (CIRI minutes of 7 February 1957, 3). The population of Sainte-Livrade was approximately four thousand in early 1956 (CIRI minutes of 17 January 1956, 9); repatriates arrived in April–May, and by early 1957 there were 1,850 repatriates total in the CAFI and the Bias centers (CIRI minutes of 7 February 1957, 3). Minutes of the meetings of the Commission interministérielle pour les rapatriés d'Indochine, SHD 1 R 238.

30. Jeanne Cressanges, *La feuille de bétel* (Paris: Casterman, 1962), n.p. This is part of a disclaimer following the dedication of the novel: "Malterre exists. Yellow and White live on either side of the cemetery. But the characters in the story are fictional. Any resemblance to real persons is purely coincidental." Throughout the novel, set in "Malterre," there are frequent references to the cemetery as the dividing line between the *corons* inhabited by the repatriates and the rest of the community.

31. Thao, "Le retour des rapatriés d'Indochine," 33.

32. The full list: defense, foreign affairs, overseas France, interior, health, labor, social affairs. Within these there was also a succession of subministries.

33. Letter from the Prefect of the Allier to the Minister of the Interior, 8 December 1964, ADA 988 W 33.

34. Most of the camp administrators were colonial civil servants who were being reassigned to positions in the metropole; some had worked in the Garde d'Indochine, others in the police or in customs. Unsigned, "Répartition des fonctionnaires des cadres locaux d'Indochine s'occupant des rapatriés d'Indochine (au 10 mars 1958)," AN CAC 19990429, carton 8.

35. Simon, *Rapatriés d'Indochine,* 264.

36. Letter from Emmanuel Bretonnière de Chèque to the Chef du service d'accueil et de reclassement des Français d'Indochine et des Français musulmans, 24 April 1964, ADA 988 W 38.

37. Ibid.

38. "Les oubliés de Vietnam-sur-Lot," 26 March 2001.

39. For more on the replication of colonial structures in *harki* camps, see Tom Charbit, "Un petit monde colonial en métropole: Le camp des harkis de Saint-Maurice-l'Ardoise (1962–1976)," *Politix* no. 4 (2006), 31–52; and Michel Roux, *Les harkis: Les oubliés de l'histoire, 1954–1991* (Paris: La Découverte, 1991), especially chapter 8, "Le contrôle 'colonial' des supplétifs rapatriés."

40. On the phenomenon of camps in France, see Marc Bernardot, *Camps d'étrangers* (Paris: Éditions du Croquant, 2008).

41. Nathalie Funès, "Lodi, le camp des oubliés," *L'Express,* 18 March 2010.

42. Ministère de l'Intérieur, "Arrêté portant règlement des centres d'accueil organisés pour l'hébergement des Rapatriés d'Indochine," 11 May 1959, ADLG 1 W 2117.

43. A letter from the departmental prefect to one of the residents of Noyant dated 9 March 1964 attests to the very real threat of expulsion on these grounds:

"You are hereby notified that given your situation and lifestyle, which has allowed you to purchase a car, you are no longer entitled to state-subsidized housing in a reception center. Please make all necessary arrangements to vacate the premises by the deadline of 30 June 1964"; ADA 988 W 33.

44. Letter from Emmanuel Bretonnière de Chèque to the Préfet de l'Allier, 19 March 1964, ADA 988 W 38. Bretonnière de Chèque justified the decision to ban such items in 1959, as at that time the residents of the center tended to have a "very pronounced mentality of dependence" and needed encouragement to find work and move on. However, in this letter he presses for such restrictions to be lifted, as the restriction on cars in particular made commuting difficult for those working farther away.

45. A. Engrand, "État de reclassement des rapatriés d'Indochine hébergés au Centre d'Accueil de Noyant," 1 December 1957, ADA 988 W 37.

46. Trinh Van Thao, "Étude d'un processus d'adaptation sociale: Portrait psycho-social du rapatrié," PhD diss., Université de la Sorbonne, 1966, 87.

47. Delvert, "Les rapatriés d'Indochine en Lot-et-Garonne," 1299.

48. "C.A.F.I. 1956–2006. Enfin l'après," *Ancrage*, hors série Indochine (April 2006), 6.

49. Letter from Henri Alquier to M. l'Inspecteur de la l'Académie de Lot-et-Garonne, 10 November 1956, ADLG (uncatalogued document). Unsigned, "Note pour Messieurs les Directeurs des centres," 15 September 1956, ADLG (uncatalogued document).

50. Ibid.

51. Commission interministérielle pour les rapatriés d'Indochine, "Procès verbal de la réunion tenue le 22 août 1957," 15, SHD 1 R 238.

52. Letter from Bernard Dutrait to the Directeur des Cités d'Accueil de Noyant d'Allier et de Saint-Hilaire, 28 March 1957, ADA 988 W 30.

53. Letter from M. Picaudé to M. le Chef du Bureau des Rapatriés d'Indochine, 16 December 1958, ADLG 1 W art. 2117.

54. "Remous au camp indochinois de Bias," *Dépêche du Midi,* 19 December 1958.

55. Telegram from Renseignements généraux in Agen to headquarters in Paris, 18 December 1958, ADLG 1 W art. 2117.

56. L. Ottaviani, Ordre de réquisition, 18 Decembre 1958, ADLG 1 W art. 2117.

57. Letter from M. Picaudé to M. le Chef du Bureau des Rapatriés d'Indochine, 16 December 1958.

58. Letter from Emmanuel Bretonnière de Chèque to the Chef du service d'accueil, 24 April 1964.

59. Letter from J.C. to M. le Haut Commissaire des Rapatriés d'Indochine accompanied by a report entitled "Les raisons de l'échec de l'administration en ce qui concerne le problème des rapatriés d'Indochine: Les principes d'une refonte administrative. Leur réalisation pratique," 23 December 1958, ADLG 1 W 2117.

60. Ibid.

61. Letter from Jacques Raphaël-Leygues to the Minister of the Interior, 26 December 1958, ADLG 1 W 2117.

62. Ibid.

63. Letter from departmental prefect's office, 12 February 1959. The letter actually states that "the residents of the camps will hereafter be subject to the same administrative structure as other French citizens"; ADLG 1 W 2117.

64. Letter from Emmanuel Bretonnière de Chèque to M. le Préfet, Chef du Service de l'Accueil et du Reclassement des Français d'Indochine et des Français Musulmans, 12 August 1964, ADA 988 W 38.

65. Emmanuel Bretonnière de Chèque, "Communiqué," 22 June 1965, ADA 988 W 38.

66. Stéphane Beaud and Gérard Noiriel, "Penser l' 'intégration' des immigrés," in Pierre-André Taguieff, ed., *Face au racisme. Tome 2: Analyses, hypothèses, perspectives* (Paris: La Découverte, 1991), 262.

67. Thao, *Étude d'un processus d'adaptation sociale*, 91.

68. "Note sur l'aspect actuel de la question des rapatriés d'Indochine," 30 October 1956, CADLC, série Asie-Océanie, sous-série Vietnam-Sud, folder 106, ff 98–106.

69. The notion of the school as facilitating integration by enforcing a common culture and heritage is common to Durkheimian sociologists; for a discussion of the impact of Durkheim on integrationist strategies, see Beaud and Noiriel, "Penser l' 'intégration' des immigrés," 261–82.

70. Letter from Bernard Dutrait to M. le Directeur du Bureau Universitaire des Statistiques, 12 February 1957, ADA 988 W 73.

71. The lack of French language skills among a population with such a large Eurasian component would seem to contradict the evidence provided by Emmanuelle Saada, Christina Firpo, and David Pomfret on the education of Eurasian children by aid societies in the 1930s and 1940s. However, several factors likely contributed to this situation, including the disruption of war to children's education, the fact that not all Eurasian children would have been under the purview of these aid societies, and the significant number of indigenous mothers of Eurasian children who spoke little French themselves. Saada, *Les enfants de la colonie: Les métis de l'Empire français entre sujétion et citoyenneté* (Paris: La Découverte, 2007); Firpo, *The Uprooted: Race, Children, and Imperialism in French Indochina, 1890–1980* (Honolulu: University of Hawai'i Press, 2016); Pomfret, *Youth and Empire: Trans-Colonial Childhoods in British and French Asia* (Stanford: Stanford University Press, 2015).

72. Commission interministérielle pour les rapatriés d'Indochine, "Procès verbal de la réunion tenue le 18 août 1955," 7, SHD 1 R 238.

73. "Rapport fait par Mlle la Directrice de l'École des Filles du Centre des Rapatriés d'Indochine de Ste Livrade," 16 September 1959, ADLG (uncatalogued document).

74. Letter from Bernard Dutrait to Mme la Directrice du Centre Féminin d'Apprentissage, 19 April 1957, ADA 988 W 73.

75. Saada, *Les enfants de la colonie;* and Firpo, *Uprooted*.

76. The impact of indigenous mothers and the absence of French fathers was addressed explicitly in 1955 by the president of the Commission interministérielle,

Léon Motais de Narbonne. In a meeting of the commission he stated that there were two categories of Eurasians: those who had been born before the war, whose fathers had been present in their lives and who had thus "remained French," and those fathered by CEFEO soldiers, who were often abandoned to their Vietnamese mothers and were thus "completely Vietnamese." He cites the "absence of paternal support" as the deciding factor in a child's "Frenchness." Commission interministérielle pour les rapatriés d'Indochine, "Procès verbal de la réunion tenue le 30 août 1955," 7–8, SHD 1 R 238.

77. Amelia Lyons addresses a similar process in *The Civilizing Mission in the Metropole: Algerian Families and the French Welfare State during Decolonization* (Stanford: Stanford University Press, 2013).

78. Letter from J.C. to M. le Haut Commissaire des Rapatriés d'Indochine, 23 December 1958, ADLG 1 W art. 2117.

79. Anne Gallois, "Vietnam-sur-Lot," *Le Point,* 17 December 1973, 65.

80. Renseignements Généraux, "Note de renseignement no. 542," 2 May 1946, ADLG 1 W art. 758.

81. Renseignements Généraux, "Note de renseignements no. 448," 14 May 1948, ADLG 1 W art. 758.

82. Simon, *Rapatriés d'Indochine,* 417–19.

83. Gendarmerie, Brigade de Sainte-Livrade, "Procès verbal d'enquête préliminaire," 2 July 1968, ADLG W Vrac Sous-préfecture de Villeneuve art. 254.

84. Capitaine M., "Rapport au sujet d'incidents sur la voie publique à Sainte-Livrade entre Eurasiens du Centre d'Accueil des Français d'Indochine à Sainte-Livrade et population locale," 28 June 1968, ADA W Vrac Sous-préfecture de Villeneuve art. 254.

85. "Climat d'émeutes à Sainte-Livrade: Une bande de jeunes voyous voulait faire la loi," *La Dépêche du Midi,* 29 June 1968, ADLG W Vrac Sous-préfecture de Villeneuve art. 254.

86. Ibid.

87. Renseignements généraux Agen, "Note d'information," 11 September 1968, ADLG W Vrac Sous-préfecture de Villeneuve art. 254.

88. There were similar incidents at the *harki* camp in Saint-Maurice-l'Ardoise: in the summer of 1975 a group of youths rebelled and took control of the camp administration offices, taking hostages in the process. The camp was closed soon thereafter. See Charbit, "Un petit monde colonial en métropole," 33.

89. J.G., "Maison des jeunes et de la culture de Sainte-Livrade-sur-Lot," 2 July 1968, ADLG W Vrac Sous-préfecture de Villeneuve art. 254.

90. Ibid.

91. Nadège Arnaud, "Sainte-Livrade-sur-Lot. CAFI: Cité ouverte," *Le Citoyen Libre,* 12 July 1991.

92. David E., "Indochine, nuit chagrine," *Sud-Ouest,* 10 February 1999.

93. Charlotte Rotman, "Le village oublié des harkis d'Indochine," *Libération,* May 15 2004, 17.

94. Booklet from the fiftieth anniversary exhibit on the CAFI, *CAFI 1956–2006 . . . De Saïgon à Sainte-Livrade.* Personal copy.

95. Anne Pascal, "Indochine en Têt," *Le Citoyen Libre,* 25 November 1988; Emmanuel Bretonnière de Chèque, Letter to M. le Directeur Départemental de l'Action Sanitaire et Sociale, 30 December 1964, ADA 988 W 34.

96. Bretonnière de Chèque, 30 December 1964.

97. SOFRES opinion poll for MRAP (1984). Cited in Alec Hargreaves, *Multi-Ethnic France: Immigration, Politics, Culture and Society,* 2nd ed. (New York and Oxford: Routledge, 2007), 144. For more on the perception of Maghrebi migrants/immigrants, and those from Algeria in particular, see Neil MacMaster, *Colonial Migrants and Racism: Algerians in France, 1900–1962* (New York: St Martin's Press, 1997).

98. Hargreaves, *Multi-Ethnic France,* 145.

99. Wallace E. Lambert et al., "Assimilation vs. Multiculturalism: Views from a Community in France," *Sociological Forum* 5, no. 3 (September 1990), 406. Respondents were asked to evaluate the two groups with respect to religious practices, personal hygiene, and family relationships, among others.

100. Jean Hugues, *Nous venons du Viêt-nam* (Paris: Syros, 1988), 20.

101. Ibid., 26.

102. Letter from the subprefect of Villeneuve-sur-Lot to M. le Préfet Pérony, Chef du Service d'Accueil et de Reclassement des Français Musulmans, 5 July 1967, ADLG W vrac Sous-préfecture de Villeneuve art. 254.

103. Gallois, "Vietnam-sur-Lot," 65.

104. Khoa, *Les Vietnamiens en France,* 187.

105. Hugues, *Nous venons du Viêt-nam,* 152.

106. J.L., "Rapport sur les Français Rapatriés," Paris, 1959, ADA 1 W art. 2117.

107. This estimate is based on INA records.

108. "'Grandeur' . . . et reconnaissance," *France observateur,* 2 July 1959.

109. *Les oubliés d'Indochine,* INF2 Dimanche, Antenne 2, 17 December 1972.

110. *Le camp des oubliés;* "Une douleur venue de l'Indochine," *Sud-Ouest,* 7 December 2004.

111. Among them are Pierre-Jean Simon and Ida Simon-Barouh, *Les génies des quatre palais* (1964); Pierre Andro, *Les oubliés de l'Indochine* (1972); Mathieu Samel, *Les fruits amers du Lot-et-Garonne* (1992), *Les enfants de Quan Am* (2004), and *CAFI: La mémoire fragmentée* (2014); Philippe Rostan, *Qué Huong/Terre natale* (2004); Marie-Christine Courtès and My Linh Nguyen, *Le camp des oubliés* (2004); Nora Genet-Lemque, *Saïgon-Sainte-Livrade: Aller simple pour l'oubli* (2007); Nadège Lobato De Faria, *Vietnam-sur-Lot* (2014).

112. Coordination des Eurasiens de Paris, "Rapport d'activité annuel, 2005–2006," www.rapatries-vietnam.org/cep-rapport-activite-2005–2006.rtf. While the association's statuts identify further goals, the centrality of these two in particular is reinforced in several editorials of the CEP-CAFI's bulletin, *Les échos du CAFI.*

113. Daniel Frêche, "Mémoire vive, mémoire vivante," *Les échos du CAFI* no. 9 (February 2013), 1.

114. Thao, *Étude d'un processus d'adaptation sociale,* 80.

115. Bruno Icher, "Abandon postcolonial," *Libération,* 7 December 2004.

116. Senate, session of 16 December 2004. Transcript consulted online at www.senat.fr.

117. *19/20* news segment, France 3, 4 June 2006, INA.

118. "C.A.F.I. 1956–2006: Enfin l'après," *Ancrage,* hors série Indochine (April 2006).

119. Dominique Foulon, "Noyant-d'Allier célèbre l'arrivée des rapatriés d'Indochine," *Carnets du Viêt Nam* 9 (October 2005), 14; Pierre Brocheux, "Sainte-Livrade: L'Émotion cinquante ans après," *Carnets du Viêt Nam* 12 (September 2006), 10.

120. Léon Nguyen, "Les cinquante ans de Noyant et de Sainte-Livrade célébrés cet été," LDH-Toulon online, August 2006.

121. Information about the project can be found online at http://cafi47.com/lieu-de-memoire/. More information on the framework for the construction of a memorial site can be found in a 2010 report by Observation Diffusion Recherche Intervention en Sociologie (ODRIS), "Proposition pour une étude de définition du Lieu de Mémoire du Cafi de Sainte Livrade sur Lot."

122. Daniel Mandouze, ARCUS agency report, "Étude pour la définition d'un lieu de mémoire au CAFI," July 2014.

123. K.P., "Renouveau pour la pagode du CAFI," *La Dépêche du Midi* online, 9 May 2015.

124. She has also published a book on the CAFI, *Petits Viêt-Nams: Histoires des camps de rapatriés français d'Indochine* (Bordeaux: Elytis, 2009).

125. Dominique Rolland, "Briques de mémoire," *Les échos du CAFI* no. 10 (January 2014), n.p.

126. A second website, www.cafi47.org, provides a similar range of materials as well as a timeline of major developments in the history of the site.

CHAPTER 6: *"LA SALE AFFAIRE"*

Copyright © 2010 by French Colonial Historical Society. Parts of this chapter originally appeared in *French Colonial History* 11 (2010), 193–209.

1. Yves Cuau, "Affaire Boudarel: L'Histoire en face," *L'Express,* 21–27 March 1991, 62.

2. Jean-Luc Einaudi mentions that the ANAI organized Beucler's intervention in *Viêt-Nam! La guerre d'Indochine, 1945–1954* (Paris: Cherche-midi, 2001), 221. General Guy Simon, then president of the ANAI, confirmed that the ANAI made extra photocopies of an invitation for several veterans, during an interview with the author on 19 March 2007.

3. This claim is frequently made by veterans, and there is no consistent indication of exactly what type of Nazi camp is being referred to. Estimations of mortality rates in the Viet Minh camps have ranged from 50% (Dalloz) to close to 70% (Bonnafous); Jacques Dalloz, *Dictionnaire de la guerre d'Indochine, 1945–1954* (Paris: Armand Colin, 2006); Robert Bonnafous, *Les prisonniers de guerre du corps*

expéditionnaire français en Extrême-Orient dans les camps Viet-minh (1945–1954) (Montpellier: Centre d'histoire militaire et d'études de défense nationale, 1985). The substantial difference in statistics can be explained in part by which groups are included in the calculation. For example, Bonnafous's statistics for prisoners of war on the French side that were missing and presumed dead list total losses for the combination of French troops, legionnaires, North African, and African troops averaging 55.87%. The inclusion of indigenous troops of the Forces terrestres d'Extrême-Orient and Forces armées viêtnamiennes forces the average to climb to 69.04%. The claims made in the press and elsewhere by veterans like Beucler comparing Viet Minh and Nazi camps do not cite any sources for their claims, but it seems likely that the original source for the comparison is Bonnafous's study, in which he draws a comparison between the above statistics and those issued by the Ministry of Veterans' Affairs of French soldiers taken prisoner by the German army by 15 July 1940. Of the 1,850,000 prisoners of war 37,054 or 2% died in captivity. He goes on to draw a number of comparisons between mortality rates in individual Viet Minh camps and individual German camps. It appears that some commentators seized this comparison and repeated it in much more general terms, comparing Viet Minh camps with Nazi "deportation" or "concentration" camps in the broadest sense, a comparison that is untenable given that mortality rates in Nazi camps reached nearly 100% in the extermination centers.

4. Jean-Jacques Beucler, "Un Français commissaire politique au service du Viêt-minh," *Le Figaro*, 19 February 1991.

5. Ibid.

6. François Léotard in an interview on the Grand-Jury RTL-*Le Monde;* quoted in "'M. Georges Boudarel relève exclusivement de ses pairs' affirme M. Lionel Jospin," *Le Monde*, 19 March 1991.

7. Henry Rousso, *Le syndrome de Vichy (1944–198 . . .)* (Paris: Seuil, 1987).

8. Hee Ko, "French Indochina War as World War II," in Alec G. Hargreaves, ed., *Memory, Empire, and Postcolonialism: Legacies of French Colonialism* (Lanham, MD: Lexington Books, 2005), 98–111.

9. For more on the *porteurs de valises,* see Marie-Pierre Ulloa's work on the Jeanson network: *Francis Jeanson: Un intellectuel en dissidence. De la Résistance à la guerre d'Algérie* (Paris: Berg, 2001).

10. For more on the GCM, see Alain Ruscio, "Le Groupe Culturel Marxiste de Saigon (1945–1950)," *Cahier d'Histoire de l'Institut Maurice Thorez* no. 31 (1979), 187–208.

11. Georges Boudarel, *Autobiographie* (Jacques Bertoin, 1991), 82.

12. Ibid., 50.

13. Medical and surgical reports on liberated prisoners of war, SHD 10 H 317. Bernard Fall takes a particularly critical view of these camps in *Street without Joy* (Harrisburg, PA: Telegraph Press, 1961).

14. Boudarel, *Autobiographie,* 409.

15. Vietnamese academics and intellectuals who criticized the regime during the same period faced imprisonment and worse. See Kim Ninh, *A World Transformed:*

The Politics of Culture in Revolutionary Vietnam, 1945–1965 (Ann Arbor: University of Michigan Press, 2002), especially chapter 4, "Intellectual Dissent: The Nhan Van Giai Pham Period," 121–63.

16. Law no. 66–409 of 18 June 1966 conferring amnesty, *Journal officiel de la République française*, 23 June 1966, 5147.

17. Yves de Sesmaisons, "L'Affaire Boudarel: L'Union fait la force," *Maolen Info* no. 31 (April 1994), 11.

18. Both are code names. Albert Clavier published his memoirs, *De l'Indochine coloniale au Vietnam libre: Je ne regrette rien* (Paris: Les Indes savantes) in 2008, recounting his experiences as a deserter who joined the Viet Minh. His account bears many similarities with Jacques Doyon's description of "Cassius" in his *Les soldats blancs de Hô Chi Minh: Les transfuges antifascistes et les communistes français dans le camp du Viêt-minh* (Paris: Fayard, 1973), which suggests that they may be one and the same.

19. Decree of the Ministry of Education 91–1000, 27 November 1991, IAO, Fonds Georges Boudarel.

20. 13–19 March and 20–26 March 1991.

21. "Boudarel, voici vos victimes," *Paris Match*, 4 April 1991, 72–77.

22. Arnaud Folch, "Gaston Klein: 'Boudarel nous a tués à petit feu . . .'" *Minute-La France*, 27 March–2 April 1991, 14–16.

23. Arnaud Folch, "Wladislas Sobanski: 'Comment j'ai failli mourir,'" *Minute-La France*, 13–19 March 1991, 6.

24. Serge de Beketch, "Ces communistes, professionnels de toutes les trahisons," *Minute-La France*, 20–26 March 1991, 4.

25. Alain Sanders, "L'Indécente arrogance de l'ex-tortionnaire," *Présent*, 23–24 March 1991.

26. Guy Birenbaum, *Le Front national en politique* (Paris: Balland, 1992), 232. See also Olivier Buffaud, "Le Front national tente de reprendre en main son électorat," *Le Monde*, 27 March 1991.

27. "Un acharnement suspect," *L'Humanité*, 18 March 1991.

28. Yves Moreau, "L'Indochine de grand-papa," *L'Humanité*, 18 March 1991.

29. Marie-France Etchegoin, "Le revenant du camp 113," *Le Nouvel observateur*, 7–13 March 1991.

30. Claude Baylé, *Prisonnier au camp 113: Le camp de Boudarel* (Paris: Perrin, 1991); Thomas Capitaine, *Captifs du Viet-Minh: Les victimes de Boudarel parlent* (Paris: Union nationale inter-universitaire, Centre d'études et de diffusion, 1991).

31. Gabriel-Xavier Culioli, "Au camp 113," *Politis*, 21–27 March 1991, 18.

32. Bernard Langlois, "Refoulé," *Politis*, 21–27 March 1991, 11.

33. Olivier Todd, "Derrière Boudarel: Le Vietnam," *Le Monde*, 25 May 1991.

34. See, for example, Dominique Le Guilledoux, "Les défenseurs de M. Georges Boudarel soulignent son engagement contre le régime de Hanoï," *Le Monde*, 20 March 1991.

35. Jean Chesneaux, "L'Affaire Boudarel: Un autre révisionisme," *Le Monde diplomatique*, May 1991.

36. Le Guilledoux, *Le Monde*, 20 March 1991.

37. This report is reproduced in Bonnafous, *Les prisonniers de guerre du corps expéditionnaire français en Extrême-Orient dans les camps Viet-minh*, 292–93.

38. Gabriel-Xavier Culioli, "Les choix de Georges Boudarel," *Politis*, 21 March 1991.

39. Malika Rebbani, "L'Affaire Boudarel," master's thesis, Université Paris VII (Jussieu), 1992, 108.

40. Michel Soudais, interview with Pierre Vidal-Naquet, "Le droit à la paix d'un homme," *Politis*, 21–27 March 1991.

41. Interview of Georges Boudarel, *Journal télévisé 20H*, Antenne 2, 20 November 1991, INA.

42. Interview of Georges Boudarel, *Journal télévisé 20H*, TF1, 15 March 1991, INA.

43. France-Inter interview with Georges Boudarel, cited in "Un acharnement suspect," *L'Humanité*, 18 March 1991.

44. The original title, *Traître au colonialisme; mais . . . ni à la République, ni à la France*, was rejected in favor of the simpler *Autobiographie*.

45. Boudarel interview, TF1, 15 March 1991.

46. Georges Boudarel, letter, "La parole aux lecteurs," *Le Nouvel observateur*, 18–24 April 1991, 58.

47. Colonel Déodat, "Sur un manifeste d'intellectuels," *Le Figaro*, 10 April 1991.

48. Ibid.

49. Jean-Jacques Beucler, *Mémoires* (Paris: France-Empire, 1991), 113.

50. Yves Daoudal, *Le dossier Boudarel, ou le procès impossible du communisme* (Paris: Perrin, 2001).

51. Beucler, *Mémoires*, 173.

52. Alain Sanders, "'Qui a protégé Boudarel? Comment se fait-il qu'on ne l'ait pas démasqué quand il est entré à l'Éducation nationale?'" *Présent*, 22 March 1991.

53. Alain Sanders, "L'Étau se resserre autour du traître," *Présent*, 20 March 1991.

54. One such message, played during a segment of the evening news on Antenne 2, was as follows: "Dirty traitor. I'm a former noncommissioned officer who fought in Indochina and who was a prisoner of the Viets. I was never in your camp, but you'll pay. We'll never, ever forget you. There's nothing left for you to do but kill yourself. Goodbye." (*Sale traître. Je suis un ancien sous-officier d'Indochine, prisonnier des Viets. Je n'ai pas été dans ton camp, mais tu paiera. On t'oubliera jamais, jamais. Tu n'as plus qu'à te suicider. Salut.*) *Journal télévisé de 20H*, 20 November 1991, INA.

55. Rebbani, "L'Affaire Boudarel," 112.

56. "Deux manifestes d'intellectuels," *Le Monde*, 16 March 1991.

57. "Pétitions pour Georges Boudarel," *Libération*, 13 March 1991.

58. There is little information on the content of these posters with the exception of the one cited in the following note, but Alain Sanders's discussion of the "cleanup commandos" mentions that all posters and graffiti in support of Boudarel was targeted by these groups. "L'Étau se resserre autour du traître," *Présent*, 20 March 1991.

59. Pictured in Christophe Agnus, "Jeunes: 'L'Indo, connais pas,'" *L'Express*, 21–27 March 1991, 77.

60. Jean-Luc Einaudi, *Viêt-nam! La guerre d'Indochine, 1945–1954* (Paris: Cherche-midi, 2001), 7.

61. As stated earlier, the charges against Boudarel had been filed in Sobanski's name with the ANAPI taking civil action.

62. For more on Henri de Turenne's "television trial," see chapter 7.

63. TF1, *Le Droit de savoir*, 27 March 1991, INA.

64. Ibid.

65. Ibid.

66. Ibid.

67. Ibid.

68. Quoted in Rebbani, "L'Affaire Boudarel," 37.

69. TF1, *Le Droit de savoir*, 27 March 1991, INA.

70. "Pourvoi no. 85-95166 de la Chambre criminelle de la Cour de cassation du 20 décembre 1985," *Bulletin criminel* no. 407 (1985). The definition of crimes against humanity has undergone a series of modifications in French law since its imprescriptibility was established in 1964. This particular decree served two purposes: to include members of the Resistance as civilian victims, which meant that Barbie's persecution of them amounted to crimes against humanity (rather than war crimes, as would have been the case if they were categorized as combatants), and to avoid any legal standing for a comparison between Barbie's actions in France and French actions during the Algerian War. For more on the evolution of crimes against humanity in French law, please see Vivian Grosswald Curran, "Politicizing the Crime against Humanity: The French Example," *Notre Dame Law Review* 78 (2003), 677–710; and Leila Sadat Wexler, "The Interpretation of the Nuremberg Principles by the French Court of Cassation: From Touvier to Barbie and Back Again," *Columbia Journal of Transnational Law* 32 (1994–95), 292–389.

71. Jacques Vergès, "L'Affaire Boudarel ou le crime contre l'humanité dans tous ses états," *L'Idiot international*, 20 March 1991.

72. Ibid.

73. Joël Le Tac, "100 libérés des camps viets racontent leur captivité," *Paris-Match*, 24–31 July 1954, 38.

74. Philippe Rochette, "La route amère de Georges Boudarel," *Libération*, 25 March 1991.

75. Culioli, "Les choix de Georges Boudarel."

76. Annie Kriegel, "L'Après-Golfe: Retour aux affaires," *Le Figaro*, 26 March 1991.

77. Soudais, "Le droit à la paix d'un homme," 17.

78. François Raoux, "Bousquet-Boudarel même combat?" *Le Quotidien de Paris*, 5 April 1991.

79. "Boudarel comme Touvier," *Minute-La France*, 6–12 March 1991.

80. Quoted in Rebbani, "L'Affaire Boudarel," 17.

81. Interview of Georges Boudarel, *Journal télévisé 20H,* Antenne 2, 20 November 1991, INA.

82. See, for example, Jean-Christophe Buisson, "Les alliés de Boudarel," *Aspects de la France,* 28 March 1991; and Arnaud Folch, "Boudarel: Les documents qui accusent," *Minute-La France,* 10–16 April 1991.

83. Interview with Jean-Marc Varaut, *Journal télévisé 20H,* Antenne 2, 14 September 1991, INA.

84. These "suitcase carriers" were those who transported documents and money for the National Liberation Front.

85. Claude Baylé, *Prisonnier au camp 113: Le camp de Boudarel* (Paris: Perrin, 1991), 25.

86. Alain Sanders, "Georges Boudarel, universitaire, ex-commissaire politique des camps vietminh...," *Présent,* 13 March 1991.

87. Jean-Pierre Bernier, "Les camps de la mort du Vietminh," *Historama* 88 (June 1991), 47.

88. A Hungarian Jew, Weinberger was deported to Buchenwald and later to Dachau; after the Second World War he joined the French Foreign Legion and served two tours of duty in Indochina. After the fall of Dien Bien Phu he was sent to a Viet Minh camp.

89. Daoudal, *Le dossier Boudarel,* 44.

90. Sanders, "'Qui a protégé Boudarel?'" 4.

91. Jean-Christophe Buisson, "Le règne de l'ignoble," *Aspects de la France,* 21 March 1991. *Aspects de la France* is the publication of the monarchist, far right organization *Action Française.*

92. Alain Griotteray, "Le véritable enjeu de l'affaire Boudarel," *Le Figaro Magazine,* 23 March 1991, 84.

93. Pierre Brocheux, "La mémoire contre l'histoire: L'Affaire Boudarel 1991–1997," paper presented at conference, "Decolonisations, Loyalties and Nations: Perspectives on the Wars of Independence in Vietnam, Indonesia, France and the Netherlands," Amsterdam, 2001.

94. Bonnafous, *Les prisonniers de guerre du corps expéditionnaire français en Extrême-Orient dans les camps Viet-minh.*

95. Frank Giroud and Lax, *Les oubliés d'Annam* (Bruxelles: Dupuis, 2003).

96. Alain Léger, "L'Affaire Boudarel: Rancoeurs contre restalinisation," *Les Temps modernes,* 1992, 63.

97. Gilles Bataillon and Jean-Philippe Béja, "L'Affaire Boudarel: Une mémoire sélective," *Esprit,* 1991, 147.

98. Chesneaux, "L'Affaire Boudarel."

99. This is a pseudonym used by Jacques Doyon in *Les soldats blancs de Hô Chi Minh.* Cross-referencing details provided in press reports of the deserters who were put on trial in 1962 with Doyon's study suggest that Vignon's real name was Roger Lucien Serve; see, for example, Alain Jallois, "Quatre déserteurs d'Indochine condamnés par le Tribunal Permanent des Forces Armées de Marseille," *Le Méridional-La France,* 15 December 1962.

100. There is some inconsistency in the press regarding the numbers. The most common numbers given are 40 deserters, 27 of whom were amnestied immediately and 13 of whom were put on trial; however, reports identify only 12 trials, suggesting that only 39 arrived in Marseilles.

101. Doyon, *Les soldats blancs de Hô Chi Minh,* 432.

102. For example, one of the flyers distributed by the Front National de la Jeunesse read "From unpatriotic re-education to [The] National [Ministry of] Education . . . No to Viet Minh universities!" Cited in Sanders, "L'Étau se reserre autour du traître."

103. The involvement of intellectuals in antiwar militancy in the context of the Franco-Algerian and American-Vietnam wars is examined in detail in David Schalk, *War and the Ivory Tower: Algeria and Vietnam* (New York: Oxford University Press, 1991).

104. For more on the importance of the affair as a catalyst for veterans speaking out about their suffering while prisoners of war, see Nicolas Séradin, "Les anciens prisonniers français de la guerre d'Indochine dans l'espace public: De l'affaire Boudarel à la reconnaissance mémorielle," *Modern and Contemporary France* 19, no. 1 (2011), 17–36.

CHAPTER 7: MISSING IN ACTION

1. Gérard Lefort, "La France occupée par l'Indochine," *Libération,* 15 April 1992.

2. Anne Andreu, "Cinéma français: La reconquête de l'Indochine," *L'Événement du jeudi,* 16–22 April 1992, 112–13.

3. Benjamin Stora, *Imaginaires de guerre: Algérie-Viêt Nam en France et aux États-Unis* (Paris: La Découverte, 1997), 34, 40–43; Delphine Robic-Diaz, *La guerre d'Indochine dans le cinéma français: Images d'un trou de mémoire* (Rennes: Presses universitaires de Rennes, 2015), 164. Both also acknowledge the impact of Second World War films on the eclipsing of Indochina.

4. For a thorough analysis of the entire corpus of films referencing the war, see Robic-Diaz, *La guerre d'Indochine dans le cinéma français.* Robic-Diaz is a specialist in cinema studies and thus includes far more analysis of the narrative and technical aspects of the films than is presented here.

5. Marc Vernet, "Si Orphée se retourne, Madame Dupont lui sourira," *Cinémathèque* no. 1 (May 1992), 92–105.

6. In addition two films released during the war did make reference to the conflict: Jack Pinoteau's *Ils étaient cinq* (1952) and Marcel Carné's *Thérèse Raquin* (1953). With respect to the total number of films released about the war, Delphine Robic-Diaz demonstrates that there were many more films that made reference to the war (both implicitly and explicitly) without being, strictly speaking, war films; *La guerre d'Indochine dans le cinéma français,* 13.

7. *Le Film français* nos. 708–9, numéro spécial hiver 1957, 16–18. *Le Film français* is one of the most reliable index of box-office statistics, though in this period it only

tracked ticket sales in Paris and eight other major cities. For this reason comparative ticket sales are also helpful: *Mort en fraude* sold 26,454 tickets in Paris in its first week, which put it in fifth place. The top-selling three films that week all sold over 50,000 tickets (*Le Film français* no. 680, 31 May 1957, 23–24). *Patrouille de choc* fared only slightly better, selling 28 785 tickets in Paris in its first week, putting it in fourth place (*Le Film français* no. 688, 26 July 1957, 15).

8. Claude Bernard-Aubert, quoted in S.D. (Simone Dubreuilh?), "Patrouille De Choc. Non! Patrouille Sans Espoir," *Les Lettres françaises*, 18–24 July 1957, 6.

9. "Hommage aux héros abandonnés d'Indochine," *La Cinématographie française*, no. 1724, cited in Frédéric Delmeulle, "Fiction cinématographique et guerre d'Indochine," *Cahiers de la Cinémathèque* no. 57, "Souvenirs d'Indochine" (October 1992), 64.

10. Claude Bernard-Aubert, *Patrouille de choc* (1957).

11. Jean Carta, "Brisons la routine ou changeons de métier," *Témoignage chrétien*, 15 August 1958.

12. Quoted in Delmeulle, "Fiction cinématographique et guerre d'Indochine," 64. For an in-depth examination of censorship and the CNC's treatment of the film, see Robic-Diaz, *La guerre d'Indochine dans le cinéma français*, 68–85.

13. Delmeulle, "Fiction cinématographique et guerre d'Indochine," 64.

14. Catherine Gaston-Mathé, *La société française au miroir de son cinéma: De la débâcle à la décolonisation* (Condé-sur-Noireau: Panoramiques-Corlet, 1996), 260.

15. According to Robic-Diaz, this is also a nod to the somewhat shady source of some of the funding for the film; *La guerre d'Indochine dans le cinéma française*, 47.

16. See, for example, reviews in *L'Aurore* of 20 July 1957 and *Paris-Presse-L'Intransigeant* of 7 July 1957.

17. See, for example, Jacques Doniol-Valcroze's review in *France observateur*, 11 July 1957.

18. Jean Hougron, *Mort en fraude* (Paris: Domat, 1953). As Robic-Diaz notes, many films about the Indochina War are based on novels; she offers the hypothesis that this is indicative of a desire among veterans to "exorcise the trauma of war by writing memoirs in a more or less fictionalized way." "La guerre d'Indochine dans le cinéma français (1945–2006): Image(s) d'un trou de mémoire," PhD diss., Université de Paris III, 2007, 24.

19. Delmeulle, "Fiction cinématographique et guerre d'Indochine," 68.

20. Quoted in Gaston-Mathé, *La société française au miroir de son cinéma*, 260.

21. Marcel Camus, *Mort en fraude* (1957).

22. This French term, from the Vietnamese *con gai* (daughter, girl, woman), became synonymous with concubine or prostitute and sometimes simply referred to an indigenous woman (though with inherently pejorative connotations).

23. Literally, a man in a relationship with a *congaï*.

24. Camus, *Mort en fraude*.

25. Hougron is credited as having contributed to the screenplay, and he may well have played a role in sharpening the critique of colonialism.

26. For more on Hougron's critique of colonial society, see Jack Yeager, "Jean Hougron's Indochina: Fantasy and Disillusionment," in Kathryn Robson and Jennifer Yee, eds., *France and "Indochina": Cultural Representations* (Lanham, MD: Lexington Books, 2005), 207–17.

27. Samuel Lachize, "A propos de 'Mort en fraude,'" *L'Humanité*, 25 May 1957.

28. Ibid.

29. Ibid.

30. Roger Fressoz, "Mort en fraude," *Témoignage chrétien*, 7 June 1957.

31. Nguyen Khac Vien, "A propos de 'Mort en fraude,'" *Les Lettres françaises*, 18–24 July 1957.

32. Henri-Georges Clouzot, "Le cinéma interdit," *L'Express*, 5 December 1953. In her extensive research in the censorship files of the *Commission de contrôle des films cinématographiques*, Delphine Robic-Diaz found no documentation suggesting official censorship measures; *La guerre d'Indochine dans le cinéma français*, 61.

33. Bénédicte Chéron, "Un cinéma d'aventure et de guerre: L'Oeuvre de Pierre Schoendoerffer. De la condition du soldat à la condition de l'homme engagé," DEA thesis, Université Paris IV (Sorbonne), 2006, 37. Chéron has since published a study of Pierre Schoendoerffer based on her doctoral dissertation: *Pierre Schoendoerffer: Un cinéma entre fiction et histoire* (Paris: CNRS, 2012).

34. Robic-Diaz, "La guerre d'Indochine dans le cinéma français" (PhD diss.), 36.

35. The film was shot in 1964 and released in 1965.

36. The setting of the film has alternately been identified as Laos and Cambodia; the voice-over in the film's opening scene states that the high command (*état-major*) of the North Cambodian sector had given orders to retreat to an outpost at Luong Ba, identified as being close to the Lao border. In the novel upon which the film is based, the setting is clearly identified as Northern Laos (Schoendoerffer, *La 317ème section* [Paris: La Table ronde, 1963], 10), and the majority of film reviews place the action in Laos. The film was shot in Cambodia.

37. As with the location the ethnicity of these auxiliaries has been identified as Lao or as Cambodian. In the novel they are clearly identified as Lao; however, the soldiers in the film were played by soldiers from the Cambodian army.

38. Jacques Dalloz, *La guerre d'Indochine, 1945–1954* (Paris: Seuil, 1987), 175.

39. See, for example, reviews of *Le facteur s'en va-t-en guerre* in *Candide* of 22 August 1966, and *L'Aurore* of 22 August 1966; as well as of *Charlie Bravo* in *Le Canard enchaîné* of 23 July 1980, and *Minute* of 30 July and 6 August 1980. Many other reviews of these two films mention *La 317ème section* in a neutral way, which nonetheless confirms its status as "the" film about the Indochina War.

40. *Le Film français* no. 1123, 17 December 1965, 5.

41. "Le plus beau film de guerre français," *Minute*, 9 April 1965, 22.

42. M.C., review of *La 317ème section*, *Le Nouvel observateur*, 1 April 1965.

43. Samuel Lachize, "Les éternels vaincus," *L'Humanité*, 7 April 1965.

44. M.C., review of *La 317ème section*.

45. Jean de Baroncelli, "La 317ème section," *Le Monde*, 2 April 1965.

46. Lachize, "Les éternels vaincus."

47. Ibid.

48. It was later revealed that the footage was in fact the result of a restaging of the battle by Russian director Roman Karmen. The footage itself has appeared in many documentaries and televised news clips since.

49. Marilyn B. Young, *The Vietnam Wars, 1945–1990* (New York: Harper Collins, 1991), 103.

50. See, for example, "Dix ans après Dien Bien Phu: La nouvelle guerre du Vietnam connaît une brusque accélération," *Le Monde*, 6 May 1964.

51. The *gégène* involves electrocuting the victim using current generated by a field radio or other device.

52. Gaston-Jean Gautier, *Le facteur s'en va-t-en guerre* (Paris: France-Empire, 1966). According to Delphine Robic-Diaz, who interviewed Bernard-Aubert, the film was not based on the novel; rather, both were the result of conversations between Bernard-Aubert and Gautier. See *La guerre d'Indochine dans le cinéma français*, 50.

53. Jean-Pierre Léonardini, review of *Le Facteur s'en va-t-en guerre*, *L'Humanité*, 25 August 1966; Marcel Martin, "Fraîche et joyeuse," *Les Lettres françaises*, 25 August 1966.

54. C.B., "Le Facteur s'en va-t-en guerre," *Le Figaro*, 22 August 1966.

55. Although out of place in this chapter chronologically speaking, *Charlie Bravo* is being discussed here in order to demonstrate the progression of Bernard-Aubert's films.

56. Oliver Stone, *Platoon* (1986).

57. In fact the film opens with an on-screen message signed by the filmmaker that states:

> This story is true. It took place a few days before the end of the first Indochina War. I am testifying about these events because long ago, on the 26th of May 1950, a French army unit massacred and razed the entirety of the village of Quinh Quang, on the Song Traly, in northern Vietnam; it did so for reasons related to the laws of war—that is, survival and strategy. I turned twenty that day, and I was there.

58. Claude Bernard-Aubert, *Charlie Bravo* (1980).

59. See, for example, Patrice de Nussac's account of this criticism in "'Charlie Bravo' relance la polémique sur la guerre d'Indochine," *Le Journal du dimanche*, 20 July 1980; see also Erwan Bergot, "Charlie-ringard," *Minute*, 6 August 1980; "'Charlie Bravo': Rien à applaudir," *Minute*, 30 July 1980.

60. De Nussac, "'Charlie Bravo' relance la polémique sur la guerre d'Indochine."

61. Georges Dascal, "Charlie Bravo," *La Vie ouvrière*, 23 July 1980.

62. Louis Chauvet, "La 317ème section," *Le Figaro*, 2 April 1965.

63. The first three episodes aired on Antenne 2 on 15, 22, and 29 January; the second three on 12, 19, and 26 February.

64. Antenne 2 produced two episodes, Central Independent Television four, and PBS the remaining seven, according to the *New York Times*. See Fox Butterfield, "TV Returns to Vietnam to Dissect the War," *New York Times*, 2 October 1983.

65. The series was entitled "Les jours héroïques de Geneviève de Galard" and appeared in the issues of 2, 3, 4, and 5 June 1954.
66. "À voix nue," special guest Henri de Turenne, part 1, France-Culture, 26 February 2007, INA.
67. Henri de Turenne, *Vietnam*, part 1, "La perle de l'empire."
68. This choice of language is particularly interesting in light of Todd Shepard's work on the Algerian War, *The Invention of Decolonization: The Algerian War and the Remaking of France* (Ithaca: Cornell University Press, 2006).
69. This is the same footage that was presented on *Cinq colonnes à la une* in 1964 as being authentic Viet Minh footage of the defeat. See chapter 1.
70. *Midi 2*, Antenne 2, 14 January 1984, INA.
71. Patrice de Beer, "Des missionnaires à Dien-Bien-Phu," *Le Monde*, 8 January 1984.
72. J.M., "Indochine 1949–1954," *L'Humanité-Dimanche*, 13 May 1984.
73. Gérard Lefort, "Histoirégéo nous fait l'Indo," *Libération*, 14–15 January 1984.
74. Noël Darbroz, "Le Vietnam englouti," *La Croix*, 14 January 1984.
75. Antoine Keomanivong, "Parti pris indochinois," *Le Figaro*, 14–15 January 1984.
76. Louis Baudoin, "Un pamphlet contre le colonialisme," *France-Soir*, 14 January 1984; "Vive Ho Chi Minh!" 21 January 1984; "Toujours la désinformation," 11 February 1984. Baudoin also published summaries of the last three episodes.
77. J.F., "L'Histoire falsifiée," *Bulletin de l'ANAI* no. 1 (1984), 2.
78. Letter to the editor, *Le Figaro*, 2 February 1984.
79. Jean-Jacques Beucler, "Le Vietnam sur l'A2: Lettre ouverte de Beucler à Henri de Turenne," *L'Est Républicain*, 17 February 1984.
80. Jean-Jacques Beucler, "Lettre ouverte à Henri de Turenne: Faire du faut avec du vrai," *Le Figaro*, 24 February 1984; Geneviève de Galard, "Dien Bien Phu à la télévision: Lettre ouverte à Henri de Turenne," *Le Figaro*, 4–5 February 1984; Pierre Schoendoerffer, "Y en a marre de tous ces mensonges!" *Figaro Magazine*, 11 February 1984, and "Trop de sourires pour l'oncle Ho!" *Paris Match*, 24 February 1984; Michel Laurillard, "Tout cela est truqué affirme Bigeard," *Le Républicain Lorrain*, 1 February 1984.
81. "Débat spécial Turenne," Antenne 2, 14 May 1984, INA.
82. Le Tien, "Bo phim su thi truyen hinh Viet Nam," *Quan Doi Nhan Dan*, 26 August 1983. The episodes aired earlier in the United States, as part of the American series, than they did in France.
83. Brigitte Friang, "Une caricature de l'histoire," *Le Figaro*, 24 February 1984. Friang had been a war correspondent in Indochina; Jacques Gandouin, "L'Oeuvre de la France," *Le Figaro*, 30 January 1984. Gandouin was private secretary (*chef de cabinet*) to Émile Bollaert, High Commissioner for Indochina, in 1947–48. He was later named to the Académie des sciences d'outre-mer.
84. Henri de Turenne, "Henri de Turenne répond," *Le Figaro*, 13 February 1984.
85. Ibid.

86. Ibid.

87. Ibid.

88. "Débat spécial Turenne," 14 May 1984.

89. Ibid.

90. Pierre Brocheux, "La mémoire contre l'histoire: L'Affaire Boudarel 1991–1997," paper presented at conference, "Decolonisations, Loyalties and Nations: Perspectives on the Wars of Independence in Vietnam, Indonesia, France and the Netherlands," Amsterdam, 2001.

91. Patrice de Beer, "La France et l'Indochine: L'Honneur d'un journaliste," *Le Monde,* 16 May 1984.

92. Ibid.

93. Ibid.

94. "Vietnam: A Teacher's Guide," *Focus on Asian Studies,* special issue, no. 1 (1983); Stanley Karnow, *Vietnam: A History* (New York: Viking Press, 1983).

95. Butterfield, "TV Returns to Vietnam to Dissect the War."

96. For a more detailed examination of the PBS and AIM documentaries, see Stephen Vlastos, "Television Wars: Representations of the Vietnam War in Television Documentaries," *Radical History Review* 36 (1986), 115–32.

97. James Banerian, *Losers Are Pirates: A Close Look at the PBS Series "Vietnam: A Television History"* (Phoenix: Sphinx, 1985).

98. For an examination of whether the film can properly be described as neorealist, see Claude Martino, *"Le rendez-vous des quais": Un film de Paul Carpita et ses histoires* (Mallemoisson: Éditions de Provence, 1996).

99. Vernet, "Si Orphée se retourne, Madame Dupont lui sourira," 100.

100. There is some disagreement with respect to the number and site of screenings prior to the seizure; in a televised interview Carpita claims that there were two screenings, while scholar Marc Vernet claims that the date of the seizure corresponds to at least the third screening. Claude Martino implies that there were numerous screenings beginning in March–April at the Rex Cinema in Marseilles and followed by screenings in June–July at the Ciné-club Action in Paris. The copy that was seized on 5 October was at the Saint-Lazare Cinema in Marseilles.

101. Vernet, "Si Orphée se retourne, Madame Dupont lui sourira," 94.

102. Fredy Le Borgne, "Censure d'hier et d'aujourd'hui," *Le Réveil des combattants* no. 533 (March 1990), 10.

103. Vernet, "Si Orphée se retourne, Madame Dupont lui sourira," 100–103.

104. Indeed it would have been difficult to have filmed any fictional scenario in the port during the war since it was the primary point of departure for troops, weapons, and supplies and the point of arrival for returning troops, the dead, and the wounded.

105. Interview with Paul Carpita and André Abrias, *La Marche du siècle,* France 3, 13 February 1991, INA.

106. Ibid.

107. Paul Carpita, *Le rendez-vous des quais* (Éditions Montparnasse, 1996; originally released 1955).

108. Ibid.
109. Ibid.
110. Ibid.
111. Jacques Dalloz, *Dictionnaire de la guerre d'Indochine, 1945–1954* (Paris: Armand Colin, 2006), 84.
112. Alfred Pacini and Dominique Pons, *Docker à Marseille* (Paris: Payot et Rivages, 1996), 75–76.
113. Ibid., 125.
114. Claude Martino adds that François Billoux, a PCF member close to Maurice Thorez, supported and "protected" Carpita and that the Communist paper *La Marseillaise* lent some of the necessary equipment for filming. Martino, *"Le rendez-vous des quais,"* 54.
115. *La Marche du siècle,* France 3, 13 February 1991.
116. Martino, *"Le rendez-vous des quais,"* 130–31.
117. Robic-Diaz, *La guerre d'Indochine dans le cinéma français,* 79–80.
118. Quoted in Claudine Galéa, "Moteur: La vie qu'on vit," *L'Humanité,* 22 July 1989.
119. Dominique de Saint Pern, "Le film que personne n'a pu voir," *L'Express,* 9 February 1990, 122.
120. Michel Boujut, "'Le Rendez-vous des quais': Un film interdit pendant trente-cinq ans," *L'Événement du jeudi,* 22 February 1990.
121. Edouard Waintrop, "Le deuxième 'Rendez-vous des quais,'" *Libération,* 13 February 1990.
122. Anna Colao, "Rendez-vous interdit," *L'Événement du jeudi,* 8 April 1993.
123. Martino, *"Le rendez-vous des quais,"* 137.
124. Ibid., 138–41.
125. Jean-Pierre Léonardini, "Retour du refoulé," *L'Humanité,* 4 March 1992.
126. Caroline Jurgenson, "Le cinéma français redécouvre l'Indochine," *Le Figaro,* 16 December 1992, 14.
127. Andreu, "Cinéma français."
128. "Les entrées à Paris," *Le Monde,* 2 April 1992.
129. Claude-Jean Philippe, "'Indochine': Une mousson d'émotions," *France-Soir,* 18 April 1992.
130. Guy Gauthier, "Indochine, rêve d'Empire," *La Revue du Cinéma* no. 483 (1992), 50–61.
131. Panivong Norindr, *Phantasmatic Indochina: French Colonial Ideology in Architecture, Film and Literature* (Durham and London: Duke University Press, 1996), 132.
132. Interview with Pierre Schoendoerffer by Alain Riou, "Schoendoerffer: Si je t'oublie, Indochine . . . ," *Le Nouvel observateur,* 27 February 1992, 20.
133. Andreu, "Cinéma français."
134. Commentators at the time of the 1992 release of the three films tended to overlook both films, presumably because Schoendoerffer's was a documentary of American soldiers and Lam Lê is of Vietnamese origin and was thus not counted as a "French" director.

135. Schoendoerffer himself insists that the film is not based on personal memories, in Pierre Schoendoerffer, Jean Noli, and Patrick Chauvel, *Diên Biên Phu: De la bataille au film* (Paris: Lincoln: Fixot, 1992); however, the film is undoubtedly shaped by his own experiences. He also cast his son, Ludovic, as an army cinematographer—a wink to his own role in the battle.

136. In fact Duras was so unhappy with Annaud's adaptation of her novel that she wrote a screenplay of her own published as *L'Amant de la Chine du Nord*. The same story is at the heart of *Un barrage contre le Pacifique, L'Amant*, and this third book, although details such as the ethnicity of the lover do change. Duras's falling out with Annaud was quite widely publicized.

137. Andreu, "Cinéma français."

138. Alison Murray-Levine makes this argument with respect to *Indochine* and two other films set in a colonial context: *Chocolat* and *Outremer*. "Women, Nostalgia, Memory: 'Chocolat,' 'Outremer,' and 'Indochine,'" *Research in African Literatures* 33, no. 2 (Summer 2002), 237.

139. Lefort, "La France occupée par l'Indochine," excerpted in the epigraph to this chapter; Rousselier, "Cinéma," *Bulletin de l'AAFV* no. 3 (June 1992), 14.

140. Interview with Pierre Schoendoerffer, *Journal de 20 heures*, Antenne 2, 1 March 1992, INA.

141. Norindr, *Phantasmatic Indochina*, 150.

142. He was also the only one of the three who agreed to return to Vietnam—both Geneviève de Galard and Marcel Bigeard declined, although the latter would eventually go on his own well-documented visit.

143. The depiction of Vietnamese as avid gamblers is a standard colonial stereotype. Significantly it is one that carried over into the repatriate camps as a subject of considerable criticism and concern from camp administrators.

144. Schoendoerffer, Noli, and Chauvel, *Diên Biên Phu*, 127.

145. He confirmed this in an interview with Vincent Rémy in *Télérama*, 4 March 1992.

146. Pierre Schoendoerffer, *Diên Biên Phu* (1992).

147. Ibid.

148. Ibid.

149. Ibid.

150. Jean-Luc Macia, "Dien Bien Phu, notre 'Apocalypse Now,'" *La Croix*, 6 March 1992.

151. Schoendoerffer et al., *Diên Biên Phu: De la bataille au film*, 120.

152. "Retour à Dien Bien Phu," TF1, 6 February 1993, INA.

153. Patrice de Plunkett, "Le caporal de l'armée morte," *Figaro Magazine*, 15 February 1992, 57.

154. "Dien Bien Phu," *Képi blanc*, March 1992, 56.

155. "Diên Biên Phu," *Képi blanc*, May 1992, 54–55.

156. Macia, "Dien Bien Phu, notre 'Apocalypse Now.'"

157. Bill Chernaud, "Cinéma," *Libération*, 4 March 1992.

158. Patrice Vautier, "Diên Biên Phu (Au feu, aux fous!)," *Le Canard enchaîné*, 4 March 1992.

159. Norindr, *Phantasmatic Indochina*, 147–49.

160. "Courrier des lecteurs," *Le Figaro*, 10 March 1992. In a lengthier letter entitled "Pourquoi nous combattons," Bernard Magnillat-Rapp challenges the idea that the fall of Dien Bien Phu brought about the end of colonialism, arguing that Vietnam had been independent since 1947.

161. 20 and 27 March.

162. Valérie Duponchelle, "'Diên Biên Phu': Le grand débat," and "Pour ou contre: Des acteurs du drame témoignent," *Le Figaro*, 26 March 1992.

163. "Pour ou contre: Des acteurs du drame témoignent," *Le Figaro*, 26 March 1992.

164. The phrase is that of Colette Boillon, "L'Offensive télévisuelle," *La Croix*, 5 March 1992.

165. *Bouillon de culture*, Antenne 2, 1 March; Danièle Rousselier, *Vietnam, la première guerre*, Antenne 2, 1 and 8 March; Patrick Jeudy, *Récits d'Indochine*, TF1, 6 March; Yves and Ada Rémy, *La mémoire et l'oubli*, France 3, 19 March.

166. Anne Andreu quotes Wargnier on this topic in "Cinéma français: La reconquête de l'Indochine."

167. This is the same term that Marguerite Duras, who was born and raised in Indochina, used to describe herself.

168. Joel David, "*Indochine* and the Dynamics of Gender," *Asian Journal of Women's Studies* 12, no. 4 (2006), 61–93.

169. Régis Wargnier, *Indochine* (1992).

170. Delphine Robic-Diaz, "Mémoires d'Indochine: Étude de la représentation cinématographique du colonialisme français en Indochine," DEA thesis, Université de Paris X (Nanterre), 2001, 2.

171. Benjamin Stora, *Imaginaires de guerre: Algérie-Viêt Nam en France et aux États-Unis* (Paris: La Découverte, 1997), 247. Stora was actually the historical consultant on the film.

172. Andreu, "Cinéma français."

173. Laurence Melville, "Vietnam Studios," *Présence du cinéma français* (March–April 1992), 35.

174. Interview with Régis Wargnier by Emmanuel de Brantes, "La légende de la congaï," *Le Quotidien de Paris*, 15 April 1992. Producer Eric Heumann also had an Indochinese connection as the grandson of a rubber plantation owner.

175. Thierry Jousse, review of *Indochine*, *Cahiers du cinéma* nos. 455–56 (May 1992), 35.

176. "Courrier des lecteurs," *Le Figaro*, 24 April 1992.

177. Ibid. This is obviously a weak comparison given that "Indochina" was not a nation. Moreover the wealth distribution was such that the majority was concentrated in the hands of the few.

178. Guy Simon, "À propos du Film 'Indochine,'" *Bulletin de l'ANAI* no. 2 (1992), 15.

179. René Cadiou, letter to the editor, *Bulletin de l'ANAI* no. 2 (1992), 15.

180. Pierre Billard, "L'Amant le film," *Le Point*, 11 January 1992.

181. Marcel Oms, "L'Amant," *Les Cahiers de la Cinémathèque* (October 1992), 93.

182. Francis Ramirez and Christian Rolot, "D'Une Indochine l'autre," *Cinémathèque* no. 2 (November 1992), 40; Norindr, *Phantasmatic Indochina*, 132.

183. Ramirez and Rolot, "D'Une Indochine l'autre," 42.

184. For a study of colonial policy regarding Eurasian children, see Emmanuelle Saada, *Les enfants de la colonie: Les métis de l'empire français entre sujétion et citoyenneté* (Paris: La Découverte, 2007). Kim Lefèvre has also published her autobiography about growing up as a *métis* in Indochina; *Métisse blanche* (Paris: B. Barrault, 1989).

185. Rachid Bouchareb's *Hors-la-loi* (2010; *Outside the Law*) does include a sustained reference to the Indochina War through the character of Messaoud, whose service in Indochina is a factor in his decision to mobilize support for the FLN during the Algerian War.

CONCLUSION

1. Daniel Lindenberg, "Guerres de mémoire en France," *Vingtième siècle* no. 42 (April–June 1994), 78.

2. Pascal Blanchard and Isabelle Veyrat-Masson, eds., *Les guerres de mémoires: La France et son histoire. Enjeux politiques, controverses historiques, stratégies médiatiques* (Paris: La Découverte, 2008).

3. *Le mal jaune*, or the "yellow sickness," refers to a nostalgia for the land and people of Indochina. See the epigraph of chapter 2 for the definition from Michel Bodin's dictionary of the Indochina War.

4. The emphasis on the oppressive nature of colonial society has been countered by groups seeking to present a positive "memory" of the colonial era, or at least of settlers, such as the Association of Rubber Plantation Owners (Amicale des planteurs d'hévéas). See the association's two publications: *Planteurs d'hévéas en Indochine: 1939–1954* (Nogent-le-Rotrou: Daupely-Gouverneur, 1996) and *Les planteurs d'hévéas en Indochine de 1950 à 1975: Contre vents et marées, souvenirs, récits et témoignages* (Panazol: Lavauzelle, 2006).

5. Carole Vann, "'Dien Bien Phu vu d'en face,' paroles de vétérans vietnamiens," *Rue 89*, 9 May 2010, www.rue89.com.

6. Existing work on memory in Vietnam has focused on these events. On the memory of the American war, see Heonik Kwon, *After the Massacre: Commemoration and Consolation in Ha My and My Lai* (Berkeley and Los Angeles: University of California Press, 2006), and *Ghosts of War in Vietnam* (New York: Cambridge University Press, 2008); on memory and commemoration more broadly speaking, see Hue-Tam Ho Tai, ed., *The Country of Memory and the Remaking of Late Socialist Vietnam* (Berkeley and Los Angeles: University of California Press, 2001). On the

period from 1954 to 1975, see Christina Schwenkel, "Exhibiting War, Reconciling Pasts: Photographic Representation and Transnational Commemoration in Contemporary Vietnam," *Journal of Vietnamese Studies* 3, no. 1 (2008), 36–77.

7. See Lien Hang T. Nguyen, "Vietnamese Historians and the First Indochina War," in Mark Atwood Lawrence and Fredrik Logevall, eds., *The First Vietnam War: Colonial Conflict and Cold War Crisis* (Cambridge: Harvard University Press, 2007), 41–55.

8. Hue-Tam Ho Tai attributes this "commemorative fever" to the unintended by-product of the economic reforms of the late 1980s. See her introduction, "Situating Memory," in *Country of Memory and the Remaking of Late Socialist Vietnam*.

9. For a more detailed analysis of the maintenance of historic sites in Dien Bien Phu, see William S. Logan, "Dien Bien Phu, Vietnam: Managing a Battle Site, Metaphoric and Actual," *Outre-Mers* 94, nos. 350–51 (2006), 175–90.

10. Clips of this performance aired on the evening news program *19/20* (national edition), France 3, 7 May 2004.

11. *La guerre d'Indochine à travers la voix des soldats du corps expéditionnaire français* (Hanoi: Nha Xuat Ban Quan Doi Nhan Dan, 2004). The texts were printed in Vietnamese and in French.

12. The Vietnamese version was published in 2009. It was recently translated into French with a preface by Jean-Pierre Rioux under the title *Dien Bien Phu vu d'en face: Paroles de bô dôi* (Paris: Nouveau Monde Éditions, 2010).

13. Pierre Journoud and Hugues Tertrais, *Paroles de Dien Bien Phu: Les survivants témoignent* (Paris: Tallandier, 2004).

BIBLIOGRAPHY

BOOKS AND ARTICLES

Académie des sciences d'outre-mer, Institut de l'Asie du sud-est and the Association nationale des anciens d'Indochine, *Indochine: Alerte à l'histoire. Ni opprobre, ni oubli*. Paris: Académie des sciences d'outre-mer, 1985.
Aldrich, Robert. *Vestiges of the Colonial Empire in France: Monuments, Museums and Colonial Memories*. New York: Palgrave Macmillan 2005.
Alleg, Henri. *La Question*. Paris: Éditions de Minuit, 1958.
Alquier, Jean-Yves et al. *Chant funèbre pour Pnom Penh et Saigon*. Paris: SPL, 1975.
Amicale des planteurs d'hévéas. *Planteurs d'hévéas en Indochine: 1939–1954*. Nogent-le-Rotrou: Daupely-Gouverneur, 1996.
———. *Les planteurs d'hévéas en Indochine de 1950 à 1975: Contre vents et marées, souvenirs, récits et témoignages*. Panazol: Lavauzelle, 2006.
L'ARAC 1917–2007: Combattants pour la vie, des voix pour l'espoir. Paris: Le Temps des cerises, 2008.
Arrighi, Jean. *Indochine, les combats oubliés*. Paris: L'Harmattan, 1992.
Ashplant, T. G., Graham Dawson, and Michel Roper, eds. *The Politics of War Memory and Commemoration*. London and New York: Routledge, 2000.
Association d'amitié franco-vietnamienne. *La guerre chimique au Sud*. Pamphlet. 1963.
———. *L'Association d'amitié franco-vietnamienne accuse . . . Crimes américains au Vietnam*. Pamphlet. 1970.
———. *Une histoire partagée: 40 ans de solidarité avec le peuple vietnamien, 1961–2001*. Supplement to *Bulletin de l'AAFV* no. 38 (June 2001).
———. *Charles Fourniau, 1921–2010: Un hommage*. 2010.
Association nationale des anciens prisonniers et internés d'Indochine. *ANAPI: Notre histoire, 1985–2003*. Paris: Atlante Éditions, 2004.
Association nationale des combattants de Diên Biên Phu. *50e anniversaire Diên Biên Phu: 1954–2004*. Booklet. 2004.
Avelane, Gérard. *L'enfer du camp 13*. Paris: Nouvelles Éditions Debresse, 1965.

Axelrad, Edouard. *Marie Casse-croûte.* Paris: Jean-Claude Lattès, 1985.

Banerian, James. *Losers Are Pirates: A Close Look at the PBS Series "Vietnam: A Television History."* Phoenix: Sphinx, 1985.

Bataillon, Gilles, and Jean-Philippe Béja. "L'Affaire Boudarel: Une mémoire sélective." *Esprit* (May 1991), 145–47.

Baylé, Claude. *Prisonnier au camp 113: Le camp de Boudarel.* Paris: Perrin, 1991.

Beaud, Stéphane, and Gérard Noiriel. "Penser l' 'intégration' des immigrés." In Pierre-André Taguieff, ed., *Face au racisme. Tome 2: Analyses, hypothèses, perspectives.* Paris: La Découverte, 1991, 261–282.

Bergot, Erwan. *Deuxième classe à Dien Bien Phu.* Paris: La Table ronde, 1964.

———. *Les Services secrets en Indochine: Les héros oubliés.* Bagneux: Le Livre de Paris, 1979.

———. *Les 170 jours de Dien Bien Phu.* Paris: Presses de la Cité, 1979.

———. *Convoi 42.* Paris: Presses de la cité, 1986.

———. *Bigeard.* Paris: Perrin, 1988.

Bernardot, Marc. *Camps d'étrangers.* Paris: Éditions du Croquant, 2008.

Bernier, Jean-Pierre. "Les camps de la mort du Vietminh," *Historama* 88 (June 1991).

———. *Il y a 50 ans: Dien Bien Phu.* Paris: Laffont, 2003.

Bertrand, Christophe, Caroline Herbelin, and Jean-François Klein, eds. *Indochine: Des territoires et des hommes (1856–1956).* Paris: Éditions Gallimard/Musée de l'Armée, 2013.

Bertrand, Romain. *Mémoires d'empire: La controverse autour du "fait colonial."* Paris: Éditions du Croquant, 2006.

Beucler, Jean-Jacques. *Quatre années chez les Viets.* Paris: Lettres du monde, 1977.

———. *Mémoires.* Paris: France-Empire, 1991.

Bigeard, Marcel. *De la brousse à la jungle.* Paris: Hachette, 1994.

Birenbaum, Guy. *Le Front national en politique.* Paris: Balland, 1992.

Blanchard, Pascal, and Isabelle Veyrat-Masson, eds. *Les Guerres de mémoires. La France et son histoire: Enjeux politiques, controverses historiques, stratégies médiatiques.* Paris: La Découverte, 2008.

Bodin, Michel. *La France et ses soldats, Indochine, 1945–1954.* Paris: L'Harmattan, 1996.

———. *Dictionnaire de la guerre d'Indochine, 1945–1954.* Paris: Economica, 2004.

Bonnafous, Robert. *Les prisonniers de guerre du corps expéditionnaire français en Extrême-Orient dans les camps Viet-minh (1945–1954).* Montpellier: Centre d'histoire militaire et d'études de défense nationale, 1985.

Bornert, Lucien. *Les rescapés de l'enfer: Les héros de Dien Bien Phu.* Paris: Nouvelles Presses Mondiales, 1954.

Boudarel, Georges, ed. *La bureaucratie au Vietnam.* Paris: L'Harmattan, 1983.

———. *Autobiographie.* Paris: Jacques Bertoin, 1991.

———. *Cents fleurs écloses dans la nuit du Vietnam: Communisme et dissidence 1954–1956.* Paris: Jacques Bertoin, 1991.

Branche, Raphaëlle. *La torture et l'armée pendant la guerre d'Algérie: 1954–1962.* Paris: Gallimard, 2001.

Brocheux, Pierre. "Les communistes et les paysans dans la révolution vietnamienne," in Pierre Brocheux et al., eds., *L'Asie du Sud-Est: Révoltes, réformes, révolutions*. Lille: Presses universitaires de Lille, 1981, 247–69.

———. "Retour sur l'Indochine, retour sur soi." *Revue française d'outre-mer* 80, no. 300 (1993), 479–87.

———. *Du conflit d'Indochine aux conflits indochinois*. Paris: Complexe, 2000.

———. *Ho Chi Minh*. Paris: Presses de Sciences Po, 2000.

———. "The Death and Resurrection of Indo-China in French Memory." *European Review* 8, no. 1 (2000), 59–64.

———. "La mémoire contre l'histoire: L'Affaire Boudarel 1991–1997," conference paper, "Decolonisations, Loyalties and Nations: Perspectives on the Wars of Independence in Vietnam, Indonesia, France and the Netherlands," Amsterdam, 2001.

———. *Ho Chi Minh: Du révolutionnaire à l'icône*. Paris: Payot, 2003.

———. "Sainte-Livrade: L'Émotion cinquante ans après." *Carnets du Viêt Nam* 12 (September 2006), 10.

———. *Histoire du Vietnam contemporain: La nation résiliente*. Paris: Fayard, 2011.

Brocheux, Pierre, and Daniel Hémery. *Indochine: La colonisation ambigüe*, 2nd ed. Paris: La Découverte, 2001. English translation: *Indochina: An Ambiguous Colonization*. Berkeley and Los Angeles: University of California Press, 2009.

Capitaine, Thomas. *Captifs du Viet Minh: Les victimes de Boudarel parlent...* Paris: Union nationale inter-universitaire, Centre d'études et de diffusion, 1991. Available online at http://archives.chez.com/index.htm.

Cenerelli, Pierre. "Revisions of Empire: The French Media and the Indochina War, 1946–1954." PhD dissertation. Brandeis University, 2000.

Chandler, David. "Paul Mus (1902–1969): A Biographical Sketch." *Journal of Vietnamese Studies* 4, no. 1 (Winter 2009), 149–91.

Chandler, David, and Christopher Goscha, eds. *L'Espace d'un regard: L'Asie de Paul Mus*. Paris: Les Indes savantes, 2006.

Charbit, Tom. "Un petit monde colonial en métropole: Le camp des harkis de Saint-Maurice-l'Ardoise (1962–1976)." *Politix* no. 4 (2006), 31–52.

Charuel, Marc. *L'Affaire Boudarel*. Paris: Éditions du Rocher, 1991.

Chéron, Bénédicte. "Un cinéma d'aventure et de guerre: L'Oeuvre de Pierre Schoendoerffer. De la condition du soldat à la condition de l'homme engagé." DEA thesis. Université Paris IV (Sorbonne), 2006.

———. *Pierre Schoendoerffer: Un cinéma entre fiction et histoire*. Paris: CNRS, 2012.

Chervel, Marc. *De la Résistance aux guerres coloniales*. Paris: L'Harmattan, 2001.

Chesneaux, Jean. *Contribution à l'histoire de la nation vietnamienne*. Paris: Éditions sociales, 1955.

Chesneaux, Jean, Georges Boudarel, and Daniel Hémery, eds. *Tradition et révolution au Vietnam*. Paris: Anthropos, 1971.

Clavier, Albert. *De l'Indochine coloniale au Vietnam libre: Je ne regrette rien*. Paris: Les Indes savantes, 2008.

Collin, Claude. *De la Résistance à la guerre d'Indochine*. Paris: Les Indes savantes, 2011.

Cooper, Nicola. "Heroes and Martyrs: The Changing Mythical Status of the French Army during the Indochinese War." In Valerie Holman and Debra Kelly, eds., *France at War in the Twentieth Century: Propaganda, Myth, and Metaphor.* New York: Berghahn Books, 2000, 126–41.

———. *France in Indochina: Colonial Encounters.* Oxford and New York: Berg, 2001.

———. "Dien Bien Phu—Fifty Years On." *Modern and Contemporary France* 12, no. 4 (2004), 445–57.

Coordination des Eurasiens de Paris. "Rapport d'activité annuel, 2005–2006." www.rapatries-vietnam.org/cep-rapport-activite-2005-2006.rtf.

Courtois, Stéphane, ed. *Livre noir du communisme: Crimes, terreur, répression.* Paris: Laffont, 1997.

Cressanges, Jeanne. *La feuille de bétel.* 2nd ed. Ottawa: Cercle du Livre de France, 1963.

Culas, Christian, and Jean-François Klein. "Introduction: Vingt ans de recherches sur le Việt Nam (1990–2010)." *Moussons* nos. 13–14 (2009), 5–26.

Curran, Vivian Grosswald. "Politicizing the Crime against Humanity: The French Example." *Notre Dame Law Review* 78 (2003), 677–710.

Cuvilliez, Joëlle, Trinh Ngoc Thai, Alain Ruscio, and Gilbert Schoon, eds. *Montreuil et le Viet Nam: Symbole de l'amitié franco-vietnamienne.* Hanoi: Nha xuat ban Chinh tri quoc gia, 2010.

D'Argenlieu, Adm. Georges Thierry. *Chronique d'Indochine, 1945–1947.* Paris: Albin Michel, 1986.

Dalloz, Jacques. *La guerre d'Indochine 1945–1954.* Paris: Seuil, 1987.

———. *Dien Bien Phu.* Paris: La Documentation française, 1991.

———. *Dictionnaire de la guerre d'Indochine, 1945–1954.* Paris: Armand Colin, 2006.

Dao Thanh Huyen et al., eds. *Dien Bien Phu vu d'en face: Paroles de bô dôi.* Paris: Nouveau Monde Éditions, 2010.

Daoudal, Yves. *Le dossier Boudarel, ou le procès impossible du communisme* Paris: Remi Perrin, 2001.

David, Joel. "*Indochine* and the Dynamics of Gender." *Asian Journal of Women's Studies* 12, no. 4 (2006), 61–93.

De Galard, Geneviève. *Une femme à Dien Bien Phu.* Paris: Éditions des Arènes, 2003.

De Lattre de Tassigny, Jean. *La ferveur et le sacrifice: Indochine 1951.* Paris: Plon, 1988.

"De l'Indochine au Vietnam." Press release for exhibit at the Musée de l'Histoire vivante.

Delmas, Henri, and Claude Martin. *Drame à Toulon—Henri Martin.* Exeter, UK: University of Exeter Press, 1998.

Delmeulle, Frédéric. "Fiction cinématographique et guerre d'Indochine." *Cahiers de la Cinémathèque* no. 57, "Souvenirs d'Indochine" (October 1992), 63–72.

Delpart, Raphaël. *Les rizières de la souffrance: Combattants français en Indochine, 1945–1954*. Neuilly-sur-Seine: M. Lafon, 2004.

Delpey, Roger. *Les soldats de la boue*. 2 vols. Paris: Karolus, 1961.

———. *Dien Bien Phu: L'Affaire (le commencement)*. Paris: Éditions de la Pensée moderne, 1974.

Delvert, Jean. "Les rapatriés d'Indochine en Lot-et-Garonne: Le CAFI de Sainte-Livrade." *Revue de l'Agenais* 132, no. 4 (2005), 1285–1311.

Devillers, Philippe. *Histoire du Viêt-Nam de 1940 à 1952*. Paris: Seuil, 1952.

———. *Paris-Saïgon-Hanoï: Les archives de la guerre, 1944–1947*. Paris: Gallimard, 1988.

———. *Vingt ans, et plus, avec le Viet-Nam: Souvenirs et écrits, 1945–1969*. Paris: Les Indes savantes, 2010.

Devillers, Philippe, and Jean Lacouture. *La fin d'une guerre: Indochine 1954*. Paris: Seuil, 1960.

———. *Viet Nam: De la guerre française à la guerre américaine*. Paris: Seuil, 1969.

Distinguin, Henry. *Une autre Indochine: Mémoires retrouvés*. Paris: La Pensée Universelle, 1992.

Dittmar, Linda, and Gene Michaud, eds. *From Hanoi to Hollywood: The Vietnam War in American Film*. New Brunswick and London: Rutgers University Press, 1990.

Doumer, Paul. *L'Indo-Chine française (Souvenirs)*. Paris: Vuibert et Nony, 1905.

Doyon, Jacques. *Les soldats blancs de Hô Chi Minh: Les transfuges antifascistes et les communistes français dans le camp du Viêt-minh*. Paris: Fayard, 1973.

Dubois, Colette. "La nation et les Français d'outre-mer: Rapatriés ou sinistrés de la décolonisation?" In Jean-Louis Miège and Collete Dubois, eds., *L'Europe retrouvée: Les migrations de la décolonisation*. Paris: L'Harmattan, 1994, 75–101.

Duras, Marguerite. *Un barrage contre le Pacifique*. Paris: Gallimard, 1950.

———. *L'Amant*. Paris: Les Éditions de Minuit, 1984.

———. *L'Amant de la Chine du Nord*. Paris: Gallimard, 1991.

Einaudi, Jean-Luc. *Viêt-nam! La guerre d'Indochine 1945–1954*. Paris: Cherche-midi, 2001.

Epain, Gérard. *Indo-Chine: Une histoire coloniale oubliée*. Paris: L'Harmattan, 2007.

Etemad, Bouda. *Possession du monde: Poids et mesures de la colonisation*. Paris: Éditions Complexe, 2000.

Evans, Martin, and Ken Lunn, eds. *War and Memory in the Twentieth Century*. Oxford: Berg, 1997.

Fall, Bernard. "Review of Paul Mus, *Sociologie d'une guerre*." *Pacific Affairs* 27, no. 2 (June 1954), 190–91.

———. *Hell in a Very Small Place: The Siege of Dien Bien Phu*. Cambridge: Da Capo Press, 2002. First published by J. B. Lippincott, 1966.

———. *Viet-Nam Witness*. London: Pall Mall Press, 1966.

———. *Street without Joy*, 4th ed. New York: Schocken Books, 1972.

Farmer, Sarah. "Oradour-sur-Glane: Memory in a Preserved Landscape." *French Historical Studies* 19, no. 1 (Spring 1995), 27–47.

———. *Martyred Village: Commemorating the 1944 Massacre at Oradour-sur-Glane*. Berkeley and Los Angeles: University of California Press, 1999.

Figuères, Léo. *Je reviens du Viet-Nam libre*. Paris: Éditions de la jeunesse, 1950.

———. *Ho Chi Minh, notre camarade: Souvenirs de militants français*. Paris: Éditions sociales, 1970.

Firpo, Christina. *The Uprooted: Race, Children, and Imperialism in French Indochina, 1890–1980*. Honolulu: University of Hawai'i Press, 2016.

Foulon, Dominique. "80 ans d'immigration vietnamienne en France." *Passions Vietnam* no. 2 (1999), 12–13.

———. "Noyant-d'Allier célèbre l'arrivée des rapatriés d'Indochine." *Carnets du Viêt Nam* 9 (October 2005), 14.

Fourniau, Charles. *Le Vietnam face à la guerre*. Paris: Éditions sociales, 1966.

———. *Annam-Tonkin 1885–1896: Lettrés et paysans vietnamiens face à la conquête coloniale*. Paris: L'Harmattan, 1989.

———. *Vietnam: Domination coloniale et résistance nationale (1858–1914)*. Paris: Les Indes savantes, 2002.

———. *Le Vietnam que j'ai vu, 1960–2000*. Paris: Les Indes savantes, 2003.

Gaston-Mathé, Catherine. *La société française au miroir de son cinéma: De la débâcle à la décolonisation*. Condé-sur-Noireau: Panoramiques-Corlet, 1996.

Gauthier, Guy. "Indochine, rêve d'Empire." *La Revue du cinéma* no. 483 (1992), 50–61.

Gautier, Gaston-Jean. *Le facteur s'en va-t-en guerre*. Paris: France-Empire, 1966.

Gay-Mazuel, Audrey. "Le Musée de l'histoire vivante: Entre lieu de mémoire politique et d'histoire, un musée en quête d'identité." Master's thesis. École du Louvre, 2003.

Gillis, John. *Commemorations: The Politics of National Identity*. Princeton: Princeton University Press, 1994.

Giroud, Frank, and Lax. *Les oubliés d'Annam*. Brussels: Dupuis, 2003.

Goscha, Christopher. *Vietnam: Un état né de la guerre, 1945–1954*. Paris: Armand Colin, 2011.

———. *Historical Dictionary of the Indochina War (1945–1954): An International and Interdisciplinary Approach*. Honolulu: University of Hawai'i Press, 2012.

———. "'So what did you learn from war?' Violent Decolonization and Paul Mus's Search for Humanity." *South East Asia Research* 20, no. 4 (December 2012), 569–93.

Gras, Yves. *Histoire de la guerre d'Indochine*. Paris: Plon, 1979.

Grauwin, Paul. *J'étais médecin à Dien Bien Phu*. Paris: France-Empire, 1954.

La guerre d'Indochine à travers la voix des soldats du corps expéditionnaire français. Hanoi: Nha Xuat Ban Quan Doi Nhan Dan, 2004.

Hagopian, Patrick. *The Vietnam War in American Memory: Veterans Memorials and the Politics of Healing*. Amherst: University of Massachusetts Press, 2009.

Halbwachs, Maurice. *Les cadres sociaux de la mémoire*. Paris: F. Alcan, 1935.

———. *On Collective Memory*. Edited and translated by Lewis Coser. Chicago: University of Chicago Press, 1992.

Hamoumou, Mohand. "Les Français-Musulmans: Rapatriés ou réfugiés?" *AWR Bulletin, Revue trimestrielle des problèmes des réfugiés* (1987), 185–201.

Harbi, Mohammed, and Benjamin Stora. *La guerre d'Algérie, 1954–2004: La fin de l'amnésie.* Paris: Robert Laffont, 2004.

Hargreaves, Alec, ed. *Memory, Empire and Postcolonialism: Legacies of French Colonialism.* Oxford: Lexington Books, 2005.

———. *Multi-Ethnic France: Immigration, Politics, Culture and Society*, 2nd ed. New York: Routledge, 2007.

"Les harkis et leurs enfants." *Hommes et migrations* no. 1135 (September 1990).

Hawley, Thomas M. *The Remains of War: Bodies, Politics, and the Search for American Soldiers Unaccounted for in Southeast Asia.* Durham and London: Duke University Press, 2005.

Hein, Jeremy. *States and International Migrants: The Incorporation of Indochinese Refugees in the United States and France.* Boulder: Westview Press, 1993.

Hémery, Daniel. *Révolutionnaires vietnamiens et pouvoir colonial en Indochine: Communistes, trotskistes, nationalistes à Saigon de 1932 à 1937.* Paris: François Maspéro, 1975.

———. "Aux origines des guerres d'indépendance vietnamiennes: Pouvoir colonial et phénomène communiste en Indochine avant la Seconde Guerre mondiale." *Le Mouvement social* no. 101 (October–December 1977), 3–35.

———. *Ho Chi Minh, de l'Indochine au Vietnam.* Paris: Gallimard, 1990.

———. "Asie du Sud-Est, 1945: Vers un nouvel impérialisme colonial? Le projet indochinois de la France au lendemain de la Seconde Guerre mondiale." In Charles-Robert Ageron, ed., *Décolonisations européennes: Actes du Colloque international Décolonisations comparées, Aix-en-Provence, 30 septembre–3 octobre 1993.* Aix-en-Provence: Université de Provence, 1995, 65–84.

"Historique et actualité de l'ANAI." Unsigned, undated. Personal copy.

Hitchcock, William. *France Restored: Cold War Diplomacy and the Quest for Leadership in Europe, 1944–1954.* Chapel Hill and London: University of North Carolina Press, 1998.

Hougron, Jean. *Mort en fraude.* Paris: Domat, 1953.

———. *La Nuit indochinoise.* Collected works from his Indochina series. 2 vols. Paris: Robert Laffont, 1989.

Hue-Tam Ho Tai, ed. *The Country of Memory and the Remaking of Late Socialist Vietnam.* Berkeley and Los Angeles: University of California Press, 2001.

Hugues, Jean. *Nous venons du Viêt-nam.* Paris: Syros, 1988.

Ingram, Norman. *The Politics of Dissent: Pacifism in France, 1919–1939.* New York: Oxford University Press, 1991.

———. "Pacifism." In Lawrence Kritzman, ed., *The Columbia History of Twentieth-Century French Thought.* New York: Columbia University Press, 2003, 76–78.

Jagielski, Jean-François. *Le soldat inconnu: Invention et postérité d'un symbole.* Paris: Imago, 2005.

Jay, Madeleine et Antoine. *Notre Indochine, 1936–1947.* Paris: Les Presses de Valmy, 1994.

Jordi, Jean-Jacques. *1962: L'Arrivée des pieds-noirs.* Paris: Autrement, 2002.

Journoud, Pierre. "Dien Bien Phu: Naissance et destin d'un mythe héroïque." In Claude d'Abzac-Épezy and Jean Martinant de Préneuf, eds., *Héros militaires, culture et société (XIXe-XXe siècles)*. "Histoire et littérature de l'Europe du Nord-Ouest" no. 52. Villeneuve d'Ascq: IRHiS-Institute des Recherches Historiques du Septentrion, 2012. Only available online: http://hleno.revues.org/251.

Journoud, Pierre, and Hugues Tertrais. *Paroles de Dien Bien Phu: Les survivants témoignent*. Paris: Tallandier, 2004.

Journoud, Pierre, and Hugues Tertrais, eds. *1954–2004: La bataille de Dien Bien Phu entre histoire et mémoire*. Paris and Saint-Denis: Société française d'histoire d'outre-mer, 2004.

Jousse, Thierry. "Review of *Indochine*." *Cahiers du cinéma* nos. 455–56 (May 1992), 35.

Karnow, Stanley. *Vietnam: A History*. New York: Viking Press, 1983.

Keith, Charles. *Catholic Vietnam: A Church from Empire to Nation*. Berkeley and Los Angeles: University of California Press, 2012.

Kelly, Gail, and David Kelly. *French Colonial Education: Essays on Vietnam and West Africa*. New York: AMS Press, 2000.

Ko, Hee. "French Indochina War as World War II." In Alec G. Hargreaves, ed., *Memory, Empire, and Postcolonialism: Legacies of French Colonialism*. Lanham, MD: Lexington Books, 2005, 98–111.

Kwon, Heonik. *After the Massacre: Commemoration and Consolation in Ha My and My Lai*. Berkeley and Los Angeles: University of California Press, 2006.

———. *Ghosts of War in Vietnam*. New York: Cambridge University Press, 2008.

Lafon, Éric. "Le musée de l'Histoire vivante de Montreuil." *Vingtième siècle* no. 106 (April–June 2010), 239–42.

Lambert, Wallace E., et al. "Assimilation vs. Multiculturalism: Views from a Community in France." *Sociological Forum* 5, no. 3 (September 1990), 387–411.

Larcher-Goscha, Agathe. "L'Enseignement et la recherche sur le Vietnam et l'Indochine à l'Université Denis Diderot-Paris VII: Expérience militante et militants d'expérience." Unpublished manuscript based on a paper given at a conference in honor of Charles Fourniau, "Hanoi-Paris-Aix-Hanoi: L'itinéraire d'un historien français du Viêt-Nam," 24–25 October 2003.

Lavigne, Raymond. *Poèmes pour Henri Martin*. Paris: Pierre Seghers, 1951.

Lawrence, Mark Atwood, and Fredrik Logevall, eds. *The First Vietnam War: Colonial Conflict and Cold War Crisis*. Cambridge: Harvard University Press, 2007.

Le Huu Khoa. *Les Vietnamiens en France: Insertion et identité*. Paris: L'Harmattan, 1985.

Lebovics, Herman. *Bringing the Empire Back Home: France in the Global Age*. Durham and London: Duke University Press, 2004.

Lefeuvre, Daniel. *Pour en finir avec la repentance coloniale*. Paris: Flammarion, 2006.

Lefèvre, Kim. *Métisse blanche*. Paris: B. Barrault, 1989.

Léger, Alain. "L'Affaire Boudarel: Rancoeurs contre restalinisation." *Les Temps modernes* (April 1992), 61–89.

Lembcke, Jerry. *The Spitting Image: Myth, Memory, and the Legacy of the Vietnam War*. New York: New York University Press, 1998.
Léotard, François. *Place de la République*. Paris: Robert Laffont, 1992.
Liauzu, Claude, ed. *Le dictionnaire de la colonisation française*. Paris: Larousse, 2007.
Lindenberg, Daniel. "Guerres de mémoire en France." *Vingtième siècle* no. 42 (1994), 77–95.
Logan, William S. "Dien Bien Phu, Vietnam: Managing a Battle Site, Metaphoric and Actual." *Outre-Mers* 94, nos. 350–51 (2006), 175–90.
Logevall, Fredrik. *Embers of War: The Fall of an Empire and the Making of America's Vietnam*. New York: Random House, 2012.
Lorenzi, Léo. *Paroles pour Xuan et Marius: Marseille et l'Indochine*. Marseilles: Mémoires Vivantes, 1999.
Lowe, David, and Tony Joel. *Remembering the Cold War Global Contest and National Stories*. Hoboken: Taylor & Francis, 2013.
Lyons, Amelia. *The Civilizing Mission in the Metropole: Algerian Families and the French Welfare State during Decolonization*. Stanford: Stanford University Press, 2013.
M.R. "Portrait de Geneviève de Galard: Des mots pour se souvenir." *Historia* (March 1992), 54–58.
MacLeod, Jenny, ed. *Defeat and Memory: Cultural Histories of Military Defeat in the Modern Era*. New York: Palgrave Macmillan, 2008.
MacMaster, Neil. *Colonial Migrants and Racism: Algerians in France, 1900–1962*. New York: St. Martin's Press, 1997.
Mandouze, Daniel. "Étude pour la définition d'un lieu de mémoire au CAFI." ARCUS agency report, July 2014.
Mann, Gregory. *Native Sons: West African Veterans and France in the Twentieth Century*. Durham: Duke University Press, 2006.
Marr, David. *Vietnam 1945: The Quest for Power*. Berkeley and Los Angeles: University of California Press, 1995.
Martino, Claude. *"Le Rendez-vous des quais." Un film de Paul Carpita et ses histoires*. Mallemoisson: Éditions de Provence, 1996.
Merlin, Martial. "Discours prononcé par M. Martial Merlin, Gouverneur Général de l'Indochine." Conseil de gouvernement de l'Indochine, Session ordinaire de 1924. Hanoi, 1924.
Millington, Chris. "Communist Veterans and Paramilitarism in 1920s France: The *Association républicaine des anciens combattants*." *Journal of War and Culture Studies*, forthcoming.
Mitterrand, François. "Déclaration lors de l'inauguration du Mémorial des guerres en Indochine." 16 February 1993. Accessed at www.vie-publique.fr/discours/.
Moinet, Jean-Philippe. *Léo et les siens: Du monastère aux affaires*. Paris: Seuil, 1995.
Moréchand, Guy. "II. Paul Mus (1902–1969)." *Bulletin de l'Ecole française d'Extrême-Orient* no. 57 (1970), 25–42.
Morgan, Joseph. *The Vietnam Lobby: The American Friends of Vietnam, 1955–1975*. Chapel Hill and London: University of North Carolina Press, 1997.

Morgan, Ted. *Valley of Death: The Tragedy at Dien Bien Phu That Led America into the Vietnam War.* New York: Random House, 2010.
Müller, Jan-Werner, ed. *Memory and Power in Post-War Europe.* Cambridge: Cambridge University Press, 2002.
Murray-Levine, Alison. "Women, Nostalgia, Memory: 'Chocolat,' 'Outremer,' and 'Indochine.'" *Research in African Literatures* 33, no. 2 (Summer 2002), 235–44.
Mus, Paul. *Viet-Nam: Sociologie d'une guerre.* Paris: Seuil, 1952.
Navarre, Henri. *Agonie de l'Indochine, 1953–1954.* Paris: Plon, 1956.
Nguyen, Léon. "Les cinquante ans de Noyant et de Sainte-Livrade célébrés cet été." *LDH-Toulon* online, 2006.
Ninh, Kim. *A World Transformed: The Politics of Culture in Revolutionary Vietnam, 1945–1965.* Ann Arbor: University of Michigan Press, 2002.
Nora, Pierre. *Les lieux de mémoire.* 3 vols. Paris: Gallimard, 1984–92.
Norindr, Panivong. *Phantasmatic Indochina: French Colonial Ideology in Architecture, Film and Literature.* Durham and London: Duke University Press, 1996.
Observation Diffusion Recherche Intervention en Sociologie (ODRIS). "Proposition pour une étude de définition du Lieu de Mémoire du Cafi de Sainte Livrade sur Lot." ODRIS, 2010.
Oscherwitz, Dayna. *Past Forward: French Cinema and the Post-Colonial Heritage.* Carbondale and Edwardsville: Southern Illinois University Press, 2010.
Pacini, Alfred, and Dominique Pons. *Docker à Marseille.* Paris: Payot & Rivages, 1996.
Parmelin, Hélène. *Matricule 2078: L'Affaire Henri Martin.* Paris: Éditeurs Français réunis, 1953.
Pirey, Philippe de. *Opération gâchis.* Paris: La Table Ronde, 1953.
Pomfret, David. *Youth and Empire: Trans-Colonial Childhoods in British and French Asia.* Stanford: Stanford University Press, 2015.
Pouget, Jean. *Le Manifeste du Camp no.1.* Paris: Fayard, 1969.
Poujade, René. *L'Indochine dans la sphère de coprospérité japonaise de 1940 à 1945.* Paris: L'Harmattan, 2007.
Prost, Antoine. *Les anciens combattants et la société française, 1914–1939.* 3 vols. Paris: Presses de la Fondation nationale des Sciences politiques, 1977.
Ramirez, Francis, and Christian Rolot. "D'une Indochine l'autre." *Cinémathèque* no. 2 (November 1992), 40–55.
Rebbani, Malika. "L'Affaire Boudarel." Master's thesis. Université Paris VII (Jussieu), 1992.
Rice-Maximin, Edward. *Accommodation and Resistance: The French Left, Indochina and the Cold War, 1944–1954.* New York: Greenwood Press, 1986.
Rignac, Paul. *Indochine: Les mensonges de l'anticolonialisme.* Paris: Indo Éditions, 2007.
———. *La guerre d'Indochine en questions.* Paris: Indo Éditions, 2009.
Rioux, Jean-Pierre, ed. *La Guerre d'Algérie et les Français.* Paris: Fayard, 1990.
Robic-Diaz, Delphine. "Mémoires d'Indochine: Étude de la représentation cinématographique du colonialisme français en Indochine." DEA thesis. Université de Paris X (Nanterre), 2001.

———. "Diên Biên Phu: Portraits de combattants sans images." *Guerres mondiales et conflits contemporains* no. 211 (July 2003), 107–21.
———. "La guerre d'Indochine dans le cinéma français (1945–2006): Image(s) d'un trou de mémoire." PhD dissertation. Université Paris III (Sorbonne Nouvelle), 2007.
———. *La guerre d'Indochine dans le cinéma français: Images d'un trou de mémoire.* Rennes: Presses universitaires de Rennes, 2015.
Robinson, W. Courtland. *Terms of Refuge: The Indochinese Exodus and the International Response.* New York: Zed Books, 1998.
Rolland, Dominique, *Petits Viêt-Nams: Histoires des camps de rapatriés français d'Indochine.* Bordeaux: Elytis, 2009.
Rousseau, Sabine. *La colombe et le napalm: Des chrétiens français contre les guerres d'Indochine et du Vietnam, 1945–1975.* Paris: CNRS, 2002.
Rousso, Henry. *Le syndrome de Vichy (1944–198 . . .).* Paris: Seuil, 1987.
Roux, Michel. *Les harkis: Les oubliés de l'histoire, 1954–1991.* Paris: La Découverte, 1991.
Roy, Jules. *La bataille dans la rizière.* Paris: Gallimard, 1953.
———. *La bataille de Dien Bien Phu.* Paris: R. Julliard, 1963.
———. *Mémoires barbares.* Paris: Albin Michel, 1989.
Ruscio, Alain. "Le Groupe Culturel Marxiste de Saigon (1945–1950)." *Cahier d'Histoire de l'Institut Maurice Thorez* no. 31 (1979), 187–208.
———. *Les communistes français et la guerre d'Indochine, 1944–1954.* Paris: L'Harmattan, 1985.
———. "Dien Bien Phu: Du coup de génie à l'aberration. Ou, Comment les contemporains ont vécu l'ultime bataille de la guerre française d'Indochine." *Revue française d'Histoire d'Outre-Mer* 72, no. 268 (1985), 335–45.
———. *Dien Bien Phu: La fin d'une illusion.* Paris: L'Harmattan, 1986.
———. "L'opinion française et la guerre d'Indochine (1945–1954): Sondages et témoignages." *Vingtième siècle* no. 29 (1991), 35–45.
———. *La guerre française d'Indochine, 1945–1954.* Paris: Complexe, 1992.
———. *La guerre "française" d'Indochine: Les sources de la connaissance. Bibliographie, filmographie, documents divers.* Paris: Les Indes savantes, 2002.
———. *Nous et moi: Grandeurs et servitudes communistes.* Paris: Tirésias, 2003.
———. *L'Affaire Henri Martin et la lutte contre la guerre d'Indochine.* Paris: Le Temps des cerises, 2005.
———. *Cambodge, an I. Journal d'un témoin, 1979–1980.* Paris: Les Indes savantes, 2008.
———. *Y a bon les colonies?* Paris: Le Temps des cerises, 2011.
Ruscio, Alain, and Charles Fourniau. "Le PCF et le déclenchement de la première guerre d'Indochine." *Cahiers d'histoire de l'Institut Maurice Thorez.* Part 1 published in no. 19 (1976), and part 2 in no. 22 (1977).
Ruscio, Alain, and Sébastien Jahan, eds. *Histoire de la colonisation: Réhabilitations, falsifications et instrumentalisations.* Paris: Les Indes savantes, 2007.
Saada, Emmanuelle. *Les enfants de la colonie: Les métis de l'Empire français entre sujétion et citoyenneté.* Paris: La Découverte, 2007.
Sainteny, Jean. *Histoire d'une paix manquée.* Paris: Amiot-Dumont, 1953.

Sartre, Jean-Paul, et al. *L'Affaire Henri Martin.* Paris: Gallimard, 1953.
Scagliola, Stef. "The Silences and Myths of a 'Dirty War': Coming to Terms with the Dutch-Indonesian Decolonisation War (1945–1949)." *European Review of History* 14, no. 2 (June 2007), 235–62.
Schalk, David. *War and the Ivory Tower: Algeria and Vietnam.* New York: Oxford University Press, 1991.
Schoendoerffer, Pierre, Jean Noli, and Patrick Chauvel. *Diên Biên Phu: De la bataille au film.* Paris: Lincoln: Fixot, 1992.
Schwenkel, Christina. "Exhibiting War, Reconciling Pasts: Photographic Representation and Transnational Commemoration in Contemporary Vietnam." *Journal of Vietnamese Studies* 3, no. 1 (2008), 36–77.
Séradin, Nicolas. "Les anciens prisonniers français de la guerre d'Indochine dans l'espace public: De l'affaire Boudarel à la reconnaissance mémorielle." *Modern and Contemporary France* 19, no. 1 (2011), 17–36.
———. "Les anciens combattants de la guerre d'Indochine, sociabilités et écritures de l'histoire." PhD dissertation. Université de Rennes 2, 2015.
Shepard, Todd. *The Invention of Decolonization: The Algerian War and the Remaking of France.* Ithaca: Cornell University Press, 2006.
Sherman, Daniel. *The Construction of Memory in Interwar France.* Chicago: University of Chicago Press, 1999.
Shipway, Martin. *The Road to War: France and Vietnam, 1944–1947.* Providence: Berghahn Books, 1996.
Simon, Guy. *Chroniques de Cochinchine (1951–1956).* Paris: Lavauzelle, 1996.
Simon, Pierre-Jean. *Rapatriés d'Indochine: Un village franco-indochinois en Bourbonnais. Aspects de la colonisation et de la décolonisation de l'Indochine orientale.* Paris: L'Harmattan/CNRS, 1981.
Simon-Barouh, Ida. *Rapatriés d'Indochine, deuxième génération: Les enfants indochinois à Noyant-d'Allier.* Paris: L'Harmattan, 1981.
Sliwinski, Marek. *Le génocide Khmer Rouge: Une analyse démographique.* Paris: L'Harmattan, 1995.
"Souvenirs d'Indochine." *Les cahiers de la cinémathèque* no. 57 (October 1992).
Spaggiari, Albert. *Faut pas rire avec les barbares.* Paris: Robert Laffont, 1977.
Stien, Louis. *Les soldats oubliés: De Cao Bang aux camps de rééducation du Viêtminh.* Paris: Albin Michel, 1993
Stora, Benjamin. *La gangrène et l'oubli: La mémoire de la guerre d'Algérie.* Paris: La Découverte, 1991.
———. *Imaginaires de guerre: Algérie-Viêt Nam en France et aux États-Unis.* Paris: La Découverte, 1997.
Tertrais, Hugues. *La piastre et le fusil: Le coût de la guerre d'Indochine, 1945–1954.* Paris: Comité pour l'histoire économique et financière de la France, 2002.
———. *Atlas des guerres d'Indochine, 1940–1990: De l'Indochine française à l'ouverture internationale.* Paris: Autrement, 2004.
Thévenet, Amédée. *Goulags indochinois: Carnets de guerre et de captivité, 1949–1952.* Paris: France-Empire, 1997.

―――. *La guerre d'Indochine racontée par ceux qui l'ont vécue: Un devoir de mémoire assumé ensemble.* Paris: France-Empire, 2001.

―――. *J'ai survécu à l'enfer des camps viêt-minh.* Paris: France-Empire, 2006.

Thomas, Martin. "People's War and the Collapse of French Indochina, 1945–1954." In Martin Thomas et al., eds., *Crises of Empire: Decolonization and Europe's Imperial States, 1918–1975.* London: Hodder Education, 2008, 182–208.

Tignères, Serges. "La guerre d'Indochine et l'opinion publique française entre 1954 et 1994: Mémoire et histoire." PhD dissertation. Université Toulouse-Le Mirail, 1999.

Tignères, Serge, and Alain Ruscio. *Dien Bien Phu: Mythes et réalités, 1954–2004. Cinquante ans de passions françaises.* Paris: Les Indes savantes, 2005.

Tønnesson, Stein. *Vietnam 1946: How the War Began.* Berkeley and Los Angeles: University of California Press, 2010.

Tran Tu Binh. *The Red Earth: A Vietnamese Memoir of Life on a Colonial Rubber Plantation.* Translated by John Spragens Jr. Athens: Ohio University Press, 1985.

Trinh Van Thao. "Étude d'un processus d'adaptation sociale: Portrait psycho-social du rapatrié." PhD dissertation. Université de Paris IV (Sorbonne), 1967.

―――. "Essai sur une sociologie du rapatriement." *Ethno-psychologie* 28, no. 1 (1973), 1–92.

―――. "Le retour des rapatriés d'Indochine: L'Expérience des centres d'accueil (1954–1960)." In Jean-Jacques and Jordi Emile Temime, eds., *Marseille et le choc des décolonisations.* Aix-en-Provence: Edisud, 1996.

Turley, William. *The Second Indochina War: A Concise Political and Military History,* 2nd ed. Lanham, MD: Rowman & Littlefield, 2009.

Ulloa, Marie-Pierre. *Francis Jeanson: Un intellectuel en dissidence. De la Résistance à la guerre d'Algérie.* Paris: Berg, 2001.

Vann, Carole. "'Dien Bien Phu vu d'en face,' paroles de vétérans vietnamiens." *Rue 89* online, 9 May 2010.

Vernet, Marc. "Si Orphée se retourne, Madame Dupont lui sourira: A propos du *Rendez-vous des quais* de Paul Carpita." *Cinémathèque* no. 1 (May 1992), 92–105.

Veyrenc, Lyliane. *Opératrice de cinéma en Indochine.* Paris: Nouvelles Éditions Debresse, 1955.

Vidal, Georges. *La grande illusion? Le parti communiste français et la défense nationale à l'époque du Front populaire (1934–1939).* Lyon: Presses universitaires de Lyon, 2006.

Vidal-Naquet, Pierre. *La torture dans la République: Essais d'histoire et de politique contemporaine (1954–1962).* Paris: Éditions de Minuit, 1972.

"Vietnam: A Teacher's Guide." *Focus on Asian Studies,* special issue, no. 1 (1983).

Vincent, Alain. *Indochine: La guerre oubliée.* Paris: A. Sutton, 2007.

Viollis, Andrée. *Indochine SOS.* Paris: Gallimard, 1935.

Vlastos, Stephen. "Television Wars: Representations of the Vietnam War in Television Documentaries." *Radical History Review* 36 (1986), 115–32.

Wadbled, Pôleth. "Construction mémorielle autour d'une situation migratoire particulière en Acquitaine: Les réfugiés et rapatriés des camps de la poudrerie de Sainte-Livrade-sur-Lot." Chapter 3 in ODRIS report, *Mémorialisation des immigrations. Pluralité des expressions, des mobilisations et des enjeux locaux à travers trois situations régionales: Acquitaine, Bretagne, et Pays de la Loire.* Prepared for the Ministère de la culture et de la communication, June 2009.

Wagner-Pacifici, Robin, and Barry Schwartz. "The Vietnam Veterans Memorial: Commemorating a Difficult Past." *American Journal of Psychology* 97, no. 2 (September 1991), 376–420.

Wahnich, Sophie. "La mémoire du CAFI, dans le contexte de sa requalification urbaine (1956–2010): De la tradition à l'accumulation." *Mouvements* hors série no. 1 (2011), 77–86.

Werth, Nicolas. "La Russie soviétique: Révolution, socialisme et dictature." *L'Histoire* no. 223 (July 1998), 8–21.

Wexler, Leila Sadat. "The Interpretation of the Nuremberg Principles by the French Court of Cassation: From Touvier to Barbie and Back Again." *Columbia Journal of Transnational Law* 32 (1994–95), 292–389.

Winter, Jay, and Emmanuel Sivan, eds. *War and Remembrance in the Twentieth Century*. Cambridge: Cambridge University Press, 2000.

Yeager, Jack. "Jean Hougron's Indochina: Fantasy and Disillusionment." In Kathryn Robson and Jennifer Yee, eds., *France and "Indochina": Cultural Representations*. Lanham, MD: Lexington Books, 2005.

Young, Marilyn B. *The Vietnam Wars, 1945–1990*. New York: HarperCollins, 1991.

Zinoman, Peter. *The Colonial Bastille: A History of Imprisonment in Vietnam, 1862–1940*. Berkeley and Los Angeles: University of California Press, 1996.

Zytnicki, Colette, and Sophie Dulucq. "Penser le passé colonial français, entre perspectives historiographiques et résurgence des mémoires." *Vingtième siècle* 86 (2005), 59–69.

NEWSPAPERS, PERIODICALS, AND ASSOCIATION BULLETINS

Aspects de la France
L'Aurore
Bulletin de l'Association d'amitié franco-vietnamienne
Bulletin de l'Association nationale des anciens et amis de l'Indochine
Le Canard enchaîné
Le Citoyen libre
Combat
Le Courrier français
La Croix (La Croix-L'Événement)
La Dépêche du Midi
Dépêche du Sud-Ouest

Les Échos du CAFI
L'Épaulette
L'Est Républicain
L'Événement du jeudi
L'Express
Le Figaro
Le Figaro littéraire
Figaro Magazine
Le Film français
Franc-Tireur
France-Asie
France-Soir
Historia
L'Humanité
Humanité-dimanche
L'Idiot international
L'Indépendant
Indochine Sud-Est Asiatique
Indochine vérités et droits
Le Journal des combattants
Le Journal d'Extrême-Orient
Le Journal du dimanche
Képi blanc
Les Lettres françaises
Libération
Maolen Info
Le Méridional (Le Méridional-La France)
Minute (Minute-La France)
Le Monde
Le Monde diplomatique
National hebdo
New York Times
Nice-Matin
Le Nouvel observateur (France observateur)
Nouvelle critique
La Nouvelle République du Centre-Ouest
La Nouvelle revue française
Paris-Match
Paris-Presse-l'Intransigeant
Le Parisien
Petit-bleu
Le Point
Politis
Présence du cinéma français

Présent
Le Progrès
Le Provençal
Quan Doi Nhan Dan
Le Quotidien de Paris
Rivarol
Regards
Le Réveil des combattants
Rouge
Rue89
Télé-observateur
Télérama
Témoignage chrétien
Tropiques
Valeurs actuelles
Var-Matin
La Vie ouvrière

DECREES, LAWS, AND STATUTES

"Décret no. 57–1108 du 8 octobre 1957 relatif à l'application des lois d'amnistie du 16 août 1947, du 5 janvier 1951 et du 6 août 1953 à certaines condamnations prononcées par des juridictions françaises sur le territoire du Cambodge." *Journal officiel de la République française*, 10 October 1957, 9682–9683.

"Décret no. 57–1109 du 8 octobre 1957 relatif à l'application des lois d'amnistie du 16 août 1947, du 5 janvier 1951 et du 6 août 1953 à certaines condamnations prononcées par des juridictions françaises sur le territoire du Laos." *Journal officiel de la République française*, 10 October 1957, 9683.

"Décret no. 57–1110 du 8 octobre 1957 relatif à l'application des lois d'amnistie du 16 août 1947, du 5 janvier 1951 et du 6 août 1953 à certaines condamnations prononcées par des juridictions françaises sur le territoire du Vietnam." *Journal officiel de la République française*, 10 October 1957, 9683.

"Décret no. 2003–925 du 26 septembre 2003 instituant une journée nationale d'hommage aux 'morts pour la France' pendant la guerre d'Algérie et les combats du Maroc et de la Tunisie, le 5 décembre de chaque année." *Journal officiel de la République française*, 28 September 2003, 16584.

"Décret no. 2005–547 du 26 mai 2005 instituant une journée nationale d'hommage aux 'morts pour la France' en Indochine, le 8 juin de chaque année." *Journal officiel de la République française*, 27 May 2005, 9218.

"Échange de lettres des 10 et 23 septembre 1986 entre le gouvernement de la République française et le gouvernement de la République socialiste du Viet-Nam relatif au rapatriement des corps de militaires français morts au Viet-Nam." *Journal officiel de la République française*, 25 April 1987, 4668–4670.

"Loi no. 59–940 du 31 juillet 1959 portant amnistie." *Journal officiel de la République française*, 5 August 1959, 7795–7797.

"Loi no. 66–409 du 18 juin 1966 portant amnistie." *Journal officiel de la République française*, 23 June 1966, 5147–5150.

"Loi no. 89–1013 du 31 décembre 1989 portant création du statut de prisonnier du Viêt-Minh." *Journal officiel de la République française*, 3 January 1990, 63.

"Loi no. 2005–158 du 23 février 2005 portant reconnaissance de la Nation et contribution nationale en faveur des Français rapatriés." *Journal officiel de la République française*, 24 February 2005, 3128.

"Proposition de loi no. 1443 visant à établir une journée nationale du souvenir des Français morts en Indochine." Assemblée nationale, 2004. Consulted online at www.assemblee-nationale.fr.

"Proposition de loi no. 283 visant à rendre inamnistiables les crimes contre l'humanité." Assemblée nationale, 2005. http://www.assemblee-nationale.fr/13/propositions/pion0382.asp.

"Pourvoi no. 85–95166 de la Chambre criminelle de la Cour de cassation du 20 décembre 1985." *Bulletin criminel* no. 407 (1985).

"Rejet du pourvoi formé par Sobanski Wladyslav." Chambre criminelle Cour de Cassation, 92–82273, 1993.

"Rejet du pourvoi formé par Sobanski Wladyslav." Chambre criminelle Cour de Cassation, 98–85902, 1999.

"Statut de prisonnier du Viêt-minh. Discussion d'un projet de loi adopté par le Sénat." *Journal officiel de la République française*, Débats de l'Assemblée nationale, 18 December 1989, 6762–6771.

ARCHIVES

Archives de l'Institut national de l'audiovisuel (Paris)

Archives départementales de l'Allier (Moulins)
    11 W 49
    988 W 29–35, 37–38, 42, 44, 56, 64, 72–75

Archives départementales de la Seine-Saint-Denis (Bobigny)
    Fonds du Parti Communiste Français

Archives départementales du Lot-et-Garonne (Agen)
    207 JX art. 329
    207 JX art. 330
    207 JX art. 339
    207 JX art. 560
    2 PRES/8/1/4
    1 PRES 282
    1 W art. 758
    1 W art. 2117
    1525 W art. 212

Series W Vrac Sous-préfecture de Villeneuve
Archives municipales de Fréjus
  87 W 3
  87 W 21
Bibliothèque de documentation internationale contemporaine (Nanterre)
Centre des archives diplomatiques de La Courneuve (La Courneuve)
  Série Asie-Océanie, sous-séries Vietnam-Nord et Vietnam-Sud
Centre des archives diplomatiques de Nantes (Nantes)
  589 PO 1
  590 PO A
Centre des archives d'outre-mer (Aix-en-Provence)
  Fonds du Cabinet du Haut Commissariat de France en Indochine
  Fonds du Conseiller Politique
  Fonds du Service de liaison avec les originaires des territoires d'Outre-mer
  Fonds privé—Archives Monguillot
  Fonds de l'Agence de la France d'Outre-mer
  Service de Protection du Corps Expéditionnaire
Centre d'histoire du travail (Nantes)
  Fonds ARAC
Institut de l'Asie Orientale (Lyons)
  Fonds Georges Boudarel
Service historique de la Défense (Paris)
  10 H 179–180, 214, 247–248, 302, 317, 320, 336, 349, 447, 970, 1041, 2388, 2761, 3134
  1 R 238
  1 K 669

FILMS AND DOCUMENTARIES (CHRONOLOGICAL)

Le rendez-vous des quais (Paul Carpita, 1955; re-released 1996)
Patrouille de choc (Claude Bernard-Aubert, 1957)
Mort en fraude (Marcel Camus, 1957)
Fort du fou (Léo Joannon, 1963)
Les parias de la gloire (Henri Decoin, 1964)
Les génies des quatre palais (Pierre Simon and Ida Simon-Barouh, 1964)
La 317ème section (Pierre Schoendoerffer, 1965)
Le Facteur s'en va-t-en guerre (Claude Bernard-Aubert, 1966)
Les oubliés de l'Indochine (Pierre Andro, 1972)
La République est morte à Dien Bien Phu (Philippe Devillers, Jean Lacouture, Jérôme Kanapa, 1974)
Charlie Bravo (Claude Bernard-Aubert, 1980)
Vietnam (Henri de Turenne, 1984). Documentary in six parts which aired on Antenne 2 on 15, 20, and 22 January, and 12, 19, and 26 February 1984.

Vietnam, la première guerre; part 1, *Doc lap;* part 2, *Le tigre et l'éléphant* (Danièle Rousselier, 1991). Aired on Antenne 2, 1 and 8 March 1992.
Récits d'Indochine: Chronique des journées de la bataille de Dien Bien Phu (Patrick Jeudy, 1992). Aired on TF1, 6 March 1992.
La mémoire et l'oubli (Yves and Ada Rémy, 1992). Aired on *Traverses,* France 3, 19 March 1992.
Indochine (Régis Wargnier, 1992)
Diên Biên Phu (Pierre Schoendoerffer, 1992)
L'Amant (Jean-Jacques Annaud, 1992)
Les fruits amers du Lot-et-Garonne (Mathieu Samel, 1992)
Les enfants de Quan Am (Mathieu Samel, 2004)
Le camp des oubliés (Marie-Christine Courtès and My Linh Nguyen, 2004)
Saïgon-Sainte-Livrade: Aller simple pour l'oubli (Nora Genet-Lemque, 2007)
Face à la mort: Les témoignages des prisonniers de Hô Chi Minh (Marcela Feraru, with the collaboration of the ANAPI, 2008)
Un Barrage contre le Pacifique (Rithy Panh, 2010)
Là-haut, un roi au-dessus des nuages (Pierre Schoendoerffer, 2010)
CAFI: La mémoire fragmentée (Mathieu Samel, 2014)
Vietnam-sur-Lot (Nadège Lobato De Faria, 2014)

INDEX

Institutions, organizations, and associations are listed under the English translation of their names. Acronyms are listed and cross-referenced.

9 March (1945). *See* Japanese coup
19 March (1962), 72, 104
8 June (1980). *See* National day of homage for the Indochina War; unknown soldier
20 July (1954). *See* Geneva Accords
7 May (1954): commemoration of, 31, 41–42, 81, 85, 92, 104; French surrender on, 20
La 317ème section (film), 27, 170, 175–79, 181, 198
AAFV. *See* Franco–Vietnamese Friendship Association
ACUF. *See* Association of the Combatants of the French Union
ACVGI. *See* Association of Veterans and Victims of the Indochina War
AEMNAI. *See* Association for the Construction of a National Monument to the *Anciens* of Indochina, Combatants and Victims of War
AEMSI. *See* Association for the Construction of a Memorial to the Soldiers of Indochina and the Victims of War
AFV. *See* France–Vietnam Association
Aldrich, Robert, 96, 110, 118
Algerian War, 1–2, 23, 69; amnesty for war crimes, 149; ARAC and, 69; Boudarel affair and, 62; commemoration of, 72, 104–5; crimes against humanity and, 160, 263n70; FNACA and, 34, 228n3; French Communist Party and, 56, 193; remembrance of, 3, 30, 87, 104, 167, 201, 208, 217n15; resettlement camps and, 126; "suitcase carriers" and, 147; torture and, 179; unknown soldier of, 93. *See also harkis; pieds-noirs*
Alliot-Marie, Michèle, 31, 105
L'Amant (film), 30, 95, 164, 167, 195–97, 201–2, 204–5, 272n136
ANAI. *See* National Association of Veterans and Friends of Indochina
ANAPI. *See* National Association of Former Prisoners and Internees in Indochina
Annaud, Jean-Jacques, 204–5, 272n136
anticolonialism, 33; AAFV and, 75, 77–78, 80–81; criticisms of, 49–50; exhibits and, 86, 110–11; film and, 173, 180, 192; French Communist Party and, 56, 193, 229n7; Georges Boudarel affair and, 147–48, 152, 154, 156–57, 165; Jacques Vergès and, 159–60; United States and, 19
anticolonial narrative, 8–10, 31, 53, 209–10, 219n32; AAFV and, 74–81; ACVGI/ARAC and, 68–74; definition of, 6–7, 54; film and, 143–44, 189–195, 206; French Communist Party and, 56; Georges Boudarel affair and, 143–44; Montreuil and, 81–86; scholars and, 57–68

anticommunism, 5, 7, 107, 152, 155, 210–11, 217n17; ANAI and, 19, 36–38, 41
anticommunist narrative, 7–9, 19, 33, 55, 58, 71–72, 87, 210–11, 109; ANAI and, 34–53; Boudarel affair and, 143, 147–48, 155, 165–66; definition of, 5–6; film and, 143–44, 184–85, 199–200; Pierre Schoendoerffer and, 175, 177, 199, 206
antiwar movement. *See* Indochina War
ARAC. *See* Association of Repatriates of Noyant d'Allier; Republican Veterans Association
Arc de Triomphe, 36, 156; ceremony of 7 May, 92; ceremony of 8 June, 31, 105; ceremony of 20 July, 72; plaque to Indochina War, 90; unknown soldier of WWI, 92
ARINA. *See* Association of Repatriates of Noyant d'Allier
Association for the Construction of a Memorial to the Soldiers of Indochina and the Victims of War (AEMSI; Association pour l'érection d'un mémorial aux soldats d'Indochine et victimes de guerre), 97–98
Association for the Construction of a National Monument to the *Anciens* of Indochina, Combatants and Victims of War (AEMNAI; Association pour l'érection d'un monument national des anciens d'Indochine, combattants et victimes de guerre), 45, 97–99, 108
Association of Repatriates of Noyant d'Allier (ARINA; Association des rapatriés de Noyant d'Allier), 139
Association of Residents and Friends of the CAFI (ARAC; Association des résidents et amis du CAFI), 119, 139–141
Association of the Combatants of the French Union (ACUF; Association des combattants de l'Union Française), 95, 106–7, 245n11
Association of Veterans and Victims of the Indochina War (ACVGI; Association des anciens combattants et victimes de la guerre d'Indochine), 10, 46, 53, 55, 69–74, 81, 233n3

Aubrac, Raymond, 62, 78, 235n37, 236n41, 241n116
August Revolution, 15, 60, 113
Auriol, Vincent, 18, 24

Bao Dai, 15, 18, 65, 112, 155, 160, 223n35
Barbusse, Henri, 69, 77, 241n128
Bastid, Hélène, 37, 41–45, 49, 113
Baylé, Claude, 48, 153, 162
Bernard-Aubert, Claude, 168–71, 175–81, 206, 268nn52,57
Beucler, Jean-Jacques, 43, 99, 102; ACVGI and, 73; ANAI and, 47, 49; anticommunist narrative and, 155; Georges Boudarel affair, 47, 145, 151, 153, 158–59, 162, 260n3; Henri de Turenne and, 185, 187–88
Bigeard, Marcel, 29, 33; anticommunist narrative and, 28, 54; battle of Dien Bien Phu, 20, 26; burial controversy, 33, 61–62; film and, 199, 201; Henri de Turenne and, 185; remembrance of Indochina War and, 26, 99, 214; television and, 27, 179, 201
boat people, 5, 28–29, 50–51, 106–7, 112, 121, 155, 182
Bonnafous, Robert, 99, 163, 260n3
Boudarel, Georges: affair, 7, 11, 28, 30, 32, 40, 47, 73, 102, 143, 145–166, 181, 187, 208, 211; AAFV and, 78, 242n134; activism of, 66, 161; 1966 amnesty, 149; ANAI and, 47; anticolonial narrative and, 153–54; anticommunist narrative and, 155; camp 113, 149; comparisons with Vichy, 161–63; crimes against humanity charges, 150, 159; defection; 148–49; *Le Droit de savoir* appearance, 157–59; experience of the colonies, 148; media and, 151–54; protests against, 155–56; scholarship of, 65–68, 150; supporters of, 156–57
Bousquet, René, 161–63
Brard, Jean-Pierre, 81, 83, 85, 233n4, 234n24
Bretonnière de Chèque, Emmanuel, 255n44
Brocheux, Pierre, 89, 163, 187; activism of, 66; scholarship of, 14, 57, 58, 65–68
Bruyère, Georges, 69

Buddhism: Memorial to the Indochina Wars and, 100; Fréjus pagoda, 98; repatriates and, 98, 124

CAFI (Centre d'accueil des Français d'Indochine), 115–17, 119, 122–25, 123*fig*, 132–33, 136–38, 251nn4,7; as site of memory, 139–43; demolition of, 142–43; 50th anniversary of, 140–42; unrest at, 128–31; conflict with *Livradais*, 134–35. *See also* reception centers; Sainte-Livrade-sur-Lot
Cambodia, 37–38, 57, 60, 101, 110, 198; colonization of, 13, 49–50, 220n8; communist regime of, 28, 87, 107; film and, 177; independence of, 12, 15, 21; refugees from, 95, 121
Camus, Marcel, 169, 172–74, 206
Carpita, Paul, 11, 164, 168–69, 189–95; censorship and, 189–90, 194, 270n100; Cinépax and, 90–91; French Communist Party and, 192–94
casualties. *See* Indochina War
Catholics: antiwar movement and, 23; exodus from north Vietnam, 112, 119, 175; in French Indochina, 13, 220n5; repatriates, 124
CEFEO. *See* French Far East Expeditionary Corps
Cenerelli, Pierre, 22
Center for Information and Documentation on Vietnam (CID-Vietnam; Centre d'information et de documentation sur le Vietnam), 60, 76–77, 86
Chesneaux, Jean, 150; AAFV and, 65, 75, 241n129; activism, 66; Georges Boudarel affair and, 152, 164; scholarship of, 57–58, 65–66
Chirac, Jacques, 31, 45, 99, 115; Memorial to the Indochina Wars and, 52, 89–90, 99–100, 102, 107–10; legacies of colonialism, 109
CID-Vietnam. *See* Center for Information and Documentation on Vietnam
CIMADE. *See* Inter-Organizational Committee in Support of Evacuees
Citadelles et maquis d'Indochine, 98, 108
Cité Hérault massacre, 15, 17

civilizing mission, 12, 14, 50, 148, 171, 184, 197, 206
Clavier, Albert, 78, 236n42, 261n18
Clouzot, Henri-Georges, 174
CNE. *See* National Franco-Vietnamese, Franco-Cambodian and Franco-Lao Aid Committee
Cold War, 2, 21, 25; decolonization and, 2; Indochina War and, 12, 18, 54, 57, 61, 68, 87, 112, 147, 209; remembrance of, 2–5, 7, 56, 70, 74, 80, 86, 209–11
colonialism, 83, 111, 158, 171, 200, 202–4, 208–9; critiques of, 54, 57, 67, 69–70, 80, 157, 159–60, 173, 205, 206; legacies of, 7–8, 25, 117, 209, 211; "positive" aspects, 36, 42, 48–51, 109, 155, 183, 186, 204
commemoration, 25–26, 32, 34–35, 217n14; ACVGI/ARAC and, 10, 46, 56, 70–72, 81; ANAI and, 35, 39–47, 51; French state and, 2, 5, 10, 89. *See also* 7 May; Geneva Accords; National day of homage for the Indochina War
crimes against humanity: colonialism and, 160; Georges Boudarel; and 146, 150, 157, 159; Ho Chi Minh and, 46; in French law, 160, 263n70; Vichy functionaries and, 161–63

Dalloz, Jacques, 22, 178, 192
d'Argenlieu, Georges Thierry, 17
de Castries, Christian, 20, 26; bunker of, 212*fig*
Decoux, Jean, 15
de Galard, Geneviève, 99, 101, 180, 182, 201, 272n142; anticommunist narrative and, 5, 54, 101; battle of Dien Bien Phu, 8–9, 20; Henri de Turenne and, 182, 185; remembrance of Indochina War and, 26, 28
de Lattre de Tassigny, Jean, 19, 101
de Turenne, Henri, 11, 27–29, 48–50, 99, 157, 163, 168, 181–88
Democratic Republic of Vietnam, 6, 16, 54, 56–57, 60, 112; AAFV and, 75–76, 78, 240n114;anticolonial narrative and, 57–58, 63; critiques of, 66–67; French deserters and, 164; repatriation of French dead and, 93–94; independence

of, 60, 160; land reform and, 59, 61, 70; repatriates and, 118
deserters (French), 150, 157, 161, 164–65, 218n24, 236n42; amnesty of, 149–50; critique of, 73
Desmoulins, Bernard, 101
Devillers, Philippe, 58, 63–65, 68, 222n29, 233n3, 234n13
Diem, Ngo Dinh. *See* Ngo Dinh Diem
Dien, Raymonde, 6, 24, 54, 56, 78, 192, 225n75, 234n16, 235n37, 241n129
Dien Bien Phu: battle of, 8, 12, 21, 25–26, 52, 70, 175, 209; commemoration of, 26–27, 30, 41–42, 80, 92, 99, 104–6, 179; film and, 179, 183–86, 198–201; François Mitterrand's trip to, 102, 198; museum and historical sites in, 211–12; role in French remembrance, 2, 29, 40, 217n10, 223n41, 226n82; Rolf Rodel's monument at, 91*fig*, 92; scholarship on, 61; Vietnamese military cemetery at, 213*fig*. *See also* Operation *Castor*
Dien Bien Phu (film), 30, 141, 164, 167, 176, 195–201, 205
dockworkers, 24, 56, 80, 164, 189–92
domino theory, 19
Doumer, Paul, 12, 221n9
DRV. *See* Democratic Republic of Vietnam
Duclos, Jacques, 82, 234n16
Dufriche, Marcel, 83
Duras, Marguerite, 12, 32, 95, 169, 197, 204, 272n136, 273n167
Dutrait, Bernard, 128, 132

EFEO. *See* French School of the Far East
Eurasian Association of Paris (CEP-CAFI; Coordination des Eurasiens de Paris-CAFI), 118–19, 139–43
Eurasian(s), 253n18; film and, 172–73, 206, 256n76; in French Indochina, 121, 132–33; repatriates, 120, 132, 134, 138;

Falco, Hubert, 111
Figuères, Léo, 233n7, 235n37, 240n105
film, 4, 11, 32, 139, 164, 166, 167–207
Firpo, Christina, 132, 256n71
FLN. *See* National Liberation Front

FNACA. *See* National Federation of Veterans of Algerian, Morocco and Tunisia
Fontainebleau conference (1946), 16, 77, 236n41
Fourniau, Charles, 54, 58–59, 141, 233n3; AAFV and, 75, 79–80; anticolonial narrative and, 58, 67–68; French Communist Party and, 55; relationship with DRV/SRV, 59–60; scholarship of, 57–59, 63
France-Viet Nam Association (AFV; Association France-Viet Nam), 23, 77
Franco-Vietnamese Friendship Association (AAFV, Association d'amitié franco-vietnamienne), 10, 59, 68, 74–81, 233n3, 234n24, 243n153; anticolonial narrative and, 77–78, 80–81, 86; commemoration and, 72, 79–81, 84–85; DRV/SRV and, 75–79, 87; film and, 197; French Communist Party and, 56, 75, 240n114; opposition to the American Vietnam War, 59, 74–76, 79, 241n121; scholars and, 55, 58, 60, 65, 75
Frank, Robert, 1, 216n5
Frêche, Daniel, 139
Fréjus, 98, 105; Monument to the Dead of Indochina, 44–45, 52, 96*fig*, 97–99; Memorial to the Indochina Wars, 10, 17, 62, 90–91, 95, 100*fig*, 101*fig*, 107, 109, 114, 118, 247n43
French Communist Party, 11, 21, 38, 151, 209; AAFV and, 55, 75, 240n114; anticolonialism, 152; anticolonial narrative and, 7, 55–56, 209; antiwar activism, 23–25, 56; ARAC and, 55, 218n22, 31–32, 69; film and, 189, 191–94; Georges Boudarel and, 148; Ho Chi Minh and, 229n7; Montreuil and, 81; Museum of Living History and, 82–84; scholars and, 58–63, 65, 67
French Far East Expeditionary Corps (CEFEO; Corps expéditionnaire français d'Extrême-Orient), 5, 15–17, 18–21, 40, 47, 52, 62, 70, 73–74, 78, 89, 91, 94, 99, 113, 149, 154, 163, 204, 209–10, 212–13, 218n22
French School of the Far East (EFEO; École française d'Extrême-Orient), 50, 63

French Union, 16, 18, 68, 75, 112, 160; military forces of, 12, 18, 21, 46, 107, 170
French Union of Veterans' and War Victims' Associations (UFAC; Union française des associations de combattants et de victimes de guerre), 72–73

Gandouin, Jacques, 185, 187, 269n83
gégène. See torture
Geneva Accords, 12, 19, 21, 119, 209; commemoration of, 10, 32, 46, 53, 55, 72, 82, 85; film and, 203; war graves and, 246n19
Gia Long (Nguyen Phuc Anh), 15
Giap, Vo Nguyen. *See* Vo Nguyen Giap
Giscard d'Estaing, Valéry, 43, 52, 88, 95, 106, 108–9, 145, 231n41
Godart, Justin, 78, 242n130
Goscha, Christopher, 63, 233n11
Gracey, Douglas, 15
Grauwin, Paul, 20, 26, 219n39

Halong Bay Accords (1948), 18, 155, 160, 210, 223n34
harkis, 51, 104, 118, 124–26, 137, 139–40, 251n6
Hémery, Daniel: activism of, 66; anticolonial narrative and, 58, 235n37; scholarship of, 14, 57, 65–68, 238n82
Ho Chi Minh, 15–16, 18, 55, 60, 63, 64, 65, 77, 161, 213, 229n7, 233n7, 236n41; anticolonial narrative and, 6, 54, 59, 78, 210; bust of (Montreuil), 10, 79, 84, 85*fig*; centenary of, 46, 79, 83, 233n3; declaration of Vietnamese independence, 39, 113, 160; film and, 183, 185; MHV exhibit on, 81, 83; room (Museum of Living History), 10, 82–84; scholarship on, 67
Hougron, Jean, 171, 173–74

immigration, 10, 118, 121, 136–38, 209; integration/assimilation and, 131–32, 136–38; museums and, 83, 89; repatriates and, 117, 138, 143; remembrance of Indochina War and, 95, 208
Indochina: colonization of, 12–14; colonial society, 14, 48–51, 67, 148, 171–73; decolonization of, 2, 12. *See also* anticolonial narrative; civilizing mission; colonialism; Indochina War; Second World War
Indochina War, 16–21; antiwar movement, 23–25; casualties of, 21, 224n50; Cold War and, 2–4, 61, 68, 74, 112, 209; decolonization and, 2–4, 138, 109; Generals' affair, 26; media coverage of, 22; migration after Dien Bien Phu, 119–120; outbreak of, 16–17; phases of, 17–21, 222n30; public opinion and, 21–25; *piastres* trafficking, 26, 226n84; withdrawal of last French Union troops (1956), 114. *See also* anticommunist narrative; anticolonial narrative; commemoration; Democratic Republic of Vietnam; Dien Bien Phu; Geneva Accords; prisoners of war; torture; Viet Minh
Indochine (film), 30, 164, 167, 195–97, 201–6
Interministerial Commission for the Repatriates of Indochina (Commission interministérielle des rapatriés d'Indochine), 121–22, 252n16, 256n76
Inter-Organizational Committee in Support of Evacuees (CIMADE Comité inter–mouvements auprès des évacués), 135
Invalides (Paris), 31, 43, 46, 88–89, 92, 99, 105

Japanese coup (9 March 1945), 15, 63, 113–14; commemoration of, 40, 42; ANAI and, 36, 39–42; remembrance of Indochina War and, 40, 112–13
Journoud, Pierre, 213, 218nn22,24, 226n82

Karmen, Roman, 27, 184
Khoa, Le Huu. *See* Le Huu Khoa
Ko, Hee, 250n101
Korean War, 19, 21, 91, 224n55

Lacouture, Jean, 64
Lamothe, Guy, 72, 240n97
Laos, 37–38, 57, 63, 148; battle of Dien Bien Phu and, 19, ; colonization of, 12–13, 15, 49–50, 220n8; communist regime of,

28, 38, 87, 107; film and, 267n36; independence of, 12, 21; refugees from, 121
Larcher-Goscha, Agathe, 66, 220n7, 233n11
Laurain, Jean, 45, 98
Law of 23 February 2005, 8, 25, 51, 53, 72, 211
Le Bras, Jean, 97–98, 104, 247n39, 248n64
Le Crenn, Joséphine, 116
Le Huu Khoa, 117, 121, 138
Lefebvre, Raymond, 69
Lefèvre, Gérard, 84
Lejeune, Émile, 140
Léotard, François, 30, 44–45, 52, 95, 97, 99, 102, 106–10, 115, 153
Lin, Maya, 101–102
Logevall, Fredrik, 17
Luccerini, Jean-Marie, 96

mal jaune, 30, 34, 209, 274n3
Marseilles, 24, 46, 56, 80, 116–17, 121, 164–65, 189–90, 192, 194, 201
Martin, Henri: AAFV and, 75, 78; affair, 24–25, 209, 225n75; anticolonial narrative and, 54, 192; antiwar protest, 6, 24–25; conference on, 31, 62, 80–81; French Communist Party and, 56; military service, 24; Vietnamese exhibits and, 211
Martino, Claude, 193–95
Mékachéra, Hamlaoui, 31, 105
Mémoire d'Indochine, 139–40
Memorial to the Indochina Wars, 10, 17, 30, 33, 39, 44, 62, 89, 95–96, 99–103, 100*fig*, 103*fig*, 114, 118, 164; inaugural speeches, 52, 90, 107–10; pedagogical center, 86, 110–12, 111*fig*
Merlin, Martial, 12
Mitterrand, François, 99, 211; inauguration of Memorial, 110; trip to Vietnam, 28, 30, 101–2, 198
modus vivendi (1946), 16
Montreuil, 10, 55, 61, 79, 81–86; 50th anniversary of Indochina War and, 31, 81, 84–86; AAFV and, 55. *See also* Ho Chi Minh; Museum of Living History
Monument to the Dead of Indochina, 44–45, 95–99, 96*fig*, 99, 114–15; anticommunist narrative and, 108–9; inauguration of, 106, 112–3

Mort en fraude (film), 168–69, 171–74, 206
Mus, Paul, 58, 63–65, 68, 219n32
Musée de l'histoire vivante. *See* Museum of Living History
Museum of Living History (MHV; Musée de l'histoire vivante), 61, 81–84, 86

National Association for the Veterans and Friends of Indochina (ANAI; Association nationale des anciens et amis de l'Indochine), 7, 9, 26, 33, 34–53, 68–69, 90; 9 March and, 39–41; ACVGI and, 46–47, 70–73, 233n3; anticommunism of, 35, 37–38, 41; anticommunist narrative and, 35, 210; commemorative dates and, 41–42, 104; exhibits and, 38, 86; film and, 204; Georges Boudarel affair and, 47–48, 145; Henri de Turenne and, 48–50, 183, 185–88; Ho Chi Minh centenary and, 46, 79; "positive" aspects of colonialism and, 36, 42, 48–51, 211; Souvenir Indochinois and, 42; state-sponsored commemoration and, 10, 29, 35, 39, 42–46, 51–52, 88, 93, 98, 103, 105, 108, 113, 210–11
National Association of Former Prisoners and Internees in Indochina (ANAPI; Association nationale des anciens prisonniers et internés d'Indochine), 35, 47, 71, 107–8, 150, 160, 229n4
National Combatants' Circle (CNC; Cercle national des combattants), 156
National day of homage for the Indochina War (8 June), 31, 41–42, 45–46, 103–105, 141
National Federation of Veterans of Algerian, Morocco and Tunisia (FNACA; Fédération nationale des anciens combattants d'Algérie, Maroc et Tunisie), 34, 104, 228n3
National Franco-Vietnamese, Franco-Cambodian and Franco-Lao Aid Committee (CNE; Comité national d'entraide franco-vietnamien, franco-cambodgien, et franco-laotien), 37
National Front, 152, 156, 181
National Liberation Front (FLN), 3, 126, 147

Nationality Convention (1955), 120
Navarre, Henri, 19, 29
Ngo Dinh Diem, 76
Nguyen Khac Vien, 174
Nguyen, Léon, 142
Nora, Pierre, 118
Norindr, Panivong, 114, 196, 198, 200, 205
Notre-Dame-de-Lorette, 42–43, 88, 92–93, 113
Noyant d'Allier, 10, 117, 122, 124–25, 127–33, 136, 139–41, 143. *See also* reception centers

Operation *Castor*, 19–20, 104

Pacini, Alfred, 71, 192
Patrouille de choc (film), 168–71, 176, 180, 196
Pham Van Dong, 60
pieds-noirs, 104, 140, 251n6
Plantier, Maurice, 43, 88, 106, 109, 113
Poivre d'Arvor, Patrick, 151, 158–59, 187
prisoners of war: CEFEO prisoners of the Viet Minh, 6, 27, 29, 40, 70, 74, 99, 107, 149, 151, 154–55, 161–63, 166, 184, 213, 231; status of prisoner of the Viet Minh, 30, 46, 99; Viet Minh POW camps, 11, 20, 61, 112, 153–54, 160, 163, 224n48, 259n3; Viet Minh prisoners of the CEFEO, 40, 154. *See also* Georges Boudarel; National Association of Prisoners and Internees in Indochina (ANAPI)
Provisional Revolutionary Government, 75, 76, 79

ralliés. See deserters
Raphaël–Leygues, Jacques, 130
reception centers for the French of Indochina, 10, 116–143, 251n7, 253n23; as sites of memory, 10, 138–143; integration/assimilation and, 131–138. *See also* CAFI; Noyant d'Allier; Sainte-Livrade-sur-Lot
refugees, 5, 28, 50, 95, 110, 117–20, 137–38, 186, 252n13. *See also* boat people
repatriates, 4, 10, 27, 116–143, 251nn2,8, 252n17, 253nn18,23. *See also* reception centers

repatriation: of French Union war dead, 29, 43, 93–95, 99
Republican Veterans' Association (ARAC; Association républicaine des anciens combattants), 10, 61, 69, 239nn85,87; ACVGI and, 71; ANAI and, 73, 233n3; anticolonial narrative and, 58, 68, 74; antiwar protest and, 70; commemoration and, 55, 62, 70, 72, 81–82, 84–85; film and, 189–90; French Communist Party and, 55–56, 69; protest of law of 23 February 2005, 72; DRV/SRV and, 69, 87
Le rendez-vous des quais (film), 11, 168–69, 189–95, 206
Resistance (WWII), 24–25, 38, 113, 115, 162; anticolonialism and, 62–63; Georges Boudarel affair and, 147; Indochina War and, 147, 209
Robert, Jean, 153, 158
Robic-Diaz, Delphine, 168, 193, 203, 265nn4,6
Rodel, Rolf: monument at Dien Bien Phu, 91*fig*, 92
Rolland, Dominique, 116, 143, 251n7
Rousselier, Danièle, 197, 201
Ruscio, Alain, 2, 17, 22, 60, 141, 233n3, 234n24, 235n33, 243n153; anticolonial narrative and, 58, 63, 79; French Communist Party and, 55, 235nn25,26; scholarship of, 61, 62–63, 68, 71, 74, 80–81, 86

Saada, Emmanuelle, 132, 256n71
Sainte-Livrade-sur-Lot, 10, 115–17, 119, 122, 124–25, 127, 131, 133–37, 141, 143, 254n29. *See also* CAFI
Sainteny, Jean, 16, 160, 222n22
Salan, Raoul, 19, 226n81
Schoendoerffer, Pierre, 26–28, 32–33, 101, 168–71, 175–81, 195–202, 205, 207, 214; anticommunist narrative and, 206; Henri de Turenne and, 185. *See also La 317ème section, Dien Bien Phu, La section Anderson*
Second World War, 71, 2, 93, 94, 133, 159–62; Indochina and, 14–16, 41; remembrance of the Indochina War and, 1, 39, 90, 106, 113–15, 147, 176, 209,

250n101; *See also* Japanese coup; Memorial to the Indochina Wars
La section Anderson (documentary), 179, 196
Simon, Guy, 36, 37, 39, 41–42, 46, 204, 230n22
Simon, Pierre-Jean, 125, 133, 251n7, 258n111
Simon-Barouh, Ida, 251n7, 258n111
Sobanski, Wladislaw, 150, 153, 157–60, 162
Socialist Republic of Vietnam (SRV), 29, 31, 44, 54–55, 58, 60, 66, 79, 93
Souchon, Jean, 44, 96
Souvenir Indochinois, 36, 42
Square of the Soldiers of Indochina (Square des combattants d'Indochine), 52, 89
SRV. *See* Socialist Republic of Vietnam
Stora, Benjamin, 168

Thao, Trinh Van. *See* Trinh Van Thao
Tignères, Serge, 2, 61, 95, 217n18, 226n80
torture: Georges Boudarel and accusations of, 145, 151–52, 154, 157; Indochina War and, 18, 23, 40, 65, 179, 181, 223n32; Japanese coup and, 39–40
Touvier, Paul, 161–63
Tran Duc Luong, 84
Trinh Van Thao, 117, 124, 131, 140

UFAC. *See* French Union of Veterans' and War Victims' Associations
University of Paris VII (Jussieu), 11, 57, 65–66, 150, 156–57
unknown soldier, 90, 92–93, 245n15; national day of homage for the Indochina War and, 45, 104; of the Algerian War, 93; of the Indochina War, 10, 29, 39, 42–44, 52, 88–89, 91–96, 98–99, 106, 108–9, 112–13, 182, 210

Vaillant–Couturier, Paul, 69
Varaut, Jean-Marc, 150, 162,
VCP. *See* Vietnamese Communist Party
Vergès, Jacques, 159–60
Vernet, Marc, 168, 189–90, 192–95, 270n100
veterans: ACVGI/ARAC and, 53–54, 68–74; ANAI and, 9, 33, 35–36, 38, 42, 95; anticolonial narrative and, 55, 63, 74, 86; anticommunist narrative and, 4–5, 28–29, 44, 53, 182; commemoration and, 2, 10, 26, 29, 31, 42, 46, 72, 88–94, 97–98, 100, 102–7, 109–11, 115, 209–10, 213–14; film and, 168, 171, 183, 185, 200–201, 204–6; French, 6, 8, 24, 26, 28, 33, 24, 47, 94, 113, 121, 192, 209–11; Georges Boudarel affair and, 145, 149, 151–53, 155, 159, 163–66; other associations of, 35, 72; travel to Vietnam, 30, 101; Vietnamese, 211, 213
Vichy regime, 14, 174; collaborators, 146–47, 161–62; Indochina and, 14, 40, 41, 113, 115; remembrance of, 3, 39, 146, 208; remembrance of the Indochina War and, 2–3, 30, 87, 161, 163
Vidal-Naquet, Pierre, 152, 154, 156, 161, 165, 235n37, 237n66
Vietnam, 15, 19, 28–30, 33, 44, 57, 60, 63, 65, 80, 87, 94–95, 99, 100–2, 108, 110, 121, 141, 155, 161, 163, 195–96, 198, 200, 202–204; AAFV and, 10, 55, 74–77, 79; ANAI and, 37–38, 43, 48, 50, 210; ARAC and, 69; colonization of, 12–13; commemoration of Indochina War, 31, 211–213; French Communist Party and, 58; French scholars and, 55, 66–68, 150, 156; independence of, 12, 21, 39, 70, 109, 113, 160; Montreuil and, 55, 81, 83–86; refugees from, 5, 28, 50, 95, 110, 186; Republic of Vietnam, 93, 169; State of Vietnam, 18, 160; Vietnamese nationalism, 63–64, 111, 202. *See also* Democratic Republic of Vietnam; Socialist Republic of Vietnam
Vietnam (documentary), 11, 27, 29, 48–49, 99, 163, 168, 181–88
Vietnam: A Television History (documentary), 182, 188
Vietnam Veterans Memorial, 95, 101–2, 217n17
Vietnam War, 17, 179–80, 206; French opposition to, 56, 59, 65–66, 75–78, 161; American remembrance of, 4, 103, 167–68; remembrance of the Indochina War and, 1–2, 28, 70, 89–90, 95, 168, 179, 200. *See also* Vietnam Veterans Memorial
Vietnamese Communist Party (VCP), 58–59, 67, 149, 174

Viet Minh, 3, 5–8, 11, 15–23, 24, 26, 33, 35, 39–42, 47, 65, 67, 71, 73–74, 78, 89, 99, 107, 110, 112–14, 118–19, 145, 147–48, 154–55, 156–57, 160–65; comparisons with French Resistance, 147, 160, 209; in film, 27, 169–73, 175–80, 184–85, 187, 199, 203. *See also* prisoners of war

Viollis, Andrée, 77–78, 154, 241n128, 242n130
Vo Nguyen Giap, 20, 102
Vu Quoc Thuc, 187

Wargnier, Régis, 203–7

www.ingramcontent.com/pod-product-compliance
Lightning Source LLC
Chambersburg PA
CBHW030522230426
43665CB00010B/729